# Ezra

# ezra

**THE BOOK OF EZRA** / A NEW TRANSLATION WITH A COMMENTARY ANTHOLOGIZED FROM TALMUDIC, MIDRASHIC, AND RABBINIC SOURCES

*Published by*

Mesorah Publications, ltd

# ספר עזרא

*Translation and Commentary by*
Rabbi Yosef Rabinowitz

*An Overview /*
*'Ezra — Molder of a New Era'*
*by* Rabbi Nosson Scherman

FIRST EDITION
*First Impression . . . November 1984*
*Second Impression . . . July 1994*

*Published and Distributed by*
**MESORAH PUBLICATIONS, Ltd.**
4401 Second Avenue
Brooklyn, New York 11232

*Distributed in Europe by*
**J. LEHMANN HEBREW BOOKSELLERS**
20 Cambridge Terrace
Gateshead, Tyne and Wear
England NE8 1RP

*Distributed in Israel by*
**SIFRIATI / A. GITLER—BOOKS**
4 Bilu Street
P.O.B. 14075
Tel Aviv 61140

*Distributed in Australia & New Zealand by*
**GOLD'S BOOK & GIFT CO.**
36 William Street
Balaclava 3183, Vic., Australia

*Distributed in South Africa by*
**KOLLEL BOOKSHOP**
22 Muller Street
Yeoville 2198, Johannesburg, South Africa

---

**THE ARTSCROLL TANACH SERIES**
**EZRA**


ISBN
0-89906-089-7 (hard cover)
0-89906-090-0 (paperback)

*Typography by CompuScribe at* ArtScroll Studios, Ltd.
*4401 Second Avenue / Brooklyn, N.Y. 11232 / (718) 921-9000*

Printed in the United States of America by Moriah Offset
*Bound by* Sefercraft Quality Bookbinders, Ltd., Brooklyn, NY

# *Publisher's Preface*

*Mesorah Publications is proud to publish the* Book of Ezra *as the newest addition to the ArtScroll Tanach Series. We are particularly gratified that Rabbi Yosef Rabinowitz, a talmid chacham and rosh yeshivah of note, continues his association with us. His previously published Mishnah* Yevamos *with the Yad Avraham commentary is a major contribution to the understanding of one of the most complex tractates in the entire Mishnah. Rabbi Rabinowitz brings the same gifts to bear on his elucidation of the* Book of Ezra. *It is a book that is insufficiently studied and understood. Especially overlooked by most students is the relationship between* Ezra *and several other books of Scripture that deal with the same period. All are interwoven, and we are proud that the ArtScroll commentary shows these relationships as Rabbi Rabinowitz elucidates the teachings of the Sages and commentators.*

*As we have stressed in our other books, the ArtScroll commentary is not meant as a substitute for the study of the sources. While this commentary, like others in the various series, will be immensely useful even to accomplished scholars and will often bring to light ideas and sources they may have overlooked, we strongly urge those who are able to study the classic seforim in the original to do so. It has been said that every droplet of ink coming from Rashi's pen is worthy of seven days of contemplation. Notwithstanding the exceptional caliber of our authors, none of us pretends to take the place of the study of the greatest minds in Jewish history.*

*Despite the work on the ArtScroll Siddurim and Rosh Hashanah and Yom Kippur Machzorim, many distinguished authors continue to work on future volumes of Tanach and Mishnah. It remains an enormous privilege for us to have a share in the renaissance of Torah study and vibrant Jewish life in the English-speaking world.*

*Rabbi Nosson Scherman / Rabbi Meir Zlotowitz*
*General Editors*

# *Author's Preface*

ה׳ לִי בְּעֹזְרָי, *Hashem is with me through my helpers (Psalms 118:7).*

*Modern men are haunted by the spectre of doubt, despite the technological explosion of the past two centuries — or perhaps because of it. The quantum growth in the quality and extent of human power during this period has been matched by a steadily shrinking perception among human beings of the presence of God, in inverse ratio to the rise in technology. And if God has abandoned us, then our suffering is haphazard and pointless; our successes are empty and ephemeral. In terms of real permanence, nothing has any value.*

*So our culture makes a fetish of 'identity' because its members aren't sure if they have any; and an institution as vital for civilization as the basic family unit, the focal point of a person's sense of belonging and inviolability, disintegrates because family members are too unsure of themselves to risk joining one another in creating enduring relationships.*

וַיִּתְעָרְבוּ בַגּוֹיִם וַיִּלְמְדוּ מַעֲשֵׂיהֶם, *But they (the Jewish people) mingled with the nations and learned their deeds (Psalms 106:35).*

*Jewish communities can be corrupted by the prevailing atmosphere and must, therefore, learn to insulate themselves against its effects. What is our reply to the modern erosion of the sense of self that is attendant upon the erosion of the sense of God?*

וּבִשְׁנַת אַחַת לְכוֹרֶשׁ מֶלֶךְ פָּרַס...הֵעִיר ה׳ אֶת־רוּחַ כֹּרֶשׁ מֶלֶךְ־פָּרַס...
*And in the first year of Cyrus, king of Persia ... Hashem aroused the good will of Cyrus, king of Persia ... (Ezra 1:1).*

*During the period in which the opening passages of the* Book of Ezra *take place, the Sanctuary in Jerusalem lay in ruin, and the nation was dispersed throughout the Persian empire. The Babylonians, who had conquered and exiled them when the First Temple was destroyed with frightful loss of life and property, had now been conquered themselves by the Persian empire, and the Jews were subject to a new set of foreign masters. All of the visible indications of God's special relationship with the Jewish people had disappeared. But even in this dark period in the life of the nation, the ideal of Jewish redemption remained as the transcendental concept of history. God would no longer overcome the enemies of the Jewish people miraculously, as in the days of the exodus from Egypt and Joshua's conquest of the Land of Israel; but the hand of Providence would yet reach into the mystic source of human motivation and move men's souls so that this ideal might be realized. God aroused the good will of King Cyrus of Persia and caused him to decree that the Jewish exiles be allowed to return to the Holy Land and rebuild the Temple.*

*This is the reply to those who would deny God's presence during the times when he chooses, in His infinite wisdom, not to reveal Himself to mortals.*

*The Divine interest never wavers; God's vigilance is cosmic, eternal. None of His creatures is isolated; no one is ever abandoned. If His presence is not apparent, then His design is implemented through surrogate means, energized by His will.*

ה׳ לִי בְּעֹזְרָי, *HASHEM is with me through my helpers (Psalms 118:7). Indeed, there is no other helper.*

*It is this theme which reverberates throughout the narrative of this book. Beginning with the founding and subsequent completion of the Temple in the face of the pernicious efforts of the enemies of the Jews; continuing with the ascension of Ezra himself, fully empowered, financially and legally, to oversee the performance of the Temple services and all other Torah laws; and closing with the exercise of these powers by Ezra to eradicate the abomination of intermarriage practiced by some of the Jewish settlers, the guiding hand of Providence is always in evidence just below the surface of events. All of these monumental accomplishments were performed under the absolute domination of the Persian emperors — all were fashioned by the compelling impulse of the Divine intelligence serving as the master architect of Jewish deliverance.*

*Thus, the* Book of Ezra *is of major significance for our times, to be studied by Jews searching for authentic Judaism.* Ezra *is a source document for developing and refining the perception of the presence of God in the sweep of history. None of us knows what merit is required to bring an end to Jewish suffering. But it may be submitted that it is this study and this perception which must one day transform unseen Providence into revealed Presence, prophetic vision into triumph and realization, unswerving faith into boundless rejoicing.*

# *Acknowledgments*

הֶחָכָם עֵינָיו בְרֹאשׁוֹ, *literally, 'The wise man has his eyes in his head' (Koheles 2:14).* Sefer Charedim *(ch. 1) interprets 'the wise man eyes his origin' — i.e., he takes note that everything stems from the Originator of the universe, the Almighty Source of all existence. My acknowledgments begin with a word of wisdom, expressing thanks to the Creator of all beings for giving me the energy and dedication necessary to complete this work.*

*Our generation is experiencing a renaissance of enthusiasm for authentic Torah living, particularly among young people, and the ArtScroll Series has played a major role at the forefront of the literature of this renaissance. It is my good fortune to be privileged to make my contribution to this literature.*

*A note of thanks to* MRS. ESTHER VAN HANDEL *of Jerusalem for her valuable editing of the initial draft, and to* RABBI YEHEZKEL DANZIGER, *of Lakewood, N.J., for his final editing and for his perceptive, stimulating comments. Thanks, also, to my good friends* REB SHEAH BRANDER *and* REB DANIEL FLEISCHMANN, *whose artistic talents have invested this book with the esthetic beauty typical of all ArtScroll publications. A final expression of deep appreciation to my dear friends* RABBI MEIR ZLOTOWITZ *and* RABBI NOSSON SCHERMAN, *general editors of the ArtScroll Series. Their constant support on a very warm, personal level made the often exacting work pleasurable, and their uncompromising dedication to the highest professional standards was instrumental in developing every facet of the book.*

אַחֲרוֹן אַחֲרוֹן חָבִיב, *Closing remarks are doubly precious. I offer an inadequate expression of thanks and appreciation to my wife* שרה שתחי׳. *May Hashem grant us the opportunity to continue sharing in the growth and fulfillment of our children,* שיחיו.

*This work*
*is dedicated*
*in loving memory*
*of my parents*
ר׳ משולם ישׂשכר ב״ר אליעזר ז״ל
פייגא רייזל בת הרב מאיר ז״ל
*May the Torah precepts articulated throughout the book*
*serve as a fitting memorial to the ideals by which they lived.*
תנצב״ה

*Yosef Rabinowitz*
*17 Cheshvan, 5745*

# *An Overview*
# *Ezra — Molder of a New Era*

# *An Overview/ Ezra — Molder of a New Era*

רָאוּי הָיָה עֶזְרָא שֶׁתִּנָּתֵן תּוֹרָה עַל יָדוֹ לְיִשְׂרָאֵל אִלְמָלֵא קוֹדְמוֹ מֹשֶׁה.

*Ezra was worthy for the Torah to have been given to Israel through him, had Moses not preceded him* (Sanhedrin 21b).

לָמָּה נִקְרָא שְׁמָן אַנְשֵׁי כְּנֶסֶת הַגְּדוֹלָה? שֶׁהֶחְזִירוּ עֲטָרָה לְיוֹשְׁנָהּ.

*Why were they called 'Men of the Great Assembly'? Because they returned* [God's] *crown as it was of old* (Yoma 69b).

קְדוּשָּׁה רִאשׁוֹנָה קִדְּשָׁהּ לְשַׁעְתָּהּ וְלֹא קִדְּשָׁהּ לֶעָתִיד לָבֹא כֵּיוָן שֶׁעָלוּ בְּנֵי הַגּוֹלָה וְהֶחְזִיקוּ בְּמִקְצָת הָאָרֶץ קִדְּשׁוּהָ קְדוּשָּׁה שְׁנִיָּה הָעוֹמֶדֶת לְעוֹלָם.

*The first holiness [i.e., the sanctification of the land pronounced by Joshua] sanctified it only for that time [when Israel was sovereign over Eretz Yisrael] but did not sanctify it for all time. When the people of the exile ascended and took possession of some of the land, they gave it a second holiness that endures forever* (Rambam, Hil. Terumos 1:5).

## I. A Mire of Complexity

The *Book of Ezra* takes place in a period of Divine aloofness, as it were. It begins during the seventy-year exile following the Destruction of the First Temple [3338-3408/422-352 B.C.E.]. The Books of *Daniel* and *Esther* tell of events that took place during the same period, and so do much of *Yechezkel, Jeremiah, Zechariah,* and *Malachi,* not to mention the lamentations of *Eichah.* With the hindsight of our knowledge that the exile *did* come to an end and the Temple *was* rebuilt, we cannot even begin to imagine the degree of doubt and despair that permeated Israel during that time. History has taught us that exile is followed by redemption, but in those times, many people wondered if a rebirth was possible.

*History has taught us that exile is followed by redemption, but in those times, many people wondered if a rebirth was possible.*

They knew that the holiness of Eretz Yisrael is such that commandments performed on its soil are of a higher qualitative order than those performed anywhere else. They knew that God directs the flow of His blessing to Israel and from there it emanates to the rest of the world *(Ramban, Leviticus* 18:25, see also to *Genesis* 33:20). They knew that compared to someone living in *Eretz Yisrael,* a person living in other lands is like someone who has no God *(Kesubos* 110b). If so, did not the exile mean that God had rejected His people and no longer wanted their service? Why else would He expel them from the source of holiness on earth?

So it was that a group of elders came to Ezekiel and asked whether they, as a nation driven by God from His land, had any more obligation to pay continued allegiance to its 'former' Master than did a divorced woman expelled from the home of her husband or a freed slave sent away from the home of his owner *(Sanhedrin* 105a; see also ArtScroll *Yechezkel,* ch. 20).

*In Babylonia, Daniel and the brightest and best of Jerusalem's youth were serving as courtiers to Nebuchadnezzar, the destroyer of the Temple.*

In Babylonia, Daniel and the brightest and best of Jerusalem's youth were serving as courtiers to Nebuchadnezzar, the destroyer of the Temple, and to his successors. There, they were subjected to a combination of blandishment and persecution designed to wean them from their religion.

At least in Babylonia, the intensive study of Torah was beginning to strike roots, but Torah was not being taught extensively in Elam. Daniel, along with Mordechai, another of those erstwhile Jewish exiles, had been taken to Elam, and there Shushan, the lavish royal capital, was built. There, the Jewish community took part in Ahasuerus' blasphemous, orgiastic celebration of what he calculated to be the dashing of the hope that Jerusalem would ever be rebuilt (see ArtScroll *Esther* and Overview).

Everywhere the scattered, powerless Jewish people saw their glorious past ebbing away and no future coming to replace it.

The *Book of Ezra* brings us to a pivotal turning point in Jewish history. It begins an epoch that is still with us, because the glories of David and Solomon were never regained, even after the Second Temple was built. There was a change in God's manner of communicating with Israel and in the leadership of the people. Just as significant, there was a change in God's manner of punishing evil and in bestowing His kindness upon the world. This too has not changed appreciably with the passage of centuries.

*There was a change in God's manner of punishing evil and in bestowing His kindness upon the world.*

Let us, therefore, begin to search amid the mists of a difficult period. If we find shafts of light and follow them, we can achieve insights not only into Ezra's time, but our own as well.

# II. When Certainty is Lacking

## *The Need for Faith*

Man craves for certainty. There are few things more perplexing than the confusion of haphazard events that tumble forth without an apparent plan. Even bad news doesn't seem quite so tragic if we understand it as part of a meaningful pattern. The Torah and Talmud tell us that good is rewarded and evil punished. If so, the person who wakes up in the morning, prays devoutly, thanks God for his life, health and nourishment, and leaves for his workplace determined to deal ethically with his associates and honestly with his customers should flourish that day. Conversely, the person whose day rests on self-indulgence and double-dealing should be struck with pain and failure. Needless to say, experience does not confirm these expectations.

*Man craves for certainty. The truth is that were such certainty to exist, it would virtually remove the challenges of life.*

The truth is that were such certainty to exist, it would virtually remove the challenges of life.

*The concept of reward and punishment is a principle of faith, not of statistical certainty.*

Rational human beings tend to do what is demonstrably successful and shun actions that bring distress. They do so in their personal and professional lives, and they would in their spiritual lives as well, if they could be sure. If lightning struck sinners, only fools would sin. But, as we all know, the concept of reward and punishment is a principle of *faith,* not of statistical certainty. When the final page is turned on the world's current state of existence and man enters the ultimate epoch of redemption and a higher spiritual life, we will see and understand how everything led toward God's ultimate goal of perfection. Then, the reward for good, the punishment for evil, and all the steps in between will be seen to have played a role in arriving at the final destiny of the universe.

*Pointless labor is drudgery; collaboration in accomplishment is exhilarating.*

When the play is complete, all its actors will recognize how their respective, seemingly unrelated, roles helped produce God's masterpiece, much as a complex machine may be composed of commodities, labor, and ingenuity from all corners of the globe. The miner in South Africa, the sailor on the Pacific, the analyst in Massachussets, the oil rigger in Alaska, the copper refiner in Chile, and the blast-furnace operator in Pittsburgh would all feel better about the sweat, pain, and frustration that accompany their rigorous occupations if they could see and enjoy the complex and magnificent machine their labor made possible. Pointless labor is drudgery; collaboration in accomplishment is exhilarating.

*Two Sides*

The eleventh of Maimonides' Thirteen Principles of Faith is:

> אֲנִי מַאֲמִין בֶּאֱמוּנָה שְׁלֵמָה שֶׁהַבּוֹרֵא יִתְבָּרַךְ שְׁמוֹ
> גּוֹמֵל טוֹב לְשׁוֹמְרֵי מִצְוֹתָיו וּמַעֲנִישׁ לְעוֹבְרֵי מִצְוֹתָיו.
>
> *I believe with complete faith that the Creator, Blessed is His Name, rewards with good those who observe His commandments, and punishes those who violate His commandments (Daily Siddur,* based on *Rambam, Comm.* to *Mishnah Sanhedrin ch. 10).*

The commentators explain that God cannot properly reward good deeds unless the doer had overcome a temptation not to do good, and He cannot punish the performance of evil deeds unless the perpetrator could have been expected to know better. In other words, man must face a roughly equal challenge whether to be a saint or sinner; truth cannot be too obvious nor can falsehood be too enticing. Only in a balanced situation can one who sins be held to account for not having overcome the lure of his senses, and one who is virtuous be commended for letting his intelligence overcome desire.

*Man must face a roughly equal challenge whether to be a saint or sinner; truth cannot be too obvious nor can falsehood be too enticing.*

Thus, intelligent people can differ sharply on how to interpret the same evidence. Some say that the complex structure of the universe dictates that there must be a Creator; others, not as willing to see the truth, argue that man's knowledge and nature's predictability remove the need for supernatural answers. To turn to a more pragmatic example, rational people are willing to deny themselves luxuries and even simple comforts in order to put away savings for the future, for children, or for worthy causes, while other rational people insist that life should be lived to the hilt, and pleasures enjoyed while one is alive and healthy.

*Rational people are willing to deny themselves luxuries and even simple comforts in order to put away savings for the future.*

It is interesting that cultured people during most of history opted for the former course, that of denying themselves today in order to have more for tomorrow. This attitude is essential to the service of God, as well, because the Torah expects us to view this world as a means to prepare for a better one. Faith in a World to Come and willingness to endure privation here to accumulate good deeds that will be rewarded there are virtual prerequisites for a life of Torah observance. Conversely, the trend in contemporary society toward instant gratification at the expense of investment for a material future has its echo in an unwillingness to sacrifice for the sake of future spiritual benefits.

*The trend toward instant gratification has its echo in an unwillingness to sacrifice.*

That history seems to record an overwhelming majority of cases when people elected not to hear

God's voice and see His hand is dismaying but should not be surprising. As *Rambam* points out in his *Guide for the Perplexed,* man is more attracted to the tangible than to the abstract. For man to deny the cravings of his animal nature in favor of the urgings of his soul is no simple task. It demands faith, will, and discipline, and for all but the most superior people, it requires the buttress of a strong social order. Not surprisingly, therefore, Jewish religious observance has been strongest when the community structure has been sound and leadership strong.

*Man is more attracted to the tangible than to the abstract.*

During World War I, the path of battling armies cut across much of Poland and Lithuania, causing the flight of hundreds of thousands of Jews, including much of the rabbinate and community leadership. Orthodox life had been under siege before the war, but it had tenaciously fought back and held its own. The ravages of the war left a vacuum where existing community structures were destroyed. The forces of assimilation, Bolshevism, Socialism, secularism, and whatnot gobbled up major chunks of power. When the War ended, it was impossible in many communities to reestablish the pre-War social order. In a spiritual sense, the Holocaust began on Tishah B'Av of 1914, when World War I broke out.

*The ravages of the war left a vacuum where existing community structures were destroyed.*

The Jewish immigration to the United States and other lands of the free world resulted in a horrendous degree of assimilation in great measure because observant, powerful community organizations did not exist and the prevailing cultures of religious tolerance and freedom made it almost impossible to build them from scratch.

This is an interesting parallel to the situation facing Ezra and his colleagues when they had to reconstruct a Jewish society that had been ravaged by destruction and dispersion.

## III. The Attribute of Justice*

*The Book of Judges*

A bulwark of Creation is the concept of מִשְׁפָּט, *Divine Justice.* In its simplest terms, this would require that good and evil should be rewarded and punished immediately. But if this were to happen the scales of equal choice would be tipped. The truth might be too obvious to permit wrong choices. So God waits. Reward and punishment will come, but the intervals will be long enough to permit the basically righteous to perceive the truth, and the basically evil to deny it. Such a period was the long one described in the *Book of Judges.* When the people succumbed to the lures of idol worship, their strength slowly ebbed and they fell under foreign domination. When they heeded the call of a righteous leader, miracles happened and God helped them once again, whereupon the chapter would conclude with a statement like וַתִּשְׁקֹט הָאָרֶץ אַרְבָּעִים שָׁנָה, *and the land was tranquil for forty years (Judges* 3:11, 5:31, 8:28; cf. 3:30).

*God waits. Reward and punishment will come, but the intervals will be long enough to permit the basically righteous to perceive the truth, and the basically evil to deny it.*

None of this happened overnight. It was a process that took years. When the cycle was complete, the victims-turned-victors paused and drew their lessons. The teachings of Moses and Joshua had been relearned and reinforced. The repentance lasted and the land was tranquil and free for forty years or more. Then, new generations that had not lived through the earlier experience, or perhaps were too young to fully absorb the lesson, reverted to the failings of their forefathers. They failed to learn from history, so they repeated it.

*A cycle of reward and punishment is a theme of the Book of Judges.*

A cycle of reward and punishment is a theme of the *Book of Judges.* From the vantage point of history, we wonder why the people didn't realize the consequences of their misdeeds before tragedy overtook them. But we have 'superior knowledge' of *their* period only because the *Book of Judges*

*This section of the Overview is based on *Daas Tevunos* and *Maamar HaGeulah* of Rabbi Moshe Chaim Luzatto.

compresses over three hundred years of history into twenty-one chapters. The extraneous factors are omitted because the prophetic eye discerns them as insignificant to the topics at hand. But we can be sure that events overwhelmed the perceptions of people in those days just as they confuse us in our time. Similarly, when the history of our era finally lurches into Messianic times, a new history book will be written with Divine influence, a book that will outline the essential events of the long exile. Like the books of the Scriptures, it will show how the Divine scheme played itself out, what mattered and what didn't, and how virtue and sin fueled the engine of history. When the climax of history arrives, people will look back and wonder why the fools of yesteryear did not realize that the spiritual struggles of the Baal Shem Tov in Mezhibozh and the Gaon in Vilna were far more significant than the heroics of conquistadors in America and the revolutionaries at the Bastille.

*Like the books of the Scriptures, it will show how the Divine scheme played itself out, what mattered and what didn't.*

It is too easy for people to rationalize events and interpret them to coincide with their own preconceived notions. According to one Midrashic interpretation, the people who built the Tower of Babel (see *Genesis* ch. 11) had the notion that they could somehow shore up the heavens to prevent another deluge. To us it seems preposterous that only some 350 years after Noah's flood, people could believe that it was a natural occurrence for the earth to be flooded by a cataclysm of sorts every 1656 years. Instead of heeding the eye-witness testimony of Noah and his children that the Flood was a Divine punishment, people said it was a natural, predictable, recurring phenomenon *(Bereishis Rabbah* 38:1; *Tanchuma, Noach).*

*The Chofetz Chaim used to insist that every natural calamity is a call and a warning to Israel to repent.*

Incredibly irrational? No doubt, but are we more rational? The *Chofetz Chaim* used to insist that every natural calamity is a call and a warning to Israel to repent. To the *Chofetz Chaim,* no natural event could be assumed to be haphazard. Yet we read about volcanic eruptions, tidal waves, tornadoes, and prolonged droughts — and all we do is feel sorry for the people who live there and congratulate ourselves on our good luck or good sense in being elsewhere. It is sad but true that we are astounded at the errors of the people of Scriptural times, but we are equally oblivious to blindness of contemporary times. At least Isaiah and Jeremiah were taken seriously enough to be scorned and threatened as enemies of the established order; in modern times, those who attempt to put natural calamities in the context of spiritual failures are not even rewarded for their pains with a chuckle.

*We are astounded at the errors of the people of Scriptural times, but we are equally oblivious to blindness of contemporary times.*

## *A New Form of Judgment*

There are times when God deems it necessary to revise the function of Justice. Let us understand that, in essence, Judgment is a form of Mercy because, eventually, it removes evil and allows good to prevail. When His rod inflicts pain, it is because His mercy means to restrain man from his destructive path of evildoing. Whenever possible, God punishes gently, lovingly. However, at times when man has earned more wrath than he can endure, God withholds His rod. For if man overwhelmingly chooses evil over a long period of time and even refuses to heed the signals of Divine punishment, God's exercise of Justice would cause unlimited destruction. The result of continued extermination of evil would be to decimate the world. This was not God's plan.

*The result of continued extermination of evil would be to decimate the world. This was not God's plan.*

It is not surprising, therefore, that the classic exercise of Judgment must be suspended in an intellectual climate that would continue to ignore its lessons. Nevertheless, despite periods of despair and spiritual degradation, God guides history to the outcome He ordained at Creation. Man's good can hasten the favorable outcome and reduce the unpleasantness along the way; his lack of goodness can make life unpleasant indeed, as history consistently reminds those who care to listen. But throughout, God's underlying desire is to shower His gifts upon man.

In his classic Kabbalistic mussar work *Tomer*

*Devorah* (ch. 1), Rabbi Moshe Cordevero writes of God's attribute of patience: לֹא הֶחֱזִיק לָעַד אַפּוֹ, *Who has not retained His wrath eternally (Micah* 7:18):

> We find that in the time of Jeroboam ben Yoash God restored the boundary of Israel [i.e., Jeroboam reconquered the northern portion of *Eretz Yisrael* from Aram *(II Kings* 14:25)]. The Jews worshiped calves, and God was merciful to them, but they did not repent. If so, why was He merciful? Because of this very attribute that He does not retain His wrath eternally. To the contrary, He softens His wrath; even while the sin [that provoked Him] still exists He does not punish; He does not punish but waits and is merciful in the hope that they will repent ... God conducts himself mildly or harshly, but all for the benefit of Israel.

*The Jews worshiped calves, and God was merciful to them, but they did not repent. If so, why was He merciful?*

God tempers His Judgment according to man's ability to endure it. When the Russian Revolution took place in 1917 and the new government made peace with Germany, a wave of relief swept the country. Among the students of the *Chofetz Chaim,* who had fled from Poland to Russia with much of his yeshivah, there was a euphoric belief that permanent peace was at hand. The elderly sage addressed his students and told them that there would be no real peace until Messiah came. He was convinced, he explained, that the widespread suffering being endured by so many Jews were the birthpangs of the Messianic age. God would not have brought such suffering upon His people unless it was the start of the process that would lead to the final redemption. It is true, the *Chofetz Chaim* insisted, that there would be intermittent periods of peace and prosperity because human beings cannot bear unrelieved agony. Therefore, God in His mercy will give man respite to recover even if he does not repent. But if need be, wars and calamities will break out again until the climax of redemption finally arrives.

*There would be intermittent periods of peace and prosperity because human beings cannot bear unrelieved agony.*

*Unpleasant Results* There are major differences, however, whether the world functions according to pure justice or whether God's mercy dictates that He withhold punishment and provide undeserved goodness. In the original scheme of Creation, the heavenly bodies and designated angels serve as the conduits to bring blessing upon the earth. When Justice functions normally — that is, in the state of regularly rewarding good and punishing evil — the heavenly blessings flow uninterruptedly to earth. Vegetation flourishes, creatures are healthy, the earth is productive. But when excessive sin causes God to refrain from punishing man lest he be destroyed, the normal flow of blessing is also impeded. True, men will survive and be nourished, but the conduits of God's goodness become constricted. At a time when evildoers must be permitted undeserved survival and success, when brazenness becomes the norm and evil's power seems to wax unbridled, God blesses the world only grudgingly. There will be only limited prosperity, or perhaps some places will prosper while others go hungry. As the Talmud *(Sotah* 48b) expresses it, at such times fruit will lack the succulent taste it was meant to have. Perhaps the fact that some fruits seem not to grow as large as the Talmud's description of them — such as typical olives and eggs that, as described by the Talmud, seem to have been much larger than they are in modern times *(Noda B'Yehudah)* — may be explained as a by-product of the diminution of blessing.

*When Justice functions normally the heavenly blessings flow uninterruptedly to earth.*

There is a far more disturbing by-product of this Divine withdrawal from direct involvement in human affairs. The growing power of evil people causes revulsion and outrage. Not only their victims, but all decent people are offended by a lack of fairness. 'How can a just God allow this to happen?' they demand. And if He permits it — as we have heard heretics argue in this century — then ח״ו perhaps God is not just, or is detached from human affairs, or lacks power, or does not exist.

*The growing power of evil people causes revulsion and outrage. Not only their victims, but all decent people are offended by a lack of fairness.*

This is known as מִדַּת מִשְׁפָּט הַקָּשֶׁה, *the Attribute of*

*Harsh Judgment*, for, indeed, the harshest judgment of all is when God's wisdom dictates that He withhold his guiding hand from the world to the point where good seems to go unrewarded and evil unrestrained. It takes powerful faith to acknowledge that even in such times, though God may seem to 'slumber,' as Scripture puts it, He is not unaware, and He will rouse Himself when the proper time comes.

*It takes powerful faith to acknowledge that even in such times He is not unaware.*

### *Beneath the Seeming Slumber*

There is another major principle in the understanding of history. God may *seem* to slumber and be detached, but He never abandons His master plan for Creation. Even when it seems to function independently of Him, He is renewing His Creation at every moment, injecting it with the goodness that will blossom into future fulfillment, not destruction. At such times, God may be so heavily concealed that even the very greatest people can fail to perceive Him.

It has been noted that the day after the Jews were expelled from Spain, Columbus set sail to discover the hemisphere that was to become a major refuge and source of support for the Jewish people in the future. It took centuries before this connection became apparent, but in the 20-20 hindsight of history, can anyone deny the fact that God was preparing the succor while He was permitting Spain its temporary moment of ascension?

*In the 20-20 hindsight of history, can anyone deny the fact that God was preparing the succor while He was permitting Spain its temporary moment of ascension?*

Only a generation after the expulsion, Spain's glow began to fade; it would never again be a significant factor in world history, but the descendants of the despised and tortured Jewish nation would follow in the wake of the explorer commissioned by Ferdinand and Isabella, the ruling couple of Spain.

When Jacob's sons came back from Egypt with the bitter news that Simon had been detained by the viceroy and that he would not be released until young Benjamin was brought to Egypt, Jacob exclaimed in despair, לָמָה הֲרֵעֹתֶם לִי, *Why did you treat me so ill? (Genesis* 43:6).

Joseph was gone. Simon was gone. Jacob's land was gripped by famine. He was not receiving prophetic insight. If Jacob were to let Benjamin, too, be dragged down to Egypt at the whim of a heartless, suspicious overlord, the last remnant of Rachel might be lost forever. Perhaps the brotherly conspiracy that led to Joseph's 'death' was repeating itself again, with Benjamin its new victim. So Jacob felt impaled by doubt and helplessness — and most of all by an impenetrable concealment of God's purpose: נִסְתְּרָה דַרְכִּי מֵה׳, *my way has been hidden from HASHEM (Isaiah 40:27).*

*So Jacob felt impaled by doubt and helplessness — and most of all by an impenetrable concealment of God's purpose.*

Can we blame him for his outburst? Surely not. But even then, when God's Judgment seemed least apparent, the future was taking shape unbeknownst to Jacob.

ר׳ לֵוִי בְּשֵׁם ר׳ חָמָא בַּר חֲנִינָא: מֵעוֹלָם לֹא אָמַר יַעֲקֹב אָבִינוּ דָבָר שֶׁל בַּטָּלָה אֶלָּא כָאן. אָמַר הקב״ה אֲנִי עוֹסֵק לְהַמְלִיךְ בְּנוֹ בְּמִצְרַיִם, וְהוּא אוֹמֵר, לָמָה הֲרֵעֹתֶם לִי.

*R' Levi [said] in the name of R' Chama ben Chanina, 'Jacob never said anything pointless except here.' Said the Holy One, Blessed is He, 'I am engaged in making his son the ruler of Egypt, and he says, "Why did you treat me so ill?!"' (Bereishis Rabbah 91:10).*

Like an embryo forming in its mother's womb, the ingredients of a new future take shape behind events that seem incompatible with any higher purpose. So it was with Jacob. The destiny of Israel was being formed. Joseph in Egypt was preparing the crucible in which Israel's nationhood would be formed. While Jacob wondered why he was being tormented, God's pledge and prophecy to Abraham were moving toward fulfillment. Jacob's family was nearing the exile and subjugation of Egypt, from which they would explode in a blaze of miracles and the revelation at Sinai. Jacob's failure to perceive this is related not to degrade him but teach his offspring the eternal lesson that God's plan moves forward inexorably, whether or not its purpose is visible.

*Jacob's family was nearing the exile and subjugation of Egypt, from which they would explode in a blaze of miracles and the revelation at Sinai.*

So it was in the days of Ezra and his comrades. Let us attempt to make our way through the darkness that shrouded God's concern for His people and the plans that were taking shape.

# IV. The Oral and Written Torah*

*Implicit in the Torah*

*It is inconceivable for the Written Torah to stand on its own without the elucidations and interpretations that God taught Moses at Sinai.*

The Torah has two parts, תּוֹרָה שֶׁבִּכְתַב וְתוֹרָה שֶׁבְּעַל פֶּה, *the Written Torah and the Oral Torah.* In terms of revelation and law, the two Torahs are complementary and inseparable. It is inconceivable for the Written Torah to stand on its own without the elucidations and interpretations that God taught Moses at Sinai. This has been amply explained in many sources. (See Overview to ArtScroll *Bereishis,* vol. I, part of which is excerpted below.)

Every original thought of every diligent student is a part of the Torah which Moses received at Sinai, and no matter how voluminous the library, its contents were part of the spiritual treasure transmitted to Israel through Moses. But this is not to say that Moses was drilled line by line in every part of Torah literature and thought. A human being makes scores of decisions every day; responsible people make more decisions of greater consequence. The choices are unconscious and obvious, according to the taste and mode of living each individual has developed. Everyone has a philosophy of life, a set of priorities, a scale of values. Most questions that arise during the day are answered intuitively because they fit into each individual's own personal pattern. It is only a rare problem that demands a thought-out response — that is the question that tests a person and demands his attention.

*Moses was taught the unity of Torah, the essential principles and laws with a clarity that implicitly contained the response to every question.*

Moses was taught the unity of Torah, the essential principles and laws with a clarity that implicitly contained the response to every question. The great sage can easily answer questions he has never heard because his knowledge is so thorough and his

*The following sections of the Overview are based on the teachings of *Rabbi Gedalyah Schorr* in *Ohr Gedalyahu.*

understanding so clear that there are no difficulties for him. The struggling student memorizes individual facts, questions and answers; the sage knows broad principles. This clear knowledge, combined with an indefatigable intensity of study and single-minded desire to master every nuance of every law became the firm basis of an unbroken oral tradition that transmitted Moses' teachings intact from generation to generation with flawless accuracy.

This was a time when the only written Torah was the Five Books of the Chumash and the Scriptures. The entire Oral Torah remained oral. When difficult questions arose, they were decided by the Great Sanhedrin, whose authority was binding. The chain of tradition during those centuries of Jewish history was transmitted intact from teacher to student, generation after generation.

*The entire Oral Torah remained oral. When difficult questions arose, they were decided by the Great Sanhedrin.*

The blossoming of the Oral Law in all its intellectual brilliance and glory as we find it recorded in the Talmud and other books did not begin until the period of the Second Temple. But Heaven forbid that anyone suggest that the Rabbinic Era which began during the Second Commonwealth produced a new or reinterpreted Torah. During the entire period from the Giving of the Law at Sinai until the opening generations of the Second Commonwealth, the Oral Law was handed down intact and free of dispute. We find no record of halachic disagreement during the entire period. During the Second Commonwealth, however, the historic intensity of study began to decline ever so slightly, with the result that disputes began to arise among the Sages *(Sanhedrin* 88b; see *Rambam's* Introduction to *Mishnah).*

*During the Second Commonwealth, the historic intensity of study began to decline.*

Only one halachic dispute arose during the first three centuries of the period, and an additional three disputes arose between Hillel and Shammai, but there are numerous disputes recorded among their students. In addition, during the long and cruel period of harsh Roman persecution, Torah study became virtually impossible except with the most extreme self-sacrifice. The result was a further tragic

*Ways had to be employed to regain what was being lost. These ways were not new.*

decline in knowledge and an impairment in the transmission of the oral tradition. Without the totally reliable teacher-to-teacher chain of Oral Law, ways had to be employed to regain what was being lost.

These ways were not new. The principles of Biblical interpretation were taught to Moses at Sinai together with the rest of the Oral Law. They are the י״ג מִדּוֹת שֶׁהַתּוֹרָה נִדְרֶשֶׁת בָּהֶם, the Thirteen Hermeneutic Principles through which the Torah is interpreted *(Sifra).* The Talmud makes extensive use of these principles; in fact, they form its heart. Through their use, it was possible to rediscover laws from the oral tradition which had become forgotten or confused.

Following the death of Moses, a substantial body of orally transmitted law was forgotten as a result of the people's grief over the loss of their teacher. The leader and sage Asniel applied the principles of Biblical exegesis and restored the lost knowledge to Israel. How did he do it? Asniel made use of established exegetical principles to regain the halachic knowledge that had been forgotten *(Temurah* 16a).

*They took the eternal tools of exegesis and used them to reveal the secrets that had always been locked within the words of the Torah.*

During the Mishnaitic and Talmudic periods, the Sages of Israel employed the same devices. They took the eternal tools of exegesis and used them to reveal the secrets that had always been locked within the words of the Torah, secrets that Moses had taught Israel and that, in turn, had been transmitted orally for over a thousand years until the oral tradition began to crumble due to outside persecution and a lack of diligence. They did nothing new and certainly made no changes in the Torah; they merely made use of hermeneutic principles that had not been needed while the tradition of study was still at its zenith.

### *Man's Potential*

There is another dimension of the difference between the Written Torah and the Oral Torah that conditions our outlook on all aspects of life. The Written Torah represents the open, revealed word of

God, the heard and recorded prophecy. Like the Ten Commandments that were heard by all Israel amid a display of Divine power that left no doubt as to Who was their Giver, the rest of the Written Torah was and is accepted by Israel because of an unbreachable faith that it is God's word. The Oral Torah represents man's ability to understand God's teaching according to His transmitted clarifications and then to build upon these Divinely given principles to cope with cases and situations never anticipated by earlier generations.

*The Written Torah represents revelation and clarity, while the Oral Torah represents murky areas where human wisdom must interpret the Torah.*

In short, the Written Torah represents revelation and clarity, while the Oral Torah represents murky areas where human wisdom must interpret the Torah and apply it to current questions. In questions of halachah, for example, the Written Torah will tell us unambiguously that it is forbidden to kindle a flame on the Sabbath; the Oral Torah will clarify the underlying principles of this commandment and then go on to consider whether electricity is considered a flame.

In matters of interpreting history, the Written Torah and the prophets not only reported events but put them in perspective. They told Israel that a drought or a deluge was not a random event, but a sign or punishment. They proclaimed that a triumph was due not to numbers or military prowess, but to God's response to Israel's prayers or repentance. When there was no prophetic proclamation, or with the beginning of the Second Temple era, when prophecy ceased to exist, it fell to the Sages to interpret events based on the lessons of the Torah.

*When prophecy ceased to exist, it fell to the Sages to interpret events based on the lessons of the Torah.*

Why the Sages? Why not political, economic, military, medical experts? For this we must return to the basic premise that the universe and its history are reflections of the Torah and cogs in the mechanism of God's plan. If so, then it stands to reason that factual findings and educated opinions of the experts must be scrutinized under the lens of the Torah. Thus it was that in the chaotic, unclear circumstances that prevailed as the Babylonian Exile ended and Jews again were permitted to return to their land and rebuild the Temple, the responsibility of leadership passed to wise men of the Oral Torah.

### *The Implanted Torah*

The *Shulchan Aruch (Orach Chaim* 139:10) explains that this concept of a dual Torah is embodied in the blessing recited upon the conclusion of the Torah reading: אֲשֶׁר נָתַן לָנוּ תּוֹרַת אֱמֶת, *Who has given us a Torah of truth* — this refers to the Written Torah; וְחַיֵּי עוֹלָם נָטַע בְּתוֹכֵנוּ, *and Who has implanted within us eternal life* — this refers to the Oral Torah. The verb referring to the Oral Torah is truly remarkable. We are told that God 'implanted it within us.' The word for planting, נָטַע, is the same verb used for planting a tree. God *planted* His law within us, meaning that we can nurture it and make it grow, just as we can turn an acorn into an oak tree.

*God planted His law within us, meaning that we can nurture it and make it grow, just as we can turn an acorn into an oak tree.*

The Oral Torah is like a flourishing seedling that grows and produces more fruit with every season. All of it grew from the first seed that was properly nurtured and cared for. To think that any year's crop is unrelated to the first planting is ludicrous, but to think that the tree can thrive if it is not nourished and tended according to its own particular needs and rules is destructive. Israel was privileged to receive God's precious gift of being able to expound the Torah and of having its human wisdom become a part of the Torah itself, because man has the capacity to uncover the secrets within God's word.

*Israel was privileged to receive God's precious gift of having its human wisdom become a part of the Torah itself.*

In his commentary to *Shulchan Aruch* (ibid.), *Vilna Gaon* cites the Talmud's interpretation *(Chagigah* 3b) of *Koheles* (12:10-11). Verse 10 tells that King Solomon sought to find דִּבְרֵי חֵפֶץ וְכָתוּב יֹשֶׁר דִּבְרֵי אֱמֶת, *words of delight, and words of truth recorded properly;* this the Talmud refers to the Written Torah. Verse 11 goes on to speak of דִּבְרֵי חֲכָמִים, *the words of the wise.* It compares their words to the דָּרְבֹנוֹת, *goads,* that prevent a plowing animal from straying out of its proper furrow. The verse also cautions that the words of the wise are as firm and immutable as מַשְׂמְרוֹת נְטוּעִים, *well-driven nails.*

It is remarkable that the verse describes inanimate, firmly anchored nails as נְטוּעִים, a word that literally means *planted.* How does one 'plant' something that cannot grow? The answer is simple: when we seek to foster the growth of Torah wisdom, we must begin with the premise that our knowledge is based on convictions that are as unyielding as a *well-driven nail.* Man can and must expound the Torah and broaden his understanding of it, but he can do so only if he builds upon God-given principles that contain the messages needed for all conditions and generations, but that do not change their essence to accommodate the changing mores and preferences of opinions and desires. Properly understood, however, the words of Torah indeed thrive and flourish like well-tended saplings.

*God-given principles contain the messages needed for all conditions, but do not change their essence to accommodate changing mores and preferences.*

## From One Shepherd

The verse concludes בַּעֲלֵי אֲסֻפּוֹת, נִתְּנוּ מֵרֹעֶה אֶחָד, [the words of the wise are sayings of] *the masters of collections, coming from one Shepherd.* The Talmud (ibid.) explains that though the Oral Torah is a collection of the teachings of many Sages who may often disagree with one another, they nevertheless all derive from one Shepherd:

> *These are disciples of the wise who sit in manifold assemblies and occupy themselves with the Torah, some pronouncing 'clean,' some pronouncing 'unclean,' some prohibiting and some permitting ... Should a man say: How [in view of the contradictory opinions held by scholars] shall I learn Torah? — The verse therefore concludes:* נִתְּנוּ מֵרֹעֶה אֶחָד, *coming from one Shepherd: One God gave them [i.e., all the various opinions do not emanate from different 'Revelations,' but have their origin in the One Torah, given by the One God]; one leader [i.e., Moses] uttered them from the mouth of the Lord of all Creation. Therefore make yourself like a hopper [which is funnelshaped and more enters than issues from it; i.e., hear all commentaries and interpretations of the Torah; then discern the Truth] and*

*All the various opinions do not emanate from different 'Revelations,' but have their origin in the One Torah.*

*develop a perceptive heart to understand the words of those who pronounce 'unclean,' and the words of those who pronounce 'clean'; the words of those who prohibit and the words of those who permit ... (Chagigah 3b).*

The concepts of Torah study and the opinions of its wise men are compared to the physical world of goads, nails, and plants. In the physical world we see countless opposites operating in complementary harmony, such as fire and water, light and darkness, centripetal and centrifugal forces. Had we not grown up with acceptance of these 'natural' occurrences, we would find their interaction incomprehensible. But since we are accustomed to the laws of nature, we do not look at these puzzling phenomena as contradictory. That is 'how it is,' and we build our principles of knowledge accordingly. To do otherwise is to act at our own peril. Even when newly discovered phenomena, such as the behavior of the rings around Saturn, seem to contradict the previously defined and proven laws of physics, we are surprised but not shattered. We know that the new facts will be assimilated into the old structure somehow, and necessary modifications and innovations will be made to adjust our mathematical formuli to reality. Because 'One Shepherd' created all in accordance with His intelligent plan, logic dictates that there must be unity in the universe and that our failure to understand it can be due only to imperfect or insufficient knowledge. Perhaps some day we will know more, perhaps not; but meanwhile the universe is not nullified because it does not conform to our current state of understanding.

*Since we are accustomed to the laws of nature, we do not look at these puzzling phenomena as contradictory.*

Similarly, the apparent proliferation of disputes in the Oral Torah — some ruling 'clean' and some ruling 'unclean,' some ruling 'guilty' and some ruling 'innocent' — must be seen in the perspective of the fact that ultimately all opinions are נִתְּנוּ מֵרֹעֶה אֶחָד, *coming from one Shepherd.* Provided that each opinion is based on the Torah itself, it remains an expression of the truth, a facet of the total fabric of

*The apparent proliferation of disputes in the Oral Torah must be seen in the perspective of the fact that ultimately all opinions are coming from one Shepherd.*

Torah knowledge, even though it contradicts other opinions. Even an opinion that is rejected by the halachah is worthy of study and respect, because it has a basis in the Torah. Perhaps, as so often happens in the Talmud and Codes, that opinion is found to prevail in a particular set of circumstances or it helps shed light and clarify the normative opinion.

*Even an opinion that is rejected is worthy of study and respect, because it has a basis in the Torah.*

# V. Ezra — Giver of Torah*

## *Delayed Journey*

כָּל זְמַן שֶׁבָּרוּךְ בֶּן נֵרִיָּה קַיָּם לֹא הִנִּיחוֹ עֶזְרָא וְעָלָה.
*As long as Baruch ben Neriah was alive, Ezra did not leave him to ascend* [*to Eretz Yisrael*] *(Megillah 16b).*

This explains why Ezra, the leading figure and the greatest of his people in those formative years, did not even come to Eretz Yisrael until *twenty-three* years after the first wave of Jews returned under the leadership of Zerubabel ben Shealtiel, scion of the Davidic dynasty, and Jeshua ben Jozadak, the *Kohen Gadol.* [See chart p. 157.] This seems strange, indeed, especially in view of his condemnation of the Levites and others who preferred the security and prosperity of Babylonia and Persia to the tribulations of rebuilding the land (8:15; *Yevamos* 86b). Why did Ezra, of all people, choose to remain behind for so long?

*Why did Ezra, of all people, choose to remain behind for so long?*

Ezra's teacher, the prophet Baruch ben Neriah, was too old and frail to make the journey to Eretz Yisrael, and as long as he lived, Ezra would not leave him *(Megillah* 16b). He stayed at Baruch's side שֶׁהָיָה צָרִיךְ לְבָרֵר תַּלְמוּדוֹ, *because he* [*Ezra*] *needed to clarify his learning* under his teacher's tutelage *(Shir HaShirim Rabbah* 5:5). It is from Ezra's decision to stay with Baruch that the Talmud *(Megillah* 16b) derives that Torah study is not interrupted even to build the Temple.

There is special significance in the fact that Ezra was the one whose experience revealed this primacy

*This section, too, is based on *Ohr Gedalyahu.*

*His Torah study was more important than the construction of the Temple, because the Temple depended upon the highest possible level of Torah knowledge.*

of Torah study. It was he whose dominant presence was to inaugurate the new era of the Oral Torah. Consequently, it was incumbent upon Ezra to perfect himself in his Torah knowledge. His Torah study was more important than the construction of the Temple, because the Temple itself, in this new phenomenon of Jewish history, depended upon the highest possible level of Torah knowledge and insight.

This emergence of Torah sages as the guiding lights of the people was not an accident of history; it was revealed in a prophecy of Zechariah ben Iddo who, together with Haggai, delivered God's command that Zerubabel and Jeshua commence building the Temple even without the king's permission (see 5:1). Zechariah was shown a vision of redemption. The Temple would be rebuilt and the *Menorah,* which symbolizes the luminescence of Torah knowledge, would once again illuminate the world. As part of his vision he saw the *Menorah* flanked by two olive trees. The angel of God told him [as interpreted by *Sanhedrin* 24a] that the olive trees symbolized the Torah scholars of Eretz Yisrael and Babylonia *(Zechariah* 4:11-14). Thus, as part of the joyous prophecy that the exile was coming to an end and the Temple would again cast its spiritual glow upon the nation, Zechariah was shown that henceforth the scholars of the age would be the prime forces in fueling the flame and assuring its survival.

*Henceforth the scholars of the age would be the prime forces in fueling the flame and assuring its survival.*

## *A Leader for a New Age*

רָאוּי הָיָה עֶזְרָא שֶׁתִּנָּתֵן תּוֹרָה עַל יָדוֹ לְיִשְׂרָאֵל אִלְמָלֵי קוֹדְמוֹ מֹשֶׁה.

*Ezra was worthy for the Torah to have been given to Israel through him, had Moses not preceded him (Sanhedrin 21b).*

At first glance it would seem that only an accident of history deprived Ezra of a mission for which he was well qualified. Had not Moses preceded him, Ezra would have been the agent to present the Torah to Israel. But, because he lived a thousand years too late, he was denied the opportunity. A sad coincidence? No, not at all. The Sages consider it important to tell us about Ezra's stature because he *was* cast in a parallel role to that of Moses. Just as Moses was the agent who transmitted the Written Torah to Israel, Ezra was the agent who, in a crucial period in our history, was the leader and catalyst in the blossoming of the Oral Torah.

*Just as Moses transmitted the Written Torah to Israel, Ezra was the leader and catalyst in the blossoming of the Oral Torah.*

בֵּית דִּינוֹ שֶׁל עֶזְרָא הֵם הַנִּקְרָאִים אַנְשֵׁי כְּנֶסֶת הַגְּדֹלָה. וְהֵם חַגַּי זְכַרְיָה וּמַלְאָכִי, דָּנִיאֵל, וַחֲנַנְיָה מִשָׁאֵל וַעֲזַרְיָה, וּנְחֶמְיָה בֶּן חֲכַלְיָה, וּמָרְדְּכַי בִּלְשָׁן, וּזְרוּבָבֶל, וְהַרְבֵּה חֲכָמִים עִמָּהֶם תַּשְׁלוּם מֵאָה וְעֶשְׂרִים זְקֵנִים.

*The court of Ezra is what is known as the Men of the Great Assembly. They were Haggai, Zechariah and Malachi, Daniel, Hananiah, Mishael and Azariah, Nechemiah ben Hachaliah, Mordechai Bilshan, Zerubabel, and many sages with them, a total of 120 elders (Rambam, Intro. to Mishneh Torah).*

During the period of the Second Temple, the principles of Scriptural exegesis and Talmudic reasoning were utilized to articulate, derive, and develop the immense body of law and logic that became the Talmud and from which the infinite body of Rabbinic literature began to flow. Since Ezra was their leader it was not a coincidence that a new era of Torah knowledge coincided with his emergence.

## The Lure of Idolatry

The אַנְשֵׁי כְּנֶסֶת הַגְּדֹלָה, *Men of the Great Assembly,* who were the leaders of Israel, knew that the *Shechinah* (Divine Presence) would not rest upon the Second Temple as it had upon the First, and that after the death of the few living prophets the age of prophecy would be over and God would no longer speak directly to Israel through His emissaries. The people were deeply distressed, not only because they longed for these sacred gifts, but because they realized that the nation's renewed vigor required some form of spiritual grandeur to compensate for the loss of the *Shechinah* and prophecy. So they prayed, insisting that they could not go ahead with

*They realized that the nation's renewed vigor required some form of spiritual grandeur to compensate for the loss of the Shechinah and prophecy.*

the construction of the Temple unless the generation was granted an intensified degree of insight into the Torah:

אַף עַל פִּי שֶׁלֹּא שָׁרְתָה שְׁכִינָה בְּבַיִת שֵׁנִי, מִכָּל מָקוֹם עִיקַּר הַתּוֹרָה וְזִיוָהּ וַהֲדָרָהּ לֹא הָיָה אֶלָּא בְּבַיִת שֵׁנִי, שֶׁלֹּא רָצוּ לִבְנוֹת עַד שֶׁהִבְטִיחָם השי״ת לְגַלּוֹת לָהֶם רָזֵי תוֹרָה.

*Even though the Divine Presence did not rest on the Second Temple, nevertheless, the main part of Torah, its splendor and its glory, was only in the period of the Second Temple, for they [i.e., the Men of the Great Assembly] did not wish to build it until HASHEM, Blessed is He, promised that He would reveal to them the secrets of the Torah (Pirkei Heichalos 27).*

*Vilna Gaon* (glosses to *Seder Olam)* explains the direct relation of the new emphasis on the Oral Torah to the loss of prophecy. During those early, troubled days when Jerusalem and the Temple were being built in fits and starts (as narrated in *Ezra* and *Nehemiah),* the Men of the Great Assembly looked to the future of the nation in the light of its downfall of the past. The First Temple and the Jewish nation — both the Ten Tribes of Samaria and the Kingdom of Judah — had crumbled spiritually because of the sin of idolatry. All the prophets from Moses onward had warned eloquently and strenuously about the pitfalls of this cardinal sin. Nevertheless, Israel succumbed, with the result that it was banished from its land and nearly destroyed as a people.

*The First Temple and the Jewish nation had crumbled spiritually because of the sin of idolatry.*

Of all the sins of the ancients, this is the hardest for modern Jews to understand. We can identify with sins of the flesh; what human being has never been tempted? We can comprehend greed for money or power and the excesses it can lead to, even bloodshed; the daily newspapers are sufficient proof that there is nothing esoteric about such moral corruption. But why were the people of Torah and spirituality tempted by images and idols that not even a child takes seriously today? And even if a rationale could be found for idolatry, as explained by

*Why were the people of Torah and spirituality tempted by images and idols that not even a child takes seriously today?*

*Rambam* and others, why should there have been such an obsessive passion for it that even prophets were ignored and murdered in the people's headlong passion to choose strange gods and pagan ceremonies over the one *God* and His Torah?

*The Price*

We will never know the answer to this question, just as a person without a sense of smell can never know the fragrance of perfume. The Talmud *(Yoma* 69b) tells us that at the outset of the Second Temple period, the Men of the Great Assembly prayed that the passion for idolatry be removed from the Jewish people. To them, idolatry was not a historical curiosity; they had seen its effects and they were aware of its attraction. They had seen it at work and wept at its effects. They knew that it was capable of destroying the new commonwealth just as it had destroyed the old. Therefore they pleaded that it no longer be a powerful lure.

*To them, idolatry was not a historical curiosity; they had seen its effects and they were aware of its attraction.*

Their prayer was answered, but at a price. Every struggle involves prizes and penalties. A person who grapples with a difficult choice between one path and another becomes stronger and better for having made the right choice, and vice versa. In ancient Eretz Yisrael, the greatest spiritual struggle people faced was that presented by the powerful attraction of idolatry. Often, the prophets of the idols seemed so right, so lofty, that it seemed blasphemous to disobey them, no matter what they preached. The Torah itself *(Deuteronomy* 13:1-4) tells us that false prophets may even perform undeniable miracles to support their case — but even then, our love for God must be so consuming that we must dismiss their preachings as nothing more than God's test, to let us prove that we are unswervingly devoted to Him. When Israel was confronted by the wile and passion of false prophets, by the tantalizing attraction of idol worship, and the nation refused to succumb, it earned the privilege of closeness to God and deeper insights into holiness. This was the essence of prophecy and הַשְׁרָאַת הַשְּׁכִינָה, *the resting of the Divine Presence* [*Shechinah*].

*False prophets may even perform undeniable miracles to support their case — but even then, our love for God must be consuming.*

Prophecy is a communication from God to man. The 'resting of the *Shechinah*' means that Godliness becomes visible in man's behavior, that a person's attitudes and actions are a direct reflection of God's will. Thus, prophecy was the fitting reward for a triumph over the strong pull toward the spiritual attraction of evil and false spirituality. When the Men of the Great Assembly accomplished the removal of the spiritual challenge of idolatry, the reward of prophecy likewise was withdrawn. Idolatry and prophecy balanced one another in the scale of strife and reward; when one was gone the other was removed.

*Prophecy was the fitting reward for a triumph over the strong pull toward the spiritual attraction of evil and false spirituality.*

Prophecy, like the Written Torah, is the direct word of God. But there is an indirect word of God as well: the Torah that permeates the mind and heart of those who immerse themselves in its study and absorb its message. As the Talmud teaches, 'From the day the Temple was destroyed, even though prophecy was taken from the prophets, it was not taken from the wise men' *(Bava Basra* 14a). *Ramban* explains that those who are wise in the Torah can derive from it God's will and intent.

## *The Kohen's Uniqueness*

In addition to his greatness in learning, piety, and leadership, Ezra was a *Kohen,* and that had an important bearing on his mission. For the teaching of the Oral Torah was the particular province of the priestly family from Israel's early days in the wilderness. *R' Tzadok HaKohen* of Lublin propounds that the first place in the Torah where a particular principle or phenomenon is found is the key to understanding its essence. The first place where the principles of the Oral Torah were used to derive the law was where Aaron proved through logic that the Rosh Chodesh *mussaf* [additional offering] should be burned if no *Kohanim* were eligible to eat it *(Leviticus* 10:16-20). This indicates that the analysis and teaching of the Oral Torah is the particular province of the *Kohanim.* That is why Aaron kindled the Tabernacle Menorah during all the forty years in the wilderness even though,

*The first place in the Torah where a particular principle or phenomenon is found is the key to understanding its essence.*

halachically, the Menorah may be kindled even by an Israelite. The Menorah represents the glow of the Oral Torah, and in the formative years of the nation, it was Aaron's role to develop that aspect of the Torah among the people.

*The Menorah represents the glow of the Oral Torah, and in the formative years of the nation, it was Aaron's role to develop that aspect of the Torah.*

Therefore, too, when the Syrian-Greeks threatened to extinguish the light of Torah from among the Jewish people and replace it with Greek culture, it was the priestly Hasmonean family that led the revolution that saved Israel as the nation of Torah. That is why they insisted on setting up and kindling a makeshift Menorah as soon as they regained the Temple. They used wood and iron because nothing else was available immediately, but they refused to delay. Their purpose was not to celebrate the military victory, but to reinforce the concept that Torah study is supreme, the main reason for their fight (see Overview to ArtScroll *Chanukah).*

*Ezra, as a Kohen, carried the banner of Aaron.*

Ezra, as a *Kohen,* carried the banner of his ancestor Aaron and emerged as the leader in a generation of giants. To conceive of the Jewish people today without the guidance, wisdom, and vision of the Men of the Great Assembly is an impossibility. They provided the strong response to unprecedented situations, and as their leader, Ezra was the key figure around whom their work revolved. It is noteworthy that *Rambam* refers to the entire assembly as Ezra's *beis din* [court].

## *The Great Assembly*

לָמָה נִקְרָא שְׁמָן אַנְשֵׁי כְנֶסֶת הַגְּדוֹלָה? שֶׁהֶחְזִירוּ עֲטָרָה לְיוֹשְׁנָהּ. אָתָא מֹשֶׁה אָמַר „הָאֵל הַגָּדוֹל הַגִּבּוֹר וְהַנּוֹרָא.״ אָתָא יִרְמְיָה וְאָמַר „נָכְרִים מְקַרְקְרִין בְּהֵיכָלוֹ — אַיֵּה נוֹרְאוֹתָיו?״ לֹא אָמַר נוֹרָא. אָתָא דָנִיאֵל אָמַר „נָכְרִים מִשְׁתַּעְבְּדִים בְּבָנָיו — אַיֵּה גְבוּרוֹתָיו?״ לֹא אָמַר גִבּוֹר. אָתוּ אִינְהוּ וְאָמְרוּ „אַדְרַבָּא זוֹ הִיא גְבוּרוֹתָיו שֶׁכּוֹבֵשׁ אֶת רְצוֹנוֹ שֶׁנּוֹתֵן אֶרֶךְ אַפַּיִם לָרְשָׁעִים. וְאֵלּוּ הֵן נוֹרְאוֹתָיו שֶׁאִלְמָלֵא מוֹרָאוֹ שֶׁל הקב״ה הֵיאָךְ אוּמָּה אַחַת יְכוֹלָה לְהִתְקַיֵּם בֵּין הָאוּמּוֹת?״

*Why were they called 'Men of the Great Assembly'? Because they returned [God's] crown as it was of old.*

*Why were they called 'Men of the Great Assembly'? Because they returned [God's] crown as it was of old. Moses had come and said 'the great, mighty, and awesome God' (Deuteronomy 10:7). Jeremiah had come and said, 'Gentiles revel in His Sanctuary, where is His awesomeness?' [Because Jeremiah could not see how God was displaying His awesomeness, when he spoke of God he] did not say 'awesome' (see Jeremiah 32:18). Daniel came and said, 'Gentiles subjugate His children — where is His might?' [Because Daniel could not see how God was displaying His might, he] did not say 'mighty' (Daniel 9:4). They [the Men of the Great Assembly] came and said, 'To the contrary — this is His might, that He suppresses His will and is slow to be angry with the wicked. And this is His awesomeness, that if not for the awe of the Holy One Blessed is He, how could a single nation survive among the nations?' (Yoma 69b).*

*Of all the achievements of the Great Assembly, the Sages singled out one for special distinction.*

Of all the achievements of the Great Assembly, the Sages singled out one for special distinction. Why was this group of men called 'great'? Because they restored the adjectives גִּבּוֹר and נוֹרָא, *mighty* and *awesome,* to the list of God's praises, and incorporated those words into the opening blessing of *Shemoneh Esrei (Yoma* 69b; see full citation above). It took the unique spiritual insight of the Talmudic Sages to isolate this as a paramount accomplishment, and if we understand it properly, this seemingly unimportant modification in the liturgy is symbolic of the full range of the Assembly's activity.

*Jeremiah and Daniel were not wrong when they failed to discern God's might and awesomeness.*

Jeremiah and Daniel were not wrong when they failed to discern God's might and awesomeness at a time when enemies cavorted in the Temple and subjugated Israel. But they were prophets, accustomed to the Written Torah, the direct word and clearly perceived hand of God, and looking at the tragic degradation of all that was holy, they could not find might or awesomeness. The Men of the Great Assembly looked with the prophecy of wisdom. It was their mission to interpret the Torah's response to history just as they would its principles to new questions in halachah.

*Earlier generations had seen God's attribute of Judgment in its simple, direct form. Good was rewarded and evil was punished.*

Earlier generations had seen God's attribute of Judgment in its simple, direct form. Good was rewarded and evil was punished. Time might go by before the judgment was executed, but sincere, perceptive people saw the connection between human deeds and Divine response. In the aftermath of the first Destruction, Judgment seemed to be suspended while its Executor slumbered. The prophets Jeremiah and Daniel could not testify to what they could not see. Where was His might? Where was His awesomeness? Where was His judgment?

The standard bearers of the Oral Torah saw a new manifestation of Judgment. It was a *harsh* judgment (see above, p. xxv), but it was a course dictated by mercy. They saw that evil had proliferated to the point where the only way God could preserve the universe was to stand back and not wipe out evildoers. Nevertheless, the Sages also realized that God's master plan would still move inexorably to completion, though its movement would be barely discernible, if at all. He was surely no less mighty and awesome than He had been when He split the Sea of Reeds or snuffed out the lives of Sennacherib's entire army. The Sages of the time perceived a new manifestation of might: who but the All-Powerful could stand patiently, impassively by while the wicked mocked Him, desecrated His Temple, and tormented His children? Silence can be as powerful as roaring anger, and forbearance for the sake of a goal demands at least as much strength as a wrathful blow. And they perceived a new manifestation of awesomeness: what awe must permeate creation if seventy raging wolves could not devour one defenseless lamb! Israel was scattered among hostile nations, but they were unable to destroy it. Truly an awesome power was protecting Israel when its statehood and armies had ceased to exist.

*Silence can be as powerful as roaring anger, and forbearance for the sake of a goal demands at least as much strength as a wrathful blow.*

Because of this insight, the Sages gave to the leaders of that generation the title 'the *Great* Assembly.' Only with their sort of penetrating understanding could Israel delve into its Torah and its history in the epoch that was then beginning.

# VI. The Land's Holiness

*Conquest*

קְדוּשָׁה רִאשׁוֹנָה קִדְּשָׁהּ לְשַׁעְתָּהּ וְלֹא קִדְּשָׁהּ לֶעָתִיד לָבֹא כֵּיוָן שֶׁעָלוּ בְּנֵי הַגּוֹלָה וְהֶחֱזִיקוּ בְּמִקְצַת הָאָרֶץ קִדְּשׁוּהָ קְדוּשָּׁה שְׁנִיָּיה הָעוֹמֶדֶת לְעוֹלָם.

*The first holiness [i.e., the sanctification of the land pronounced by Joshua] sanctified it only for that time [when Israel was sovereign over Eretz Yisrael] but did not sanctify it for all time (Chagigah 3b). When the people of the exile ascended and took possession of some of the land, they gave it a second holiness that endures forever (Rambam, Hil. Terumos 1:5).*

*When the people of the exile ascended and took possession of some of the land, they gave it a second holiness that endures forever.*

In an important sense, the new nature of the Jewish experience that began in the Second Temple era, muted and subdued though it was, had a more permanent effect than that of the miraculous conquests of Joshua and David.

*Rambam* (ibid.) explains that the first sanctification was put into effect by כִּבּוּשׁ, *conquest,* and therefore became nullified when Israel was no longer sovereign over its land. The second sanctification, however, did not result from conquest, because Eretz Yisrael was part of the Persian Empire and the Jews were permitted to settle there only by the sufferance of Cyrus. That sanctification was based on חֲזָקָה, *possession,* i.e., the fact that Jews were again living in Eretz Yisrael. Since then, there have always been at least some Jews on the land, even in times when it was incredibly dangerous for them to be there.

*That sanctification was based on the fact that Jews were again living in Eretz Yisrael.*

It is true, of course, as *Kessef Mishnah* states, that even during the First Commonwealth, there was חֲזָקָה, *possession,* even though the land had been conquered originally. Since a handful of Jews remained in the land even during the exile, why should the loss of Jewish sovereignty have nullified the sanctification? In the case of the First Temple, though Israel did have possession of the land, it was not habitation but conquest that they relied upon to make it theirs and give it holiness. It is true, as *Kessef Mishnah* argues, that there was Jewish possession as well, but it was incidental to the conquest. The Jewish people based their dominion and sanctification on the sovereignty born of conquest. But once the land was conquered by Assyria in the north and later by Babylonia in the south, Jewish sovereignty ended, and with it the sort of possession upon which the Jews relied.

*In the case of the First Temple, though Israel did have possession of the land, it was not habitation but conquest that they relied upon to make it theirs and give it holiness.*

## *A New Era*

In the case of the Second Temple, however, the directness of conquest was lacking, just as the clarity of the Written Torah and prophecy were lacking. Ezra and his colleagues endowed the land with sanctity because it was possessed by the people of Israel. *Yerushalmi Shevi'is* (6:1, 17b) expounds that the Second Commonwealth was superior to the First in the respect that Israel's original possession of the land could come about only under circumstances of independence, whereas the Second Commonwealth achieved its status despite foreign domination. Less perceptible — yes. Less pleasing to those who feel that nationhood must have the trappings of invincibility — most certainly! But there was a powerful virtue in this kind of sanctification, for it has survived conquest, destruction, and exile. The holiness of Eretz Yisrael today derives from Ezra's settlement, not Joshua's conquest *(see R' Chaim Soloveitchik, Chiddushei HaGrach, Gittin).*

*The Second Commonwealth achieved its status despite foreign domination.*

*Rabbi Samson Raphael Hirsch (Horeb)* explains the basic difference between the premises upon which the two commonwealths were built. Joshua proclaimed sanctification and based nationhood upon political independence. That is why the sanctity could not survive the loss of sovereignty. But Ezra's world was different. Cyrus ruled the world, not Zerubabel. Israel could not hope to regain its land by conquest; never was it ordained that they would. Two centuries earlier, Isaiah had prophesied that Cyrus would build the Temple *(Isaiah* 45:1-3), implying plainly that Israel would not have the power to do so, as indeed, it didn't. What, then, would be Israel's role? Ezra understood that Israel's new role was to forge a *spiritual* nationhood. It would derive nurture from Eretz Yisrael by living there and by living up to the ideals set forth by the Torah and expounded by the Sages. Instead of the political independence of the First Commonwealth, Ezra based Israel's future on spiritual independence. Only during the relatively brief period of the Hasmonean dynasty was the Second Commonwealth a strong political and military power (see ArtScroll *Chanukah),* but no nation on earth has so consistently been a spiritual superpower, even in exile and degradation.

*Ezra understood that Israel's new role was to forge a spiritual nationhood.*

# VII. Three Prophecies

*Perplexities*

There were three prophecies concerning the Second Temple and, as is often the case with such Divine messages, their definite meaning was nebulous until they were fulfilled. The first was delivered by Isaiah:

כֹּה אָמַר ה׳ לִמְשִׁיחוֹ לְכוֹרֶשׁ ... לְמַעַן עַבְדִּי יַעֲקֹב וְיִשְׂרָאֵל בְּחִירִי ... הוּא יִבְנֶה עִירִי וְגָלוּתִי יְשַׁלֵּחַ ...

*So said God to His anointed, to Cyrus ... For the sake of Jacob My servant and Israel My chosen ... he shall build My city and he shall free My captives (Isaiah 45).*

Cyrus, who wept and groaned over the Temple's destruction *(Seder Eliyahu Rabbah,* 19), became God's chosen instrument to fulfill the ancient prophecy and bring the glory of the Divine Presence back to the holy mountain where Abraham bound Isaac to the altar, where Jacob beheld the heavenly ladder, where David set his hopes, and where Solomon build the Temple of God. It was the Divine

*Cyrus, who wept and groaned over the Temple's destruction, became God's chosen instrument to fulfill the ancient prophecy.*

will that Cyrus, not the Jews, build the House of God and bring its children back to its holy environs. But Cyrus lacked the will or wisdom to seize the privilege; instead he gave it to the Jewish people (*Megillah* 12a). The righteous Persian monarch decreed that the Jews might go home again — and only 42,360 heeded his call! Forty-two thousand heard the call of prophecy but millions stayed behind.

*But Cyrus lacked the will or wisdom to seize the privilege; instead he gave it to the Jewish people.*

There were two other prophecies, so similar that they could almost be considered as one, but they were different:

כִּי כֹה אָמַר ה׳ כִּי לְפִי מְלֹאת לְבָבֶל שִׁבְעִים שָׁנָה אֶפְקֹד אֶתְכֶם וַהֲקִימֹתִי עֲלֵיכֶם אֶת דְּבָרִי הַטּוֹב לְהָשִׁיב אֶתְכֶם אֶל הַמָּקוֹם הַזֶּה.

*For thus said* HASHEM, *'After seventy years of Babylon are completed, I will remember you and establish My good word concerning you to return you to this place' (Jeremiah 29:10).*

אֲנִי דָנִיֵּאל בִּינֹתִי בַּסְּפָרִים מִסְפַּר הַשָּׁנִים אֲשֶׁר הָיָה דְבַר ה׳ אֶל יִרְמְיָה הַנָּבִיא לְמַלֹּאות לְחָרְבוֹת יְרוּשָׁלַיִם שִׁבְעִים שָׁנָה.

*I, Daniel, considered in the books the number of years whereof the word of* HASHEM *came to Jeremiah the prophet that he would complete seventy years of the ruins of Jerusalem (Daniel 9:2).*

Both Jeremiah and Daniel said that the Babylonian exile would end after seventy years, but there was a difference between the two prophecies. Jeremiah spoke of 'seventy years of Babylon,' implying that the seventy-year period depended on the chronology of Babylonian history. Daniel, on the other hand, spoke of the ruins of Jerusalem, implying that the end of the exile would be counted from the Destruction. Did the two prophecies contradict one another? How could both be correct?

*Both Jeremiah and Daniel said that the Babylonian exile would end after seventy years, but there was a difference between the two prophecies.*

King Nebuchadnezzar of Babylonia conquered Eretz Yisrael in the year 3319 from Creation. In the seventieth year from that conquest, 3390, Cyrus gave the electrifying announcement with which the

*Book of Ezra* begins: the Jews were permitted — urged — to return to their land and rebuild their Temple. It was seventy years since Babylonia's ascendancy over Eretz Yisrael, an event that perhaps could also be understood as 'ruins of Jerusalem,' because the glory of the Holy City had been tarnished, not to return.

But only a few years later, in 3392, Ahasuerus became king and ordered that the construction of the Temple be stopped (see ch. 5).

*We can imagine the consternation of Israel. What of Isaiah's prophecy that Cyrus, as God's anointed, would build the Temple?*

We can imagine the consternation of Israel. What of Isaiah's prophecy that Cyrus, as God's anointed, would build the Temple? If, indeed — as seemed undeniable — Jeremiah's seventy years were counted from the conquest, then apparently the promise had been aborted. Had God banished Israel forever from His presence? Had a sinful Jewish nation forfeited its chosenness?

## *Clarity*

Then, in 3408, exactly seventy years after the destruction of Jerusalem, the prophets Haggai and Zechariah declared to Zerubabel and Jeshua that God willed them to complete the building of the Temple without waiting for royal permission (5:1). They complied and not long after, Darius, the new Persian king — the son of Ahasuerus and Esther — ratified their decision.

*Cyrus had fallen short of the august role he could have had, but he had still performed a noble deed.*

Now, the meanings of the three prophecies were clear. Cyrus had fallen short of the august role he could have had, but he had still performed a noble deed by initiating the building of the Temple. Cyrus was given a lofty mission and a proud title — he was called God's anointed because he was assigned by the Author of history to follow in the footsteps of David and Solomon by building the Temple and ending Israel's exile *(Isaiah* 45:1,13). But Cyrus failed to seize the opportunity fully. Instead of carrying out his task, he merely gave permission and support to the Jews who wished to go — and even that was half-hearted and fleeting, as the *Book of Ezra* tells us.

אָמַר לֵיהּ הקב״ה לְמָשִׁיחַ, קוֹבֵל אֲנִי לְךָ עַל כּוֹרֶשׁ.
אֲנִי אָמַרְתִּי הוּא יִבְנֶה עִירִי וִיקַבֵּץ גָּלְיוֹתַי, וְהוּא אָמַר

מִי בָכֶם מִכָּל עַמּוֹ וְיָעַל.

*The Holy One Blessed is He said to Messiah, 'I grieve to you regarding Cyrus. I said he would built My city and gather in My exiles, but he said, "Anyone among you of His entire people ... let him go up"' (Megillah 12a).*

Cyrus fell short of his potential. Nevertheless, he performed a vital task, because by allowing Jews to go back home he set in motion the פְּקִידָה, God's *remembrance* of His exiled children. Jeremiah had said that God would 'remember' Israel 'after seventy years of Babylon are completed.' As R' Moshe Chaim Luzatto explains *(Maamar HaGeulah)*, the term פְּקִידָה, *remembrance*, refers to the beginning of the process: When God 'remembers' His people, a process begins that may take many years, sometimes even centuries to complete. In a sense, he explains, the remembrance that began with Cyrus is still developing, because the Second Commonwealth was not a complete redemption. It was the beginning of a new era and the new bulwark of the Oral Torah that insures Israel's survival to this day and that will maintain Israel's spiritual strength until the coming of Messiah, may it be speedily in our days.

*Remembrance refers to the beginning of the process: When God 'remembers' His people, a process begins that may take years, sometimes even centuries.*

Only a short time after Cyrus' magnanimous gesture, his successor ordered a halt to the construction (4:21). However, God's 'remembrance' had begun and continued to develop despite royal displeasure. Eighteen years after Cyrus' initial decree, Darius ordered that the Second Temple work be completed (ch. 5).

The change of languages in the *Book of Ezra* is an indication of the importance attached to Cyrus' accomplishment. Several times, the Book switches between Hebrew to Aramaic. An examination of the text reveals that royal Persian documents and decrees are given in Aramaic while the narrative and the conversation of the Jews is given in Hebrew. The exception to this is the first chapter, where Cyrus' royal decree permitting the Jews to settle in Eretz Yisrael and rebuild the Temple is stated in Hebrew, a surprising change of the pattern. But it is understandable in the light of Cyrus' prophetically foretold mission. His decree was a fulfillment of God's preordained task for His 'anointed.' Therefore Scripture gives it in the sacred tongue, Hebrew (*Rabbi Yehezkel Danziger*).

*The dual periods of seventy years coincided perfectly with the events from which they were dated.*

The dual periods of seventy years coincided perfectly with the events from which they were dated. Seventy years after Jewish sovereignty was ended by Nebuchadnezzar, a measure of it was returned by Cyrus. And seventy years after the Temple was destroyed, the Second Temple began taking shape by order of Haggai and Zechariah's prophecy and, later, Darius' decree.

# VIII. Repentance and Redemption

### *Rationalization Born of Lust*

*Repentance should ideally involve a challenge by and a triumph over the very temptations that caused the exile in the first place.*

Every exile is caused by a specific sin or set of sins, and the exile continues until Israel repents and atones for them. For repentance to be complete, it should ideally involve a challenge by and a triumph over the very temptations that caused the exile in the first place. The First Commonwealth was brought down by the cardinal sins of idolatry, adultery, and murder.

A statement of our Sages gives us an insight into the nature of people and their reaction to sin.

לֹא עָבְדוּ יִשְׂרָאֵל עֲבוֹדָה זָרָה אֶלָּא לְהַתִּיר לָהֶם עֲרָיוֹת בְּפַרְהֶסְיָא.

*Israel worshiped idols only as a means to permit itself public immorality (Sanhedrin 63b).*

Normal human self-respect dictates that people seek to defend their actions. They may cite existentialism, the 'new' morality, the law of the jungle or whatever other 'philosophy' is currently fashionable — but there will always be some rationalization.

The nation of Israel in the period of the First Temple began to experience an uncontrollable urge for immorality. That the flesh is weak is not a new phenomenon. But how does one justify such behavior — especially by the nation of Torah, the nation that knew full well that God equates morality with holiness? *(Vayikra Rabbah).* We have seen what secular society has done when faced with this dilemma in the second half of the twentieth century; it has ridiculed shame and morality as symptoms of dishonesty and hypocrisy. It has transformed the word 'love' from a sublime emotion into a synonym for animalism. Jews smitten with lust during the Temple period turned to idols to legitimate their drives. The Jewish religion imposed high standards of behavior — but the idols winked at immorality, so idolaters flourished. When righteous people attempted to bar their path, the idolaters even resorted to murder. So the three cardinal sins — all born of lust — infiltrated Jewish holiness with impurity, driving the Divine Presence from the land and resulting in the Destruction and exile *(Michtav MeEliyahu).*

*The Jewish religion imposed high standards of behavior — but the idols winked at immorality, so idolaters flourished.*

As a result they were exiled to Babylonia, Media, and Persia — all lands that were distinguished primarily for their immersion in sensuality. If Israel was to repent immorality and the grievous sins that came in its wake, it would be forced to do so in a region that was inhospitable to self-control. Only then could it prove itself. Nor was it easy, even though the nation still had in its memory the terrors of the Destruction. A significant number of the people married non-Jewish wives in Babylonia. Shockingly, even the sons of Jeshua the *Kohen Gadol* married women who were halachically forbidden to *Kohanim (Sanhedrin* 93a).

*If Israel was to repent immorality, it would be forced to do so in a region that was inhospitable to self-control.*

The aftereffects of the lust that brought on the Destruction were felt not only in the exile, but even in its aftermath, for a significant number of those who were brave and dedicated enough to return to Eretz Yisrael could not resist the temptation to marry non-Jewish women *after* having returned to the land. Ezra's primary mission, when his teacher Baruch ben Neriah died and Ezra hurried to join his brethren in

Eretz Yisrael, was to purge the nation of this vestige of immorality.

As soon as Ezra and his entourage arrived in the land, the Jewish leaders came to him with the sad plaint that the returnees from Babylonia had not shed their gentile wives. It was not Ezra who discovered the calamity; the leaders appealed to him for help. Obviously, the heads of the nation, who must have included Zerubabel and Jeshua, were powerless up to Ezra's arrival. Ezra wept and fasted. He recited a public confession for the sins of his nation, and the people wept with him. They were moved and voluntarily accepted his plea to purify themselves and purge the vestiges of the immorality that lingered through the exile (see ch. 9,10).

### *The Inner Israel*

Lest we think that the returnees did not merit redemption of even an incomplete nature, let us look at their response to Ezra's urgings. The people listened to his call that they abandon their non-Jewish wives and families, and unanimously they agreed to make the enormous sacrifice for the sake of the nation and its Torah. Only someone who loves a wife and children can appreciate their emotional ordeal, but the nation that descends from Abraham and Isaac who freely went to the *Akeidah* if that was God's will — such a nation knows that there are higher loyalties, and sacrifices that are worth making.

*Only someone who loves a wife and children can appreciate their emotional ordeal.*

*Maharal,* based on many sayings of the Sages, teaches that the sins of Israel besmirch its exterior, but do not reach into its פְּנִימִיּוּת, *inner essence.* Deep inside the Jewish heart is a place that remains pure. It may be heavily insulated with overlays of habitual sins that usually make people impervious, even sharply antagonistic to the call of repentance. Nevertheless, there is a major difference between an evil person who has been trained to do good deeds and a good person who has been trained to sin. Each one has a veneer — strip away the veneer of good from the evil person and the veneer of evil from the good one, and you are left with the true human being. When Israel returned to its land, many of its sons brought along foreign daughters, but the sinners were like a smooth vase covered with dust. The outer filth is not a part of the vase — it is not even firmly attached. A few swipes of a cloth remove the grime and reveal the beauty of the vase. So, too, Ezra and his court were dealing with an essentially pure and virtuous nation. The response of even the ostensible sinners proved it.

*Ezra and his court were dealing with an essentially pure and virtuous nation. The response of even the ostensible sinners proved it.*

### *The Lesson of Shemittah*

Another sin, though not in itself responsible for the exile, had to be atoned for before it could end. For centuries before the exile, the people had failed to observe properly the prohibitions against working the fields during Sabbatical and Jubilee years. A total of seventy such years had been violated, prior to the Destruction. As a result, Eretz Yisrael lay desolate and fallow for the seventy years of the Babylonian exile to atone for the seventy years of rest that had been denied it *(Leviticus* 26:34-35, see *Rashi).*

The Sabbatical year teaches a special lesson, one that was of particular importance in paving the way for the insights Israel had to have in the Second Commonwealth and beyond. *Shemittah* [the Sabbatical year] is one of the commandments that has the particular function of teaching that God alone controls nature. Without such faith, how could rational people refrain from planting for a full year? With the conclusion of the era of prophecy and the beginning of the new emphasis on the Oral Torah, Israel had to emphasize as never before the search for meaning and the hand of God where they had seemed to be hidden. Over was the age of open miracles and of direct, clear communication by God through prophets. From Ezra's time onward, the secrets of halachah and history had to be derived from the Torah through study and analysis.

*Shemittah is one of the commandments that has the particular function of teaching that God alone controls nature.*

The miracle of Purim, for example — which occurred during the painful years when the Temple construction had been suspended — is the prime lesson of God's control of 'normal,' 'everyday' events (see Overview to ArtScroll *Esther).* Such

*Such awareness was crucial to the new existence of the Jewish people.*

awareness was crucial to the new existence of the Jewish people, and the lessons of Purim were an essential prelude to the new mode of Jewish life. Therefore, it had to be demonstrated to them that the land could not be theirs unless it had the *Shemittah* rest, which was constant proof that plow and sower are but God's means — and surely not His only means to provide His faithful ones with sustenance.

❦ ❦ ❦

*Theirs are the lessons that maintained Israel's faith and vigor despite constant wanderings and buffetings.*

We still live in Ezra's world and we try to see it through the lens his *beis din* shaped for us. Ezra and the Men of the Great Assembly returned the crown of God's greatness to its former splendor by teaching posterity to seek His active, beneficent hand behind the mists of history and the ephemeral ascendancy of the wicked. Theirs are the lessons that maintained Israel's faith and vigor despite constant wanderings and buffetings. And theirs is the inner flame that will illuminate the universe when the Final Redemption is at hand.

*Rabbi Nosson Scherman*
*Cheshvan 5745*

# ספר עזרא

## Prologue

Jeremiah, bearer of the prophetic vision of the Jewish exile and the devastation of Jerusalem, also foretold of the redemption of the Jews from Babylon and their return to the holy city.

כִּי־כֹה אָמַר ה׳ כִּי לְפִי מְלֹאת לְבָבֶל שִׁבְעִים שָׁנָה אֶפְקֹד אֶתְכֶם וַהֲקִמֹתִי עֲלֵיכֶם אֶת־דְּבָרִי הַטּוֹב לְהָשִׁיב אֶתְכֶם אֶל־הַמָּקוֹם הַזֶּה.

*For thus says HASHEM: For after seventy years of Babylon are completed, I shall remember you and uphold My good word concerning you, to restore you to this place (Jeremiah* 29:10).

The prophet, however, did not clarify how the seventy years of Babylon would be calculated. The Babylonian ascendancy over the Jewish people began in the year 3320 (440 B.C.E.), when King Yehoyakim [Jehoiakim] and his subjects were overwhelmed by the mighty legions of Nebuchadnezzar. It culminated eighteen years later, on the ninth of *Av* in the year 3338 (422 B.C.E.), when the Babylonian armies again swept across the Jewish kingdom, this time ravaging the Temple and the city of Jerusalem, and driving the people into exile in the distant land of Babylon [see *Rashi* to *Ezra,* 1:1]. Would the seventy years of Babylon be counted from the subjugation of Yehoyakim or from the destruction of the Temple?

Years later, when the Temple and the sacred city had lain in ruins for over half a century, Daniel studied Jeremiah's stirring prophecy — and was distraught.

בִּשְׁנַת אַחַת לְדָרְיָוֶשׁ בֶּן־אֲחַשְׁוֵרוֹשׁ מִזֶּרַע מָדָי אֲשֶׁר הָמְלַךְ עַל מַלְכוּת כַּשְׂדִּים ... אֲנִי דָּנִיֵּאל בִּינֹתִי בַּסְּפָרִים מִסְפַּר הַשָּׁנִים אֲשֶׁר הָיָה דְבַר־ה׳ אֶל־יִרְמְיָה הַנָּבִיא לְמַלֹּאות לְחָרְבוֹת יְרוּשָׁלַיִם שִׁבְעִים שָׁנָה.

*In the first year of Darius, the son of Ahasuerus, of the seed of Media,*[1] *who was made king over the kingdom of the Chaldeans ... I, Daniel, contemplated the calculation, the number of years about which the word of HASHEM had come to the prophet Jeremiah, to complete the seventy years from the ruins of Jerusalem (Daniel* 9:1,2).

The seventieth year following the fall of Yehoyakim was apparently at hand, and the royal house of Nebuchadnezzar had indeed expired; but Darius the Mede, who had conquered Babylon, made no move to withdraw the restrictions imposed by the Babylonian masters whom he had replaced. Daniel, therefore, drew the compelling conclusion that the seventy years of Babylon could not be reckoned from the original conquest of Judea. The calculation would begin from a later period, that of the final, catastrophic stage of the Babylonian enslavement — the destruction of the Sanctuary and the holy city. Based on this conclusion, Daniel referred to the fulfillment of Jeremiah's prophecy as the completion of the *seventy years from the ruins of Jerusalem (Daniel* 9:2) — not seventy years from the conquest of Yehoyakim, but from the ruination of Jerusalem, an event which had transpired fully eighteen years after Judah had first been vanquished. To complete the seventy years from the ruins of Jerusalem, the return to Zion would have to await the passage of eighteen additional years *(Rashi, Daniel* 9:1,2; see ArtScroll *Daniel).*

1. Darius, son of Ahasuerus the Mede, conquered the Babylonian-Chaldean empire at the death of Belshazzar, the last of the Babylonian kings *(Daniel* 5:30, 8:1). Darius' father, Ahasuerus the Mede, should not be confused with King Ahasuerus of the *Book of Esther,* who later ruled over the Persian empire *(Rashi, Daniel* 9:1).

Covered with ashes and wrapped in sackcloth, a grieved Daniel recited his confessional prayer for the restoration of the Temple and the city bearing the sacred name *(Daniel* 9). His prayers were heard [see *Vilna Gaon*, comm. to *Shir HaShirim* 5:5]. The angel Gabriel informed Daniel that the first stage of redemption would start at once; the restoration of the city and the Temple would *begin* seventy years after the capture of Yehoyakim.[1] The *completion* of the entire Sanctuary would be subject to the eighteen-year delay, but the initial settlement of the city and the laying of the Temple foundation would take place precisely seventy years after the downfall of Yehoyakim, or fifty-two years after the ruination of Jerusalem. Gabriel's reply is recorded in *Daniel:*

... וְהָאִישׁ גַּבְרִיאֵל ... וַיְדַבֵּר עִמִּי ... לְהָשִׁיב וְלִבְנוֹת יְרוּשָׁלַםִ עַד־מָשִׁיחַ נָגִיד שָׁבֻעִים שִׁבְעָה ...

*... And the man Gabriel ... spoke to me ...* [*that*] *to return and build Jerusalem until anointing the prince will be seven weeks ...* (*Daniel* 9:21-25).

When the week, i.e. the seven-year *shemittah* cycle, will have occurred seven times [forty-nine years], the anointed prince, Cyrus, would sanction the rebuilding of Jerusalem. [The additional three years which completed the fifty-two-year period remain unmentioned, since the date is given in terms of the number of *shemittah* cycles, each of which is a unit of seven years *(Rashi).*]

Shortly thereafter, Darius the Mede was slain in battle *(Rashi* to *Daniel* 6:29). His son-in-law, the virtuous Cyrus, was immediately crowned on the battlefield and the mystic veil of Providence was swept aside, revealing the momentous drama which now unfolds across the pages of the *Book of Ezra.*

## Chronology of the Period

| King | Country | Years of Rule[2] From Creation | B.C.E. | Comment |
|---|---|---|---|---|
| Nebuchadnezzar | Babylon | 3319-3363 | 441-397 | Destroyed Jerusalem |
| Evil Merodach | Babylon | 3363-3386 | 397-374 | Freed king Yechonyah |
| Belshazzar | Babylon | 3386-3389 | 374-371 | Last Babylonian king |
| Darius the Mede | Persia-Media | 3389-3390 | 371-370 | Defeated Belshazzar |
| Cyrus | Persia-Media | 3390-3393 | 370-367 | Authorized return of exiles and rebuilding of Temple |
| Ahasuerus | Persia-Media | 3393-3407 | 367-353 | Husband of Esther |
| Darius the Persian | Persia-Media | 3407-3442 | 353-318 | Esther's son; authorized Temple's completion |

1. The Sages note that Jeremiah's prophetic words had been: After seventy years of Babylon ... I shall *remember* you. Remembrance denotes a partial, but not yet complete, restoration (*Megillah* 12a).

2. These dates are based on *Seder Olam* and the Talmud *(Megillah* 11b-12a with *Rashi).* However, the Jewish calendar currently in use adds one year to the Talmudic chronology. Thus, *Seder Olam's* date of 3338 for the Destruction would really be 3339 under the current calendar. This does *not* mean, of course, that there is any disagreement over when the respective events happened. The discrepancy results from the different starting points used in these Creation calendars. While the Talmudic mode uses Adam's birth on the sixth day of Creation (1 Tishrei) as its starting point, our calendar begins on the Tishrei preceding Adam's birth by a full year, thus including the first five days of Creation in the first year. Nevertheless, we have retained the dates of *Seder Olam* simply because they are so familiar that it would have been confusing for us to change them. This is especially true for the date of the Destruction of the First Temple, which many people have memorized as 3338. For this

## ⊸§ The Authorship of the Book of Ezra

The *Book of Ezra*, as defined in the order of the Scriptures and in the Talmudic literature, incorporates the *Book of Nehemiah* as well [see *Gilyon HaShas, Succah* 12a].

Ezra, the Rabbis assert, was the author of the volume bearing his name: 'Ezra composed his book' *(Bava Basra* 15a). However, an apparently conflicting Rabbinical statement indicates that Nehemiah, not Ezra, composed the *Book of Ezra. Sanhedrin* 93b states: 'All of *Ezra* was composed by Nehemiah ... Why, then, does the book not carry his name? Because he sought credit for himself, requesting in his prayers that God recognize his good deeds [see *Nehemiah* 5:19]. R' Yosef said: Because he recounted the misdeeds of those who preceded him.' [Nehemiah remarked that the governors who preceded him had imposed heavy taxes on the people; see *Nehemiah* 5:15.]

This discrepancy is resolved by *Rashi (Sanhedrin* 93b). To the Talmud's statement that all of *Ezra* was composed by Nehemiah, *Rashi* interjects: 'The major portion of *Ezra* and *Nehemiah.*' Evidently troubled by the conflict with *Bava Basra's* statement that Ezra composed his book, *Rashi* determined that the statement: 'All of Ezra was composed by Nehemiah,' is not intended literally, but as a reference to that section of the work now known as the *Book of Nehemiah.* In the order of Scripture, however, both *Ezra* and *Nehemiah* are regarded as *one* book, which is called *Ezra.* The *Nehemiah* portion of the book is nearly double the *Ezra* portion. Because it comprises the bulk of the combined book of *Ezra/Nehemiah*, the Talmud refers to it by the term 'all of *Ezra*,' although the reference is only to *Nehemiah.* Indeed, *Rashi* remarks in his opening comment to the *Book of Nehemiah:* 'From this point on, this book was composed by Nehemiah' [see *Chochmas Shlomo, Bava Basra,* 15a].

reason, we have not tampered with these familiar dates. [A well-known mnemonic device has been used for this date: the word שָׁלַח, *He sent away;* i.e., God sent away the Jewish nation. The word שָׁלַח has the numerical value of 338.] For a fuller discussion of this matter see ArtScroll, *History of the Jewish People — The Second Temple Era,* pp. 213-14, and *Sheelos U'Teshuvos R' Levi ibn Chaviv (Ralbach)* §143, p. 50-1 in Lemberg ed.

Since this reason is obviously not relevant to the dates of the secular calendar, which provide the frame of historical reference for most people, we have allowed for the discrepancy between our Creation calendar and that of *Seder Olam* in those dates. For example, the date of the Destruction is given as 3338 from Creation but the secular date (422 B.C.E.) is based on the assumption that 3338 of *Seder Olam* is the year 3339 of our Creation calendar. To do otherwise would have been a falsification of history.

It should be noted that in calculating years B.C.E., one cannot subtract from the year 3760 [which is the starting point of the secular calendar (5744-1984=3760)] because calendars never use the digit zero, so that 3760 is 1 B.C.E. One must rather subtract from the year 3761 after Creation.

א א וּבִשְׁנַת אַחַת לְכוֹרֶשׁ מֶלֶךְ פָּרַס לִכְלוֹת
א דְּבַר־יהוה מִפִּי יִרְמְיָה הֵעִיר יהוה אֶת־רוּחַ

# I

### The Proclamation

1. וּבִשְׁנַת — *And in the year.* The *Book of Ezra* opens with the conjunctive ו, *vav,* suggesting an association with an earlier book of Scripture.

According to *Rashi, Ezra* is a continuation of *Daniel.* Noting that *Ezra* follows *Daniel* in the order of the Scriptures *(Bava Basra* 14b),[1] *Rashi* links the two books by referring to Daniel's contemplation of Jeremiah's prophetic message of redemption, and his [Daniel's] fervent confessional prayers over the people's transgressions which had caused the destruction of the Temple and the Babylonian captivity *(Daniel* 9). The *Book of Ezra, Rashi* continues, opens in the first year of Cyrus, with the fulfillment of the prophecy over which Daniel agonized — referred to as *the word of Hashem from the mouth of Jeremiah* [see above in the prologue]. Thus, *Ezra* follows *Daniel,* and the two are joined by a *vav.*

*Ramban (Exodus* 1:1; *Sefer HaGeulah)* and *Malbim* differ with *Rashi's* explanation of the opening *vav.* They contend that *Ezra* is linked with *Chronicles,* since the opening verses of *Ezra* and the final sentences of *Chronicles* are identical.

[This view, however, seems to be contradicted by the arrangement of the Scriptures in *Bava Basra* 14b, where *Ezra* appears before *Chronicles.* However, *Rambam (Sefer Torah* 7) deletes *Ezra* entirely from the enumeration of the order of Scriptures. [Evidently, this was *Rambam's* version of the text in *Bava Basra* 14b.] This version indicates the absorption of *Ezra* into another book — perhaps *Chronicles* — thereby justifying the linkage of *Ezra* with *Chronicles* by *Ramban* and *Malbim.*

*Tur* and *Shulchan Aruch (Yoreh Deah* 282) do not follow *Rambam,* listing *Ezra* before *Chronicles.*

However, *Radak* to *Joshua* 1:1 states that it is the Biblical style to begin a book or an episode with a *vav* and that this does not necessarily indicate a link with any previous episode.

אַחַת — *The first.* This does not mean his first year as king of Persia, for Cyrus had long been the Persian monarch, but the first year of his rule over the Babylonian empire after the death of his father-in-law Darius the Mede *(Ibn Ezra).*

[In *Isaiah* 45:1-5 the prophet declares that God empowered Cyrus to conquer Babylon in order to deliver the Jewish people from Babylonian exile (see *Rashi* there). Thus, the passage may be understood in terms of Cyrus' elevation

1. [Actually, the Talmud in *Bava Basra* places the *Book of Esther* between *Daniel* and *Ezra. Rashi* (there) explains that this order was chosen because the events then follow in chronological order. The events of *Daniel* take place from the times of King Nebuchadnezzar, through the reign of Darius the Mede; the *Book of Esther* during the days of Ahasuerus the Persian, who reigned a number of years after Darius the Mede [see chart in prologue]; and *Ezra* in the period of Ahasuerus' successor, Darius the Persian. This apparently contradicts *Rashi's* linkage of *Ezra* with *Daniel.*

It should be noted, however, that the *Book of Ezra* begins with the proclamation issued by Ahasuerus' predecessor, King Cyrus, and continues with the events which followed during Cyrus' reign. [The Ahasuerus of the *Book of Esther* is later mentioned fleetingly. See 4:6.] Darius, who ruled after Ahasuerus, does not appear in *Ezra* until the close of the fourth chapter (4:24).

Based on this observation, it would seem that *Rashi's* meaning is that although the *Book of Ezra* does not follow immediately after the *Book of Daniel,* the two are linked thematically. *Ezra's* opening chapters recounting the fulfillment of Jeremiah's prophecy through Cyrus follow Daniel's preoccupation with the same prophecy. Nevertheless, *Bava Basra* places the *Book of Esther* between *Daniel* and *Ezra* because Ahasuerus and the Purim story precede King Darius and the activities described in the latter portion of the *Book of Ezra.*]

I
1 *And in the first year of Cyrus, king of Persia, upon the conclusion of HASHEM's word by the mouth of*
The Proclamation *Jeremiah, HASHEM aroused the good will of Cyrus,*

to the role of redeemer. *The first year of Cyrus* refers to the first year that Cyrus, through his conquest of Babylon, assumed his role as the instrument of redemption.]

לְכוֹרֶשׁ — *Cyrus* [*Koresh*]. Cyrus, king of Persia, accompanied his father-in-law, Darius king of Media, in the conquest of the Babylonian empire. Darius replaced Belshazzar, last of the Babylonian kings *(Daniel* 5:30, 6:1), and ruled for one year. He died in battle, and was immediately succeeded by his son-in-law, Cyrus[1] *(Rashi* from *Yossipon, Daniel* 6:29) in the year 3390.

Cyrus' dominion included the Land of Israel, with its amalgam of gentile nationals [see 4:9,10]. He permitted the return of the Jewish exiles from Babylon, where they had been banished when the Babylonians destroyed the Temple over half a century earlier [see prologue]. His reign lasted three years *(Rashi, Megillah* 11b from *Seder Olam).* He was followed by Ahasuerus, the husband of Queen Esther, who was succeeded by their son Darius *(Rashi).* [See table.]

The name *Cyrus* — in Hebrew, כֹּרֶשׁ, *Koresh* — has the same letters as כשר, *kosher. Rashi* (4:7) comments that the name *Koresh* therefore indicates that Cyrus was a virtuous *(kosher)* king. *Ibn Ezra* adds that his name was given in recognition of his virtuous behavior towards the Jewish people.

*Rashi* here quotes the *Talmud:* [He was named] *Koresh* becuase he was a virtuous [kosher] king ... What was his true name? Darius (*Rosh Hashanah* 3b).

These Talmudic remarks concern Darius, son of Esther and Ahasuerus. Darius reigned some fourteen years after Cyrus, and presided over the completion of the Temple [see *Rashi, Haggai* 1:1]. His name does not appear in the *Book of Ezra* until 4:24. He is referred to in Scripture as Darius, and it is only through Rabbinic tradition *(Rosh Hashanah* 3b) that we are informed that he was surnamed *Koresh* because of his virtue. Yet *Rashi* invokes the Talmudic statement concerning Darius, in relation to the Cyrus mentioned here. Evidently, *Rashi* feels that the Talmudic explanation of Darius' surname *Koresh* may be applied as well to his virtuous predecessor, King Cyrus [*Koresh*].

לִכְלוֹת דְּבַר־ה׳ מִפִּי יִרְמְיָה — *Upon the conclusion of HASHEM's word by the mouth of Jeremiah.* This occurred at the conclusion of the seventy-year period about which Jeremiah prophesied: *After seventy years of Babylon are completed: I shall remember you ... to restore you to this place (Jeremiah* 29:10) *(Rashi).*[2]

[The prophecy was not literally *by the mouth of Jeremiah,* but was transmitted in a letter dispatched by the prophet to the Babylonian exiles *(Jeremiah* 29:11).]

*Rashi* to *Megillah* 12a (based on *Seder Olam* and *Megillah* 11b, 12a) interprets *seventy years of Babylon* to mean seventy years of Jewish subjugation to Babylon, and computes these years from the year 3320 [see table] — the second year of the reign of Nebuchadnezzar, founder of the Babylonian empire, when his conquest of the Jewish kingdom took place. Nebuchadnezzar's rule over the Jews lasted over forty-three years. His son and successor, Evil Merodach, completed the forty-fourth year and reigned for twenty-two years afterward. He was followed by Belshazzar, last of the Babylonians, whose rule lasted three years. His kingdom was conquered by Darius the Mede, who reigned for one year, completing the passage of seventy years from the Babylonian conquest of the Jewish people. [Although Darius was not of Babylonian descent, his rule is included in the seventy years. Evidently, *seventy years of Babylon*

1. The historical tradition that Cyrus king of Persia was the son-in-law of Darius king of Media is quoted by *Ibn Ezra (Daniel* 6:1) as well. See ArtScroll *Daniel* 6:1.
2. See *Rambam* in *Moreh* [Guide] II:45 for a different understanding of this verse.

א כֹּרֶשׁ מֶלֶךְ־פָּרַס וַיַּעֲבֶר־קוֹל בְּכָל־מַלְכוּתוֹ
ב ב וְגַם־בְּמִכְתָּב לֵאמֹר: כֹּה אָמַר כֹּרֶשׁ מֶלֶךְ
פָּרַס כֹּל מַמְלְכוֹת הָאָרֶץ נָתַן לִי יהוה אֱלֹהֵי

refers to the passage of seventy years from the Babylonian conquest, but does not necessarily mean seventy years under the sovereignty of Babylonian kings.] Cyrus, who followed Darius, immediately granted permission for the Temple's reconstruction.

However, *R' Yeshayah MiTrani* begins the computation of the seventy years of Babylon with the *first* year of Nebuchadnezzar's rule. His reign lasted over forty-four years. His successor, Evil Merodach, completed the forty-fifth year, and continued on the throne for another twenty-one years, and part of a twenty-second year. He was followed by Belshazzar, who completed the twenty-second year and ruled for two years thereafter. Darius succeeded him for one year, completing the passage of a total of seventy years from the establishment of the Babylonian Empire.

הֵעִיר ה׳ אֶת־רוּחַ כֹּרֶשׁ — *HASHEM aroused the good will of Cyrus. Ralbag* suggests that Cyrus was inspired by a dream in which it was revealed that God had given him all the kingdoms of earth, and now commanded him to build the Temple in Jerusalem.

*Malbim* cites *Josephus*, who relates that when Cyrus learned of the miraculous downfall of Belshazzar [see *Daniel* 5],[1] he vowed to rebuild the Sanctuary.

**The Seventy Years of Babylon**

*(according to Rashi)*

| King | Rule over Jews | B.C.E. | No. of Years |
|---|---|---|---|
| Nebuchadnezzar | 3320-3363 (midyear) | 440-397 (midyear) | 43½ |
| Evil Merodach | 3363 (midyear)-3386 | 397 (midyear)-374 | 22½ |
| Belshazzar | 3386-3389 | 374-371 | 3 |
| Darius | 3389-3390 | 371-370 | 1 |
| | | | **Total:** 70 |

*(according to R' Yeshayah MiTrani)*

| King | Rule over Jews | B.C.E. | No. of Years |
|---|---|---|---|
| Nebuchadnezzar | 3319-3363 (midyear) | 441-397 (midyear) | 44½ |
| Evil Merodach | 3363 (mid.)-3385 (mid.) | 397 (mid.)-375 (mid.) | 22 |
| Belshazzar | 3385-3388 | 375 (mid.)-372 | 2½ |
| Darius | 3388-3389 | 372-371 | 1 |
| | | | **Total:** 70 |

1. The Babylonian monarch Belshazzar and his forces had defeated the invading armies led by Darius the Mede and Cyrus (*Rashi, Daniel* 5:1). At the victory celebration, Belshazzar and his entourage drank from the sacred Temple vessels which Nebuchadnezzar had taken during the sack of the Temple in Jerusalem. A hand then appeared miraculously, and spelled out a mysterious message, which Daniel interpreted as the prediction of Belshazzar's downfall. Later the same night Belshazzar was murdered [by one of his own attendants *(R' Saadiah Gaon)*].

*king of Persia; and he issued a proclamation throughout his kingdom — and in writing as well — saying:*

2 *So says Cyrus, king of Persia: All the kingdoms of earth has* HASHEM, *God of heaven, delivered to me,*

Another explanation given by *Malbim* is that Cyrus was inspired by the words of *Isaiah* (44:28): *My shepherd Cyrus shall fulfill My every wish, and shall proclaim, 'Let Jerusalem be rebuilt and the Sanctuary be founded.'*

וַיַּעֲבֶר־קוֹל בְּכָל־מַלְכוּתוֹ וְגַם־בְּמִכְתָּב — *And he issued a proclamation throughout his kingdom — and in writing as well.* The proclamation was announced orally and distributed in written form, with the royal seal *(Ibn Ezra).*

*Malbim* comments that the proclamation was committed to writing to insure its implementation. According to Persian law, a written decree of the king could not be rescinded, as stated in *Esther* 8:8: *For an edict which is written in the king's name, and sealed with the royal signet, may not be revoked.*[1]

*Malbim* also notes that this documentation of Cyrus' proclamation proved to be of great significance in the eventual restoration of the Temple. After the first wave of Jewish exiles returned to the Holy Land and laid the Temple's foundation (chs. 2,3), Cyrus accepted the slander of the enemies of Judah and Benjamin, and ordered the construction halted (ch. 4). Eighteen years later, Darius sanctioned the resumption of the Temple construction based upon the discovery in the royal archives of a copy of Cyrus' original proclamation (6:12). Thus it was only through the documentation of Cyrus' decree that Darius was later able to justify his sanctioning of the resumption of the Temple's construction.

**2.** כֹּה אָמַר כֹּרֶשׁ מֶלֶךְ פָּרַס — *So says Cyrus, king of Persia.* The Rabbis teach that the Persian king's sponsorship of the return to Jerusalem was evidence of Jewish unworthiness in the eyes of God. A more deserving generation would have merited a return to the land free from alien domination. The Sages state in *Berachos* 41a: 'Ezra's generation was destined for a redemption as miraculous as that of Joshua's days [when the greatly outnumbered Jewish army conquered Eretz Yisrael in a series of miraculous victories; see *Joshua*], but their misdeeds prevailed.' *Rashi* (there) explains that this unworthiness made the return to Zion contingent upon Cyrus' permission, and caused those who returned to suffer the domination of Cyrus' successors, Ahasuerus [of the *Book of Esther*] and Darius [Ahasuerus's son who completed the construction of the Temple; see ch. 6].

Darius and Cyrus renewed their attack, and this time succeeded in conquering the Babylonian capital (*Daniel* 5).

1. This comment is apparently contradicted by subsequent events (ch. 4), when the enemies of Judah and Benjamin persuaded the king to withdraw his sanction for the Temple's reconstruction. *Malbim,* however, reconciles the apparent contradiction, explaining that the enemies convinced the king, through a slanderous misrepresentation of the activities in Jerusalem, that the Jews had grossly overstepped the terms of the edict. The decree had specified that they were granted permission only to rebuild the Temple. Instead, the enemies alleged, they were actually rebuilding and fortifying the entire city with its surrounding walls, indicating that they planned a rebellion. The king accepted the slander and halted the work in Jerusalem because he assumed that the construction taking place was unauthorized by his edict. Thus, the enemies were successful in circumventing the objective of the proclamation without actually repealing it [see comm. ch. 4].

א הַשָּׁמַיִם וְהוּא־פָקַד עָלַי לִבְנוֹת־לוֹ בַּיִת
ג בִּירוּשָׁלַםִ אֲשֶׁר בִּיהוּדָה: ג מִי־בָכֶם מִכָּל־עַמּוֹ
יְהִי אֱלֹהָיו עִמּוֹ וְיַעַל לִירוּשָׁלַםִ אֲשֶׁר

כֹּל מַמְלְכוֹת הָאָרֶץ נָתַן לִי ה׳ — *All the kingdoms of earth has HASHEM ... delivered to me.* God has placed all the kingdoms under my rule *(Rashi)*, and I am, therefore, obliged to fulfill his command *(Metzudos)*.

Cyrus did not actually rule over all mankind. He exaggerated deliberately to enhance his prestige (*Megillah* 11b).

אֱלֹהֵי הַשָּׁמַיִם — *God of heaven. Ibn Ezra* and *Malbim* note that Cyrus refrained from describing *HASHEM* as God of heaven *and earth* because of his erroneous belief that *HASHEM* does not intervene in earthly affairs, but relegates the dominion over earth to man. This is indicated, as well, by the statement: *All the kingdoms of earth has HASHEM delivered to me*, i.e., Cyrus thought that the power to influence the destiny of the kingdoms of earth was related to himself in particular *(Ibn Ezra; Malbim)*. [Where Jerusalem was concerned, however, Cyrus did acknowledge that Divine guidance was in effect. See comm. to v.3.]

וְהוּא־פָקַד עָלַי — *And He has commanded me.* The command was not given directly, but through the prophet Isaiah (44:28): [*HASHEM*] *Who says of Cyrus, 'My shepherd shall fulfill My every wish, and shall proclaim, "Let Jerusalem be rebuilt and the Sanctuary be founded," '* and (45:1), *So says HASHEM of his illustrious Cyrus: 'I have strengthened his right arm' (Rashi)*.

לִבְנוֹת־לוֹ בַיִת בִּירוּשָׁלָיִם — *To build Him a Temple in Jerusalem.* According to R' Yochanan *(Yoma* 9b), the *Shechinah*, Divine Presence, did not reside in the Second Temple as it had in the First, because the Second Temple was built through the efforts of Persian kings Cyrus, and later Darius, whereas the first was constructed by King Solomon.

This opinion is based on the Biblical passage describing the blessing bestowed by Noah upon his two sons — Shem, the ancestor of the Jewish people, and Japheth, forefather of the Persians: *May God extend Japheth, but He will dwell in the tents of Shem (Genesis* 9:27). R' Yochanan interprets: Although God shall extend Japheth, He shall dwell only in the tents of Shem *(Yoma* 9b, 10a).

[The interpretation may be understood as follows: Japheth's creative impulse will, with God's inspiration, extend to the sacred area generally reserved for Shem. I.e., Japheth's Persian progeny will construct a sanctuary. Nevertheless, He shall dwell only in the tents of Shem — Japheth's sanctuary will not be God's dwelling place, for the *Shechinah* shall reside only in the Temple erected by King Solomon and the Jewish descendants of Shem (see *Rashi, Genesis* 9:27).]

The prophetic ordination of Cyrus as the restorer of the Temple does not conflict with the Rabbis' assertion that the *Shechinah* would not reside in a Temple built by a Persian. Although the Second Temple would not achieve the very highest level of sanctity, it would serve as the focal point of the Jewish attachment to God. When He saw that the Jews were deserving of such a sanctuary, God made it known, through His prophet, that they would be given the *Beis HaMikdash* and that Cyrus would be the instrument for the fulfillment of Providential design.

Reish Lakish disagrees, attributing the loss of the *Shechinah* to the fact that the entire nation did not return from Babylon *(Yoma* 9b), as it is written: *The entire congregation* [*of returnees*] ... *forty-two thousand three hundred sixty.* This was a small minority of the community of exiles.

**3.** מִי־בָכֶם מִכָּל־עַמּוֹ — *Anyone among you of His entire people.* Cyrus' procla-

I *and He has commanded me to build Him a Temple in*
3 *Jerusalem which is in Judah.* 3 *Anyone among you of*
*His entire people, may his God be with him, let him*
*go up to Jerusalem which is in Judah, and build the*

mation was worded to address all of Cyrus' subjects, including the non-Jews, inviting the Jews among them to go up to Jerusalem to build the Temple *(Rashi).* Although only the Jews were qualified to perform the work of construction, Cyrus obligated the gentiles to share in the building of the Temple. They were to help send the Jews to Jerusalem *(Malbim).*

[This obligation is spelled out further in verse 4 where the gentiles were instructed to provide financial support for the Jewish immigrants.]

יְהִי אֱלֹהָיו עִמּוֹ — *May his God be with him.* The translation follows *Rashi,* who understands this phrase as a blessing invoking Divine assistance, interjected by Cyrus into the invitation to the Jews to emigrate.

*Ibn Ezra* disagrees with *Rashi,* rendering יְהִי אֱלֹהָיו עִמּוֹ, *with whom his God was* [*Ibn Ezra* understands יְהִי, *May He* (future tense), as הָיָה, *was* (past tense)]; i.e., whom God had blessed with the wealth with which to go up to Jerusalem. The entire sentence thus reads: *Any among you of His people with whom his God has been* [whom God endowed with wealth enough to go up] — *let him go up to Jerusalem.*

In *Ibn Ezra's* view, then, Cyrus began the proclamation by urging emigration for those Jews wealthy enough to afford the trip. The closing statement of the proclamation (v. 4) provides that those Jews who could not afford to emigrate were to receive the necessary funds from their gentile neighbors.

[See further ArtScroll *Divrei HaYamim/Chronicles* II 36:23.]

וְיַעַל לִירוּשָׁלַיִם — *Let him go up to Jerusalem.* [Because of the holiness of the land, a trip to Eretz Yisrael is described by Scripture as 'going up' to a higher place. As the Sages expound, the Sanctuary is loftier than all of the Land of Israel, and the Land of Israel is elevated over all lands (*Kiddushin* 69a). Cyrus was evidently aware of this, and did not hesitate to express his awareness publicly.]

The Midrash relates that the king subsequently withdrew the grant permitting the Jews to go up to Jerusalem because of economic considerations. Cyrus learned that the emigration of the Jewish goldsmiths and silversmiths had wrought economic havoc. He decreed, therefore, that any Jews who had not yet crossed the Euphrates [the river Euphrates separated the Land of Israel from Babylon — *Rashi* to 4:10] could not leave Babylon to return to Jerusalem (*Shir HaShirim Rabbah,* 5:5; see also *Koheles Rabbah,* 10:13 and *Pesikta* to *Esther Rabbah,* 8).

[It should be noted that this halt to emigration affected only the Babylonian Jews who had not yet emigrated, but was unrelated to the general halt of Temple construction brought about later by the enemies of Judah and Benjamin, described below in ch. 4.]

אֲשֶׁר בִּיהוּדָה — *Which is in Judah.* Since *Jerusalem, which is in Judah,* has already been mentioned (v. 2), the repetition of the phrase here seems unnecessary. *Ramban (Sefer HaGeulah)* resolves this difficulty in discussing the failure of the majority of the exiles to return to Zion. [The number of returnees — 42,360 (see 2:64) — constituted only a fraction of the exiled Jewish community.] Cyrus' authorization, *Ramban* suggests, was granted only to those Babylonian exiles who had, or whose ancestors had, lived in the kingdom of Judah in pre-exilic times, but not to members of the Ten Tribes,

א ד

בִּיהוּדָה וְיִבֶן אֶת־בֵּית יהוה אֱלֹהֵי יִשְׂרָאֵל
ד הוּא הָאֱלֹהִים אֲשֶׁר בִּירוּשָׁלָם׃ וְכָל־הַנִּשְׁאָר
מִכָּל־הַמְּקֹמוֹת אֲשֶׁר הוּא גָר־שָׁם יְנַשְּׂאוּהוּ
אַנְשֵׁי מְקֹמוֹ בְּכֶסֶף וּבְזָהָב וּבִרְכוּשׁ וּבִבְהֵמָה
עִם־הַנְּדָבָה לְבֵית הָאֱלֹהִים אֲשֶׁר בִּירוּשָׁלָם׃

who had been exiled much earlier.[1] Since the king's permission was extended only to subjects of the Judean kingdom, the proclamation specified the return to Jerusalem *in Judah*.

וְיִבֶן — *And build*. This rendition follows *Rashi*, who interprets the proclamation as a reference to those going up intending to build.

*Malbim*, however, understands the verse to mean: *May his God be with him* [i.e., assist him] *to go up to Jerusalem and to build the Temple*. Cyrus invoked God's assistance for both their journey to Jerusalem and the building of the Temple.

The Talmud *(Megillah* 12a) censures Cyrus for his failure to labor personally for the restoration of the Temple. 'I [*Hashem*] lament the behavior of Cyrus. I proclaimed, *"He shall build My Temple and gather in My exiles,"* yet [instead of participating in the construction *(Rashi)*] he merely announced *"Any among you of his people ... let him go up."* '

As a source for this criticism, the Talmud *(Megillah*, ibid.) quotes *Isaiah* (45:1-4) *'So says HASHEM ... about Cyrus, I sustained his right arm, prostrated the nations before him ... yet he did not know Me.'* He did not fulfill My wishes (*Rashi* there). He permitted them to go, but cast off the yoke of personal effort.

Nevertheless, Cyrus was richly rewarded for his sanctioning of the restoration of the Temple. The Midrash relates that Nebuchadnezzar, king of Babylon, had amassed an immense fortune during the course of his conquests. In his extreme avarice, he wished to prevent his own son from falling heir to his wealth, and he buried it beneath the waters of the Euphrates. When Cyrus issued the decree sanctioning the construction of the Temple, God revealed to him the resting place of this vast treasure (*Esther Rabbah* 2:1).

בֵּית ה׳ אֱלֹהֵי יִשְׂרָאֵל — *The Temple of HASHEM, God of Israel.* The Second Sanctuary was the Temple only of the God of Israel, but the final, everlasting Sanctuary of the future will serve as a house of worship for all mankind, as described by *Isaiah* (56:7): *For my Temple will be known as a House of Prayer for all peoples (Malbim).*

הוּא הָאֱלֹהִים אֲשֶׁר בִּירוּשָׁלָם — *He is the God — which is in Jerusalem.* The translation follows *Rashi* and *Ibn Ezra*, who understand the phrase אֲשֶׁר בִּירוּשָׁלָם, *which is in Jerusalem*, as a description of the location of the Temple, not of God, whose Presence is universal. Their reading is, *to build the Temple of HASHEM — He is the God — which is in Jerusalem.* The intervening

1. In the days of King Rehoboam, son of Solomon, the majority of the people — ten tribes — seceded, and the Jewish nation was divided into two kingdoms. One was the kingdom of Judah, which included the Temple in Jerusalem. This kingdom consisted of the tribes of Judah and Benjamin, and was governed by the descendants of the House of David. The other was the kingdom of Israel, made up of the ten remaining tribes and ruled over by a series of kings, beginning with Jereboam, son of Nebat [see *I Kings*, ch. 12].

The Ten Tribes were the first to be exiled, at the hands of the king of Assyria [*II Kings*, ch. 17]. The Judean kingdom, however, remained intact until the Babylonian conquest, when the Temple was destroyed and the people exiled to Babylon [*II Kings*, ch. 25].

I
4

*Temple of HASHEM, God of Israel — He is the God! — which is in Jerusalem.* 4 *And anyone who remains in whatever place he dwells, let the inhabitants of that place bestow upon him gifts of silver, gold, valuables, and animals; together with the contribution for the Temple of God in Jerusalem.*

phrase, הוּא הָאֱלֹהִים, *He is the God*, was interjected parenthetically by Cyrus as a declaration of his belief in the supremacy of the God of Israel: 'He is *the* God!'

The natural flow of the text, however, would indicate that the translation should be, *He is the God Who is in Jerusalem*. This is *Metzudos'* rendition. [Apparently, this version was rejected by *Rashi* and *Ibn Ezra* because it limits the presence of God to the city of Jerusalem.] *Metzudos'* interpretation is borne out by *Shemos Rabbah* (2:2): Consider what Cyrus said — *He is the God Who is in Jerusalem*. Although it is desolate, God does not abandon it.

*Malbim* also considers the phrase to be a reflection of Cyrus' limited understanding of the Divine ways. Cyrus thought that Divine Providence was limited to Jerusalem, while the remainder of the world was entrusted to the influence of the stars. *Koheles Rabbah* (10:13) supports this interpretation, remarking that the passage, *His talk begins as foolishness (Eccles.* 10:13), refers to Cyrus' statement that *He is the God Who is in Jerusalem*. [Only a fool could fail to observe the universal evidence of the hand of Providence and declare that God's power is limited to Jerusalem.]

**4.** וְכָל־הַנִּשְׁאָר מִכָּל־הַמְּקֹמוֹת אֲשֶׁר־הוּא גָר־שָׁם — *And anyone who remains in whatever place he dwells*. Should any Jew be forced to remain because of his poverty *(Rashi)*.

[The next phrase, where *the inhabitants of that place* are instructed to provide gifts so that those remaining may go up, indicates that the obstacle to returning was poverty.]

אַנְשֵׁי מְקֹמוֹ — *Let the inhabitants of that place*. This refers to the gentile inhabitants *(Rashi)*.

יְנַשְּׂאוּהוּ ... בְּכֶסֶף וּבְזָהָב — *Bestow upon him gifts of silver, gold*. The decree *to bestow upon him* is not merely a suggestion, but a command. The reason for bestowing gifts was to enable even the poorest Jews to go up to Jerusalem *(Rashi)*.

*Ibn Ezra* translates יְנַשְּׂאוּהוּ, *shall raise him up*. The lowly pauper is uplifted by wealth *(Ibn Ezra)*.

*Malbim* suggests an additional nuance — the inhabitants shall raise his spirit. Should some remain behind for lack of the self-assurance required for this bold project — then let their spirits be lifted through the support shown by their countrymen.[1] Thus, the inhabitants were instructed to furnish moral as well as financial backing for the returning exiles.

עִם־הַנְּדָבָה לְבֵית הָאֱלֹהִים — *Together with the contribution for the Temple of God*. In addition to the gifts which they were to bestow upon the remaining Jews to enable them to ascend to Jerusalem, the gentile inhabitants were to give their own contributions for the Temple of God to the Jews, who would bring the gifts to Jerusalem. Some of the gentiles

1. See *Ramban* to *Exodus* 35:21: *And they came* [to build the Tabernacle] *all those whose hearts uplifted them (Exodus* 35:21). The Israelites wandering in the desert were untutored and unskilled in any of the crafts; but they were *prideful in the ways of God*. Their hearts raised them up, and they presented themselves with supreme self-confidence, volunteering to execute the exquisite artistry required in the construction of the Tabernacle.

א ה ויָּק֡וּמוּ רָאשֵׁ֣י הָאָב֗וֹת לִֽיהוּדָה֙ וּבִנְיָמִ֔ן
ה־ו וְהַכֹּהֲנִ֖ים וְהַלְוִיִּ֑ם לְכֹ֨ל הֵעִ֤יר הָֽאֱלֹהִים֙ אֶת־
רוּח֔וֹ לַעֲל֣וֹת לִבְנ֔וֹת אֶת־בֵּ֥ית יְהוָ֖ה אֲשֶׁ֥ר
ו בִּירֽוּשָׁלִָֽם׃ וְכָל־סְבִיבֹֽתֵיהֶם֙ חִזְּק֣וּ בִֽידֵיהֶ֔ם

did indeed contribute toward the Temple's construction *(Rashi)*.

*Malbim* explains that Cyrus felt some Jews might refrain from ascending to Jerusalem because they were unable to present a donation for the Temple's construction. He therefore ordered the gentiles to send contributions with the Jews, so that none need refrain from ascending.

### ◂§ The Response

**5.** וַיָּקוּמוּ — *Thereupon* [lit. *and*] ... *rose up*. The Midrash *(Shir HaShirim Rabbah* 5:5) teaches that the response to the call for the renewal of the Temple stands as a source of Jewish merit. קַמְתִּי אֲנִי לִפְתֹּחַ לְדוֹדִי, *I arose to open for my Beloved (Song of Songs* 5:5) — It was I [Israel] who arose, not the other nations.

*Radal* views this as a reference to the fact that it was the Jewish people, not the Persian Cyrus, who actively arose to renew the Temple. God had proclaimed, *'He (Cyrus) shall build My Temple'*; Cyrus, however, merely permitted the Jews to rebuild it, but did not actively participate himself. [See comm. 1:3.]

According to *Yefei Kol*, the Midrashic statement that the other nations did not rise refers not to Cyrus, but to the *enemies of Judah and Benjamin* (4:1) — the idolatrous Samaritans, whose proposal to assist in the construction of the Temple was rejected. Israel arose to restore the Temple, but not the Samaritans. Their offer was a ruse masking purely destructive designs (see *Rashi* to 4:2; *Arachin* 5b).

רָאשֵׁי הָאָבוֹת — *The heads of the families* [lit. *of the fathers*]. Each of the tribes of Israel was divided into families, each with its own leader *(Metzudos)*.

לִיהוּדָה וּבִנְיָמִן וְהַכֹּהֲנִים וְהַלְוִיִּם — *Of Judah and Benjamin, and the Kohanim, and the Levites*. The opinion of *Tosafos (Arachin* 32a) is that some members of all the twelve tribes went up to the Land of Israel. However, only the tribes of Judah, Benjamin, and Levi are mentioned specifically in the text, because they comprised the preponderant majority of the returnees.[1] [See chapter 2 for the breakdown of the returning exiles by tribes. The *Kohanim*, Levites, Judeans, and Benjaminites numbered about 29,000, while all the others numbered only 13,000. See comm. to 2:64.]

*Ramban (Sefer HaGeulah)* contends that the Ten Tribes remained in the diaspora, except for small elements of Ephraim and Manasseh who now returned and took up residence in the cities of Judah and Benjamin. The others failed to return because Cyrus' permission was specifically limited to those who had previously inhabited the Judean territories [see comm., v. 3. See further, ArtScroll comm. to *Divrei HaYamim/Chronicles I* 9:2 and 3].

Alternatively, the others did not return because they were bound by their oath that the redemption not be unduly hastened. The exiled nation had sworn not to return to the Holy Land without Divinely revealed authorization. [See *Shir HaShirim Rabbah* 2:18: *I adjure you, O nations* — He caused

1. The Midrash explains why these tribes were particularly responsive: Judah responded because it was the royal tribe [King David and his descendants, who established the Temple and preserved it as the nation's most prized possession, were from Judah]; Benjamin, because the Temple stood on its ancestral soil [see *Rashi, Deut.* 33:12]; the *Kohanim*, because they performed the sacrificial rites; and the Levites, because they stood upon the platform at the Temple and chanted during the services (*Shir HaShirim Rabbah* 5:5).

I
5-6
*The Response*

5 *Thereupon, the heads of the families of Judah and Benjamin, and the Kohanim, and the Levites rose up, with all whom God inspired to go up and build the Temple of* HASHEM *in Jerusalem.* 6 *And all their*

Israel to swear not to rebel against the monarchies.] The Babylonian exiles were released from the oath by Jeremiah's prophecy of their return to Zion [*for after seventy years of Babylon ... I shall remember you (Jeremiah* 29:10); see prologue], but the Ten Tribes who had been taken captive before the rise of the Babylonian empire were not included in the prophetic message. They remained bound by the solemn pledge prohibiting their premature departure from the diaspora *(Sefer HaGeulah).*

לְכֹל הֵעִיר הָאֱלֹהִים אֶת־רוּחוֹ — *With all whom God inspired* [lit. *aroused his spirit*]. *Rashi* renders לְכֹל, *with all*, interpreting the entire verse as a single statement: *Thereupon, the heads of the families of Judah and Benjamin, the Kohanim, and the Levites rose up,* [*together*] *with all whom God inspired to go up to build the Temple.*

*Malbim*, however, divides the verse, and translates לְכֹל, *to all.* The passage reads as follows: *Thereupon, the heads of the families of Judah and Benjamin, and the Kohanim and Levites rose up. To all* [of these] *God granted inspiration to go up and build the Temple in Jerusalem.*

*Malbim* correlates the two sentences by explaining that Providential assistance is provided only after independent human endeavor has begun. This assistance enables those to whom it is granted to overcome ordinarily insurmountable obstacles. First the people, led by the elders of Judah and Benjamin, rose up spontaneously. Only then did God respond, furnishing the spark of Divine inspiration which moved them to go up and build the Temple. [Because they were now Divinely inspired, they would persevere even in the face of the most discouraging circumstances.]

לַעֲלוֹת לִבְנוֹת — *To go up and build.* The inspiration was twofold: (a) *to go up,* i.e., to undertake the arduous journey to Jerusalem; and (b) *to build*, i.e., to begin the construction of the Temple *(Malbim).*

The Talmud notes that Ezra did not respond to Cyrus' call, and remained in Babylon until after the reconstruction of the Temple [see ch. 7]. This was because he was a disciple of Baruch ben Neriah and he would not leave his teacher as long as he still lived. From this the Rabbis infer that the *mitzvah* of studying Torah is greater even than that of building the Temple (*Megillah* 16b).

But why did Baruch ben Neriah not ascend? Because he was aged and infirm, and could not withstand the rigors of the journey (*Shir HaShirim Rabbah* 5:5).

6. וְכָל־סְבִיבֹתֵיהֶם — *And all their neighbors* [lit. *all who were around them*]. Their gentile neighbors supported the Jews so they would be able to go up to Jerusalem *(Rashi).*

[This corresponds with *Rashi's* remark (v. 4) that Cyrus instructed the non-Jews to provide the financial aid necessary for the Jewish emigration. His instructions were now carried out.]

חִזְּקוּ בִידֵיהֶם — *Supported them* [lit. *strengthened in their hands*]. The familiar idiom חִזְּקוּ יְדֵיהֶם, *they strengthened their hands*, is altered in this passage to חִזְּקוּ בִידֵיהֶם, lit. *they strengthened 'in' their hands.*

*Malbim* observes that the expression 'strengthening the hands' is appropriate in reference to the feeble and the irresolute — those whose hands are weak. The exiles, however, were not wanting in inner resolution; they were simply in need of funds. Thus, in presenting the gifts, the gentiles did not strengthen the hands' of their Jewish

בִּכְלֵי־כֶסֶף בַּזָּהָב בָּרְכוּשׁ וּבַבְּהֵמָה
וּבַמִּגְדָּנוֹת לְבַד עַל־כָּל־הִתְנַדֵּב׃
ז וְהַמֶּלֶךְ כּוֹרֶשׁ הוֹצִיא אֶת־כְּלֵי בֵית־יְהוָה
אֲשֶׁר הוֹצִיא נְבוּכַדְנֶצַּר מִירוּשָׁלַםִ וַיִּתְּנֵם
ח בְּבֵית אֱלֹהָיו׃ וַיּוֹצִיאֵם כּוֹרֶשׁ מֶלֶךְ פָּרַס עַל־

neighbors. They merely placed monetary assistance *in* the hands of Jews who were already fortified with the required determination.

וּבַבְּהֵמָה — *Animals.* For transport *(Ibn Ezra).*

וּבַמִּגְדָּנוֹת — *And precious goods.* This is a general term for the costly, highest-quality items of any category, such as clothing, food, or jewels *(Ralbag; Metzudos).*

לְבַד עַל־כָּל־הִתְנַדֵּב — *Besides all that was contributed.* The treasure given to them by the king's decree was besides the contributions for the construction of the Temple volunteered by the gentile neighbors[1] *(Rashi).* The silver, gold, valuables, and animals were to provide the finances and the transport for the trip *(Malbim).*

**7. The Temple Vessels**

כְּלֵי בֵית־ה׳ — *The vessels of the Temple of HASHEM.* According to *Rashi,* this was the fulfillment of Jeremiah's prophecy *(Jeremiah* 21:21-22): *Concerning the vessels remaining in the Temple ... they shall be transported to Babylon, and shall remain there until the day when I will remember them ... and restore them to this place* (i.e., during the days of Cyrus — *Rashi).*

Nebuchadnezzar exiled the Jews and plundered the Temple on three occasions [see table]. In the year 3326, he banished King Yehoyakim [Jehoiakim] and *conveyed ... some of the vessels of the Temple of HASHEM to Babylon (II Chronicles* 36:7). The next year, he brought King Yehoyachin [Jehoiachin] to Babylon *with the precious vessels of the Temple of HASHEM* (ibid. v. 10). Eleven years later, on the ninth of Av 3338, he destroyed the Temple, drove King Zidkiyahu [Zedekiah] and the nation into exile, and carried off all the remaining Temple vessels to Babylon (ibid. v. 18; see *Megillah* 11b). Which of the vessels did Cyrus now return?

**Table according to Rashi**

| Exile | Year | King |
|---|---|---|
| First | 3326 | Yehoyakim |
| Second | 3327 | Yehoyachin |
| Third | 3338 | Zidkiyahu |

According to *Rashi* and *Radak* *(Jeremiah* 27:22), Jeremiah's prophecy foretelling the eventual restoration of the vessels refers to their return by Cyrus. Since this prophecy, which predicts the removal of the vessels still

1. The Talmud *(Arachin* 5b, 6a) stipulates that contributions for the establishment of the Temple may not be accepted from non-Jewish sources. This precept is based on the refusal of the elders of Israel to permit the participation of the Samaritans in the construction of the Temple (4:3). Yet Cyrus' assistance was instrumental in the construction of the Temple, and the exiles returned to Jerusalem bearing gifts for the Temple of God contributed by their gentile neighbors.

*Tosafos* justifies this by referring to the word of the prophet Isaiah (ch. 44), wherein Cyrus is extolled as the builder of the city of Jerusalem and the restorer of the Temple. The assistance rendered by Cyrus and those under his sovereignty could be accepted because it was the fulfillment of the stated will of Heaven [see comm. and footnote to 4:3].

*neighbors supported them with silver utensils, gold, valuables, animals, and precious goods, besides all that was contributed.*

*The Temple Vessels*

7 *King Cyrus removed the vessels of the Temple of* HASHEM, *which Nebuchadnezzar had removed from Jerusalem and placed in the temple of his gods.*
8 *Cyrus, king of Persia, had them removed by*

remaining in the Temple followed by their eventual restoration, was spoken after the first two exiles, it is clear that in *Rashi's* and *Radak's* opinions, the vessels brought to Babylon in the third exile were returned by Cyrus.

An additional clue can be gleaned from *Daniel* 1:2, which specifies that the vessels despoiled during the first exile were deposited by Nebuchadnezzar *in the treasury of his gods.* This corresponds with the description of the returned vessels in our verse: *which Nebuchadnezzar had ... placed in the temple of his gods.* [This seems inconsistent with *II Chronicles* 36:7, which records that Nebuchadnezzar brought the vessels *to his palace.* Perhaps the treasury of Nebuchadnezzar's gods was housed in his palace.] Evidently then, Cyrus also returned the utensils taken in the *first* exile.

Whereas the vessels confiscated during the first and last Judean exiles were clearly returned by Cyrus, the fate of those utensils taken during the second exile is not certain.

*Ramban* (to *Megillah* 11b), however, disagrees with *Rashi,* citing the statement in the Talmud (ibid.) that Ahasuerus used the Temple goblets *(Esther* 1:7) taken by Nebuchadnezzar. Since this took place some years *after* the return described here, it follows that Cyrus did not restore all the Temple vessels. He returned only those vessels which Nebuchadnezzar had plundered during the first Judean exile, when Yehoyakim was banished, not the vessels mentioned in Jeremiah's prophecy. Those vessels, which were not removed from the Temple until its destruction, were later returned when the Temple was completed by King Darius [see below 7:19, 8:28]. In this way, each set of vessels remained in the exile for seventy years.

**8.** וַיּוֹצִיאֵם כּוֹרֶשׁ — *Cyrus ... had them removed.* Cyrus first removed the Temple vessels from Nebuchadnezzar's temple and placed them in his own treasury (v. 7). He then had them removed from there (v. 8) by his treasurer, Mithredath, and delivered to Sheshbazzar *(Malbim).*

Cyrus did not convey the vessels directly from the pagan temple to the Temple in Jerusalem, because it is unseemly for utensils retained in a house of idolatry to be presented for use in the Temple of God. The king, therefore, first dissociated the vessels from the source of corruption — the temple of Nebuchadnezzar's gods — and placed them in his own treasury.

This was similar[1] to the act of בִּטּוּל, *nullification,* of the defilement invested in an object by its use in a pagan ritual. The vessels were now rendered fit for use in the Temple services, and Cyrus had them removed from his own treasury — not from the pollutive dominion of the house of idolatry — to Sheshbazzar as a Temple contribution *(Malbim).*

1. Nullification of idolatry is generally performed through an overt act of either damaging the vessel or casting it away, thereby demonstrating the disavowal of its further idolatrous use. See *Avodah Zarah* 52b, 53a.

א ט־יא

יַ֣ד מִתְרְדָ֣ת הַגִּזְבָּ֑ר וַֽיִּסְפְּרֵם֙ לְשֵׁשְׁבַּצַּ֔ר
ט הַנָּשִׂ֖יא לִיהוּדָֽה׃ וְאֵ֖לֶּה מִסְפָּרָ֑ם
אֲגַרְטְלֵ֨י זָהָ֜ב שְׁלֹשִׁ֗ים אֲגַרְטְלֵי־כֶ֙סֶף֙ אָ֔לֶף
י מַחֲלָפִ֖ים תִּשְׁעָ֥ה וְעֶשְׂרִֽים׃ כְּפוֹרֵ֤י זָהָב֙
שְׁלֹשִׁ֔ים כְּפ֤וֹרֵי כֶ֙סֶף֙ מִשְׁנִ֔ים אַרְבַּ֥ע מֵא֖וֹת
יא וַעֲשָׂרָ֑ה כֵּלִ֥ים אֲחֵרִ֖ים אָֽלֶף׃ כָּל־כֵּלִים֙ לַזָּהָ֣ב

מִתְרְדָת הַגִּזְבָּר — *Mithredath the treasurer. R' Yeshayah MiTrani* identifies Mithredath as a Levite who was the administrator of all the king's treasure houses.

According to *Ralbag,* he was the official keeper of the Temple vessels taken from Jerusalem.

וַיִּסְפְּרֵם — *Who then counted them over.* They were given over to Sheshbazzar to transport to Jerusalem *(Rashi).*

לְשֵׁשְׁבַּצַּר הַנָּשִׂיא לִיהוּדָה — *To Sheshbazzar, the prince of Judah. Rashi,* citing the Midrash *(Yalkut,* ch. 5), asserts that the Judean prince was actually Daniel. The name *Sheshbazzar* is derived from the Hebrew שֵׁשׁ [*shesh*], *six,* and בַּצַּר [*bazzar*], *in affliction,* denoting the six afflictions[1] of Daniel's times.

*Rashi* points out that Sheshbazzar was the prince of the tribe of Judah. [At this time there was no prince of the *kingdom* of Judah.]

*Ibn Ezra, Ralbag,* and *Metzudos,* however, contend that Sheshbazzar was either the Chaldean or Persian name of Zerubabel, chief of the returning exiles [see 2:2; *Haggai* 1:1].

[Zerubabel, a scion of the royal house of Judah (see comm. to 2:2), was the leader of the exiles. Therefore, the title *prince of Judah* was fitting for him, and the king would naturally have chosen him for the guardianship of the Temple vessels.]

9. אֲגַרְטְלֵי זָהָב ... אֲגַרְטְלֵי־כֶסֶף — *Golden utensils ... silver utensils.* The translation follows *Rashi.*

*R' Yeshayah MiTrani* and *Metzudos* translate אֲגַרְטְלֵי as *wash basins,* from which water was poured in washing the hands of the *Kohanim* during the Temple ritual.

*Talmud Yerushalmi (Yoma* 3:5) explains that these utensils were bowls for the blood of the Temple sacrifices: the אֲגַרְטְלֵי זָהָב, *golden bowls,* were for the sacrificial lambs, and the אֲגַרְטְלֵי כֶסֶף, *silver bowls,* for the sacrificial bulls.

*Korban HaEidah* explains the *Yerushalmi's* interpretation. אֲגַרְטְלָה, is constructed from אֲגַר, *to gather,* and טְלֶה, *lamb.* אֲגַרְטְלָה is the vessel wherein the essence of the lamb — its blood — is gathered. Hence אֲגַרְטְלֵי זָהָב are golden bowls for the sacrificial lambs.

In the phrase אֲגַרְטְלֵי כֶסֶף אָלֶף, *one thousand silver utensils,* the word אָלֶף [lit. *one thousand*] may sometimes mean *cattle* [as in שְׁגַר אֲלָפֶיךָ, *the offspring of your cattle;* see *Deut.* 7:13], thus suggesting that the silver utensils were used for the Temple services involving bulls.

*Korban HaEidah* further notes that the bowls used for the sacrificial cows had to be much larger than those used for the lambs, because bulls have much more blood than lambs. Since golden bowls of such great size would have been very costly, the vessels used

1. *Yalkut (Ezra* 5) lists the six afflictions:
(a) Daniel was cast into the den of lions (*Daniel* 6:17);
(b) Hananiah, Mishael, and Azariah were thrown into the fiery furnace (*Daniel* 3:21);
(c) The lives of Daniel and his companions were menaced (*Daniel* 2:13) [Nebuchadnezzar threatened to kill all the wise men of Babylon unless they would interpret his dream, which he could not even recall];
(d-f) Portions of the Jewish nation were exiled on three separate occasions [see comm., v. 7], culminating in the destruction of the Sanctuary (II *Chronicles* 36).

I
9-11 Mithredath the treasurer, who then counted them
over to Sheshbazzar, the prince of Judah. 9 This was
their number: thirty golden utensils, one thousand
silver utensils, twenty-nine knives, 10 thirty golden
bowls, four hundred and ten secondary silver bowls,
and one thousand other vessels. 11 The total of all the

for the bulls were of silver. The smaller utensils used for the lambs were made of gold.

מַחֲלָפִים — *Knives.* The Mishnah (*Middos* 4:7) mentions a chamber in the Temple called בֵּית הַחֲלִיפוֹת, where [damaged] knives were stored *(Rashi;* see *Yerushalmi, Yoma* 3:8).

*Korban HaEidah* to *Yerushalmi* there suggests that the origin of this word is from the root חלף, *to exchange* or *transform.* The slaughterer's knife produces the ultimate exchange — the transformation of life into death.

**10.** כְּפוֹרֵי זָהָב — *Golden bowls.* These bowls were also used for conveying the sacrificial blood to the altar. כְּפוֹר is derived from the Aramaic כפר, *to wipe.* The *Kohanim* cleansed their hands by wiping them along the edges of these bowls. Hence כְּפוֹרֵי literally means *wiping bowls*[1] *(Rashi; Metzudos;* see *Menachos* 7:8).

כְּפוֹרֵי כֶסֶף מִשְׁנִים — *Secondary silver bowls.* The silver bowls were second in value *(Ibn Ezra). Malbim* agrees, citing *I Samuel* 15:9, מֵיטַב הַצֹּאן ... וְהַמִּשְׁנִים, *the superlative sheep ... and the secondary ones.*[2]

*R' Yeshayah MiTrani* renders coupled silver bowls, referring, evidently, to utensils used in pairs.

Yet another translation appears in *Metzudos: doubled silver bowls,* the kind which could be used from either of two sides. [The bowls consisted of two convex sections joined at the base.]

**11.** כָּל־כֵּלִים ... חֲמֵשֶׁת אֲלָפִים וְאַרְבַּע מֵאוֹת — *The total of all the ... vessels was five thousand four hundred.* This is not consistent with the number of utensils catalogued above (vs. 9,10), which comes to less than half this sum. *Rashi* reconciles the discrepancy by explaining that those listed above comprised only the most precious of all the vessels contributed. There were also a great number of less valuable vessels. Together, the total was 5400.

*Ibn Ezra* offers a similar solution. The list of utensils recorded above refers to the larger vessels. The sum total of 5400 recorded here includes the smaller utensils as well. In support of this approach, *Ibn Ezra* notes that the passage in *II Chronicles* (36:18), which recounts the plundering of the Temple, also refers to large and small vessels: *All of the vessels of the Temple of God, large and small,* [*Nebuchadnezzar*] *brought to Babylon.*

*R' Yeshayah MiTrani* differs with the preceding explanations. In his opinion, the 5400 vessels recorded here were given *in addition* to those enumerated previously. *Malbim* agrees, but with the

1. Similarly, *Rashi* to *Genesis* 32:21 translates אוּלַי אֲכַפְּרָה פָנָיו, *perhaps I shall wipe away his rage. Ramban,* however, objects to *Rashi's* interpretation, contending that the Aramaic term כְּפוֹרֵי זָהָב, *golden wiping bowls,* is characteristic of the *Book of Ezra,* which abounds with Aramaic expressions, but is hardly appropriate for the pure Hebrew phraseology of *Genesis. Ramban,* therefore, proposes a new interpretation of the passage. In the Hebrew, כַּפָּרָה is synonymous with פִּדְיוֹן, *redemption.* He renders אוּלַי אֲכַפְּרָה פָנָיו as *perhaps I shall redeem myself, that I may gaze upon his countenance.*

2. *Rashi (I Samuel* 15:9) interprets הַמִּשְׁנִים as *the doubly fleshy ones* [sheep], and remarks that the word is unparalleled in the Scripture. Evidently, *Rashi* means that מִשְׁנִים interpreted as *doubly large and opulent* is unparalleled in the Scripture.

ב
א־ב

וְלַכֵּסֶף חֲמֵשֶׁת אֲלָפִים וְאַרְבַּע מֵאוֹת הַכֹּל הֶעֱלָה שֵׁשְׁבַּצַּר עִם הֵעָלוֹת הַגּוֹלָה מִבָּבֶל לִירוּשָׁלָםִ׃

א וְאֵלֶּה ׀ בְּנֵי הַמְּדִינָה הָעֹלִים מִשְּׁבִי הַגּוֹלָה
אֲשֶׁר הֶגְלָה °נבוכדנצור מֶלֶךְ־בָּבֶל לְבָבֶל °נְבוּכַדְנֶצַּר ק׳
וַיָּשׁוּבוּ לִירוּשָׁלַםִ וִיהוּדָה אִישׁ לְעִירוֹ׃
ב אֲשֶׁר־בָּאוּ עִם־זְרֻבָּבֶל יֵשׁוּעַ נְחֶמְיָה שְׂרָיָה

following variation: The vessels listed previously had been confiscated by Nebuchadnezzar during the plundering of the First Temple, and were now taken from the Temple of his gods. The additional 5400 did not come from the First Temple, but were presented as Cyrus' personal gift.

# II

**1.** וְאֵלֶּה בְּנֵי הַמְּדִינָה — *These are the children of the province.* The verse refers to the Jews from the province of Israel who had been exiled to Babylon and now ascended from the exile *(Rashi).*

*Ibn Ezra,* however, disagrees with *Rashi* and identifies *the province* as Babylon. The *children of the province* are the Jews who were living in exile in the province of Babylon.

אֲשֶׁר הֶגְלָה נְבוּכַדְנֶצַּר מֶלֶךְ־בָּבֶל לְבָבֶל — *Which Nebuchadnezzar king of Babylon had exiled to Babylon.* [For a record of the various stages of the Babylonian exile, see comm. 1:7.]

וַיָּשׁוּבוּ לִירוּשָׁלַםִ וִיהוּדָה אִישׁ לְעִירוֹ — *They now returned to Jerusalem, and [the children of] Judah, each to his city.* The translation follows *Rashi,* who explains that *Judah* is not another destination but another category of people — the Judean immigrants who returned to their ancestral cities.

*Metzudos,* however, punctuates the sentence differently: The children of the province *now returned to Jerusalem and [to the land of] Judah, each to his city.*

[Perhaps *Rashi* rejects this approach because such a construction would require that the text read: לִירוּשָׁלַיִם וְלִיהוּדָה, *to Jerusalem and 'to' Judah.* This is, indeed, the reading in the parallel passage in *Nehemiah* (7:6). There *Rashi* interpolates: *to 'the province of' Judah. Metzudos,* however, interprets both verses as referring to the province rather than the people of Judah.]

*Malbim* agrees with *Metzudos* that our verse can be understood in the light of its counterpart in *Nehemiah,* and explains why the prefix ל, *to,* is omitted from the word וִיהוּדָה here. His opinion [see comm. to v. 3-35, s.v. *The Judeans and Benjaminites*] is that the *Book of Ezra* lists the spiritual leaders of the community, whose primary destination was the Sanctuary and the sacred city of Jerusalem. From there they ventured to establish homes elsewhere in the less exalted territory of Judah. Thus, their passage is described as the return *to Jerusalem and Judah.* The usage of the proposition *to* in relation to Jerusalem alone identifies the holy city as their primary objective; their eventual settlement in the Judean province was a relatively secondary act. The *Book of Nehemiah,* however, recounts the return of the less distinguished immigrants, too. They also ascended to Jerusalem, but they were equally prompted by the desire to settle the territory of Judah. Their journey is therefore characterized as the return *to Jerusalem and 'to' Judah.*

*golden and silver vessels was five thousand four hundred. All were brought up by Sheshbazzar with the ascension of the exile from Babylon to Jerusalem.*

*These are the children of the province ascending from the captivity of the exile, which Nebuchadnezzar king of Babylon had exiled to Babylon; they now returned to Jerusalem, and [the children of] Judah, each to his city.* 2 *Those who had come with Zerubabel, Jeshua, Nehemiah, Seraiah,*

Although our verse records that the people returned *each to his city,* the Talmud *(Chulin* 7a) notes that not all the old cities were resettled. Many cities which had been conquered by the Jews who came up from Egypt were left unsettled by the Babylonian immigrants so that they might sustain the destitute during *shemittah* [the sabbatical year of the land).

[The Land of Israel may not be cultivated, nor its crops harvested, during the year of *shemittah,* which occurs every seventh year *(Leviticus* 25:1-7). This prohibition applies only to the land sanctified by national Jewish occupation under the leadership of a prophet or Jewish monarch *(Rambam, Hil. Terumos* 1:2). Eretz Yisrael was first sanctified by Joshua and the people when they vanquished the Canaanite nations and took possession of the land [see *Joshua*]. This sanctification, however, was not permanent. It expired at the destruction of the First Temple, when the nation was exiled and the land left unoccupied (ibid. 1:5) — and with the loss of sanctity, the laws of *shemittah* also expired. The second sanctification, with its accompanying *shemittah* regulations, was instituted in the days of Ezra, when the Jews who came up from Babylon resettled the land. Fearing that the poor would be left in desperate straits should the entire land lie fallow every seventh year, the settlers refrained from taking control of certain cities so that the sanctity of those areas would not be renewed. Since their exemption from the *shemittah* restraints remained intact, they could be worked freely during the *shemittah* period to feed the destitute.]

**2.** אֲשֶׁר־בָּאוּ — *Those who had come.* Those who had come down to the Babylonian exile with Zerubabel *(Rashi)* [not those who came *now* to Jerusalem. Our phrase describes the past history of those who now returned. They had been exiled with Zerubabel. Now, upon their return from the exile, they are listed here].

This interpretation evidently conflicts with the Talmudic statement *(Sanhedrin* 38a) that Zerubabel did not go into exile from Israel, but was born in Babylon. [See comm. s.v. *Zerubabel.*] Perhaps *Rashi* derives his interpretation by contrasting the tenses in verse 1 and our verse. In describing the going up from Babylon (v. 1), the present tense (ascending) is used. But in our verse, the verb is in the past tense *(had come),* indicating that they *had come* with Zerubabel at some period preceding the return from captivity — i.e., they *had come* down to the Babylonian exile with him.

The parallel list of the returning exiles in *Nehemiah's* introductory passages reads in the present tense *(Nehemiah* 7:7). *Rashi* there comments that the reference is to the exiles who returned from captivity with Zerubabel.[1]

According to *R' Yeshayah MiTrani* and *Metzudos,* however, our passage refers to those who *now* came with Zerubabel from the Babylonian exile to the Land of Israel.

זְרֻבָּבֶל — *Zerubabel.* Zerubabel was a descendant of the Judean king Yehoyachin [Jehoiachin] *(I Chronicles* 3:17-19). He is widely referred to as

1. *Maharsha* (to *Megillah* 16b) explains the difference in the tenses between *Nehemiah* and here as an allusion to the fact that some of the people mentioned in this verse came twice: once during the initial emigration, after which they returned to Babylon, and again with Nehemiah.

Zerubabel ben Shealtiel (3:2, 5:2, *Haggai* 1:1, 2:2, 2:23), and he appears as a major Jewish leader during the restoration of the Second Temple (see 3:2, 4:3, 5:2). Addressing him as the governor of Judah, God informs Zerubabel that He has chosen him for future greatness *(Haggai* 2:21,23).

The Talmud *(Sanhedrin* 38a) identifies Zerubabel as Nehemiah ben Hachaliah, author and leading personality of the *Book of Nehemiah.* The name זְרֻבָּבֶל [Zeru-babel] is a contraction of the Hebrew words נִזְרַע בְּבָבֶל, meaning *conceived* [lit. *implanted*] *in Babylon.* Nehemiah was designated Zerubabel to commemorate his birth in Babylon.

The *Book of Ezra* places Zerubabel in Jerusalem during the entire period of the Temple reconstruction, beginning with Cyrus' proclamation, extending through the interval of intervention by the enemies of Judah and Benjamin, and closing with the successful renewal of the reconstruction effort in the second year of the reign of the Persian king, Darius. Throughout this time, Zerubabel played a principal role in all of the communal affairs in Jerusalem [see *Ezra* 3:2, 4:3, 5:2]. The *Book of Nehemiah,* however, relates that Nehemiah learned of the privations in Jerusalem and emigrated to the Holy Land in Darius' twentieth year [see *Rashi* to *Nehemiah* 1:1]. Where was Zerubabel-Nehemiah during the interval between the second and twentieth years of Darius?

Apparently, Zerubabel had departed from Jerusalem sometime after the construction of the Temple, which was completed in Darius' sixth year *(Ezra* 6:15). He settled in Shushan, where he reappears in the *Book of Nehemiah* under the name Nehemiah ben Hachaliah. He returned to Israel in Darius' twentieth year.

*R' Yaakov Emden* (in his notes to *Sanhedrin* 38a) raises two additional difficulties to the proposition that Zerubabel was actually Nehemiah. First, Zerubabel is listed together with Nehemiah in our passage. Second, Zerubabel and Nehemiah are mentioned together in *Nehemiah* (12:47): *During the days of Zerubabel and the days of Nehemiah.* The reference to *the days of Nehemiah* indicates that the person named was the national leader.

[The first objection may be countered, however, by assuming that the Nehemiah mentioned here (Ezra) is not the author of the *Book of Nehemiah.* The second may also be reconciled. *During the days of Zerubabel and the days of Nehemiah* may be understood as *during the days of Zerubabel,* i.e., *the days of Nehemiah,* meaning that Nehemiah and Zerubabel were the same person.]

However, *Rambam* (Introduction to *Commentary on Mishnah,* and Introduction to *Mishneh Torah), Meiri* (Introduction to *Avos), Abarbanel,* and *R' Ovadiah Bertinoro (Avos* 1:1) assume that Zerubabel and Nehemiah were not the same person. [See *B'Shaar HaMelech* by *R' Chaim Konievsky* who cites *Targum* to *Shir HaShirim* in support of *Rambam's* view.]

*Ibn Ezra* (3:2) offers an additional interpretation of the name. *Zerubabel* represents the words שָׁרוּי בְּבָבֶל, *residing in Babylon,* referring to Israel's exile in Babylon.

יֵשׁוּעַ — *Jeshua. Ibn Ezra* and *Metzudos* identify him as the *Kohen Gadol* (High Priest) Jehoshua ben Jehozadak. *Ezra* 3:2 mentions that *Jeshua ben Jozadak, and his brothers, the Kohanim,* erected the altar for the fledgling community; and the prophet Haggai (chs. 1,2) urged the *Kohen Gadol* Jehoshua ben Jehozadak to complete the construction of the Temple.

נְחֶמְיָה — *Nehemiah.* [See comm. to s.v. זרבבל.]

*Ralbag* identifies this Nehemiah as the author of the *Book of Nehemiah.*

[*Nehemiah* 1:1 recounts that Nehemiah was in Shushan serving as a minister to the king (2:1). Accordingly, he must have left Jerusalem at some point and returned to Persia, as did Mordechai. See below.]

שְׂרָיָה רְעֵלָיָה — *Seraiah, Reelaiah.* In *Nehemiah* (7:7) these two names are omitted and replaced by three names — עֲזַרְיָה, רַעַמְיָה, נַחֲמָנִי: *Azariah, Raamiah, Nahamani. Ibn Ezra* (there) states that Azariah and Raamiah are identical with Seraiah and Reelaiah of our verse, i.e., they were each known by more than one name. Although *Ezra* refers to them as Seraiah and Reelaiah, *Nehemiah* records them by their other names — Azariah and Raamiah. This occurs frequently in Scripture *(Metzudos)*. [See *I Chronicles*, chs. 1-9, ArtScroll ed.] Nahamani, who is not listed in our verse, was still a young man at the time of the return and had not yet achieved the prominence warranting special mention. Thirty-six years later, when Nehemiah recorded this list a second time, he had become a recognized leader of the community, and Nehemiah inserted his name *(Metzudos* to *Nehemiah* 7:66).

מָרְדְּכַי — *Mordechai.* This was Mordechai ben Yair *(Esther* 2:5), cousin of Queen Esther, and Jewish leader during the events of Purim *(Megillah* 16b).

[According to *Rashi*, all of those listed in this chapter (vs. 3-61) originally came from the Land of Israel to the Babylonian exile. *Rashi*, however, does not specify *when* they came to Babylon. Was it during the exile of King Yehoyakim, the banishment of King Yehoyachin, or the final expulsion, in the times of King Zidkiyah [see *II Kings* 24, 25; comm. 1:1]. This question is clarified by the inclusion of Mordechai among the notables with whom the returnees had come to Babylon. Since the *Book of Esther* (2:6) states that Mordechai had been exiled with Yehoyachin, it follows that the other returnees, too, had been banished with Yehoyachin.]

*R' Yeshayah MiTrani* notes that although Mordechai now emigrated to Jerusalem, he evidently did not settle there permanently, for he later appeared in the Persian capital of Shushan during the reign of King Ahasuerus (2:5; *Esther* 1:1) who succeeded Cyrus and ruled for fourteen years *(Megillah* 11b). When the reconstruction of the Temple was discontinued, Mordechai departed from the Holy Land. *Ralbag* explains that Mordechai journeyed to Persia in order to gain the good graces of the king and convince him to permit the completion of the Temple.

Although here Mordechai's name is listed fifth, in Nehemiah's roster of those who emigrated to Jerusalem *(Nehemiah* 7:7) it appears sixth. The Sages observed that Mordechai's standing among the foremost Torah luminaries of the age had diminished. He was the fifth greatest sage at the time of Cyrus' proclamation [when Ezra's list was compiled], but only the sixth when Nehemiah's list appeared over three decades later. The Rabbis attribute this reduction to Mordechai's ministerial activities, which began at the time of the Purim miracle when King Ahasuerus elevated him to an exalted rank in the Persian court *(Esther* 10:3). His influence was vital for the preservation of the entire Jewish community, but his diligence in the study of Torah necessarily diminished. As a result, his standing among the leading Torah sages fell, and he was lowered to the sixth position in Nehemiah's list. The Talmud draws the conclusion from this that the study of Torah surpasses even the protection of lives[1] *(Megillah* 16b).

בִּלְשָׁן — *Bilshan.* The Talmud *(Menachos* 65a) states that *Bilshan* was a supplementary name for Mordechai, denoting his mastery of language. *Bilshan* is a contraction of the words בָּיִל לִישָׁנֵי, *he mixed languages.* Mordechai could understand the most cryptic remarks through word comparisons and associations. The Rabbis cite several instances of halachic decisions which hinged upon the interpretation of obscure statements. With his genius for word linkage, Mordechai was able to uncover their

1. The general rule that saving a life takes precedence over all the Torah's precepts except for the three cardinal sins applies only where there is an imminent threat to life. In Mordechai's case, that threat had already been averted with the death of Haman and the destruction of his followers. Mordechai, however, continued to occupy the post of chief minister in order to guard against any *potential* future threats. Although this, too, was a great *mitzvah*, it did not take precedence over the study and teaching of Torah, since no clear threat actually existed at that time *(R' Yosef Chaim* in *Ben Yehoyada* to *Megillah* there).

true meaning. Mordechai was also called פְּתַחְיָה (*Pethahiah,* to open or unlock), because he 'unlocked words'; i.e., he was expert in the art of comparing and extrapolating meanings in all of the seventy tongues (Mishnah, *Shekalim* 5:1).

Others suggest that *Bilshan* is simply the name of another person *(Ibn Ezra; Malbim).*

מִסְפָּר — *Mispar.* This is the name of a person *(Rashi; Ibn Ezra).* In *Nehemiah* (7:7) the name is given as מִסְפֶּרֶת, *Mispereth.*

*Yalkut Shimoni* takes Mispar Bigvai as one name and asserts that he was a member of the tribe of Levi, and was still within his mother's womb during the ascent from Babylon described in this passage.

*Radal (Bamidbar Rabbah* 3:20) explains that this is derived from the literal meaning of מִסְפָּר, *number,* and בִּגְוַי, *within.* He was *numbered* or *counted* while *within* the womb.[1]

רְחוּם — *Rehum.* In *Nehemiah* his name is given as נְחוּם, *Nehum.* Such minor changes in names are common *(Metzudos* to *Nehemiah).*

מִסְפַּר — *The number of.* Whereas the word *Mispar* above [*Mispar Bigvai*] is a name, the word *mispar* here is rendered *the number of (Rashi).*

אַנְשֵׁי — *The dignitaries* [lit. *men*] *of.* This translation follows *Rashi's* principle *(Numbers* 13:3) that wherever the term אֲנָשִׁים [lit. *men*] is mentioned in the Scripture, it denotes eminence.

The *dignitaries* are those already mentioned in the verse. Since these distinguished personages led the others, they are classified separately. Those less eminent are counted in the verses (3-61) which follow. The sense of v. 1-3 is then: *The following are the people of the province* (who had followed the dignitaries Zerubabel, Jeshua ...): *the children of Parosh ... (Rashi).*

*Machzor Vitry,* in the preface to his commentary on *Avos,* considers all those mentioned in this verse as members of the אַנְשֵׁי כְּנֶסֶת הַגְּדוֹלָה, *Men of the Great Assembly.*

The oral tradition enumerates additional great national figures who emigrated from the Babylonian exile. R' Yochanan said: Three prophets went up with them from exile *(Zevachim* 62a). *Rashi* explains that the three were Haggai, Zechariah, and Malachi.

*Pirkei d' R' Eliezer* (ch. 38) and *Yalkut Shimoni (II Kings* 17) indicate that Ezra also returned now to the Land of Israel with Zerubabel. [Ezra's emigration to the Holy Land is first recorded in 7:1-6, one year after the completion of the Temple. *Pirkei d' R' Eliezer* and *Yalkut* assume, apparently, that Ezra later returned to Babylon and then ascended to Jerusalem a second time, during the year following the Temple's construction. *Seder HaDoros* (3408, p. 132) cites a similar opinion.]

This is clearly disputed, however, by the Talmud *(Megillah* 16b) and by *Midrash Shir HaShirim* (5:5), which maintain that Ezra did not leave Babylon until the year following the construction of the Temple, as recorded in 7:1-6.

### ◆§ The Returnees

**3-35.** The *Book of Nehemiah* (7:5-73) records the discovery of a register of those who returned to the Holy Land

1. The Sages comment that this corresponds with the Scriptural custom of counting the Levites during their early youth. R' Judah ben Shalom the Levite said: 'The Holy One, Blessed is He, regularly enumerates the Tribe of Levi in their infancy. Yocheved, Levi's daughter, was borne down to Egypt in the womb, and is numbered among the *seventy souls who came with Jacob to Egypt (Genesis* 46:26). *Mispar Bigvai* was counted with those ascending from the exile ... and the members of the tribe of Levi were enumerated in the desert *(Numbers* 3:15) from the age of one month [the census of the rest of Israel excluded those of less than twenty years] *(Yalkut Shimoni).*

from the Babylonian exile which closely parallels the list furnished in our chapter. There are, however, a number of discrepancies between the two lists. In several instances names are spelled differently, but in all these cases the changes are very minor and of the sort that occur commonly throughout Scripture where lists of names are repeated. There are also instances where names mentioned in the list here are omitted in the *Nehemiah* list, and vice versa. Some of these may be cases of the same person being listed under two different names. [A discussion of the ways in which names change in Scripture may be found in the Introduction and first nine chapters of *I Chronicles*, ArtScroll ed.]

Another discrepancy is between the numbers for the various family members given in the two lists. In most instances of disagreement the number in *Nehemiah* is the larger one. It is noteworthy, though, that the totals for the various categories (the Nethinites and descendants of the servants of Solomon — v. 58; the entire congregation — v. 63; the livestock — vs. 66, 67) agree. [The actual differences between the two lists will be pointed out in the commentary to each verse.]

Several explanations of these discrepancies have been given. *Rashi (Nehemiah* 7:7) does not attempt to resolve the differences, but remarks that care was taken only in establishing the total for the entire emigration. In that respect the two lists agree perfectly. Scripture, however, was not concerned with the differences in the individual numbers.

[Perhaps *Rashi* may be understood in the following way: Although he agrees with the other commentators (see their explanations below) that the discrepancies may be reconciled in a number of ways, *Rashi* cannot satisfactorily explain why Scripture left the two lists in apparent contradiction, without stating plainly how the conflicts may be resolved. In answer to this point, *Rashi* asserts that the differences in individual numbers are of no major significance, so their reconciliation is left to the reader's understanding.]

Other commentators, however, offer various explanations for the discrepancies. *Ibn Ezra* and *Metzudos* (to *Nehemiah)* explain that although Nehemiah states that the document he found was written at the time of the original settlement, he updated the number of settlers to reflect the population of the Jewish community at the time of his writing. Since this occurred thirty-six years later, it is not surprising that the sizes of the various families had changed through deaths and births. In general, the birth rate exceeded the death rate, so that the numbers in *Nehemiah* generally exceed those in *Ezra*. However, though the total population at the time of Nehemiah's writing almost certainly exceeded that of the original immigration, Nehemiah was careful to give the original *total* in his account as well, in order to reflect accurately the conditions of the original settlement *(Metzudos)*.

*Ralbag* (to *Nehemiah)* explains that some of those listed in *Ezra* at the time of their arrival in the Holy Land were later joined by additional family members; or, in some cases, the emigrants themselves returned to the exile. The *Nehemiah* list records those actually forming the permanent settlement.

*Malbim* takes note of yet another discrepancy. Although the account in *Nehemiah* also begins with the preface: *These are the children ... of the exile, which Nebuchadnezzar king of Babylon had exiled,* our verse contains the additional phrase לְבָבֶל, *to Babylon,* which is not found in *Nehemiah*.

*Malbim* explains the discrepancies by considering the different stages of exile. Nebuchadnezzar first exiled the leading personalities — the nobility, the wealthy, the powerful [see *II Kings* 24:14]. Later, when the Temple was destroyed, he exiled King Zidkiyah and

ד אַלְפַּיִם מֵאָה שִׁבְעִים וּשְׁנָיִם: בְּנֵי שְׁפַטְיָה
ה שְׁלֹשׁ מֵאוֹת שִׁבְעִים וּשְׁנָיִם: בְּנֵי אָרַח שְׁבַע
ו מֵאוֹת חֲמִשָּׁה וְשִׁבְעִים: בְּנֵי־פַחַת מוֹאָב
לִבְנֵי יֵשׁוּעַ יוֹאָב אַלְפַּיִם שְׁמֹנֶה מֵאוֹת
ז וּשְׁנֵים עָשָׂר: בְּנֵי עֵילָם אֶלֶף מָאתַיִם
ח חֲמִשִּׁים וְאַרְבָּעָה: בְּנֵי זַתּוּא תְּשַׁע מֵאוֹת
ט וְאַרְבָּעִים וַחֲמִשָּׁה: בְּנֵי זַכָּי שְׁבַע מֵאוֹת
י וְשִׁשִּׁים: בְּנֵי בָנִי שֵׁשׁ מֵאוֹת אַרְבָּעִים וּשְׁנָיִם:
יא־יב בְּנֵי בֵבָי שֵׁשׁ מֵאוֹת עֶשְׂרִים וּשְׁלֹשָׁה: בְּנֵי
יג עַזְגָּד אֶלֶף מָאתַיִם עֶשְׂרִים וּשְׁנָיִם: בְּנֵי
יד אֲדֹנִיקָם שֵׁשׁ מֵאוֹת שִׁשִּׁים וְשִׁשָּׁה: בְּנֵי בִגְוָי

the lesser levels of the Jewish people. *Ezra* lists the distinguished captives who were exiled earlier. Nebuchadnezzar treated them respectfully, establishing them in the capital city of Babylon. They belonged to the exile which Nebuchadnezzar *had exiled to Babylon* (our verse), the royal capital. [Even among these notables, however, some were of undistinguished origin. See below v. 59.] *Nehemiah's* larger list includes the less distinguished Jews who were banished with King Zidkiyah. Nebuchadnezzar held them in disdain and exiled them to the distant territories of the Babylonian empire. They are characterized as members of the exile whom Nebuchadnezzar *had exiled* — not to Babylon, the capital city, but to some anonymous destination in the expanse of the Babylonian empire. These became part of the larger *Nehemiah* numbers. The few instances where the number in *Nehemiah* is smaller reflects those who returned to Babylon when the construction of the Temple was halted.

### The Judeans and Benjaminites

**3.** בְּנֵי פַרְעֹשׁ — *The children of Parosh.* Some of the immigrants are identified by the name of their family patriarch [e.g., *the childen of Parosh*]; others, by the city of their extraction [e.g., *the children of Bethlehem* in v. 21] *(Rashi).*

*Malbim* reasons that those coming as members of a family unit which included residents of different cities are listed according to the family heads. Those who did not emigrate as members of a large family group are categorized by the cities of their derivation.

The families of Parosh, Arah (v. 5), the governor of Moab (v. 6), Zattu (v. 8) and Adin (v. 15) were from the tribe of Judah *(Taanis* 26a, *Rashi; Tosafos, Eruvin* 41a), while Senaah (v. 35) was of the tribe of Benjamin. These families later contributed the firewood for the Temple altar *(Nehemiah* 10:35). They were, therefore, awarded the exclusive privilege of supplying firewood for the altar during specific periods of the year *(Taanis* 4:4, 28a).

**5.** בְּנֵי אָרַח — *The children of Arah.* See comm., v. 3. In *Nehemiah* (7:10) their number is given as only 652.

**6.** בְּנֵי־פַחַת מוֹאָב — *The children of the governor of Moab.* פַּחַת מוֹאָב is not a name; it means *the governor of Moab (Metzudos; Tosafos, Taanis* 28a).

*The Judeans and Benjaminites*

*of Israel.* 3 *The children of Parosh, two thousand one*
*hundred and seventy-two.* 4 *The children of*
*Shephatiah, three hundred and seventy-two.* 5 *The*
*children of Arah, seven hundred and seventy-five.*
6 *The children of the governor of Moab — of the*
*children of Jeshua and Joab — two thousand eight*
*hundred and twelve.* 7 *The children of Elam, one*
*thousand two hundred and fifty-four.* 8 *The children*
*of Zattu, nine hundred and forty-five.* 9 *The children*
*of Zaccai, seven hundred and sixty.* 10 *The children of*
*Bani, six hundred and forty-two.* 11 *The children of*
*Bebai, six hundred and twenty-three.* 12 *The children*
*of Azgad, one thousand two hundred and twenty-*
*two.* 13 *The children of Adonikam, six hundred and*
*sixty-six.* 14 *The children of Bigvai, two thousand and*

According to one opinion in the Talmud (*Taanis* 28a), this family was descended from King David. Another Talmudic view is that they were the descendants of his nephew and chief of staff, Joab, son of David's sister Zeruiah. *Tosafos* explains that the family members are referred to as *the children of the governor of Moab* because both David and Joab traced their lineage to the Moabite princess Ruth (see *Rashi, Judges* 3:209). [The story of her conversion and marriage to Boaz, as well as the birth of David, are recorded in the *Book of Ruth.*]

In *Nehemiah* (7:11) their number is given as 2818.

לִבְנֵי יֵשׁוּעַ יוֹאָב — *Of the children of Jeshua* [*and*] *Joab. Metzudos* and *Malbim* read the passage as follows: *The children of the governor of Moab* [who were] *the children of* [his descendants] — *Jeshua and Joab* [numbered] — *2812.* [The governor of Moab was the head of the clan. The families of two of his descendants, Jeshua and Joab, emigrated to Jerusalem.]

*Ibn Ezra* conjectures that Jeshua and Joab were ancestors of *the governor of Moab.* The verse is then understood: *The children of the governor of Moab* [who were therefore also] *the descendants of* [his ancestors] *Jeshua and Joab* [numbered] *2812.*

[Evidently, *Ibn Ezra* does not identify the *governor of Moab* as Ruth. Perhaps, in his view, the reference is to King David himself. Since David was a sovereign who was descended from the Moabitess Ruth, he is entitled *the governor of Moab.*]

**8.** בְּנֵי זַתּוּא — *The children of Zattu.* See comm., v. 3.

In *Nehemiah* (7:13) their number is given as only 845.

**10.** בְּנֵי בָנִי — *The children of Bani.* In *Nehemiah* (v. 15), this name is given as בִּנּוּי, *Binnui,* and their number is 648.

**11.** בְּנֵי בֵבָי — *The children of Bebai.* In *Nehemiah* (v. 16) — 628.

**12.** בְּנֵי עַזְגָּד — *The children of Azgad.* In *Nehemiah* (v. 17) — 2,322.

**13.** בְּנֵי אֲדֹנִיקָם — *The children of Adonikam.* In *Nehemiah* (v. 18) — 667.

**14.** בְּנֵי בִגְוָי — *The children of Bigvai.* In *Nehemiah* (v. 19) — 2067.

טו אַלְפַּיִם חֲמִשִּׁים וְשִׁשָּׁה: בְּנֵי עָדִין אַרְבַּע
טז מֵאוֹת חֲמִשִּׁים וְאַרְבָּעָה: בְּנֵי־אָטֵר לִיחִזְקִיָּה
יז תִּשְׁעִים וּשְׁמֹנָה: בְּנֵי בֵצָי שְׁלֹשׁ מֵאוֹת
יח עֶשְׂרִים וּשְׁלֹשָׁה: בְּנֵי יוֹרָה מֵאָה וּשְׁנֵים
יט עָשָׂר: בְּנֵי חָשֻׁם מָאתַיִם עֶשְׂרִים וּשְׁלֹשָׁה:
כ-כא בְּנֵי גִבָּר תִּשְׁעִים וַחֲמִשָּׁה: בְּנֵי בֵית־לָחֶם
כב מֵאָה עֶשְׂרִים וּשְׁלֹשָׁה: אַנְשֵׁי נְטֹפָה חֲמִשִּׁים
כג וְשִׁשָּׁה: אַנְשֵׁי עֲנָתוֹת מֵאָה עֶשְׂרִים וּשְׁמֹנָה:
כד-כה בְּנֵי עַזְמָוֶת אַרְבָּעִים וּשְׁנָיִם: בְּנֵי קִרְיַת עָרִים
כְּפִירָה וּבְאֵרוֹת שְׁבַע מֵאוֹת וְאַרְבָּעִים
כו וּשְׁלֹשָׁה: בְּנֵי הָרָמָה וָגָבַע שֵׁשׁ מֵאוֹת
כז עֶשְׂרִים וְאֶחָד: אַנְשֵׁי מִכְמָס מֵאָה עֶשְׂרִים

**15.** בְּנֵי עָדִין — *The children of Adin.* See comm., v. 3.

*Rashi (Taanis* 28a) remarks that Adin was entitled Adino HaEtzni, a name listed in *II Samuel* 23:8 among the heroes of David's kingdom. This title portrays the marvelously divergent facets of his character. *Adino,* meaning *to enfold,* refers to his method of studying Torah. He would *fold* his limbs and recline in a posture of complete physical repose and absolute intellectual absorption. *HaEtzni,* meaning *of wood,* denotes his approach to warfare. When engaged in battle, he was as tough and unyielding as a *block of wood.*

In R' Yose's opinion, Adin was actually Joab ben Zeruiah. R' Yehudah maintains that Adin was King David himself.

In *Nehemiah* their number is given as 655.

**16.** בְּנֵי־אָטֵר לִיחִזְקִיָּה — *The children of Ater — of Hezekiah. Ibn Ezra* feels that Hezekiah was the head of the family. *Metzudos* agrees, interpreting: *The children of Ater* [who was a descendant] *of Hezekiah.*

*Malbim's* understanding is that Ater was the family head, and the children of his descendant Hezekiah went up to the Holy Land.

An alternate explanation is: *The children of Ater* [together with the children] *of Hezekiah (Metzudos).*

**17.** בְּנֵי בֵצָי — *The children of Bezai.* In *Nehemiah* (v. 23) — 324.

**18.** בְּנֵי יוֹרָה — *The children of Jorah.* This family is not mentioned in *Nehemiah.* There is a family בְּנֵי חָרִיף, *the children of Harif,* mentioned there (v. 24) in approximately the same position in the list, which is not mentioned here, and their number is also 112. *Ibn Ezra* (there) suggests that they may be identical with the family of Jorah listed here.

**19.** בְּנֵי חָשֻׁם — *The children of Hashum.* In *Nehemiah* (v. 22) — 328.

**20.** בְּנֵי גִבָּר — *The children of Gibbar.* [In *Nehemiah* (v. 25) a family בְּנֵי גִבְעוֹן, *The children of Gibeon,* is mentioned at this point in the list and their number is also 95. Perhaps this is the same family.]

II
15-28

*fifty-six.* 15 *The children of Adin, four hundred and*
*fifty-four.* 16 *The children of Ater — of Hezekiah —*
*ninety-eight.* 17 *The children of Bezai, three hundred*
*and twenty-three.* 18 *The children of Jorah, one*
*hundred and twelve.* 19 *The children of Hashum, two*
*hundred and twenty-three.* 20 *The children of Gibbar,*
*ninety-five.* 21 *The children of Bethlehem, one*
*hundred and twenty-three.* 22 *The people of*
*Netophah, fifty-six.* 23 *The people of Anathoth, one*
*hundred and twenty-eight.* 24 *The children of*
*Azmaveth, forty-two.* 25 *The children of Kiriath*
*Arim, Kefirah, and Beeroth, seven hundred and*
*forty-three.* 26 *The children of Haramah and Geba,*
*six hundred and twenty-one.* 27 *The people of*
*Michmas, one hundred and twenty-two.* 28 *The*

**21.** בְּנֵי בֵית־לָחֶם — *The children of Bethlehem.* These are the inhabitants of the city of Bethlehem *(Malbim;* see comm., v. 3).

**22.** אַנְשֵׁי נְטֹפָה — *The people of Netophah.* In *Nehemiah* (v. 26) they are included in one group with the sons of Bethlehem — *The people of Bethlehem and Netophah, one hundred and eighty-eight.* The total there is ten greater than here.

In *I Chronicles* 2:54 we learn that the inhabitants of both cities were descendants of the same person — Salma — and it may be for this reason that they are listed together.

**23.** עֲנָתוֹת — *Anathoth.* The city of Anathoth was the home of the prophet Jeremiah *(Jeremiah* 1:1). It was situated in the territory of the tribe of Benjamin, and was among the cities given to the *Kohanim* in the days of Joshua *(Joshua* 21:18, *I Chronicles* 6:45).

*Yalkut Shimoni* notes that the people of Anathoth had conspired to murder Jeremiah *(Jeremiah* 11:19), and were therefore placed under a prophetic curse of total destruction: *The young men shall die by the sword, their sons and daughters by famine. Nothing shall remain of them (Jeremiah* 11:21,22). Yet they now appear among those re-establishing themselves in the Holy Land. *Yalkut* explains that because they repented, the imprecation was lifted, and the people of Anathoth merited a privileged position in the ranks of the returning exiles.

**24.** בְּנֵי עַזְמָוֶת — *The children of Azmaveth.* In *Nehemiah* (v. 28) they are referred to as אַנְשֵׁי בֵית עַזְמָוֶת, *The people of the house of Azmaveth.*

**25.** בְּנֵי קִרְיַת עָרִים כְּפִירָה וּבְאֵרוֹת — *The children of Kiriath Arim, Kefirah, and Beeroth. Ibn Ezra* explains: *the children of Kiriath Arim, the children of Kefirah, and the children of Beeroth.*

In *Nehemiah* (v. 29) they are listed as אַנְשֵׁי קִרְיַת יְעָרִים, *The people of Kiriath Jearim.*

[In *Joshua* 18:14, *Kiriath Jearim* is mentioned as a city belonging to the Tribe of Judah *(Metzudos). I Samuel* (6:21, 7:12) tells how the sacred Ark was brought to this city.]

**26.** בְּנֵי הָרָמָה — *The children of Haramah.* In *Nehemiah* (v. 30) — אַנְשֵׁי הָרָמָה, *The people of Haramah.*

כח וּשְׁנָיִם: אַנְשֵׁי בֵית־אֵל וְהָעָי מָאתַיִם עֶשְׂרִים
כט-ל וּשְׁלֹשָׁה: בְּנֵי נְבוֹ חֲמִשִּׁים וּשְׁנָיִם: בְּנֵי
לא מַגְבִּישׁ מֵאָה חֲמִשִּׁים וְשִׁשָּׁה: בְּנֵי עֵילָם
לב אַחֵר אֶלֶף מָאתַיִם חֲמִשִּׁים וְאַרְבָּעָה: בְּנֵי
לג חָרִם שְׁלֹשׁ מֵאוֹת וְעֶשְׂרִים: בְּנֵי־לֹד חָדִיד
לד וְאוֹנוֹ שְׁבַע מֵאוֹת עֶשְׂרִים וַחֲמִשָּׁה: בְּנֵי
לה יְרֵחוֹ שְׁלֹשׁ מֵאוֹת אַרְבָּעִים וַחֲמִשָּׁה: בְּנֵי
סְנָאָה שְׁלֹשֶׁת אֲלָפִים וְשֵׁשׁ מֵאוֹת וּשְׁלֹשִׁים:
לו הַכֹּהֲנִים בְּנֵי יְדַעְיָה לְבֵית יֵשׁוּעַ תְּשַׁע מֵאוֹת
לז שִׁבְעִים וּשְׁלֹשָׁה: בְּנֵי אִמֵּר אֶלֶף חֲמִשִּׁים
לח וּשְׁנָיִם: בְּנֵי פַשְׁחוּר אֶלֶף מָאתַיִם אַרְבָּעִים
לט וְשִׁבְעָה: בְּנֵי חָרִם אֶלֶף וְשִׁבְעָה עָשָׂר:

**28.** אַנְשֵׁי בֵית־אֵל וְהָעָי — *The people of Beth El and Ai.* In *Nehemiah* (v. 32) — 123.

**29.** בְּנֵי נְבוֹ — *The children of Nebo. Nebo* was the name of a person, not a place *(Ibn Ezra).*

*Nehemiah* (v. 33) refers to them as *the people of Nebo Aher,* and *Metzudos* (there) assumes it to be a city.

**30-33.** The names *Magbish, Elam, Harim, Lod, Hadid,* and *Ono* refer to persons rather than places *(Ibn Ezra).*

**31.** עֵילָם אַחֵר — *A different Elam.* This Elam was different from the Elam mentioned above (v. 7) — although, coincidentally, the number of returnees listed is identical *(Metzudos).*

**33.** בְּנֵי־לֹד חָדִיד וְאוֹנוֹ — *The children of Lod, Hadid, and Ono.* In *Nehemiah* (v. 37) — 721.

**34.** יְרֵחוֹ — *Jericho.* This was the walled city vanquished by Joshua *(Ibn Ezra;* see *Joshua* 6).

**35.** בְּנֵי סְנָאָה — *The children of Senaah.* The children of Senaah were members of the tribe of Benjamin *(Tosafos, Eruvin* 41a). They were among the donors of the Temple firewood in the early days of the Second Temple, and were given the exclusive right to celebrate the Temple wood-offering annually on the tenth of Av *(Taanis* 26a; see comm., v. 3).

In *Nehemiah* (v. 38) their number is 3930.

### 36-39. The Kohanim

**36.** הַכֹּהֲנִים — *The Kohanim. Rashi* notes that all those registered above (vs. 3-35) belonged to the tribes of Judah and Benjamin.

Having completed the list of the two tribes, the text now turns to the *Kohanim* and Levites (vs. 36-42).

This sequence — first Judah and Benjamin, then the *Kohanim* and Levites — corresponds with the order followed in 1:5 in describing those who responded to Cyrus' proclamation: *Thereupon, the heads of the families of Judah and Benjamin and the Kohanim* and the Levites rose up.

בְּנֵי יְדַעְיָה לְבֵית יֵשׁוּעַ — *The children of Jedaiah — of the house of Jeshua.* Jedaiah was a descendant of Jeshua *(Metzudos).*

II
29-39

*people of Beth El and Ai, two hundred and twenty-*
*three.* 29 *The children of Nebo, fifty-two.* 30 *The*
*children of Magbish, one hundred and fifty-six.*
31 *The children of a different Elam, one thousand two*
*hundred and fifty-four.* 32 *The children of Harim,*
*three hundred and twenty.* 33 *The children of Lod,*
*Hadid, and Ono, seven hundred and twenty-five.*
34 *The children of Jericho, three hundred and forty-*
*five.* 35 *The children of Senaah, three thousand six*
*hundred and thirty.* 36 *The Kohanim: The children of*
*Jedaiah — of the house of Jeshua — nine hundred and*
*seventy-three.* 37 *The children of Immer, one*
*thousand fifty-two.* 38 *The children of Pashhur, one*
*thousand two hundred and forty-seven.* 39 *The*
*children of Harim, one thousand and seventeen.*

*The Kohanim*

According to *Malbim,* the order of ancestry was reversed — Jedaiah was the family patriarch, and Jeshua was his descendant. The returnees were members of Jeshua's household (see comm., v. 6).

The Talmud *(Taanis* 27a) observes that of the twenty-four families of *Kohanim* who had served in the first Temple [see *I Chronicles* 24:18], only four now heeded Cyrus' call and went up from Exile — the families of Jedaiah, Harim, Immer, and Pashhur.

The *Kohanim* who performed the sacrificial rituals during the first Temple were divided by King David into twenty-four family groups *(I Chronicles* ch. 24), each of which officiated at the Temple services for a period of one week [see *Rambam, Klei HaMikdash* 4:3]. The sequence of alternating weeks of service for the groups was determined in King David's time by the drawing of lots *(I Chronicles* 24), and remained fixed throughout the duration of the First Temple.

When Cyrus called for the construction of the Second Temple, and only the four families of *Kohanim* mentioned here emigrated, the prophets among them divided each family into six groups. The total then corresponded to the twenty-four companies of *Kohanim* who had served in the First Temple. As in the case of the First Temple, each group was assigned to the Temple for one week, and the order of rotation was decided by lots. The system of rotation thus determined was binding throughout the period of the Second Temple, as shown in the following example.

The family of Jehoiarib preceded Jedaiah in the order of service in the First Temple *(I Chronicles* 24:7). But Jehoiarib's group did not heed Cyrus' invitation, whereas the children of Jedaiah emigrated. Should Jehoiarib have later gone up to Jerusalem and joined the *Kohanim* at the Temple, he would have been subordinate to Jedaiah; i.e. he would have followed Jedaiah's turn of service. Jehoiarib had forfeited his primary position among the *Kohanim* by failing to respond to Cyrus' proclamation *(Taanis* 27a,b).

**38.** בְּנֵי פַשְׁחוּר — *The children of Pashhur. Rashi* to *Taanis* 27a is perplexed by the Talmudic statement that the family of Pashhur served in the First Temple, since that name does not appear in *I Chronicles* ch. 24 among the families of *Kohanim* appointed to the Temple service. *Bach* explains that the Pashhur family appears in *Chronicles* under some different name.

**39.** בְּנֵי חָרִם — *The children of Harim.*

מ הַלְוִיִּם בְּנֵי־יֵשׁוּעַ וְקַדְמִיאֵל לִבְנֵי הוֹדַוְיָה
מא שִׁבְעִים וְאַרְבָּעָה: הַמְשֹׁרְרִים בְּנֵי אָסָף מֵאָה
מב עֶשְׂרִים וּשְׁמֹנָה: בְּנֵי הַשֹּׁעֲרִים בְּנֵי־שַׁלּוּם
בְּנֵי־אָטֵר בְּנֵי־טַלְמוֹן בְּנֵי־עַקּוּב בְּנֵי חֲטִיטָא
בְּנֵי שֹׁבָי הַכֹּל מֵאָה שְׁלֹשִׁים וְתִשְׁעָה:
מג הַנְּתִינִים בְּנֵי־צִיחָא בְנֵי־חֲשׂוּפָא בְּנֵי
מד טַבָּעוֹת: בְּנֵי־קֵרֹס בְּנֵי־סִיעֲהָא בְּנֵי פָדוֹן:
מה־מו בְּנֵי־לְבָנָה בְנֵי־חֲגָבָה בְּנֵי עַקּוּב: בְּנֵי־חָגָב
°שַׁלְמַי ק׳ מז בְּנֵי־°שמלי בְּנֵי חָנָן: בְּנֵי־גִדֵּל בְּנֵי־גַחַר בְּנֵי
מח־מט רְאָיָה: בְּנֵי־רְצִין בְּנֵי־נְקוֹדָא בְּנֵי גַזָּם: בְּנֵי־
נ עֻזָּא בְנֵי־פָסֵחַ בְּנֵי בֵסָי: בְּנֵי־אַסְנָה בְנֵי־

This is not the Harim mentioned in v. 32 but a family of *Kohanim (Metzudos).*

**40-42. The Levites**

**40.** בְּנֵי־יֵשׁוּעַ וְקַדְמִיאֵל לִבְנֵי הוֹדַוְיָה — *The children of Jeshua and Kadmiel — of the children of Hodaviah.* Jeshua and Kadmiel were themselves descended from Hodaviah *(Ibn Ezra; Metzudos).*

**41.** הַמְשֹׁרְרִים — *The singers,* i.e., the Levite singers *(Rashi).*

The Levites were required to fulfill three duties at the Temple: They served as guards, standing watch at specific areas on the Temple grounds; they were the gatekeepers, opening the Temple gates in the morning and closing them at night; and they stood upon a special platform and sang *Hashem's* praises while the sacrifices were brought. [See *Middos* 1:1; *Arachin* 11a; *Rambam, Klei HaMikdash* 3:2.]

In *Nehemiah* (v. 44) their number is given as 148.

**42.** הַשֹּׁעֲרִים — *The gatekeepers.* I.e., the Levite keepers of the Temple gates *(Rashi)* [see comm. v. 41]. These had been the guardians of the First Temple gates before the exile [but were not now gatekeepers, as the Temple still lay in ruins *(Metzudos)*].

In *Nehemiah* (v. 45) their number is given as 138.

**43-54. The Nethinites**

**43.** הַנְּתִינִים — *The Nethinites.* The Nethinites and the base-born (vs. 59,60) were disqualified from intermarrying with other Jews. [They could marry only within their own group or with other disqualified groups.]

The Talmud *(Kiddushin* 69a,b, 70) asserts that all of the disqualified members of the Babylonian Jewish community emigrated to the Holy Land under Ezra's instructions. *Rashi* explains that Ezra observed that the Rabbinical leadership was leaving Babylon and ascending to the Holy Land, leaving no one to properly examine the marital qualifications of those remaining in Babylon. Fearing that this would lead to desecration of the marriage precepts, Ezra instructed all of those who were disqualified from marrying into the community to leave Babylon and settle in the Land of Israel. There, the many sages would guide the people and guard against improper marriages.

The original Nethinites lived in the Land of Israel in the city of Gibeon at the time of Joshua's conquest of the Holy Land. They belonged to the Hivite nation — one of the seven peoples whom the Israelites were to supplant [see

II
40-50

*The Levites*

*The Nethinites*

40 *The Levites: The children of Jeshua and Kadmiel —*
*of the children of Hodaviah — seventy-four.* 41 *The*
*singers, the sons of Asaph, one hundred twenty-*
*eight.* 42 *The children of the gatekeepers: The*
*children of Shallum, the children of Ater, the children of Talmon, the children of Akkub, the children of Hatita, the children of Shobai; their total*
*— one hundred and thirty-nine.* 43 *The Nethinites:*
*the children of Ziha, the children of Hasufa, the*
*children of Tabbaoth.* 44 *The children of Keros, the*
*children of Siaha, the children of Padon.* 45 *The*
*children of Lebanah, the children of Hagabah, the*
*children of Akkub.* 46 *The children of Hagab, the*
*children of Salmai, the children of Hanan.* 47 *The*
*children of Giddel, the children of Gahar, the*
*children of Reaiah.* 48 *The children of Rezin, the*
*children of Nekoda, the children of Gazzam.* 49 *The*
*children of Uzza, the children of Paseah, the children*
*of Besai.* 50 *The children of Asnah, the children of*

*Joshua* 3:10]. Fearing the Israelite conquerors, who had already leveled Jericho (*Joshua* 6) and devastated the city of Ai (*Joshua* 8), the Gibeonites disguised themselves as travelers from a distant land and approached Joshua and the elders of Israel seeking a covenant with them. They succeeded in eliciting from Joshua a covenant guaranteeing their safety, backed by a solemn oath taken by the elders. The ruse was soon discovered, but to avoid public desecration of the Name of God the treaty was honored and the Gibeonites were spared. Joshua then designated them as woodcutters and water carriers for the community and the altar (*Joshua* 9).

*Metzudos* explains that the word *Nethinites* means *those designated,* from the root נתן, *to place* or *designate.* They were so called because Joshua *designated them ... woodcutters and water carriers for the community and for the altar of God* (*Joshua* 9:27).

*Ibn Ezra,* however, suggests that the title *Nethinites,* meaning *those designated,* originated with King David, not Joshua. His source is *Ezra* 8:20: *of the Nethinites whom David ... had designated for the service of the Levites,* which indicates that they were so named because King David *designated* them as servants. They had previously been known as *Gibeonites,* after Gibeon, the city of their origin [see *Joshua* 9:3]. *Ralbag* adds that they were employed by David for quarrying, woodcutting, and preparing other materials for eventual use in the construction of the Temple.

*Rashi's* opinion is that Joshua also issued an edict forbidding the Nethinites to marry within the Jewish community, although they had converted to Judaism. The prohibition was to have lasted only as long as the Temple stood. But when King David discovered the Nethinites' barbaric disposition (*II Samuel* 21), he made the marriage injunction permanent (*Rashi, Yevamos* 78b, 79a; *Kesubos* 29a; see *Rambam, Isurei Biah* 12:23).

*R' Tam* disagrees, contending that the members of the Jewish community were already Biblically enjoined from marrying the

ב °נפוסים ק׳ נא מְעוּנִים בְּנֵי °נפיסים: בְּנֵי־בַקְבּוּק בְּנֵי־
נא־נט נב חֲקוּפָא בְנֵי חַרְחוּר: בְּנֵי־בַצְלוּת בְּנֵי־מְחִידָא
נג בְּנֵי חַרְשָׁא: בְּנֵי־בַרְקוֹס בְּנֵי־סִיסְרָא בְּנֵי־
נד־נה תָמַח: בְּנֵי נְצִיחַ בְּנֵי חֲטִיפָא: בְּנֵי עַבְדֵי
שְׁלֹמֹה בְּנֵי־סֹטַי בְּנֵי־הַסֹּפֶרֶת בְּנֵי פְרוּדָא:
נו־נז בְּנֵי־יַעְלָה בְנֵי־דַרְקוֹן בְּנֵי גִדֵּל: בְּנֵי שְׁפַטְיָה
נח בְנֵי־חַטִּיל בְּנֵי פֹּכֶרֶת הַצְּבָיִים בְּנֵי אָמִי: כָּל־
הַנְּתִינִים וּבְנֵי עַבְדֵי שְׁלֹמֹה שְׁלֹשׁ מֵאוֹת
נט תִּשְׁעִים וּשְׁנָיִם: וְאֵלֶּה
הָעֹלִים מִתֵּל מֶלַח תֵּל חַרְשָׁא כְּרוּב

Nethinites. They belonged to the Hivite nation, one of the seven peoples dwelling in the Holy Land concerning whom *Deuteronomy* 7:3 states: *You shall not marry them.* [*R' Tam* assumes that this prohibition applies even after they have converted.[1]] According to *R' Tam*, Joshua [and later King David] decreed only that the Nethinites were to be employed as servants to the people and the altar, but he was not involved in the marriage prohibition (*Tosafos, Yevamos* 79a; *Kesubos* 29a).

**50.** בְּנֵי־מְעוּנִים בְּנֵי נְפוּסִים — *The children of Meunim, the children of Nephusim. Meunim* and *Nephusim* are the names of individuals (*Ibn Ezra).*

[The *im* ending is generally a suffix denoting the plural. *Ibn Ezra* does not translate in that sense here because if the interpretation of *Meunim* were *those who came from the city of Meun,* the reading would be *the children of* הַמְּעוּנִים, *'the' Meunim.*]

**51.** בַקְבּוּק ... חֲקוּפָא ... חַרְחוּר — *Bakbuk ... Hakupha ... Harhur.* The Midrash observes: There are some whose names are ugly, but whose deeds are becoming. These are the exiles — *the children of Bakbuk ... Hakupha ... Harhur* — who were meritorious and ascended to the Land and built the Temple (*Bereishis Rabbah* 71:3).

The commentators explain: *Bakbuk* is associated with *pikpuk,* meaning *contradiction* or *obstruction (Minchas Kehunah);* or it means a *vessel,* empty of content *(Rashash). Hakupha* is derived from *takof, attacking* or *assailing (Minchas Kehunah);* or from *kof,* the *ape* or *beast (Razav). Harhur* denotes *instigation* or *incitement* of strife *(Minchas Kehunah).*

Names in Scripture indicate personality traits. [See *Names and their Significance in Scripture,* preface to the ArtScroll edition of *I Chronicles.*] Thus, the exiles' evil-sounding names — strife, emptiness, and beastliness — imply a natural tendency towards wickedness. But the actions of the children of Bakbuk, Hakupha, and Harhur belied the meaning of their names. They conquered their wicked inclinations and acted meritoriously by ascending to Jerusalem and building the Temple.

### 55-58. Descendants of Solomon's Slaves

**55.** בְּנֵי עַבְדֵי שְׁלֹמֹה — *The children of Solomon's slaves.* This does not mean literally the children of King Solomon's slaves, but their descendants *(Rashi).*

1. *Ran* (to *Kiddushin* 69a) is of the opinion that even if the prohibition applies to converts, it does not extend to their children (who were born as Jews). Consequently, their continued disqualification was due to David's edict, not to Biblical law. He postulates that this may be *Rashi's* opinion as well.

Meunim, the children of Nephusim. 51 The children
of Bakbuk, the children of Hakupha, the children of
Harhur. 52 The children of Bazluth, the children of
Mehida, the children of Harsha. 53 The children of
Barkos, the children of Sisera, the children of Tamah.
54 The children of Neziah, the children of Hatipha.
*Descendants of Solomon's Slaves* 55 The children of Solomon's slaves: The children of
Sotai, the children of Hassofereth, the children of
Peruda. 56 The children of Jaalah, the children of
Darkon, the children of Giddel. 57 The children of
Shephatiah, the children of Hattil, the children of
Pochereth Hazzebaim, the children of Ami. 58 All of
the Nethinites and the children of Solomon's slaves —
*The Base-born* three hundred and ninety-two. 59 The following went
up from Tel Melah and Tel Harsha: Cherub, Addan,

[Since four hundred and sixty-two years had passed since Solomon had built the First Temple, these could hardly have been the children of the slaves of Solomon and could only have been the slaves' distant descendants.]

בְּנֵי־הַסֹּפֶרֶת — *The children of Hassofereth.* According to *Malbim, Hassofereth* is a person's name, the ה being part of the name.

*Ibn Ezra,* however, feels that it may be translated *the woman scribe.*

**58.** כָּל־הַנְּתִינִים וּבְנֵי עַבְדֵי שְׁלֹמֹה — *All of the Nethinites and the children of Solomon's slaves.* These two groups are listed together among the returning exiles because they shared a common descent from the heathen peoples who inhabited ancient Palestine. The original Nethinites were members of the Hivite nation *(Joshua* 9:7), and King Solomon *(I Kings* 9:20-21) took his slaves from the Emorites, Hittites, Perizzites, Hivites and Jebusites who remained in the Land *(Ralbag; Malbim).*

**59-60. The Base-born**

**59.** תֵּל מֶלַח תֵּל חַרְשָׁא — *Tel Melah and Tel Harsha.* The Talmud *(Kiddushin* 70a) lists three types of base-born immigrants who, according to the *halachah,* were not permitted to marry into the community: (1) Those known to be illegitimate *(mamzerim)* [children born from adultery or incest; see *Yevamos* 49a]; (2) those whose mothers are known to have been Jewish but who could not identify their fathers (שְׁתוּקִי), and thus *may* have been illegitimate; and (3) foundlings (אֲסוּפִי), who may be illegitimate because both parents are unknown. Another possibility is that their mothers may have been non-Jews, in which case the foundlings were themselves gentiles [since only the child of a Jewish mother is considered Jewish (see *Rambam, Isurei Biah* 12:7, 15:3)]. The Talmud sees reference to all three of these groups in our verse.

[Tel Melah and Tel Harsha are the only Babylonian cities mentioned in the entire chapter. (Bethlehem, Anathoth, Kiriath Arim and others mentioned in vs. 21, 23 and 25 were cities in Israel.) This indicated to the Rabbis that the names refer homiletically to the nature of the immigrants described as going up from Tel Melah and Tel Harsha *(Maharsha).*]

ב אַדָּן אִמֵּר וְלֹא יָכְלוּ לְהַגִּיד בֵּית־אֲבוֹתָם
ס־סב ס וְזַרְעָם אִם מִיִּשְׂרָאֵל הֵם: בְּנֵי־דְלָיָה בְנֵי־
טוֹבִיָּה בְּנֵי נְקוֹדָא שֵׁשׁ מֵאוֹת חֲמִשִּׁים
סא וּשְׁנָיִם: וּמִבְּנֵי הַכֹּהֲנִים בְּנֵי חֳבַיָּה
בְּנֵי הַקּוֹץ בְּנֵי בַרְזִלַּי אֲשֶׁר לָקַח מִבְּנוֹת
סב בַּרְזִלַּי הַגִּלְעָדִי אִשָּׁה וַיִּקָּרֵא עַל־שְׁמָם: אֵלֶּה
בִּקְשׁוּ כְתָבָם הַמִּתְיַחְשִׂים וְלֹא נִמְצָאוּ

The first name, *Tel Melah* [lit. *mound of salt*], refers to the known illegitimates. The immigrants from Tel Melah were descended from persons likened to the immoral inhabitants of Sodom,[1] which was turned into a mound of salt *(Genesis* 19). These people were the known *mamzerim* and were therefore prohibited from marrying into the community *(Kiddushin* 70a).

The second name, Tel Harsha, means *mound of the mute* (from חֵרֵשׁ, *a mute),* and alludes to those who could not identify their fathers (שְׁתוּקֵי). Such a child is *muted,* or silenced, by its mother when calling to its father. Thus, he is unsure of his father's identity. Since children of unknown paternity may be *mamzerim,* they are prohibited from marrying into the community *(Kiddushin* 70a).[2]

The closing phrase of the passage — *They could not state whether they were of Israelite ancestry* — is a reference to the foundlings who were abandoned by both parents, and may have been *mamzerim* or possibly gentiles.

כְּרוּב אַדָּן אִמֵּר — *Cherub, Addan, and Immer.*[3] According to *Rashi,* these are names of immigrants who came up from Tel Melah and Tel Harsha. The sense of our verse is: *The following people went up from Tel Melah and Tel Harsha: Cherub, Addan, and Immer. They* [Cherub, Addan, and Immer] *could not state whether they were of Israelite ancestry.* The following verse lists the names of additional emigrants from Tel Melah and Tel Harsha.

*Metzudos'* view differs. In his opinion, Cherub, Addan, and Immer are all names of places in Babylon. Verses 59 and 60 read: *The following were those going up from Tel Melah, Tel Harsha, Cherub, Addan, and Immer, who could not state whether they were of Israelite ancestry: the children of Delaiah, the children of Tobiah ...*

1. *Rashi* there points out that according to the Sodomite legal code, a man guilty of striking another's wife and causing her to miscarry was required to compensate by impregnating his victim. [In doing this, however, he fathered an illegitimate child.]

*Maharsha* cites the evidence of Sodomite licentiousness in the Biblical account of their attempt to sexually assault the guests of Lot *(Genesis* 19:5). *They* [the men of Sodom] *called out to Lot and said to him, 'Where are the men who came to you tonight? Bring them out to us that we may know them.'*

2. The Sages make another comment based on the literal interpretation of this passage, with Tel Melah translated *a mound of salt,* and Tel Harsha, *a mound of plowing,* from חָרַשׁ, *to plow.* A man who marries an unsuitable wife [whom he is forbidden to marry because she cannot state whether she is of Israelite ancestry *(Rashi)*] is likened to one who plows [*Harsha*] an entire world, only to plant it with salt [*Melah*], as it is written: *The following were those going up from Tel Melah and Tel Harsha ... they could not state whether they were of Israelite ancestry (Kiddushin* 70a).

3. The Talmud *(Kiddushin* 70a) comments that these names teach us God's expectations of

II
60-62

*and Immer; but they could not state whether they*
*were of Israelite ancestry.* 60 *The children of Delaiah,*
*the children of Tobiah, the children of Nekoda, six*
*hundred and fifty-two.* 61 *Of the children of the*
*Kohanim: the children of Habaiah, the children of*
*Hakkoz, the children of Barzillai, who married one of*
*the daughters of Barzillai the Gileadite and assumed*
*their name.* 62 *These searched for their genealogical*
*record, but they could not be found, and they were*

*The Family of Barzillai*

וְלֹא יָכְלוּ לְהַגִּיד בֵּית־אֲבוֹתָם וְזַרְעָם אִם מִיִּשְׂרָאֵל הֵם — *But they could not state whether they were of Israelite ancestry* [lit. *the house of their fathers and their seed whether they were of Israel*]. The Talmud asserts that this refers to foundlings of unknown parentage. These foundlings were therefore disqualified from marrying into the community *(Kiddushin* 70a).

*Maharsha* presents an additional interpretation. In the phrase *whether they were of Israel,* the word אִם, *whether,* may be read homiletically as אֵם, *mother.* The passage now reads *they could not state* [*their*] *mother,* i.e. they could not identify their mothers, and were thus of questionable Israelite ancestry.

According to *Rashi* (here), the passage includes those who could not locate the genealogical records certifying their Jewish origins. According to *R' Yeshayah MiTrani,* the verse refers to the descendants of those who had actually intermarried with non-Jews. *Ralbag* adds that they had abandoned their Jewish names and thus could not trace their Jewish family origins, since each family was identified by its Jewish name. They had forgotten the Jewish names which indicated the *house of their fathers,* the family group to which they belonged.

**60.** בְּנֵי־דְלָיָה בְנֵי־טוֹבִיָּה בְּנֵי נְקוֹדָא — *The children of Delaiah, the children of Tobiah, the children of Nekoda.* In *Nehemiah* (v. 62) their number is given as 642.

### 61-62. The Family of Barzillai

**61.** בְּנֵי בַרְזִלַּי אֲשֶׁר לָקַח מִבְּנוֹת בַּרְזִלַּי — *The children of Barzillai, who married one of the daughters of Barzillai.* These descendants of Barzillai were not actually descended from his sons, but from a son-in-law who assumed his name when he married one of his daughters *(Rashi).*

**62.** אֵלֶּה בִּקְשׁוּ כְתָבָם הַמִּתְיַחְשִׂים — *These searched for their genealogical record.* The search was required because

the Jewish people's sanctity, and his displeasure at their licentiousness. The name *Cherub* is symbolic of angelic chastity [*Ezekiel* 10 describes the angels as having *the face of the cherub (Rashi* to *Kiddushin,* ibid.)]. And, according to *Maharsha,* they also symbolize marital fidelity, as represented by the two golden cherubs placed in the inner sanctuary facing one another *(Exodus* 25:20), in portrayal of absolute conjugal devotion [see *Rashi, Bava Basra* 99a]. *Addan* is read *Adon,* meaning *Master.* It refers to the Master of Creation. *Immer* suggests the verb *Amar,* meaning *He said* or *remarked.* The order of the names is rearranged to *Amar Adon, 'Cherub,'* which may be understood homiletically as, 'the Master of the universe remarked: "I presumed that Israel would be esteemed before me as the cherub — but they have likened themselves to the leopard" ' [who mates indiscriminately *(Rashi)*].

A different Rabbinic exposition of the same passage states that the names reveal God's affection for even the most grievous sinners. *Amar Adon, 'Cherub.'* The Master of the universe remarked: 'They are as esteemed before me as the cherub, although they have likened themselves to the leopard' *(Kiddushin* 70a).

ב
סג

סג וַיְגֹאֲלוּ מִן־הַכְּהֻנָּה׃ וַיֹּאמֶר הַתִּרְשָׁתָא לָהֶם אֲשֶׁר לֹא־יֹאכְלוּ מִקֹּדֶשׁ הַקֳּדָשִׁים עַד עֲמֹד

*Kohanim* are forbidden to marry a woman who is a proselyte or is descended from proselytes, unless one of her ancestors was of original Jewish lineage. Furthermore, a child born of such a forbidden priestly marriage is disqualified from the *Kehunah* [see *Rambam, Isurei Biah* 19:12]. Barzillai was a proselyte. His wife's origins were unknown, raising the possibility that she, too, was a proselyte, and the *Kohanim* were enjoined from marrying their daughters. Hence the *Kohanim* who had married the daughters of Barzillai were suspected of having violated the priestly canon, causing the disqualification of their descendants. It therefore became necessary for those descendants — *the children of Barzillai* — to produce records certifying that Barzillai's daughters were not descended from proselytic ancestry alone *(Beis HaBechirah, Kiddushin* 69b).

*Malbim* explains that the doubt concerning the children of Barzillai arose from the fact that besides the family of *Kohanim* entitled *the children of Barzillai,* there was also an Israelite clan known by the same name. The *children of Barzillai* who now presented themselves as *Kohanim* were required to certify that they belonged to the priestly family and not the Israelite clan. In addition, it was suspected that some of those who were actually *Kohanim* had believed, mistakenly, that they were members of the Israelite Barzillais and had, in consequence, married women forbidden to *Kohanim.* By doing so they disqualified their children from the *Kehunah.* Thus it was also necessary for the *children of Barzillai* to prove that their ancestors had adhered to the special marriage restrictions which apply to the *Kohanim.*

וְלֹא נִמְצָאוּ — *But they could not be found.* The records could not be found *(Rashi).*

*Rashi* interprets *they* as a reference to the *records.* This interpretation, however, raises a grammatical problem, since *record* in our verse is singular, whereas *they* is plural. *Ibn Ezra* suggests that a single object made up of several parts is sometimes treated as a plural. Such an object is the family genealogical record, which consists of a single list comprising many individuals. It may, therefore, be referred to with the plural usage *they.*

וַיְגֹאֲלוּ — *And they were disqualified.* Because they could not produce the genealogical records identifying them as *Kohanim,* they were found repugnant and expelled from the *Kehunah.*

[The root גאל — spelled with an *alef* — means *repugnant.* געל, with an *ayin,* refers to expulsion. Since the letters *alef* and *ayin* may be homiletically interchanged, the word וַיְגֹאֲלוּ is subject to a dual rendition: וַיְגֹאֲלוּ, *they were found repugnant,* and וַיְגֹעֲלוּ, *they were expelled. Rashi* cites both interpretations — they were *found repugnant* and *expelled.*]

מִן־הַכְּהֻנָּה — *From the priesthood.* They could not take part in the Temple rituals with the other *Kohanim (Rashi).* [But they were permitted to continue receiving certain tithes given to *Kohanim.* See comm., v. 63.]

**63.** הַתִּרְשָׁתָא — *Hatirshatha. Rashi* identifies Hatirshatha as Nehemiah. [See *Nehemiah* 8:9 — *Nehemiah, who is Hatirshatha;* see also comm., v. 2.] *Rashi* also cites the Rabbinic analysis *(Yerushalmi, Kiddushin* 4:1) of the name *Hatirshatha:* הִתִּיר, *he permitted,* שְׁתָא, *to drink.* Nehemiah was granted permission to drink wine which had been touched by a heathen. Although the Sages had prohibited the drinking of such wine [see *Rambam, Maachalos*

II
63

*banned from the priesthood.* 63 *And Hatirshatha instructed them to refrain from eating of the sacrificial food until there arose a Kohen of the Urim*

*Asuros* 11:3], they removed the restriction in the extraordinary circumstance of Nehemiah,[1] whose office as royal butler to Darius required that he taste the wine prior to placing it before the king (see *Nehemiah* 2:1).

*Ibn Ezra* suggests that Hatirshatha was a Chaldean title conferred upon men of great power and influence, similar to prince or satrap.

מִקֹּדֶשׁ הַקֳּדָשִׁים — *Of the sacrificial food* [lit. *of the holy of the holies*]. The disqualified *Kohanim* were forbidden to eat the *Kohen's* portion of the sacrifices *(Rashi).* The inference is that only the sacrificial portions were forbidden to them but not the *terumah* (produce portion given to the *Kohen)* levied on the produce of the Land.

*Rashi's* interpretation follows the Talmudic opinion *(Kiddushin* 69b) which states that Hatirshatha disqualified these *Kohanim* only from eating the sacrificial portions, but permitted them to partake of *terumah. Rashi* (there) explains that, according to this view, the *holy of holies* refers to the sacrificial portions because they are *holy* food taken from *the holy* sacrifices. The term *holy of holies,* however, is inapplicable to *terumah.* Although this levy is itself *holy,* it is taken from the crops harvested by the farmers for their own personal use. Thus, it is not *of the holies.*

Although both the sacrificial portions and *terumah* may not be consumed by non-*Kohanim* [i.e., Levites, Israelites and disqualified *Kohanim (Kiddushin* 69b)], a distinction was made between the two. The basis for this distinction, the Talmud reasons, is the legal principle of *chazakah — maintenance of the status quo in cases of doubt* [see *Chulin* 10b]. According to this principle, when an uncertain halachic (Torah law) situation remains unresolved, the original legal status prevails — i.e., no previous practices are abrogated, and no innovations are introduced. In the case of the agricultural tithes, these questionable *Kohanim* had eaten them throughout the Babylonian exile.[2] When the return to the Land prompted investigations which cast doubt upon the ancestry of some *Kohanim* and that uncertainty could not be resolved, the decision was rendered in accordance with the principle of *chazakah* — the previous practice concerning *terumah* would prevail. All these *Kohanim* could continue eating this tithe, as they had done before the subject of their legitimacy was raised. However, the sacrificial portion now being reinstated would be forbidden to those of doubtful ancestry, since this was an innovation [sacrifices not having been brought during the exile years when there was no Temple] *(Kiddushin* 69b).

A different Talmudic interpretation states that the questionable *Kohanim* were forbidden from partaking even from *terumah.* However, this prohibition applied only to Biblically required *terumah;* they were permitted to continue eating *terumah* made

1. *R' Yeshayah MiTrani* states that permission was granted because of the danger to Nehemiah's life should he have refused the king's order to drink. [Although even Biblical prohibitions may be transgressed to save a life, a special dispensation was needed to allow Nehemiah to take the office and place himself in a position where he would be forced to drink the wine. This permission was granted to him so that he could work for the welfare of his people.]

2. Although produce grown outside the Land of Israel is Biblically exempt from the tithe, Rabbinic legislation made such tithing obligatory in Babylon. (See *Rambam, Terumos* 1:1.)

ב סד כֹּהֵן לְאוּרִים וּלְתֻמִּים: כָּל־הַקָּהָל כְּאֶחָד
סד אַרְבַּע רִבּוֹא אַלְפַּיִם שְׁלֹשׁ־מֵאוֹת שִׁשִּׁים:

obligatory by Rabbinic decree.[1] Accordingly, Hatirshatha's restriction was directed against the eating of both sacrificial tithes and *terumah*. Thus our phrase is interpreted *the holy* [*and*] *the holies*. *Terumah* is entitled *the holy* [food], as in *Leviticus* 22:10: *all strangers may not eat 'the holy'* (i.e., *terumah*); and the sacrificial portions are entitled *the holies*, as in *Leviticus* 22:12: *Should the daughter of a Kohen marry a stranger, she may not eat the tithe of 'the holies'* [i.e., the *Kohen's* portion of the sacrifices].[2]

According to this opinion, the principle of *chazakah* permitted the *terumah* prescribed Rabbinically, but prohibited that required by Biblical law. The reasoning is as follows: Since the doubtful *Kohanim* had partaken of the Rabbinically prescribed *terumah* in Babylon, they could continue this practice and eat the Rabbinically required *terumah* in the Holy Land. But Biblically ordained *terumah* was now innovated, i.e., reinstated, with the return to the Land of Israel. Because the rule of *chazakah* proscribes innovations in case of uncertainty, the questionable *Kohanim* could not partake of Biblical *terumah* (*Kiddushin* 69b).

כֹּהֵן לְאוּרִים וּלְתֻמִּים — *The Kohen of the Urim V'Tumim.* The *Urim V'Tumim* was a parchment bearing the Ineffable Name of God which was inserted into the חֹשֶׁן מִשְׁפָּט [*Choshen Mishpat*], breastplate worn by the *Kohen Gadol* (*Exodus* 38:30).[3] When he requested Divine instruction, certain letters of the names of the twelve tribes inscribed on the breastplate would light up, spelling out the prophetic message (*Rashi, Exodus* 28:30).

The *Kohen* of the *Urim V'Tumim* is therefore the *Kohen Gadol* (High Priest). He could elicit, through the

1. The Biblical requirement to give *terumah* from produce applies only to produce grown in Eretz Yisrael. The Rabbis at the time of the exile and in the early years of the Second Temple decreed that this requirement be extended, first to Babylon — because it was a center of Jewish activity relatively close to Israel — and then to the lands immediately bordering on Israel — Ammon, Moab, and Egypt (*Rambam, Terumos* 1:1). The Biblical requirement is further limited, according to some opinions (*Rashi* to *Kiddushin* 69b) to grains, wine (grapes) and olive oil, while the *terumah* requirement for other fruits is only Rabbinic. Others disagree (see *Rambam, Terumos* 2:1 and *Kesef Mishneh* there). *Terumah* from vegetables, according to all opinions, is only Rabbinic.

2. There is a question, however, whether any Biblical requirement for *terumah* existed during the period of the Second Temple at all. Based on a dispute recorded in the Talmud (*Yevamos* 81b-82b), *Rambam* (*Terumos* 1:26) rules that even in Eretz Yisrael the Biblical requirement applies only when all [or at least most] of Israel lives there. This situation never existed during the period of the Second Temple. Accordingly, the question of whether the doubtful *Kohanim* were allowed to eat Biblical *terumah* or only Rabbinic *terumah* would seem to have been an essentially academic one. Nehemiah, anticipating the eventual return of all Jews to Israel, and hence the restoration of the Biblical requirement of *terumah*, may have disqualified these questionable *Kohanim* from eating the Biblical *terumah*; in practice, however, the question was moot because the conditions for restoring the Biblical requirement of *terumah* were never met.

*Ravad* (ibid.) and others dispute this ruling and assert that there was a Biblical requirement for *terumah* during the period of the Second Temple even though most Jews did not live in Israel. Accordingly, this question had practical significance (see further, *Gra* to *Yoreh Deah* 331:3).

3. This is *Rashi's* opinion (*Exodus* 28:30) and is accepted by *Ramban* (ibid.), who adds that it was written by Moses in a manner entrusted by God to him alone. *Ritva* (*Yoma* 73b) says that it was Divinely written and given to Moses.

*Rambam* (*Klei HaMikdash* 10:10 and *Beis HaBechirah* 4:1) seems to be of the opinion that it was the breastplate itself (see *Kesef Mishneh* there). His son, *R' Avraham*, in his commentary to *Exodus*, feels that *Urim V'Tumim* was the general name of the precious stones affixed to the

*The Total*

*V'Tumim.* [64] *The entire congregation together was forty-two thousand three hundred and sixty.*

*Urim V'Tumim,* the Divine revelation necessary to clarify the standing of these doubtful *Kohanim (Ralbag; Metzudos).*

*Rashi,* citing *Sotah* 48b, states that this phrase refers to the Messianic era, since the *Urim V'Tumim* had disappeared during the destruction of the First Temple and was never restored in the Second Temple. The reference, therefore, is not to any *Kohen* of the Second Temple, but to the *Kohen Gadol* who will arise during the Messianic era, when the final Temple will be constructed and the *Urim V'Tumim* will be restored. Until that time, Hatirshatha informed these *Kohanim,* the doubts regarding their legitimacy would persist.[1]

*R' Yeshayah MiTrani* identifies *the Kohen* of the *Urim V'Tumim* as the escort of the Messiah — the prophet Elijah. *Malbim,* however, feels that the passage may be understood in relation to the *Kohen Gadol* of the Second Temple, contending that although the *Urim V'Tumim* was never actually reinstated, it would have been restored had the nation been found worthy. Thus, during the early period of the return from Babylon, when Hatirshatha made his statement to the *Kohanim,* the people still hoped that the *Kohen* of the *Urim V'Tumim* would arise in their times.

### ◆§ The Total

**64.** כָּל־הַקָּהָל כְּאֶחָד אַרְבַּע רִבּוֹא אַלְפַּיִם שְׁלֹשׁ־מֵאוֹת שִׁשִּׁים — *The entire congregation together* [lit. *as one*] *was forty-two thousand three hundred and sixty.* Noting that the sum of 42,360 exceeds

breastplate [see further ArtScroll *Mishnah Yoma* 7:5 and Appendix II there, p. 168].

1. The Talmud *(Yoma* 21b) lists the *Urim V'Tumim* among the five things that were present in the First Temple but not in the Second Temple. This needs to be clarified in light of what we know about the *Urim V'Tumim* (see previous footnote). According to *Rambam* [who understands the *Urim V'Tumim* to be the breastplate itself (or, according to *R' Avraham,* the precious stones on it)]. The *Urim V'Tumim* was itself one of the vestments which the *Kohen Gadol* was required to wear. Thus, it could not have been absent during the Second Temple, for without the breastplate and its stones, the *Kohen Gadol* would be מְחוּסַר בְּגָדִים, *lacking vestments,* and hence unfit to perform the service (see *Mishnah Zevachim* 2:1, *Gemara* there 18a).

*Rambam,* sensing this difficulty, says *(Klei HaMikdash* 10:10):

> They made an *Urim V'Tumim* during the Second Temple in order to complete [the total of] eight vestments, though they did not inquire of them. Why did they not inquire of them? Because there was no sacred spirit [i.e., no prophecy; cf. *Moreh Nevuchim* 2:45] and any *Kohen* who does not speak with the sacred spirit and upon whom the Divine Presence does not rest is not inquired of.

As *R' Avraham* explains this view, the *Urim V'Tumim* itself did exist in the Second Temple. It was only its prophetic power which was lacking. Thus, the meaning of our verse is: *Until a Kohen* [fit to make use] *of the Urim V'Tumim* [i.e., its prophetic power].

According to *Rashi* only the parchment with the Divine Name written on it was missing during the Second Temple. Thus, the *Kohen Gadol* was not lacking in vestments since the *Urim V'Tumim* was not a vestment, but something inserted *into* a vestment. According to this school of thought, why was there not an *Urim V'Tumim* during the Second Temple?

*Abarbanel* (to *Exodus* 28) says that when King Josiah hid the Ark *(Yoma* 52b) he also hid Moses' *Urim V'Tumim.* This is best understood according to *Ritva* (previous footnote) who asserts that the *Urim V'Tumim* was given to Moses by God, hence it was irreplaceable. According to *Ramban's* view that Moses wrote the Divine Name in the *Urim V'Tumim,* it was replaceable, but since Moses received secret instructions on how to write the Divine Name, it could not be duplicated. Although *Ramban* states that Moses revealed this secret to the greatest of the Jewish sages to whom he transmitted the mysteries of the Torah, it may be that

סה מִלְּבַד עַבְדֵיהֶם וְאַמְהֹתֵיהֶם אֵלֶּה שִׁבְעַת
אֲלָפִים שְׁלֹשׁ מֵאוֹת שְׁלֹשִׁים וְשִׁבְעָה וְלָהֶם
סו מְשֹׁרְרִים וּמְשֹׁרְרוֹת מָאתָיִם׃ סוּסֵיהֶם שְׁבַע
מֵאוֹת שְׁלֹשִׁים וְשִׁשָּׁה פִּרְדֵיהֶם מָאתַיִם
סז אַרְבָּעִים וַחֲמִשָּׁה׃ גְּמַלֵּיהֶם אַרְבַּע מֵאוֹת
שְׁלֹשִׁים וַחֲמִשָּׁה חֲמֹרִים שֵׁשֶׁת אֲלָפִים
סח שְׁבַע מֵאוֹת וְעֶשְׂרִים׃ וּמֵרָאשֵׁי
הָאָבוֹת בְּבוֹאָם לְבֵית יהוה אֲשֶׁר בִּירוּשָׁלִָם
הִתְנַדְּבוּ לְבֵית הָאֱלֹהִים לְהַעֲמִידוֹ עַל־
סט מְכוֹנוֹ׃ כְּכֹחָם נָתְנוּ לְאוֹצַר הַמְּלָאכָה

the total of those listed above (vs. 3-60) by almost 13,000, *Rashi* (from *Seder Olam* ch. 29) explains that those specified were only from Judah, Benjamin, *Kohanim*, Levites and those of questionable ancestry. Almost 13,000 additional exiles from the ten remaining tribes also returned. These are not enumerated separately, but are included in the sum total of 42,360.

*Malbim's* opinion is that only the first to emigrate are enumerated above (vs. 3-60). The total of 42,360 includes settlers who arrived later.

The 42,360 returnees, accompanied by over 7,000 servants and 200 musicians (v. 65), were only a small segment of the exiled Jewish people. What happened to the rest of the nation?

According to *Ramban* (to *Megillah* 2a), the 42,360 were followed by many others. The fledgling community grew rapidly, and soon the majority of the people, including the *Men of the Great Assembly* [the supreme national legislative and judicial body mentioned in *Avos* 1:1], inhabited the land. Some fifteen years later, when Haman remarked to King Ahasuerus, *'There is a certain people scattered abroad and dispersed among the peoples in all the provinces of your realm'* (*Esther* 3:8), he was referring not to the entire nation, but only to that portion of the people still in the diaspora.

*Ran* (there), however, disagrees, citing Haman's statement as conclusive evidence that the bulk of the Jewish community was *scattered abroad and dispersed ... in all the provinces.* He contends, therefore, that only those enumerated in Scripture settled in the Holy Land, while the multitudes did not respond to Cyrus' edict.

*Metzudos'* view in *Nehemiah* 1:2 coincides with *Ran's.* [In Darius' twentieth year, a number of years after Haman's time] Nehemiah said: *I questioned* [those who came from Judah to Persia] *concerning the Jewish refugees who still remained* [in Judah] *from the captivity. Metzudos* explains that the Jews living in the Land of Israel were referred to as merely the remainder of the captivity because the majority of the exiles still dwelt in the Babylonian captivity. Thus, according to *Metzudos,* the great majority of the Jewish people had not ascended from exile even after

with the passage of time the secret was lost and the *Urim V'Tumim* could no longer be replaced.

*The Animals*

*The Leaders' Contribution*

[65] *Besides their male and female slaves, who numbered seven thousand three hundred and thirty-seven; and they had two hundred male and female singers.* [66] *Their horses, seven hundred and thirty-six; their mules, two hundred and forty-five.* [67] *Their camels, four hundred and thirty-five; donkeys, six thousand seven hundred and twenty.* [68] *And some of the heads of the families, when they came to [the site of] the Temple of HASHEM in Jerusalem, contributed for the Temple of God to establish it on its foundation.* [69] *They contributed to the work-treasury according to their means: sixty-one*

both Haman and Ahasuerus disappeared from the scene.

**65.** מִלְּבַד עַבְדֵיהֶם וְאַמְהֹתֵיהֶם — *Besides their male and female slaves.* These were not included in the count of the congregation (v. 64) *(Rashi).*

וְלָהֶם מְשֹׁרְרִים וּמְשֹׁרְרוֹת מָאתָיִם — *And they had two hundred male and female singers.* Singers accompanied the returnees, so that the journey up from Babylon to the Land of Israel would be made with great rejoicing *(Rashi).* The singers offered songs of praise to God *(Ibn Ezra).*

מָאתָיִם — *Two hundred.* In *Nehemiah* (7:67) the number is given as two hundred and forty-five. *Metzudos* (there) conjectures that the additional forty-five were minors at the time of the return. Having grown up in the interim, they were counted by Nehemiah.

### 66-67. The Animals

**66.** סוּסֵיהֶם שְׁבַע מֵאוֹת שְׁלֹשִׁים וְשִׁשָּׁה — *Their horses, seven hundred and thirty-six.* The Midrash *(Ruth Rabbah* 1:5) contrasts Ezra's description of the exiles' return to Israel with the account of Elimelech's abandonment of the Land *(Ruth* 1:7): Observe how the Holy One, Blessed is He, cherishes the return to the Land ... [In *Ezra*] it is written: *their horses ... their mules ... their camels ...* [In *Ruth,*] however, it is written: *A man went forth ...* Because he [Elimelech] forsook the Land of Israel, Scripture omits any mention of his possessions.

### 68-69. The Leaders' Contribution

**68.** וּמֵרָאשֵׁי הָאָבוֹת — *And some of the heads of the families* [lit. *heads of the fathers*]. *Ibn Ezra* notes: *Some,* but not *all.*

בְּבוֹאָם לְבֵית ה׳ — *When they came to [the site of] the Temple of HASHEM.* *Metzudos* remarks that since the Temple was not yet rebuilt, the reference is not to the Temple itself but to its site.

*Ibn Ezra,* however, proposes an alternative, translating *when they came 'for' the Temple,* i.e., for the purpose of building the Temple.

**69.** אוֹצַר הַמְּלָאכָה — *The work-treasury.* This was the treasury used for storing the gold and silver which would be needed in the work of constructing the Temple *(Metzudos).*

*Ramban* (to *Exodus* 36:6) cites a number of passages where מְלָאכָה [lit. *work*] is translated *valuables,* referring to money or materials. Accordingly, אוֹצַר הַמְּלָאכָה may be translated *the treasury of valuables.*

ב זָהָב דַּרְכְּמוֹנִים שֵׁשׁ־רִבֹּאות וָאֶלֶף וְכֶסֶף
ע מָנִים חֲמֵשֶׁת אֲלָפִים וְכָתְנֹת כֹּהֲנִים
ע מֵאָה: וַיֵּשְׁבוּ הַכֹּהֲנִים וְהַלְוִיִּם וּמִן־הָעָם
וְהַמְשֹׁרְרִים וְהַשּׁוֹעֲרִים וְהַנְּתִינִים בְּעָרֵיהֶם
ג א וְכָל־יִשְׂרָאֵל בְּעָרֵיהֶם: וַיִּגַּע
א־ב הַחֹדֶשׁ הַשְּׁבִיעִי וּבְנֵי יִשְׂרָאֵל בֶּעָרִים
ב וַיֵּאָסְפוּ הָעָם כְּאִישׁ אֶחָד אֶל־יְרוּשָׁלִָם: וַיָּקָם
יֵשׁוּעַ בֶּן־יוֹצָדָק וְאֶחָיו הַכֹּהֲנִים וּזְרֻבָּבֶל בֶּן־

זָהָב דַּרְכְּמוֹנִים שֵׁשׁ־רִבֹּאות וָאֶלֶף וְכֶסֶף מָנִים חֲמֵשֶׁת אֲלָפִים — *Sixty-one thousand golden darkemons, five thousand silver manehs. Darkemon* is the name of a gold coin *(Rashi). Ralbag* identifies the *darkemon* as the gold dinar.

The gifts of the family heads chronicled in *Nehemiah* (7:71) total only twenty thousand *darkemons* and twenty-two hundred silver *manehs.* Thus, it may be concluded that the far greater sum mentioned here was not donated solely by the heads of the families mentioned in the preceding passage, but was the aggregate of everyone's contributions. [Some of the contributions of others are listed separately in *Nehemiah.*]

*Metzudos* and *Malbim* (there) suggest that the contributions listed in *Nehemiah* are in addition to those listed here. They were made either by small groups arriving shortly after the first major wave of returnees *(Malbim)* or by those coming with Nehemiah years later. Although the Temple had already been built by that time, the new contributions were used for repairs or for additional construction *(Metzudos).*

וְכָתְנֹת כֹּהֲנִים — *And ... priestly tunics.* The tunics were to be worn by the *Kohanim* during the Temple services *(Rashi).*

**70.** וּמִן־הָעָם ... בְּעָרֵיהֶם וְכָל־יִשְׂרָאֵל בְּעָרֵיהֶם — *And some of the people ... in their cities; and all of Israel in their cities. Metzudos* states that *some of the people* refers to the members of the tribes of Judah and Benjamin; *all of Israel* to the returnees from the other tribes.

*Malbim* explains that the people did not settle in Jerusalem because the lack of food required them to engage immediately in agriculture. In addition, they had not yet gained permission to reconstruct the protective walls surrounding the city. All of the immigrants, therefore, returned to their ancestral cities.

# III

**1.** וַיִּגַּע הַחֹדֶשׁ הַשְּׁבִיעִי — *The seventh month arrived.* I.e., the month of Tishrei[1] [during which the holidays of Rosh Hashanah, Yom Kippur, and Succos are celebrated] *(Rashi).*

*Malbim* notes that the simple form of

1. Although the new year begins with Tishrei, it is seventh in the order of months beginning with the month of Nissan. *Ramban (Exodus* 12:2) explains that the Nissan order is followed throughout Scripture in commemoration of the Exodus from Egypt, which took place on the fifteenth of Nissan. This is in keeping with the Biblical statement: *This month* [*Nissan*] *is, for you, the beginning of* [*the*] *months; first, for you, of the months of the year (Exodus* 12:2).

*thousand gold darkemons, five thousand silver*
*manehs, and one hundred priestly tunics.* 70 *The*
*Kohanim and Levites and some of the people, and the*
*singers, gatekeepers, and Nethinites settled in their*
*cities; and all of Israel in their cities.*



*The seventh month arrived, and the children of*
*Israel were in the cities; then the people*
*assembled as one man to Jerusalem.* 2 *Then Jeshua*
*the son of Jozadak arose, and his brethren the*
*Kohanim, and Zerubabel the son of Shealtiel and his*

*The Return to Jerusalem*

the verb *arrived* — וַיִּגַּע [usually meaning *touched*] — is used rather than the more common form — וַיַּגִּיעַ — to imply that the people gathered in Jerusalem several days *before* the New Moon [when the seventh month was close, but had not yet arrived]. This was in anticipation of the celebration of the New Year and the ensuing festivals at the Temple.

*Ibn Ezra* remarks that the word חֹדֶשׁ, from חָדָשׁ, *new*, is used to describe the monthly lunar cycle because the moon *renews* itself after its disappearance.

וּבְנֵי יִשְׂרָאֵל בֶּעָרִים וַיֵּאָסְפוּ הָעָם — *And the children of Israel were in the cities; then the people assembled.* What did the children of Israel in the cities do? They assembled *(Rashi).* [The second phrase — וַיֵּאָסְפוּ הָעָם, *then the people assembled* — refers to the Children of Israel in the cities.]

כְּאִישׁ אֶחָד — *As one man.* They came in unity, as if they were a single person *(Rashi).* [See also *Rashi* to *Numbers* 14:15, s.v. כאיש אחד.]

They assembled speedily, as if only one man had come to Jerusalem *(Ibn Ezra; Metzudos).*

**2.** יֵשׁוּעַ בֶּן־יוֹצָדָק — *Jeshua the son of Jozadak.* Jeshua was *Kohen Gadol* (High Priest) at the restoration of the Second Temple. He is referred to by the prophets Haggai and Zechariah as *Joshua the Kohen Gadol (Haggai* 1:1; *Zechariah* 3:1; see comm. 2:2).

Jeshua's father, Jozadak, [also known as Jehozadak — *Haggai* 1:1] was a brother of Ezra *(Radak* and *Ibn Ezra* to *Haggai* 1:1). [Both Ezra and Jehozadak were sons of Seraiah. This may be seen by comparing the list of Ezra's lineage *(Ezra* 7:1-5) with Jehozadak's *(I Chronicles* 5:29-41).] He served as *Kohen Gadol* during the First Temple (*Shir HaShirim Rabbah* 5:4), seems to have been its last *Kohen Gadol (Ibn Ezra, Haggai* 1:1), and was among the Judeans exiled by Nebuchadnezzar *(I Chronicles* 5:41).[1]

The Midrash *(Shir HaShirim Rabbah* 5:4) remarks that inasmuch as Jehozadak's son Jeshua was heir to the High Priesthood, he was favored by God for the office over his uncle Ezra, despite the latter's superior virtue.[2] Reish Lakish said: The sanctity of the Temple was preserved because Ezra did not go up [to the Holy Land] then, for had Ezra ascended then the Accuser could have offered reproach, saying that Ezra was more worthy of the position of

1. *II Kings* 25:18 states that Seraiah — Jehozadak's father — was כֹּהֵן הָרֹאשׁ, *Kohen Gadol* (see commentaries there) and that he was executed by Nebuchadnezzar immediately after the destruction of the Temple. Evidently, Jehozadak succeeded his father sometime during the latter's lifetime.

2. *Sefer HaYuchasin* gives a different explanation for the appointment of Jeshua over Ezra.

ג שְׁאַלְתִּיאֵל וְאֶחָיו וַיִּבְנוּ אֶת־מִזְבַּח אֱלֹהֵי
ג יִשְׂרָאֵל לְהַעֲלוֹת עָלָיו עֹלוֹת כַּכָּתוּב
ג בְּתוֹרַת מֹשֶׁה אִישׁ־הָאֱלֹהִים׃ וַיָּכִינוּ הַמִּזְבֵּחַ
°מְכוֹנָתָיו ק׳ עַל־°מְכוֹנֹתוֹ כִּי בְּאֵימָה עֲלֵיהֶם מֵעַמֵּי

*Kohen Gadol* than Jeshua ben Jehozadak. Though Jeshua was the son of the [previous] *Kohen Gadol,* Ezra was supremely qualified because of his consummate virtue ... R' Simon said: The Holy One, Blessed is He, does not easily uproot the ancestral link.'[1]

וּזְרֻבָּבֶל בֶּן־שְׁאַלְתִּיאֵל — *And Zerubabel the son of Shealtiel.* Zerubabel was the leader of the returning exiles. See comm. 2:2.

Both Zerubabel and Shealtiel are listed among the descendants of the Judean king Yehoyachin [Jehoiachin] in *I Chronicles* 3:17-19 (where he is called Yechoniah), but the commentaries differ concerning the relationship between them. According to *Radak* and *Metzudos* there, Shealtiel was the father of Pedaiah and grandfather of Zerubabel. In several places in Scripture we find grandchildren referred to as children and it is in this sense that Ezra calls him Zerubabel the son of Shealtiel. *Radak (Haggai* 1:1) speculates that Shealtiel may have been a much more important and famous figure than his son Pedaiah and for that reason his illustrious grandson Zerubabel was known as the son of Shealtiel. *Ibn Ezra* maintains, however, that Shealtiel and Pedaiah, father of Zerubabel, were brothers. Zerubabel is entitled *the son of Shealtiel* because he was raised by his uncle.

The Talmud identifies Zerubabel as Nehemiah ben Hachaliah and explains that the name *Zerubabel ben Shealtiel* is a homiletical description of his birth and lineage. *Zeru-babel* is constructed from the Hebrew words נִזְרַע בְּבָבֶל, meaning *implanted* or *conceived in Babylon,* for Nehemiah was conceived [and born] in Babylon. *Shealtiel* alludes to Nehemiah's ancestor, who was a son of King Yehoyachin. The name comes from the Hebrew words, **שֶׁנִּשְׁאַל** עַל **אֱלָתוֹ אֵל**, *God petitioned for revocation of His oath.* The Talmud explains: God had sworn that the sinful Yehoyachin

He explains that since Ezra did not return at the time of Zerubabel when the reconstruction of the Temple began and when the sacrificial service was restored, Jeshua, who did return then, was made *Kohen Gadol. Radak* to *Haggai* 1:1 seems to accept this view as well. [After having installed Jeshua in the position, it would have been improper to remove him to give the position to Ezra.]

1. The Midrash's statement that Ezra was not the son of a *Kohen Gadol* presents difficulties, since *II Kings* 25:18 describes Seraiah (Ezra's father) as כֹּהֵן הָרֹאשׁ [lit. *Head Kohen*]. Furthermore, most commentators assume the list in *I Chronicles* 5:29-41 to be the line of the *Kohanim Gedolim* (see ArtScroll commentary there).

Accordingly, the Midrash must be understood as meaning that although Ezra was also the son of a *Kohen Gadol,* he was not the son of the last *Kohen Gadol.* The line of the *Kehunah Gedolah* had already passed to Ezra's older brother Jehozadak during the First Temple, and Jehozadak's son Jeshua was therefore his proper successor.

Although no Talmudic or Midrashic source states clearly that Ezra ever served as *Kohen Gadol, Rambam* (Introduction to *Mishneh Torah)* and *Meiri* (Introduction to *Avos)* say that Ezra did serve as *Kohen Gadol. Rambam's* source many have been the Mishnah in *Parah* (3:5) which states that Ezra made the first *parah adumah* (red heifer; see *Numbers* chap. 19) of the Second Temple. Since all the other *Kohanim* credited there with making a *parah adumah* during the Second Temple period were *Kohanim Gedolim* [and presumably attended to the matter during their terms], it may be inferred that Ezra, too, was a *Kohen Gadol.* However, his

III
3

*brethren, and they built the altar of the God of Israel to offer burnt offerings upon it, as is written in the Torah of Moses, the man of God.* 3 *And they established the altar on its foundations — for the fear*

(there referred to as Chaniahu[1]) would never have a child [see *Jeremiah* 22:30]. However, when the Judean king repented in his Babylonian dungeon, the decree was withdrawn. God, so to speak,[2] then petitioned the heavenly tribunal for revocation of his oath.

[Revocation of a restrictive oath may be awarded by a Rabbinical court if the petitioner professes absolute remorse for his prohibitive declaration or if he asserts that present circumstances broaden the scope of the prohibition beyond its original intent. See *Chaggigah* 10a.]

The child subsequently born was named Shealtiel, and his descendant Nehemiah is described as *ben Shealtiel,* the descendant of him whose existence was contingent upon the revocation of God's oath (*Sanhedrin* 37b, 38a). [See further in *I Chronicles* 3:17, ArtScroll edition.]

עֹלוֹת — *Burnt offerings.* Burnt offerings were completely burnt upon the altar (*Zevachim* 53b), whereas other sacrifices were only partially burnt and the rest eaten. *Metzudos* states that this passage refers to the *tamid, daily burnt offerings,* which were offered every morning and afternoon (v. 3).

**3.** וַיָּכִינוּ הַמִּזְבֵּחַ ... וַיַּעַל — *And they established the altar ... and they offered.* They established the altar[3] in order to offer burnt offerings because they feared the peoples of the land (*Rashi*).

עַל מְכוֹנָתוֹ — *On its foundations.* The Sages assert that this altar was larger than the one used in the First Temple. R' Yose said: The altar was originally only twenty-eight cubits by twenty-eight cubits, but when the exiles returned they added four cubits to the south and four to the west ... (*Middos* 3:1). The Talmud explains that they were able to do so because the size of the altar, within certain limits, is not Biblically fixed (*Zevachim* 62a). The Talmud (there) adds: 'Rabbah bar bar Chanah said in the name of R' Yochanan: Three prophets [Haggai, Zechariah, and Malachi (*Rashi*)] ascended with them from the exile. One testified as to the altar [i.e., its size —

tenure as *Kohen Gadol* can not have been long since he is not listed by the Talmud in *Yoma* 9a among those who served lengthy terms as *Kohen Gadol* (*Kuntres B'Shaar HaMelech* by *R' Chaim Kunievsky*).

1. The prefix *Yeho-* and the suffixes *-iah* and *-iahu* are freely interchanged throughout Scripture, especially in the names of the kings. (See ArtScroll commentary to *Divrei HaYamim/Chronicles I* 3:11.) Thus Yehoyachin, Yechoniah, and Chaniahu are all identical with either the prefix or suffix being added to the root *yachin* or its abbreviated form *chan.*

2. Since revocation of an oath is based on the remorse of the oath-taker or the development of unforeseen circumstances — situations which cannot apply to an Omniscient God — it is obvious that this statement of the Sages is an anthropomorphism. Yechoniah, by his absolute repentance, had become like another person, and the original decree was no longer warranted (*Rambam, Hil. Teshuvah* 7:6). When *Hashem* saw this, He forgave him and rescinded His decree. The Sages, as is their custom, figuratively describe this action in human terms — as if the circumstance of Yechoniah's repentance caused *Hashem* to petition for a revocation of His oath.

3. There were two altars in the Temple. One was the *outer altar,* which was used for burning the sacrifices and stood in the *azarah* (main courtyard). The other was the *inner altar,* used for burning incense and placed in the Temple building. The reference in our passage is to the *outer altar* upon which the sacrifices were offered. See *Rambam, Beis HaBechirah* 1:5,6.

ג הָאֲרָצוֹת °ויעל עָלָיו עֹלוֹת לַיהוָה עֹלוֹת °וַיַּעֲלוּ ק׳
ד־ה ד לַבֹּקֶר וְלָעָרֶב׃ וַיַּעֲשׂוּ אֶת־חַג הַסֻּכּוֹת
כַּכָּתוּב וְעֹלַת יוֹם בְּיוֹם בְּמִסְפָּר כְּמִשְׁפַּט
ה דְּבַר־יוֹם בְּיוֹמוֹ׃ וְאַחֲרֵי־כֵן עֹלַת תָּמִיד
וְלֶחֳדָשִׁים וּלְכָל־מוֹעֲדֵי יְהוָה הַמְקֻדָּשִׁים

*Rashi*], one as to its place [i.e., its exact position in the Temple courtyard — *Rashi*], and one [to the law] that sacrifices may be offered [at that site] even in the absence of the Temple structure.'

The location of the altar is extremely precise, and it may never be varied ... It is a universal tradition that the place upon which David and Solomon built the altar ... is the spot where Abraham constructed the altar and bound Isaac (*Genesis* 22:9) ... where Noah built [his altar] when he went forth from the ark (*Genesis* 8:20). This is the altar upon which Cain and Abel presented their offerings (*Genesis* 4:34). Here Adam brought a sacrifice when he was created and it was from this soil that he was created. Man, the Sages remarked, was fashioned from the soil of his [eventual] absolution (*Rambam, Beis HaBechirah* 2:1-2).

כִּי בְאֵימָה עֲלֵיהֶם מֵעַמֵּי הָאֲרָצוֹת — *For the fear of the peoples of the land was upon them.* They feared that the peoples of the land would interfere with their labors and slander them before the king. Hence they sought immediately to establish visible evidence that they enjoyed royal favor. They quickly built the altar and offered sacrifices, hoping that these activities, which could have been accomplished only with the king's acquiescence, would deter their enemies (*Rashi*).

*Ibn Ezra* differs, contending that the sacrifices were brought in order to invoke Divine protection against the hostile peoples of the land whom the Jewish settlers feared.

*Malbim* offers a third opinion, noting that the altar was built and the sacrifices brought only after all the children of Israel had gathered in Jerusalem (v. 1). Why were the sacrifices not reinstituted immediately upon the settlers' return to the Holy Land? Our verse provides the explanation. The delay was necessary because they feared the peoples of the land. They waited, therefore, until all the children of Israel had gathered in Jerusalem, in the hope that the strength of their numbers would discourage hostility.

וַיַּעַל — *And they offered up.*

The written form (כְּתִיב) of this word differs from its pronunciation (קְרִי). The written version is the singular וַיַּעַל, *and he offered up.* The pronunciation is the plural וַיַּעֲלוּ, *and they offered up. Ibn Ezra* explains that only one person — the *Kohen Gadol* Jeshua — actually offered the sacrifices, but he was assisted by a number of his fellow *Kohanim.* Since the offering was accomplished by an individual through group involvement, it is described with a word written in the singular and pronounced in the plural.

עֹלוֹת לַבֹּקֶר וְלָעָרֶב — *Burnt offerings for the morning and the afternoon.* This refers to the *tamid,* the daily sacrifice brought each morning and afternoon (*Rashi;* see *Numbers* 28:1-9).

**4.** וַיַּעֲשׂוּ אֶת־חַג הַסֻּכּוֹת — *They then observed the festival of Tabernacles.* I.e., by bringing the prescribed offerings of the festival (*Metzudos*).

כַּכָּתוּב — *As it is written.* As written in *Numbers* (29:12-32), fourteen young sheep and two rams were sacrificed daily during the seven-day festival. In

*of the peoples of the land was upon them — and they*
*offered up burnt offerings upon it: burnt offerings*
*for the morning and the afternoon.* 4 *They then*
*observed the festival of Tabernacles as it is written:*
*the specified number of burnt offerings of each day in*
*its day, according to the law of each day.* 5 *And*
*afterward, the daily burnt offerings, those of the New*
*Moons and of all* HASHEM*'s sanctified festivals; and*

addition, a total of seventy bulls were offered throughout the holiday, beginning with thirteen on the first day and decreasing each day by one until the seventh and final day when seven bulls were offered.

וְעֹלַת יוֹם בְּיוֹם בְּמִסְפָּר — *The specified number of burnt offerings of each day in its day.* They celebrated the festival of Succos [Tabernacles] by bringing the number of burnt offerings specified for each day. [The letter *vav,* usually translated *and,* is not to be taken in its usual sense *(Metzudos).*]

כְּמִשְׁפַּט דְּבַר־יוֹם בְּיוֹמוֹ — *According to the law of each day.* This is apparently a repetition of the previous phrase. It would seem that *Rashi* considers our verse to be a paraphrase of the verse in *Numbers* 29:18, בְּמִסְפָּרָם כַּמִּשְׁפָּט [see commentators there]. *Malbim,* however, explains the first phrase, *The specified number of burnt offerings of each day,* as referring to the fourteen rams sacrificed daily. The phrase, *according to the law of each day,* alludes to the seventy sacrificial bulls brought in descending order throughout the holiday.

**5.** וְאַחֲרֵי־כֵן עֹלַת תָּמִיד — *And afterward, the daily burnt offerings.* After Succos, the daily offerings [see comm., v. 3] were brought regularly *(Rashi).*

According to *R' Yeshayah MiTrani,* however, *afterward* does not refer to the period following the holiday, but to the morning after each day's sacrifices had been consumed. [Although sacrifices could only be offered during the day, they could be burnt throughout the night *(Berachos* 2a).] *Afterward* (i.e., the next morning, after the previous day's sacrifices had finally been consumed), the morning *tamid* was brought. At their appropriate times, the sacrifices mentioned next in our verse were offered as well — *Rosh Chodesh* (New Moon) and festival offerings, and donations.

וּלְכָל־מוֹעֲדֵי ה׳ הַמְקֻדָּשִׁים — *And of all* HASHEM*'s sanctified festivals.* The sacrifices pertaining to the remaining festivals [Pesach and Shavuos] were brought in their appropriate times *(Rashi).*

*Malbim* notes that the Jewish settlers were able to offer the festival sacrifices only during the ensuing Pesach and Shavuos holidays. Later, the king's sanction was rescinded and the sacrificial services were halted [see 4:24].

הַמְקֻדָּשִׁים — *Sanctified.* The term הַמְקֻדָּשִׁים, *sanctified,* is used rather than קְדוֹשִׁים, *holy,* because the festivals were sanctified, or proclaimed as holy, by Rabbinic decree *(Ibn Ezra).*

The Rabbinic court determines when the festivals fall by decreeing which day is the first of the month. This is based on the Scripturally ordained method for determining the first day of the new month, which may begin either on the thirtieth or the thirty-first day of the previous month. The supreme Rabbinic tribunal must proclaim one of these two days as the beginning of the

ו וּלְכֹ֛ל מִתְנַדֵּ֥ב נְדָבָ֖ה לַֽיהוָֽה׃ מִיּ֤וֹם אֶחָד֙
לַחֹ֣דֶשׁ הַשְּׁבִיעִ֔י הֵחֵ֕לּוּ לְהַעֲל֥וֹת עֹל֖וֹת
ז לַֽיהוָ֑ה וְהֵיכַ֥ל יְהוָ֖ה לֹ֥א יֻסָּֽד׃ וַיִּתְּנוּ־כֶ֕סֶף
לַחֹצְבִ֖ים וְלֶחָרָשִׁ֑ים וּמַאֲכָ֨ל וּמִשְׁתֶּ֜ה וָשֶׁ֗מֶן
לַצִּדֹנִים֙ וְלַצֹּרִ֔ים לְהָבִ֡יא עֲצֵי֩ אֲרָזִ֨ים מִן־
הַלְּבָנ֜וֹן אֶל־יָ֣ם יָפ֗וֹא כְּרִשְׁי֛וֹן כּ֥וֹרֶשׁ מֶֽלֶךְ־
ח פָּרַ֖ס עֲלֵיהֶֽם׃ וּבַשָּׁנָ֣ה הַשֵּׁנִ֗ית
לְבוֹאָ֞ם אֶל־בֵּ֤ית הָֽאֱלֹהִים֙ לִיר֣וּשָׁלִַ֔ם בַּחֹ֖דֶשׁ
הַשֵּׁנִ֑י הֵחֵ֡לּוּ זְרֻבָּבֶ֣ל בֶּן־שְׁ֠אַלְתִּיאֵל וְיֵשׁ֨וּעַ
בֶּן־יוֹצָדָ֜ק וּשְׁאָ֥ר אֲחֵיהֶ֣ם ׀ הַכֹּהֲנִ֣ים וְהַלְוִיִּ֗ם

month, based on testimony verifying the sighting of the new moon (*Rosh Hashanah* 23b, 24a). Since all of the festivals fall on certain days of specific months, the Rabbis, by fixing the opening day of the month, in effect select the particular day of the festival, thereby causing that day to be sacred.

וּלְכֹל מִתְנַדֵּב נְדָבָה לַה׳ — *And for everyone who contributed a voluntary offering to HASHEM.* These offerings were given to the *Kohanim* to be sacrificed *(Rashi).*

6. הֵחֵלּוּ לְהַעֲלוֹת עֹלוֹת לַה׳ — *They commenced offering burnt offerings to HASHEM.* On the first day of the seventh month a sporadic beginning was made. After the festival of Succos, it was expanded into a full schedule *(Metzudos).*

וְהֵיכַל ה׳ לֹא יֻסָּד — *But the foundation of HASHEM's Sanctuary was not yet laid.* The altar was built and the offerings brought prior to the construction of the Temple, despite the stringent Biblical prohibition against sacrificing outside the Temple [see *Leviticus* 17:3,4; *Rambam, Maaseh HaKorbanos* 18:1-5]. This remarkable circumstance merits considerable discussion in the Rabbinic literature. The Talmud states that special testimony was needed to authorize the bringing of these sacrifices. One of the three prophets who returned with them from the Babylonian exile [see above v. 3] testified that the sacrifices may be offered on the altar (when it is on its original site) even in the absence of the Temple structure[1] *(Zevachim* 62a).

The justification for bringing sacrifices in the absence of the Temple is expressed in the Mishnaic principle of *perpetual sanctification.* R' Yehoshua said: I have heard that the sacrifices may be offered even in the absence of the Temple ... since the original sanctification [of the Temple by King Solomon] is perpetually effective (*Eduyos* 8:6). *Rambam (Beis HaBechirah* 6:14-16) elaborates: Solomon consecrated the [Temple] courtyard and Jerusalem for all time; therefore the sacrifices may be offered although the Temple does not stand ... Why do I maintain that the sanctification of the Temple and Jerusalem is eternally effective? Because they became sacred through the visitation of the Divine Presence, and the Divine Presence is without end.'

*Ravad* (there) disagrees, deciding in favor of the Mishnaic opinion which rejects R' Yehoshua's principle of perpetual sanctifica-

1. This has aroused periodic speculation among the later Rabbinic authorities concerning the feasibility of bringing sacrifices in post-exilic and even contemporary times. For a detailed analysis of the issue, see *Kaftor VaFerach* ch. 6; *Yaavetz* [responsa] 89; *Chasam Sofer,* vol. *Yoreh Deah* [responsa] 236; *Binyan Zion* 1.

*for everyone who contributed a voluntary offering to*
*HASHEM.* 6 *From the first day of the seventh month*
*they commenced offering burnt offerings to HASHEM,*
*but the foundation of HASHEM's Sanctuary was not*
*yet laid.* 7 *They then paid silver to the quarriers and*
*carpenters, and food, drink, and oil to the Sidonians*
*and Tyrians, to transport cedar wood from Lebanon*
*to the sea of Jaffa, as authorized for them by Cyrus,*
*king of Persia.* 8 *In the second year of their arrival at*
*the Temple of God in Jerusalem, in the second*
*month, Zerubabel the son of Shealtiel, Jeshua son of*
*Jozadak, and the rest of their brethren, the Kohanim*

*The Temple Construction Begins*

tion. *Ravad* maintains that King Solomon's sanctification was limited to the duration of the Temple structure [see *Shevuos* 16a]. How, then, could the sacrifices have been offered before the construction of the Second Temple, as described in our verse? *Shevuos* (ibid.) suggests the possibility that curtains were set up along the boundaries of the Temple walls during construction, and the sacrifices were brought within the confines of these legally acceptable walls.

**7.** עֲצֵי אֲרָזִים מִן־הַלְּבָנוֹן — *Cedar wood from Lebanon.* Cedar wood was used in the construction of the First Temple *(I Kings* 5-19,20; 6:15-18) and the palaces of King David *(II Samuel* 5:11) and King Solomon *(I Kings* 7:1-12). It grew in Lebanon and the Sidonians [of the kingdom of Tyre] were its master craftsmen *(I Kings* 5:20). The same payment of food for labor was used in the construction of the First Temple as well.

כִּרְשְׁיוֹן כּוֹרֶשׁ — *As authorized ... by Cyrus.* This refers to Cyrus' decree authorizing the construction of the Temple *(Rashi).*

*Malbim,* however, explains that the authorization was used only for the transport of the cedar wood mentioned in this passage. The wood for the Temple was a gift of the king, as provided under the clause in Cyrus' proclamations stating that *the Temple expenditure will be provided by the royal estate* [6:4; 6:2-4 provides details of Cyrus' decree omitted from the opening verses of *Ezra.* The forests of Lebanon belonged to the king's preserve, and their cedar wood was appropriated only by royal decree (see *Nehemiah* 2:8)].

### ◆§ The Temple Construction Begins

**8.** לְבוֹאָם אֶל בֵּית־הָאֱלֹהִים — *Of their arrival at the Temple of God.* [I.e., of their arrival at the Temple site. The Temple itself was not yet standing. See comm. 2:6.]

בַּחֹדֶשׁ הַשֵּׁנִי — *In the second month.* The month of Iyar *(Rashi).*

[It seems likely that the year is reckoned not from their arrival but from the first of Nissan — i.e., the first of Nissan marked the beginning of the *second year* although it was only about seven months after their arrival in the Holy Land. This is the common Scriptural system of dating. See *Rosh Hashanah* 1:1. Thus the event described here took place only seven months after the people first gathered in Jerusalem to celebrate the festival of Succos (v. 1).]

הֵחֵלּוּ — *Commenced.* They began building the Temple *(Metzudos).*

ג
ט־י

וְכָל־הַבָּאִים֙ מֵהַשְּׁבִי֙ יְרוּשָׁלִַ֔ם וַיַּֽעֲמִ֨ידוּ אֶת־
הַלְוִיִּ֜ם מִבֶּ֨ן עֶשְׂרִ֤ים שָׁנָה֙ וָמַ֔עְלָה לְנַצֵּ֖חַ עַל־
ט מְלֶ֥אכֶת בֵּית־יְהוָֽה׃ וַיַּעֲמֹ֣ד יֵשׁ֡וּעַ בָּנָ֣יו וְ֠אֶחָיו
קַדְמִיאֵ֨ל וּבָנָ֤יו בְּנֵי־יְהוּדָה֙ כְּאֶחָ֔ד לְנַצֵּ֖חַ עַל־
עֹשֵׂ֣ה הַמְּלָאכָ֑ה בְּבֵ֖ית הָאֱלֹהִ֑ים בְּנֵי֙ חֵֽנָדָ֔ד
י בְּנֵיהֶ֥ם וַאֲחֵיהֶ֖ם הַלְוִיִּֽם׃ וְיִסְּד֥וּ הַבֹּנִ֖ים אֶת־
הֵיכַ֣ל יְהוָ֑ה וַיַּעֲמִ֨ידוּ הַכֹּהֲנִ֜ים מְלֻבָּשִׁ֗ים

מִבֶּן עֶשְׂרִים שָׁנָה וָמַעְלָה — *Aged twenty and above.* Precedent for taking Levites from the age of twenty for service in the Temple comes from King David *(I Chronicles* 23:24-32).

*Numbers* 4:43 teaches that the Levites entered the service of the Temple at age thirty and began training at twenty-five *(Numbers* 8:24 as explained by *Rashi* from Talmud *Chullin* 24a). This, however, applied only as long as a primary part of the Levites' task was to carry the Ark and the other utensils of the Tabernacle. Once the Ark arrived at its permanent home in Jerusalem, and the only tasks remaining to the Levites were to guard and maintain the Temple and sing, the Levites entered service at age twenty, as established by David *(Ramban* to *Numbers* 8:24 and in *Sefer HaMitzvos, Shoresh* 3; *Gra* and *Malbim* to *I Chronicles* 23:24; see ArtScroll comm. there).

לְנַצֵּחַ עַל־מְלֶאכֶת בֵּית־ה׳ — *To sing during the work of the Temple of* HASHEM. The translation follows *Rashi.*

*Metzudos* explains that although לְנַצֵּחַ is ordinarily rendered *to conquer,* it is also used to denote choral singing, since in the choral arrangement members of the group 'conquer' one another by alternately singing loudest.

*Ibn Ezra, Radak (Shorashim),* and *Ralbag,* however, translate *to oversee* (i.e., to strengthen and expedite) *the work of the Temple of* HASHEM. The Levites aged twenty and above were engaged to supervise the Temple labor force and hasten the labor so that the work would be completed before *the peoples of the land* [see v. 3, above] could interrupt it *(Ralbag).*

9. יֵשׁוּעַ בָּנָיו — *Jeshua ... and his sons.* Although not in the text, the word *and* is understood *(Ibn Ezra).*

קַדְמִיאֵל וּבָנָיו בְּנֵי יְהוּדָה — *Kadmiel and his sons — the sons of Judah.* Kadmiel's descent from Judah distinguishes him from Kadmiel mentioned in *Nehemiah* 10:10, who was descended from Henadad *(Malbim).*[1]

לְנַצֵּחַ — *To sing. Rashi* renders לְנַצֵּחַ as he does in the preceding verse.

This rendition, however, poses a problem. The previous passage indicates that *all* of the Levites sang in the chorus, but this verse specifies only a few individuals as choristers — Jeshua, Kadmiel, Henadad and their sons and brethren. Evidently, *Rashi's* understanding is that the previous verse states the general arrangement — *all* of the Levites were engaged as choristers. The present passage describes how this was implemented — Jeshua, Kadmiel, Henadad and their sons and brethren were the first actually to sing before the laborers.

*Rashi's* view corresponds with the Talmudic interpretation presented in *Arachin* 13b. The Mishnah rules that Levite minors, although generally disqualified from performing the

1. The names *Jeshua* and *Kadmiel* are identical with the names of two Levites listed above (2:40). There, however, they are identified as the *sons of Hodaviah,* while our verse describes them as the *sons of Judah.*

*and the Levites, and all those who came to Jerusalem
from the captivity commenced; and they stationed
the Levites aged twenty and above to sing during the
work of the Temple of HASHEM.* 9 *Then Jeshua arose,
and his sons and brethren, Kadmiel and his sons —
the sons of Judah, as one, to sing before the workers
in the Temple of God; also, the sons of Henadad,
their Levite sons and brethren.* 10 *And the builders
laid the foundation of the Sanctuary of HASHEM, and
they stationed the Kohanim, elegantly attired, with*

Levitical tasks, may join in harmonizing the chanting of the Temple liturgy. The Talmud explains that this ruling is deduced from our passage. *Tosafos* attributes the derivation specifically to the closing words, *their Levite sons.* Since the text has already specified Jeshua *and his sons,* Kadmiel *and his sons,* Henadad *and his sons,* the final statement, *their Levite sons,* seems repetitious. The redundancy indicates a novel connotation — their Levite *minor* sons also joined in the singing.

Thus, the Talmud obviously interprets לְנַצֵּחַ in our verse as a reference to singing.

*Metzudos* and *Malbim,* however, while agreeing with *Rashi* in the preceding passage, maintain that the same term in our verse has a different meaning [since the term in v. 8 includes all the Levites, whereas here לְנַצֵּחַ refers only to certain families and their friends]. They render לְנַצֵּחַ here *to oversee* the Temple laborers and *to enforce* the work requirements [from the root נצח — *to conquer*]. *Then Joshua arose ... to supervise the workers in the Temple of God.*

*Ralbag* understands both verses in this sense. He explains that the Levites as a whole were charged with overseeing all the various aspects of the project, while those mentioned here were specifically responsible for supervising and urging on the workers.

This is indicated by the change in phrasing from v. 8 to v. 9. The Levites were appointed to *oversee the work of the Temple of HASHEM* (v. 8), whereas those mentioned in v. 9 undertook to oversee *the workers.*

בְּנֵי חֵנָדָד — *Also, the sons of Henadad.* The word *also* is implied *(Ibn Ezra).*

**10.** וְיִסְּדוּ הַבֹּנִים אֶת־הֵיכַל ה׳ — *And the builders laid the foundation of the Sanctuary of HASHEM.* The builders laid the Sanctuary foundation while the Levites sang (v. 9) *(Rashi).* [*Rashi* reads this verse as a continuation of the preceding passage ... *Jeshua and his sons and brethren ... stood as one to sing before the workers ... and the builders laid the foundation ...*]

וַיַּעֲמִידוּ הַכֹּהֲנִים — *And they stationed the Kohanim.* While the builders laid the foundation for the Sanctuary, the *Kohanim* were stationed ... *(Rashi).*

מְלֻבָּשִׁים — *Elegantly attired.* Although the word literally means *dressed, Rashi* explains that in the context of this verse it means that the *Kohanim* wore elegant clothing [since otherwise, there is no need for the verse to state that they were dressed]. He pointedly does not state that they wore the special priestly garments [shirt, breeches, belt, and turban; see *Rashi, Exodus* 28:40]. *Ibn Ezra,* however, asserts that they were indeed dressed in the special priestly vestments generally worn during the sacrificial services, although they were now merely engaged in sounding the trumpets during the laying of the foundation. Accordingly, the word should be rendered as *formally attired.*

בַּחֲצֹצְרוֹת וְהַלְוִיִּם בְּנֵי־אָסָף בַּמְצִלְתַּיִם
לְהַלֵּל אֶת־יהוה עַל־יְדֵי דָּוִיד מֶלֶךְ־יִשְׂרָאֵל׃
יא וַיַּעֲנוּ בְּהַלֵּל וּבְהוֹדֹת לַיהוה כִּי טוֹב כִּי־
לְעוֹלָם חַסְדּוֹ עַל־יִשְׂרָאֵל וְכָל־הָעָם הֵרִיעוּ
תְרוּעָה גְדוֹלָה בְהַלֵּל לַיהוה עַל הוּסַד בֵּית־
יב יהוה׃ וְרַבִּים מֵהַכֹּהֲנִים וְהַלְוִיִּם וְרָאשֵׁי
הָאָבוֹת הַזְּקֵנִים אֲשֶׁר רָאוּ אֶת־הַבַּיִת
הָרִאשׁוֹן בְּיָסְדוֹ זֶה הַבַּיִת בְּעֵינֵיהֶם בֹּכִים

*Malbim* relates the two interpretations to a halachic disagreement involving *Rambam* and *Ravad*. *Rambam* (*Klei HaMikdash* 8:12) prohibits the wearing of the priestly vestments at any time save during the performance of the sacrificial rituals. This view coincides with *Rashi's* interpretation that the *Kohanim* who sounded the trumpets during the Temple construction were attired with elegance and distinction — but not in their vestments. *Ravad* (ibid.), however, states that the *Kohanim* were permitted to wear their vestments in the Temple at all times. This corresponds to *Ibn Ezra's* opinion that the *Kohanim* who sounded the trumpets on the Temple grounds wore the priestly vestments, although they were not performing the sacrificial rituals.

In an alternative approach, *Malbim* justifies the wearing of the special vestments even according to *Rambam*. When the *Kohanim* don their vestments for the purpose of performing the sacrificial rituals, they may continue to wear them even after the sacrifices have been concluded. The *Kohanim* who sounded the trumpets had donned the ceremonial attire while performing the morning's sacrificial services [see v. 5], and continued to wear them while playing the trumpets during the founding of the Temple.

בַּחֲצֹצְרוֹת — *With trumpets.* Although the special sounding of the trumpets in the Temple was reserved for the festivals [see *Rambam, Klei HaMikdash* 3:5], the present occasion warranted their use because the Rabbinic court deemed it appropriate to invest the celebration of the founding of the Temple with festival status. The rejoicing was therefore accompanied by the festive sounding of the trumpets (*Malbim*).

וְהַלְוִיִּם בְּנֵי־אָסָף — *And the Levites, the sons of Asaph.* This is the family of Levites listed above (2:41) as having been choristers in the First Temple (*Rashi*).

*I Chronicles* 6:16,17 tells that David appointed Levites to sing in the Temple of *Hashem*. One of the three head choristers was Asaph. Additionally, Asaph was placed in charge of the daily song service which took place before the Ark of *Hashem* which David had brought to Jerusalem (*I Chronicles* 16:5; see ArtScroll commentary there). Asaph (who was presumably the ancestor of this family of choristers) also played the cymbals during that daily service.

עַל־יְדֵי דָּוִיד — *Through* [lit. *by the hands of*] *David.* The Levites sang King David's compositions [from the *Book of Psalms*] (*Rashi*).

*Ibn Ezra*, however, renders *with the melodies of David*, because the melody is drawn from the instrument by the hands.

**11.** וַיַּעֲנוּ — *And they sang responsively.* The songs were sung responsively, with the leader singing the first part of a verse and the people responding with the second part (*Rashi;* see his commentary to *Exodus* 15:21).

*Metzudos* translates, *they raised their voices* [see *Deut.* 27:14 — וְעָנוּ הַלְוִיִּם... קוֹל רָם, *Let the Levites exclaim with raised voices; Rashi, Deut.* 26:5].

*trumpets, and the Levites, the sons of Asaph, with*
*cymbals, to exalt* HASHEM *through David, king of*
*Israel.* 11 *And they sang responsively with exaltation*
*and thanks to* HASHEM, *for it is good, for His*
*benevolence towards Israel is eternal. And all the*
*people burst into a great shout of exaltation of*
HASHEM *— for the laying of the foundation of the*
*Temple of* HASHEM. 12 *But many of the Kohanim,*
*Levites and heads of the families, elders who had*
*beheld the First Temple upon its foundation, wept*

*Joy and Grief*

בְּהַלֵּל וּבְהוֹדֹת — *With exaltation and thanks.* [To extol God.] The translation follows *Rashi.*

*Exaltation* denotes praise of God. *Thanks* is an expression of gratitude for his kindness *(Malbim).*

כִּי טוֹב — *For it is good.* For it is good to thank HASHEM. [This was part of their song] *(Rashi; Metzudos).*

*Malbim,* however, translates: *That He* [God] *is good.*

כִּי־לְעוֹלָם חַסְדּוֹ עַל־יִשְׂרָאֵל — *For His benevolence towards Israel is eternal.* These words were also sung by the Levites *(Metzudos).*

*Malbim* observes that the opening portion of this passage, *And they sang ... with exaltation and thanks to* HASHEM, describes the words of the song which follow. *Exaltation,* the praise of God's objective goodness, is expressed by the phrase *that He* [*God*] *is good. Thanks,* gratitude to God for His kind acts, are conveyed in the statement *for His benevolence towards Israel is eternal.*

וְכָל־הָעָם — *And all the people.* I.e., the Israelites *(Rashi)* [that is, all the people except for the *Kohanim* and Levites, who were involved in their own singing and music playing, as mentioned previously].

בְּהַלֵּל לַה׳ — *Of exaltation of* HASHEM. The Levites' song at the beginning of the verse includes both exaltation and thanks, whereas the people's great shout expresses only exaltation — but not thanks. *Malbim* explains that the song of thanks was in gratitude for the founding of the new Temple. But not all the people could join in this, since many of them had witnessed the First Temple, and now wept at the inadequacy of the present one [see v. 12].

עַל הוּסַד בֵּית־ה׳ — *For the laying of the foundation of the Temple of* HASHEM. All the aforementioned rejoicing [trumpet blowing, singing, and shouting of praise] was over the laying of the foundation *(Rashi).*

### ◆§ Joy and Grief

**12.** בְּיָסְדוֹ — *Upon its foundation.* The translation follows *Rashi.*

[This is an idiom meaning *when it still stood.*]

However, *Ralbag, Ibn Ezra* and *Metzudos* relate the word בְּיָסְדוֹ to the following phrase: *Many ... who had beheld the First Temple wept loudly when they witnessed 'the laying of the foundation' of the present Temple.*

זֶה הַבַּיִת בְּעֵינֵיהֶם — *When they witnessed the present Temple* [lit. *the present Temple with their eyes*]. *Malbim* explains the word בְּעֵינֵיהֶם, literally *with their eyes,* as referring back to the first phrase as well: *Many ... who had beheld the First Temple 'with their eyes' wept loudly when they beheld the present Temple 'with their eyes.'*

בֹּכִים — *Wept* [lit. *would weep*]. They

ג בְּקוֹל גָּדוֹל וְרַבִּים בִּתְרוּעָה בְשִׂמְחָה לְהָרִים
יג קוֹל׃ וְאֵין הָעָם מַכִּירִים קוֹל תְּרוּעַת
הַשִּׂמְחָה לְקוֹל בְּכִי הָעָם כִּי הָעָם
מְרִיעִים תְּרוּעָה גְדוֹלָה וְהַקּוֹל נִשְׁמַע עַד־
לְמֵרָחוֹק׃

ד א־ב
א וַיִּשְׁמְעוּ צָרֵי יְהוּדָה וּבִנְיָמִן כִּי־בְנֵי הַגּוֹלָה
ב בּוֹנִים הֵיכָל לַיהוָה אֱלֹהֵי יִשְׂרָאֵל׃ וַיִּגְּשׁוּ
אֶל־זְרֻבָּבֶל וְאֶל־רָאשֵׁי הָאָבוֹת וַיֹּאמְרוּ לָהֶם

would weep whenever they beheld the new Temple *(Rashi).*

[*Rashi* deduces this, apparently, from the usage of the present tense בֹּכִים, *are weeping*, rather than the past tense בָּכוּ, *wept.* The present tense suggests constant weeping.]

Various explanations for the causes of the weeping are given. *Rashi* and *Metzudos* indicate that the elders wept because the Second Temple was not as large as the first. *Ralbag* states that the stones used for the new foundation were smaller than those of Solomon's Temple, though the size was the same.

*R' Yeshayah MiTrani* explains that the disappointment with the new Temple was of a more general nature — for the Second Temple was 'as nothing' compared with the first. [This remark is based on the passage in *Haggai* (2:3) — *Who remains among you who beheld this Temple in its former glory? That which you observe at present is 'as nothing' by comparison.*] The Midrash *(Pesikta Rabbasi* 36) states that the Divine Presence did not rest upon the Second Temple as it had upon the First. *Yoma* (21b) elaborates: The following were present in the First Temple, but lacking in the second — the Ark with its covering and its cherubs, the heavenly flame [which miraculously kept the altar firewood burning], the Divine Presence, the sacred spirit [of prophecy *(Rashi)*] and the *Urim V'Tumim* [explained in comm. to 2:63].

וְרַבִּים בִּתְרוּעָה בְשִׂמְחָה לְהָרִים קוֹל — *While many raised their voices in shouts*[1] *of joy.* Those who had not beheld the First Temple rejoiced over their deliverance from exile *(Rashi).*[2]

[*Rashi's* comment indicates that the *shouts of joy* were not over the founding of the Temple, as the context of the entire chapter implies, but in reaction to the deliverance from exile. This novel interpretation is based, evidently, on the contrast between the final phrase of this verse and the closing words of the preceding passage. The previous verse ended by stating that the singing and shouting were *for the laying of the foundation of the Temple of* HASHEM. The present passage, however, does not contain an explanatory phrase. This omission apparently prompted *Rashi* to conclude that the motivation for the shouts of joy mentioned in our verse was not the laying of the foundation but the deliverance from exile.]

**13.** לְקוֹל בְּכִי הָעָם — *Because of the*

1. See *Joshua* 6:5, where the context of the verse clearly indicates that תְּרוּעָה means *shouts* and not *trumpet blasts* [as it usually does]. See also Talmud, *Taanis* 14a.
2. In *Rashi's* opinion (comm. 2:2), the returnees named above (2:2-61) were exiled from the Holy Land with Zerubabel. Who then, were the settlers who had *not* yet beheld the first Sanctuary and now rejoiced? Perhaps they were the 13,000 immigrants included in the total of 42,360 (2:64), but not listed by name with the Levites and members of Judah and Benjamin who were exiled with Zerubabel. See comm. 2:64.

III
13 *loudly when they witnessed the present Temple; while many raised their voices in shouts of joy.* 13 *The people could not discern the sound of the joyful shouting because of the clamor of the people's weeping; for the people raised a great shout — but the clamor was heard from afar.*

IV
1-2
*The Enemies of Judah and Benjamin*

*Now the enemies of Judah and Benjamin heard that the people of the exile were building a Sanctuary for* HASHEM, *God of Israel.* 2 *They approached Zerubabel and the heads of the families and said to*

*clamor of the people's weeping.* The sound of joyful shouting was not discerned because of the greater clamor of the weeping *(Rashi).* This interpretation is supported by the Talmud's observation (*Temurah* 15b) that the clamor of the weeping was louder than the sounds of rejoicing. From this the Talmud deduces that the elders who had beheld the First Sanctuary and therefore wept, outnumbered those who had not witnessed the First Temple and now rejoiced.

*Malbim* proposes another approach. Neither the sound of the weeping nor that of the rejoicing could be distinguished. He renders the translation: *The people could not distinguish the sound of the joyful shouting 'from' the clamor of the people's weeping* [see following comm.].

כִּי הָעָם מְרִיעִים תְּרוּעָה גְדוֹלָה וְהַקּוֹל נִשְׁמַע עַד־לְמֵרָחוֹק — *For the people raised a great shout — but the clamor was heard from afar.* The translation follows *Rashi. The shout* refers to the joy, while the *clamor* refers to the weeping.

*Metzudos* renders כִּי, *although,* rather than *for.* Although the rejoicers raised a great shout, the clamor of the weepers was heard from afar, and overpowered the sounds of rejoicing.

*Malbim,* differing with both *Rashi* and *Metzudos,* translates מְרִיעִים תְּרוּעָה, *sounded a trumpet blast,* as in וְהַעֲבַרְתָּ שׁוֹפַר תְּרוּעָה — *Proclaim* [*with*] *the shofar blast (Leviticus* 25:9). The people sounded a trumpet blast powerful enough to be heard from afar, which overshadowed the sounds of rejoicing and of weeping, so that neither could be discerned.

# IV

### ⌘ The Enemies of Judah and Benjamin

**1.** צָרֵי יְהוּדָה וּבִנְיָמִן — *The enemies of Judah and Benjamin. Rashi* identifies them as the people whom the Assyrian king Sennacherib had transplanted to the Land of Israel [185 years earlier] and settled in the province of Samaria. These are the people known in the Talmud as כּוּתִים, *Cuthites,* and in general literature as Samaritans.

[*Rashi's* comment is based on vs. 9-10, where they are characterized as the peoples whom Asenappar (Sennacherib) had exiled and settled in Samaria.]

*II Kings* 17:24-41 relates that the transplanted pagan peoples were attacked by lions because they did not keep *the law of the God of the Land,* i.e., Jewish law. Consequently they converted to Judaism, but continued their idol worship (vs. 20-41 there). The Talmud

ד נִבְנֶה עִמָּכֶם כִּי כָכֶם נִדְרוֹשׁ לֵאלֹהֵיכֶם
ג °ולא | אֲנַחְנוּ זֹבְחִים מִימֵי אֵסַר חַדֹּן מֶלֶךְ °וְלוֹ ק׳
ג אַשּׁוּר הַמַּעֲלֶה אֹתָנוּ פֹּה׃ וַיֹּאמֶר לָהֶם
זְרֻבָּבֶל וְיֵשׁוּעַ וּשְׁאָר רָאשֵׁי הָאָבוֹת
לְיִשְׂרָאֵל לֹא־לָכֶם וָלָנוּ לִבְנוֹת בַּיִת

refers to them as Cuthites (see *Kesubos* 29a), after the land of *Cutha* from which some of them originated, and records a Rabbinic dispute concerning the legitimacy of their conversion. One opinion is that the Cuthites were true proselytes. According to another opinion, however, they were merely 'proselytes of the lions,' whose conversion was an insincere response to the lions' attacks and therefore invalid. Accordingly, they were not really Jews[1] *(Sanhedrin* 85b).

**2.** נִבְנֶה עִמָּכֶם — *Let us build with you.* The offer to help was a ruse. Their true objective was to disrupt the reconstruction of the Temple *(Rashi).* Their intention was to infiltrate the inner councils of the Temple builders in order to discover their plans and frustrate them *(Metzudos).*

[The Scriptural basis for this view is the epithet *enemies of Judah and Benjamin,* used in the text to describe them at the very time that they made this 'friendly' overture to Zerubabel and the leaders. This indicates that although they offered to aid in the construction, they were, in reality, adversaries.]

The Rabbis have a similar appraisal of their motivation. The Talmud *(Arachin* 5b) states that they were rebuffed by the Jewish leaders (v. 3) because their purpose was to *hinder* the builders (v. 4) and eventually halt the work of reconstruction. In addition, *Sifri (Haazinu* 331) states that the passage, *I shall visit vengeance upon My enemies (Deut.* 32:4), refers to God's intention to punish the Cuthites (v. 1) of whom it is written: *Now the enemies of Judah and Benjamin heard that the people of the exile were building a Sanctuary* ... [Clearly *Sifri* feels that the enemies' offer of help was deserving of God's vengeance.]

*Shir HaShirim Rabbah* (5:1) also alludes to the enemies' negative intentions. On the verse there (5:5), *I arose to open for my Beloved,* it declares: I arose [to answer Cyrus' call to build a Temple for God], but the gentile nations did not respond similarly [i.e., their true intentions were destructive] *(Yefeh Kol, Maharzav).*

כִּי כָכֶם נִדְרוֹשׁ לֵאלֹהֵיכֶם וְלוֹ אֲנַחְנוּ זוֹבְחִים — *For like you, we seek your God, and we have sacrificed to Him.* The verse is read וְלוֹ, *to Him,* we have offered sacrifices, but written וְלֹא, *we have not offered sacrifices.* Both statements are true. We have offered sacrifices to Him [*Hashem*], *and have not* offered sacrifices to anyone else. The Samaritans claimed to worship *Hashem* exclusively *(Ibn Ezra).*

*Malbim* disagrees. Although they gave preeminence to the God of Israel, they also indulged in idolatry, as portrayed by *II Kings* 17:33, which describes the pagans whom Sennacherib had brought to Samaria: *They* [the heathens] *feared* HASHEM, *but they worshiped their gods.* They now wished

1. Both opinions agree that an insincere conversion [i.e., one in which there is no intent to observe the Torah's commandments] is not valid. The opinion which considers the Samaritans valid proselytes holds that they later became sincerely Torah observant and converted properly *(Tosafos* to *Yevamos* 24b and *Chulin* 3b).

IV
3

*them: Let us build with you, for like you, we seek your God, and we have sacrificed to Him since the days of Esar Haddon, king of Assyria, who brought us up to here.*

3 *Zerubabel, Jeshua, and the rest of the family heads of Israel replied to them: It is not for you and us to build the Temple of our God; but we [alone]*

to join with the Jewish people in the practice of this dual worship, hoping to entice them by stressing the favored status of the Jewish God with the statement *we have sacrificed to Him,* i.e., mainly to Him.

אֵסַר חַדֹּן — *Esar Haddon.* Esar Haddon was Sennacherib's son and successor, as related in *Isaiah* 37:38 — *While he prostrated himself in the Temple of his god Nisroch, his sons Adramelech and Sharezer smote him ... and his son Esar Haddon succeeded him on the throne (Rashi).*

הַמַּעֲלֶה אֹתָנוּ פֹּה — *Who brought us up to here. II Kings* (17:24) does not name the king of Assyria who brought the Samaritans to Israel. Verse 10 (below) states that the king who brought them to Samaria was Asenappar, identified by all the commentators as Sennacherib *(Rashi; Ralbag; Metzudos).* However, our verse seems to say that it was Esar Haddon who brought them.

*Metzudos* (to v. 10) explains that Sennacherib ordered the transfer which Esar Haddon then implemented.

**3.** לֹא-לָכֶם וָלָנוּ לִבְנוֹת בַּיִת לֵאלֹהֵינוּ — *It is not for you and us to build the Temple of our God.* Based on this passage, the Talmud *(Arachin* 5b, 6a) rules that contributions for the establishment of the Temple may not be accepted from non-Jewish sources (see comm. 1:6). According to R' Meir, this rule applies even to donations for Temple repairs. R' Yehudah disagrees, applying the restriction only to the original construction of the Temple, but permitting donations to be accepted from non-Jews for the upkeep of the Temple.

One explanation given for R' Yehudah's distinction is that the restriction against accepting contributions from gentiles is because gentiles offering to aid in the construction of the Temple are suspected of secretly intending to prevent its establishment, as in the case of the Cuthites *(Rashi).* Or, that the non-Jewish contributors might later claim rights to the Temple they had helped create *(Tosafos).*

Despite the injunction against accepting gentile help, Cyrus' assistance was instrumental in establishing the Second Temple. The exiles also brought gifts to the Temple of God contributed by their gentile neighbors (1:6). *Tosafos* justifies this by referring to the prophet *Isaiah* (ch. 44), who extolled Cyrus as the rebuilder of Jerusalem and the restorer of the Temple. Thus, the assistance rendered by Cyrus and those under his sovereignty could be accepted because it was the fulfillment of the stated will of Heaven *(comm.* ibid.; see *Nehemiah* 2:20)[1] [see comm. to 1:2].

1. This does not contradict the Talmud's assertion that the *Shechinah* did not reside in the Second Temple because it was built by the Persian kings Cyrus and Darius [see comm. to 1:2]. Isaiah's prophecy authorized Cyrus as the instrument of the Divine will, but only in the context of the *partial* redemption of the Jewish people, whereby they were found unworthy of resettling the land and rebuilding the Temple in freedom from Persian subjugation. Under these circumstances of limited redemption, God selected Cyrus to provide the support necessary for the reconstruction of the Temple. Such a Temple, however, was flawed in its sanctity, inasmuch as it was not built solely by Jews, and it did not merit Divine visitation.

ד ד־ז

לֵאלֹהֵינוּ כִּי אֲנַחְנוּ יַחַד נִבְנֶה לַיהוָה
אֱלֹהֵי יִשְׂרָאֵל כַּאֲשֶׁר צִוָּנוּ הַמֶּלֶךְ כּוֹרֶשׁ
ד מֶלֶךְ־פָּרָס: וַיְהִי עַם הָאָרֶץ מְרַפִּים יְדֵי עַם־
ה יְהוּדָה °ומבלהים אוֹתָם לִבְנוֹת: וְסֹכְרִים
עֲלֵיהֶם יוֹעֲצִים לְהָפֵר עֲצָתָם כָּל־יְמֵי
כּוֹרֶשׁ מֶלֶךְ פָּרַס וְעַד־מַלְכוּת דָּרְיָוֶשׁ
ו מֶלֶךְ־פָּרָס: וּבְמַלְכוּת אֲחַשְׁוֵרוֹשׁ בִּתְחִלַּת
מַלְכוּתוֹ כָּתְבוּ שִׂטְנָה עַל־יֹשְׁבֵי יְהוּדָה
ז וִירוּשָׁלִָם: וּבִימֵי

°וּמְבַהֲלִים ק׳

כִּי — *But.*

The translation follows *Rashi*. [The sense of the passage is we will not build with you *but* alone.]

יַחַד — [*alone*] ... *Together.*

The entire Jewish people, together, will build the Temple *(Ibn Ezra).*

נִבְנֶה לַה׳ — *Will build ... for* HASHEM.

We will build the Temple for *Hashem (Metzudos).*

אֱלֹהֵי יִשְׂרָאֵל — *God of Israel. Malbim* explains that the gentile nations are placed under the aegis of celestial intermediaries who operate by the dictates of the Divine will. Because of this system the early pagans developed the idolatrous practice of dual worship. They thought, erroneously, that the heavenly intermediaries possessed independent powers and should therefore be worshiped, whereas in reality they merely served as instruments of God's will. But the Israelites are favored with direct Providential guidance, without intermediaries. Thus they were free of one of the major causes of the false worship of associate gods which preoccupied the ancient peoples.[1] The Jewish leaders stressed, therefore, that the Jewish people would build the Temple for the God of Israel, Who alone directly supervises every turn in the course of Jewish destiny [see *Malbim, II Kings* 17:25-41].

See also *Taanis* 10a: Eretz Yisrael is watered (with rainfall) by the Holy One, Blessed is He, Himself, but the rest of the world through an intermediary.

כַּאֲשֶׁר צִוָּנוּ הַמֶּלֶךְ כּוֹרֶשׁ — *As King Cyrus ... has commanded us. Malbim* explains that the Samaritans claimed that all residents of the Holy Land had a right to share equally in the construction of the Temple dedicated to the worship of the *God of the Land* [see *II Kings* 17:26]. In response, the Jewish leaders cited Cyrus' proclamation wherein it was explicitly stated that the Temple would be rebuilt for the worship of God by the people of Israel — but not by the pagan inhabitants of the land. *Anyone among you of His entire people ... and let him build the Temple of* HASHEM, *God of Israel* (1:3).

### Disruption

**4.** וַיְהִי עַם הָאָרֶץ — *And the people of the land.* When the Samaritan people of the land — the enemies of Judah and

1. See *Deut.* 4:19, 20: *Lest you lift your eyes heavenward and behold the sun, the moon, the stars, and all the heavenly hosts. And you stray and bow to them and worship them — for* HASHEM *your God has apportioned them to all the nations ... but* HASHEM *took you and delivered you ... that you may be the nation of His heritage.* Cf. *Ramban's* remarks there.

**IV**
**4-6**

*Disruption*

*will build together for* H*ASHEM*, *God of Israel, as King*
*Cyrus the king of Persia has commanded us.* 4 *And*
*the people of the land hindered the people of Judah*
*and frightened them from building.* 5 *And they hired*
*advisors against them to disrupt their plans,*
*throughout the days of Cyrus, king of Persia, until*
*the reign of Darius, king of Persia.* 6 *And during the*
*reign of Ahasuerus, at the beginning of his reign,*
*they wrote a calumny against the inhabitants of*
*Judah and Jerusalem.*

Benjamin mentioned in v. 1 *(Rashi)* — were rebuffed, they began to disrupt the construction of the Temple *(Malbim).*

מְרַפִּים יְדֵי עַם־יְהוּדָה — *hindered* [lit. *weakened the hands of*] *the people of Judah.* [This idiom is the opposite of the expression חִזְּקוּ בִידֵיהֶם, *supported them,* found above (1:6).]

The hindrances caused the Jews to lose their enthusiasm for the rebuilding *(Malbim).*

וּמְבַהֲלִים אוֹתָם לִבְנוֹת — *And frightened them from building* [lit. *to build*]. The translation follows *Rashi*, who understands לִבְנוֹת as מִלִּבְנוֹת, *from building.*

**5.** וְסֹכְרִים — *And they hired.* The letters ס and שׂ are interchangeable. Thus סֹכְרִים is understood as שֹׂכְרִים, *hired (Rashi).*

יוֹעֲצִים לְהָפֵר עֲצָתָם — *Advisors ... to disrupt their plans.* The advisors were to counsel them on how to frustrate the Jewish plans for construction *(Rashi).* And they were to speak to the king and convince him to revoke the permission granted to the Jews *(Metzudos).*

כָּל־יְמֵי כּוֹרֶשׁ ... עַד מַלְכוּת דָּרְיָוֶשׁ — *Throughout the days of Cyrus ... until the reign of Darius.* They maintained their pressure and successfully halted the Temple construction throughout the reigns of Cyrus and his successor Ahasuerus, until the second year of Darius, who followed Ahasuerus on the throne *(Rashi).*

**6.** אֲחַשְׁוֵרוֹשׁ — *Ahasuerus.* He was Cyrus' successor and the husband of Queen Esther *(Rashi).*

כָּתְבוּ שִׂטְנָה — *They wrote a calumny.* שִׂטְנָה is from the word שָׂטָן, *Satan,* lit. *the Accuser (Ibn Ezra; Metzudos).* The purpose of this slanderous accusation was to halt the reconstruction of the Temple *(Rashi).*

*Yalkut Shimoni*, quoting *Seder Olam*, identifies the composers of the attacks as Haman's ten sons, who were later hanged at the time of the Jewish Purim victory [see *Esther* 9:6-10]. When Cyrus died and Ahasuerus succeeded him, the Temple work had already been halted through the intervention of the Samaritans (v. 24). Haman, who was soon elevated to an exalted position in Ahasuerus' court *(Esther* 3:1), took measures to prevent resumption of the Temple restoration. [*Targum Esther* 3:1 states that Haman had previously journeyed from Shushan to Jerusalem in order to disrupt the construction of the Temple.] His sons wrote to the provincial governors of the Holy Land, instructing them, in the name of the king, to thwart any attempt at construction *(Rashi* to *Esther* 9:10).

The Talmud *(Megillah* 11a) regards Ahasuerus himself as a co-conspirator in the slander, remarking: 'Ahasuerus was akin to Nebuchadnezzar ... [Nebuchadnezzar] destroyed [the Temple], and [Ahasuerus] sought to destroy [the Temple], as it is written: *And during the*

ד אַרְתַּחְשַׁשְׂתָּא כְּתַב בִּשְׁלָם מִתְרְדָת טָבְאֵל
ח וּשְׁאָר כְּנָוָתֹו עַל־אַרְתַּחְשַׁשְׂתְּא מֶלֶךְ פָּרָס
וּכְתָב הַנִּשְׁתְּוָן כָּתוּב אֲרָמִית וּמְתֻרְגָּם
אֲרָמִית: ח רְחוּם בְּעֵל־
טְעֵם וְשִׁמְשַׁי סָפְרָא כְּתַבוּ אִגְּרָה חֲדָה עַל־

*reign of Ahasuerus ... they wrote a calumny against the inhabitants of Judah and Jerusalem.' Rashi* (ibid.) explains that Ahasuerus was included among the accusers.

*Targum (Esther* 1:1) relates that the wicked queen Vashti persuaded Ahasuerus to halt the construction. Both suffered Divine retribution: Vashti was executed; Ahasuerus lost much of his empire and died prematurely.

**7.** אַרְתַּחְשַׁשְׂתָּא — *Artahshasta. Rashi* (citing *Rosh Hashanah* 3b) identifies him as Cyrus, king of Persia, who had originally issued the proclamation that sanctioned the reconstruction of the Temple (1:1-4). Artahshasta was a royal title of Persian monarchs *(Rosh Hashanah* 3b).[1].

Indeed, his true name, the Talmud asserts, was neither Cyrus nor Artahshasta, but Darius[2] [not to be confused with Darius the Mede, Cyrus' predecessor *(Daniel* 6:1), nor with Darius, son of Ahasuerus and Esther, who ascended the throne fourteen years after Cyrus' death and restored the Temple].

*Rashi* notes that the numerical values of Cyrus [כֹּרֶשׁ] and Darius [דָּרְיָוֶשׁ] are each 520. Because of his virtue, he was given the name *Koresh* [Cyrus], a derivative of the Hebrew word *kosher, virtuous.*

[According to *Rashi,* the events portrayed in vs. 7-24 — the letter to Artahshasta and his ensuing decree halting the construction of the Temple — took place *before* the slanderous attack of the reign of Ahasuerus described in verse 6, since Cyrus' rule preceded that of Ahasuerus. In this view, the chronological order of the events of our chapter is as follows: Verses 4 and 5 relate the general history of the incessant activities of the people of the land against the Jewish builders, from the days of Cyrus through the times of Ahasuerus and Darius. Verse 6 portrays the writing of the calumny during the reign of Ahasuerus (by the sons of Haman and Ahasuerus, who feared that the Temple construction might be resumed). Verses 7-24 return to the time of Cyrus, describing the original letter written by the people of the land to King Cyrus, and his resulting ban on the Temple restoration.]

However, *Ibn Ezra, Ralbag* and *R' Yeshayah MiTrani* think that the Artahshasta mentioned in this verse is not Cyrus, but Ahasuerus, whose name appears in v. 6, and that the calumny mentioned in v. 6 is elaborated upon in v. 7. It began with the letter written by Mithredath Tabeel to Artahshasta/-Ahasuerus, urging the retraction of permission to resume construction of the Temple.

[In *R' Yeshayah's* opinion, the order of events of our chapter is as follows: Verses 4 and 5 give the general record of the opposition of the people of the land to the building of the Temple during the days of Cyrus, Ahasuerus, and Darius. Verse 6 describes the writing of the calumny during the reign of Ahasue-

1. This name is spelled differently in different places in this book. In chapter 7, it appears with a *samech* — אַרְתַּחְשַׁסְתְּא. In our verse it is vowelized first with a *kametz* [תָּא] — and then without a *sheva* [תְא]. The commentators consider all of them to be variant spellings of the same royal title. The English transliteration follows the Hebrew in each case.

2. In classical times, and even occasionally in modern times, kings often had several names, some of which duplicated those of their fathers.

IV
7

7 *In the days of Artahshasta, Mithredath Tabeel and the rest of his companions wrote in peace to Artahshast, king of Persia. The text of the letter in Aramaic script and in the Aramaic language.*
8 *Rehum the secretary and Shimshai the scribe wrote*

rus. Verses 7-24 provide the details of this slander, beginning with Mithredath Tabeel's letter to Artahshasta/Ahasuerus, and ending with the king's reply supporting their opposition to the Jewish builders.]

כְּתַב — *Wrote.* The principal writer was Mithredath Tabeel. The others merely joined in his plot *(Metzudos).* [This may explain why the verb is in the singular.]

בִּשְׁלָם — *In peace.* They wrote a letter containing a peaceful message *(Rashi).*

[Apparently the meaning is that they presented their case as loyal subjects of the king, concerned only with the peace of the empire.]

*Malbim,* however, states that בִּשְׁלָם was the name of one of the persons who wrote the letter. His reading is: *Bishlam, Mithredath and Tabeel and the rest of their companions wrote to Artahshasta.*

מִתְרְדָת טָבְאֵל — *Mithredath Tabeel.* Mithredath Tabeel was the name of one of the enemies *(Rashi). R' Yeshayah MiTrani* is of the opinion that he was the satrap who ruled over the gentile residents of Samaria.

*Malbim* believes that Mithredath and Tabeel were two different people. This is the opinion of *Ralbag* as well.

עַל — *To* [lit. *on*]. The translation follows *Rashi,* who interprets עַל — lit. *on* — as אֶל, *to.*

וּכְתָב הַנִּשְׁתְּוָן — *The text of the letter.* This translation follows *Rashi* and *Ralbag,* who render הַנִּשְׁתְּוָן, *the letter.* Other commentators differ in their interpretation of this word.

*Ibn Ezra* suggests that נִשְׁתְּוָן is derived from שָׁוֶה, *equal.* He translates כְּתָב הַנִּשְׁתְּוָן, *balanced text,* meaning that both the characters and the language were Aramaic. He also offers another translation of נִשְׁתְּוָן — *seal.*

According to *Radak* and *Metzudos,* נִשְׁתְּוָן is translated as *lucid;* thus, the *lucid letter.* [The letter was clear and explicit — either in the unambiguous terms of its accusation, or in its clarity of expression, i.e., it being written in the Aramaic script and language.]

*Malbim* translates כְּתָב הַנִּשְׁתְּוָן as *the original text.* [נִשְׁתְּוָן, from the root שוה, *equal.* The original draft is the one to which the translation is compared to determine its accuracy.] Thus: *The original letter was written in Aramaic script and in the Aramaic language* [the native tongue of the Samaritans]. It was then translated into Persian by Rehum and Shimshai (v. 8).

According to a minority Talmudic opinion *(Sanhedrin* 21b, 22a), the translation of כְּתָב הַנִּשְׁתְּוָן is *the changed script,* and it refers to the new alphabet which came into use during the times of Ezra. The five books of Moses were originally written in the ancient Hebrew alphabet *(Kesav Ivri,* Hebrew script), with the stipulation that new alphabetic characters would be introduced at a later date. This stipulation is intimated by the Biblical phrase מִשְׁנֵה תּוֹרָה, homiletically interpreted as *the changed Torah (Deut.* 17:18), implying that the letters of the Torah would some day be changed. The change was introduced [by Divine revelation *(Rashi* to *Sanhedrin* 22a, *Yefeh Mareh, Yerushalmi Megillah* 1:7], during the times of Daniel, when the angel Gabriel wrote on King Belshazzar's wall a message intelligible only to Daniel.[1] The mysterious letters were in

1. The likeness of a human hand inscribed a mysterious message on the wall of Belshazzar's palace. Called upon to interpret the 'handwriting on the wall,' Daniel informed the king that it foretold his downfall. That night Belshazzar was murdered, and his kingdom fell to the Medes *(Daniel* 5).

ד
ט

ט יְרוּשְׁלֶם לְאַרְתַּחְשַׁשְׁתְּא מַלְכָּא כְּנֵמָא׃ אֱדַיִן
רְחוּם בְּעֵל־טְעֵם וְשִׁמְשַׁי סָפְרָא וּשְׁאָר
כְּנָוָתְהוֹן דִּינָיֵא וַאֲפַרְסַתְכָיֵא טַרְפְּלָיֵא
אֲפָרְסָיֵא °ארכוי בַבְלָיֵא שׁוּשַׁנְכָיֵא °דהוא

°אַרְכְּוָיֵא ק׳
°דֶּהָיֵא ק׳

the hitherto unknown *Kesav Ashuri,* Assyrian script,[1] so called because it was brought up from Assyria (*Sanhedrin* 22a) [that is, it became widely used by the Babylonian-Assyrian peoples among whom Daniel and his fellow Jews lived *(Yefeh Mareh)*]. Ezra introduced the new script into the Scriptures. This was the *changed Torah* alluded to in *Deuteronomy* 17:18.[2] The Samaritans now corresponded with the king in the *changed script* — the Assyrian script which had lately been adopted by the Jews.

Our verse specifies that the writing was done with Aramaic symbols — which seems to contradict the assertion that the Assyrian script was used. *Yefeh Mareh (Yerushalmi Megillah* 1:7) explains that the Arameans became absorbed into the Babylonian-Assyrian peoples. Thus, the Assyrian script and the Aramaic symbols were identical.

The Talmudic rendering of כְּתָב הַנִּשְׁתְּוָן as *the changed script* is a minority opinion, controverted by other Talmudic Sages. In their view, the Biblical alphabet was never changed. The term מִשְׁנֵה תּוֹרָה is not translated as *the changed Torah,* but the *doubled Torah.* The doubled Torah refers to the two Torah Scrolls which the king was required to have [see *Rambam (Hil. Melachim* 3:1)]. *R' Chananel (Sanhedrin* 22a) states that the latter view (denying that the Biblical alphabet was changed) is the prevailing one. [Since none of the commentaries to *Ezra* cited above in this passage make mention of the translation of כְּתָב הַנִּשְׁתְּוָן as *the changed script,* it is apparent that they, too, share *R' Chananel's* view that this represents a minority opinion.]

**8.** רְחוּם בְּעֵל־טְעֵם — *Rehum the secretary.* Rehum, a master of literary style, composed the letter *(Rashi; Metzudos).*

*Ibn Ezra* translates *counselor,* i.e. the one who advised the Samaritans how to proceed (see comm. to v. 5).

According to *Malbim,* however, Rehum and Shimshai were not Samaritans but translators in the service of the king.

וְשִׁמְשַׁי — *And Shimshai.* Shimshai was a son of Haman, the oppressor of the Jews *(Rashi).*

Later, as scribe to Ahasuerus, he sought to prevent the king from discovering how Mordecai had saved his life by reporting the plot against him *(Megillah* 16a, *Rashi* there). [See comm., v. 6.]

סָפְרָא — *The scribe.* Shimshai was the scribe who wrote the letter dictated to him by Rehum *(Rashi; Metzudos).*

1. The following illustration depicts both the Hebrew and the Assyrian alphabets:

2. *Ritva (Megillah* 2b) maintains that the change from the Hebrew script to the Assyrian Script did not apply to the words of the Torah revealed to Moses at Sinai, for the Ten Commandments and Moses' Torah Scrolls were written in the symbols that later came to be known as the Assyrian script. The 'changed Torah' refers only to the Torah scrolls written by the people for their own use. In those, the Hebrew script was used from the days of Moses until Ezra, when it was changed to the basic Torah alphabet originally presented to Moses at the Sinai revelation — the Assyrian script. See essay on this subject by R' Nosson Scherman in the appendix to ArtScroll's *Wisdom of the Alphabet.*

*a letter concerning Jerusalem to King Artahshasta, as we will state.* 9 *Then Rehum the secretary, Shimshai the scribe, and the rest of their companions: the Dinites, Apharsathechites, Tarpelites, Apharsites, Archevites, Babylonians, Shushanites, Dehaites and*

כְּתַבוּ אִגְּרָה חֲדָה — *Wrote a letter.* Verse 6 tells of an accusatory letter written by Mithredath Tabeel, while this verse seems to mention yet another letter written by Rehum and Shimshai. *Rashi* explains that Mithredath Tabeel did not actually execute the letter himself but instructed his fellow Samaritans, Rehum and Shimshai, to write it. Thus, verses 7 and 8 describe the same letter.

*R' Yeshayah MiTrani* disagrees, explaining that indeed Mithredath Tabeel wrote one letter, while Rehum and Shimshai collaborated on yet a second one.

עַל־יְרוּשְׁלֶם — *Concerning* [lit. *on*] *Jerusalem.* The letter concerned the construction of the Temple in Jerusalem *(Rashi).*

*Metzudos* retains the literal translation *upon Jerusalem.* They wrote a letter heaping slander *upon Jerusalem.*

*Malbim* proposes a novel explanation of the two letters. Mithredath composed the original letter in the Aramaic tongue (v. 7). Rehum and Shimshai were employed as the king's translators. When they rendered the letter into Persian to be presented to the king (see comm. to v. 7), they altered it to give the impression that the Jews were also rebelliously fortifying Jerusalem (v. 12).

כְּנֵמָא — *As we will state.* The actual text of the letter begins below in v. 11 with the words: *Your servants.* Scripture, though, first identifies all the parties to the letter (vs. 9-10) *(Rashi).*

*R' Yeshayah MiTrani* disagrees, rendering כְּנֵמָא, *as follows.* According to him, the text of the letter begins with the names listed in vs. 9 and 10. They are not merely a list of those who sent the accusation but are the opening words of the letter, wherein the correspondents introduced themselves by name to the king.

*Malbim* adds that it was normal protocol when a petition was presented to the king for the names of the king's translators to appear first, followed by a list of the petitioners. Thus the names of Rehum and Shimshai (who were the translators according to *Malbim)* are followed by Mithredath, Tabeel, and their companions. The letter was, in effect, signed at the top rather than the bottom.

9. דִּינָיֵא וַאֲפַרְסַתְכָיֵא — *The Dinites, Apharsathechites.* This passage lists the names of gentile people whom King Sennacherib had settled in Samaria. They all agreed to the correspondence with the king *(Rashi).*

*Malbim,* following his previously stated view, conjectures that the translators, Rehum and Shimshai, inserted the names of all of the gentile peoples dwelling in the Holy Land so that the king would be impressed by the universal objection to the restoration of Jerusalem, or that Mithredath actually gathered the signatures of the inhabitants of the Samaritan cities authorizing him to petition the king on their behalf.

אֲפָרְסָיֵא — *Apharsites.* These were Persians [אֲפְרַס being the Aramaic equivalent of the Hebrew פָּרַס] *(Rashi).*

According to *R' Yeshayah MiTrani,* they were natives of an area called Aphares.

אַרְכְּוָיֵא — *Archevites.* These were the inhabitants of Erech, which is mentioned in *Genesis* 10:10 *(Rashi).*

שׁוּשַׁנְכָיֵא — *Shushanites.* They came from Shushan, the capital city of the

י עֶלְמָיֵא׃ וּשְׁאָר אֻמַּיָּא דִּי הַגְלִי אָסְנַפַּר רַבָּא
וְיַקִּירָא וְהוֹתֵב הִמּוֹ בְּקִרְיָה דִּי שָׁמְרָיִן וּשְׁאָר
יא עֲבַר־נַהֲרָה וּכְעֶנֶת׃ דְּנָה
פַּרְשֶׁגֶן אִגַּרְתָּא דִּי שְׁלַחוּ עֲלוֹהִי עַל־
°עַבְדָךְ ק׳ אַרְתַּחְשַׁשְׂתְּא מַלְכָּא °עבדיך אֱנָשׁ עֲבַר־
יב נַהֲרָה וּכְעֶנֶת׃ יְדִיעַ
לֶהֱוֵא לְמַלְכָּא דִּי יְהוּדָיֵא דִּי סְלִקוּ מִן־
לְוָתָךְ עֲלֶינָא אֲתוֹ לִירוּשְׁלֶם קִרְיְתָא

Persian empire (*Rashi;* see *Esther* 1:2).

שׁוּשַׁנְכָיֵא דֶּהָיֵא עֵלְמָיֵא — *Shushanites, Dehaites and Elamites.* The translation follows *Rashi. Malbim,* however, renders this as *Shushanites who are also called Elamites,* since the city of Shushan was located in the province of Elam (see *Daniel* 8:2).

**10.** וּשְׁאָר אֻמַּיָּא — *And the rest of the nations.* They, too, agreed to the petition (*Rashi*).

אָסְנַפַּר — *Asenappar. Rashi,* based on the Talmud (*Sanhedrin* 94a), identifies Asenappar as the Assyrian king Sennacherib. *Metzudos* adds that Asenappar was the name by which he was known to the Persians. This is supported by the Rabbis (*Sanhedrin* 94a) who list Asenappar among the Scriptural names for Sennacherib. See *Yadayim* 4:4 and *Berachos* 28b.

Asenappar/Sennacherib's policy of bringing foreign peoples to the Holy Land was implemented by his son Esar Haddon. Hence the latter is referred to above (v. 2) as the king who brought them to Israel, since it was he who actually transported them (*Metzudos;* see comm. v. 2).

רַבָּא וְיַקִּירָא — *Great and venerated. Rashi* cites *Isaiah* 36:4: *Thus speaks the great king, King of Assyria.*

The Talmud (*Sanhedrin* 94a) remarks that this Scriptural expression of high esteem for Sennacherib/Asenappar was given in recognition of his deference towards the Holy Land. R' Yochanan said: Why did this evil man [Sennacherib] merit the title *great and venerated?*[1]? Because he did not demean the Land of Israel, as it is written (*II Kings* 18:32): *Until I* [Sennacherib] *shall come and transport you* [the Jewish people] *to a land such as yours.*

*Rashi* explains that the exile was described as to a land such as yours, but not as a land greater than yours.

וּשְׁאָר עֲבַר־נַהֲרָה — *With the rest of the Trans-River.* Israel was referred to by the Persians as the Trans-River territory. The Euphrates River separated Israel from Babylon. Thus, in relation to Babylon the Holy Land lay beyond the river, and those who settled there were known as the dwellers of Trans-River. The letter stated that the accusation was endorsed not only by those brought by Asenappar but by all the peoples of the Trans-River (*Rashi*).

1. This question of the Talmud tends to support *Rashi's* view (see comm. to v. 8) that the actual text of the letter does not begin until v. 11. Accordingly, the reference to Sennacherib/Asenappar as *great and venerated* is a Scriptural description of him. However, according to those commentaries which consider the text of the letter to begin in v. 9, this reference is a Samaritan description of him, not a Scriptural one. Yet, the point is still valid. There is no need for Scripture to quote this part of the letter and thereby accord such an honor to this evil man. Apparently, Scripture feels that he merited this honor.

*Elamites.* 10 *And the rest of the nations whom the great and venerated Asenappar had exiled and settled in the cities of Samaria; with the rest of the Trans-River and Che'eneth.*

*The Letter*

11 *This is the text of the letter which they dispatched to him, to King Artahshast: Your servants are the people of the Trans-River and Che'eneth.* 12 *Let the King be informed that the Jews who went up from you to us have arrived in*

וּכְעֶנֶת — *And Che'eneth.* Che'eneth was the name of yet another people *(Ibn Ezra)* who agreed to send the letter to the king *(Rashi). Metzudos* adds that Che'eneth was a large city centrally located among the gentile peoples of Samaria.

*Ralbag* renders this as: *Whom Asenappar ... had settled in the cities of Samaria, the rest of the Trans-River territories and Che'eneth.*

*Radak* and *R' Yeshayah MiTrani* contend that כְּעֶנֶת is derived from the word כְּעֵת, *at the time.* The time, or date, of the dispatch was recorded at this point in the letter. Scripture, however, does not record the date, stating merely וּכְעֶנֶת, *a date.*

### ◆§ The Letter

**11.** פַּרְשֶׁגֶן אִגַּרְתָּא — *The text of the letter.* The translation follows *Rashi,* who equates this word with פַּתְשֶׁגֶן *(Esther* 3:14). *Ibn Ezra,* however, translates: *The essence of the letter.*

אִגַּרְתָּא — *The letter.* [אִגַּרְתָּא may be singular or plural.]

According to *Rashi,* only *one* letter was sent by Mithredath Tabeel, Rehum and Shimshai [see comm., v. 8]. The translation reads: *This is the text of the letter.*

In *R' Yeshayah's MiTrani's* opinion, however, two letters were written to the king, one by Mithredath, and a second by Rehum and Shimshai [see comm., v. 8]. Accordingly, our verse reads: *This is the text of the letters,* i.e., the following passages provide the essential contents of both letters.

עַבְדָךְ — *Your servants are.* This is the opening phrase of the letter, introducing all of the gentile inhabitants of the Holy Land as the petitioners *(Rashi).*

According to *Malbim* the quotation of the letter actually began in v. 9 (see comm. there) with the listing of the signatories. However, the actual *text* of the letter begins in this verse. Therefore the phrase, *Your servants are the people of the Trans-River and Che'eneth,* is repeated.

אֱנָשׁ — *The people* [lit. *person*]. Although the word אֱנָשׁ is singular, it is used here as a collective noun *(R' Yeshayah MiTrani).* [Compare *Genesis* 32:6: וַיְהִי־לִי שׁוֹר וַחֲמוֹר, *I have acquired oxen* (lit. *an ox) and donkeys* (lit. *a donkey).*]

עֲבַר־נַהֲרָה וּכְעֶנֶת — *The Trans-River and Che'eneth.* This phrase includes [in short form *(Malbim)*] all the peoples listed above (vs. 9, 10) *(Rashi).*

**12.** מִן־לְוָתָךְ — *From you.* That is, the Jews whom you, as king of Persia, permitted to ascend to Jerusalem *(Rashi).*

This indicates that Artahshast, to whom the correspondence was addressed, is indeed Cyrus, the monarch who had granted permission for the Jews to ascend to Jerusalem (1:1-4). According to those commentators who identify Artahshast as Ahasuerus [see comm., v. 7], the interpretation of this passage is, *the Jews who went up from your country (Malbim).*

ד מָרָדְתָּא וּבְאִישְׁתָּא בָּנַיִן °ושורי אשכללו
יג וְאֻשַּׁיָּא יַחִיטוּ׃ כְּעַן יְדִיעַ לֶהֱוֵא לְמַלְכָּא דִּי
הֵן קִרְיְתָא דָךְ תִּתְבְּנֵא וְשׁוּרַיָּא יִשְׁתַּכְלְלוּן
מִנְדָּה־בְלוֹ וַהֲלָךְ לָא יִנְתְּנוּן וְאַפְּתֹם מַלְכִים

°וְשׁוּרַיָּא שַׁכְלִלוּ ק׳
יג

בָּנַיִן — *They are constructing. Malbim* proposes an ingenious explanation of the workings of the slanderous letter. His exposition answers the following questions:

— According to Persian law, a royal decree was irreversible [see *Esther* 8:8]. Thus Cyrus' proclamation granting permission to restore the Temple could not have been rescinded. How then could the king demand that the work on the Temple be stopped (v. 21)?

— How could the Jews be accused of rebellion (vs. 12-16), when they were engaged in nothing more seditious than the authorized reconstruction of their Temple?

— How did Mithredath and his accomplices dare to overtly misrepresent the Jewish activities in Jerusalem [and, according to *Malbim's* own interpretation of v. 8 (see above), how could Rehum and Shimshai falsify the translation of Mithredath's letter] when such lies could have been easily discovered and would have incurred the king's wrath?

As *Malbim* explains it, the plotters set out to devise a text which would at once falsely slander the Jews and yet permit its authors to exonerate themselves should the falsehood come to light. They settled on the Aramaic phraseology of our verse, which may be translated two ways, depending on the punctuation:

(a) [The Jews] *have arrived in Jerusalem,* [historically] *a rebellious, villainous city. They are constructing, have laid the foundations for the ramparts, and are linking the walls.* The latter half of the passage refers to the Temple. It describes truthfully the innocuous, authorized activity of restoring the Sanctuary in which the Jews were actually engaged.

(b) [The Jews] *have arrived in Jerusalem. A rebellious, villainous city they are constructing; they have laid the foundations for the ramparts, and are linking the walls.* This translation does not describe the restoration of the Temple, but the construction of the city of Jerusalem and the laying of foundations for its walls. Thus they informed the king that the Jews were busily reconstructing the city and fortifying its walls, activities which were illegal, unauthorized by Cyrus' proclamation, and which indicated Jewish insubordination and a growing threat to the king's dominion.

Rehum and Shimshai chose translation (b). They presented to Artahshast a petition claiming that the Jewish settlers had grossly overstepped the conditions set forth in Cyrus' proclamation; that they were, in fact, preparing a rebellion; that the reconstruction of the city of Jerusalem should be halted. Although the royal decree permitting the Temple restoration could not be rescinded, the abuse of its privileges for the purpose of revolution should cause the whole project to be suppressed.

At the same time the originators of the accusation — Mithredath and his accomplices — could argue, if necessary, that they had merely reported, in their native Aramaic, that the Jews were constructing their Temple, in accordance with translation (a). The Persian translators, they would say, had misunderstood, and had rendered into Persian an erroneous translation.

Thus the Samaritans were able to dispatch a slanderous letter, falsely accusing the Jews of treason, without fear of recrimination [see comm., v. 21].

שׁוּרַיָּא ... אֻשַּׁיָּא — *Ramparts ... walls.*

IV
13

*Jerusalem. They are constructing a rebellious and villainous city; they have laid the foundations for the ramparts, and are linking the walls.* 13 *Now let the King be informed that should this city be built and the ramparts be founded, then the levies, taxes and tithes will no longer be paid, and the royal duty will*

*Rashi* translates שׁוּרַיָּא as חוֹמוֹת, *[fortified] walls,* i.e. those surrounding a city. [See *Targum* to *Lev.* 25:29 who translates עִיר חוֹמָה as קַרְתָּא מַקְפָא שׁוּר, *a city surrounded by walls.*] אֻשַּׁיָּא is rendered by *Rashi* as כְּתָלִים, [house] *walls.* [See *Targum* to *Lev.* 14:37. See also *Joshua* 2:15.] [Apparently, the accusation was that a foundation had been laid for outer walls to surround the city and that even the walls of the city's houses were being linked to form, in effect, a second, inner wall.]

*Ibn Ezra,* however, followed by *Metzudos,* translates אֻשַּׁיָּא as *foundations.* See below.

שַׁכְלִלוּ — *They have laid the foundations.* The translation follows *Rashi. Metzudos,* however, translates *they wish to complete.*

וְאֻשַּׁיָּא יַחִיטוּ — *And are linking the walls. Rashi* comments that יַחִיטוּ, *stringing together* or *linking,* stems from the word חוּט, *string.*

*Ibn Ezra* suggests another translation: *and they have taken measurements.* [This too is based on the translation of יַחִיטוּ as *stringing.* Strings were the basic measuring devices.] They are measuring and leveling for the construction of a wall atop this foundation.

*Metzudos* translates אֻשַּׁיָּא, *foundations. They are linking the foundations* — they are reinforcing and adding to the foundations to create a complete, interlocked network.

**13.** וְשׁוּרַיָּא יִשְׁתַּכְלְלוּן — *And the ramparts be founded.* Since the accusation stated that the foundations had already been laid, *Rashi* interprets this phrase as: *Should well-founded walls surround the city. Metzudos,* who understood the previous statement to mean that they wish to complete the walls, renders this as *should the walls be completed.*

מִנְדָּה־בְלוֹ וַהֲלָךְ — *Levies, taxes and tithes.* These were various duties, including a personal tax *(Rashi).*

*R' Asher (Nedarim* 62b) is more explicit. מִנְדָּה, *levies,* was the property tax, levied upon landed estates; בְּלוֹ, *taxes,* the personal head tax paid by each individual; and הֲלָךְ, *tithes,* the animal tithe — one tenth of all livestock was given to the king.

According to *Ibn Ezra,* בְּלוֹ was a province tax, imposed collectively on the community. הֲלָךְ, from the Hebrew הלך, *to go* or *travel,* was the traveler's toll, exacted from those using the royal roads.

*R' Yeshayah MiTrani,* however, explains הֲלָךְ as the tribute paid to the king when he traveled to visit his subjects.

לָא יִנְתְּנוּן — *Will no longer be paid.*

*Midrash Rabbah (Genesis* 64:10) relates that a similar incident took place when the oppressive empire [i.e., the Roman Empire in the years after the destruction of the Second Temple — see *Tzemach Dovid* V. II year 3880, *Seder HaDoros* in *Seder Tanaim* letter *yud*] was considering granting the Jews permission to rebuild the Temple. The Samaritans warned that the Jews would refuse to pay the taxes, and the king replied that he was powerless to halt the Temple construction, since a royal decree could not be repealed. Thereupon, the Samaritans suggested that the king demand that the Temple site be changed, or its size altered — proposals that the Jews would certainly reject. This was done, with the desired results, and the reconstruction was suspended.

When the people learned that permission

ד

יד־יז

תְהַנְזִק׃ יד כְּעַן כָּל־קֳבֵל דִּי־מְלַח הֵיכְלָא
מְלַחְנָא וְעַרְוַת מַלְכָּא לָא־אֲרִיךְ לַנָא
לְמֶחֱזֵא עַל־דְּנָה שְׁלַחְנָא וְהוֹדַעְנָא לְמַלְכָּא׃
טו דִּי יְבַקַּר בִּסְפַר דָּכְרָנַיָּא דִּי אֲבָהָתָךְ
וּתְהַשְׁכַּח בִּסְפַר דָּכְרָנַיָּא וְתִנְדַּע דִּי קִרְיְתָא
דָךְ קִרְיָא מָרָדָא וּמְהַנְזְקַת מַלְכִין וּמְדִנָן
וְאֶשְׁתַּדּוּר עָבְדִין בְּגַוַּהּ מִן־יוֹמָת עָלְמָא עַל־
טז דְּנָה קִרְיְתָא דָךְ הָחָרְבַת׃ מְהוֹדְעִין אֲנַחְנָה
לְמַלְכָּא דִּי הֵן קִרְיְתָא דָךְ תִּתְבְּנֵא וְשׁוּרַיָּה
יִשְׁתַּכְלְלוּן לָקֳבֵל דְּנָה חֲלָק בַּעֲבַר נַהֲרָא לָא
יז אִיתַי לָךְ׃ פִּתְגָמָא שְׁלַח מַלְכָּא
עַל־רְחוּם בְּעֵל־טְעֵם וְשִׁמְשַׁי סָפְרָא וּשְׁאָר
כְּנָוָתְהוֹן דִּי יָתְבִין בְּשָׁמְרָיִן וּשְׁאָר עֲבַר־

to build the Temple had been withdrawn, they wept, and planned an insurrection against the king. The Rabbis [realizing the folly of such a move] dispatched R' Yehoshua ben Chananiah to calm the people. 'Once,' R' Yehoshua told them, 'a lion suffered from a bone lodged in its throat. It was extracted by a long-beaked bird, who then requested a reward. "It is sufficient," said the lion, "that you emerged from the lion's mouth unscathed." It is sufficient, concluded R' Yehoshua, that we emerged from the clutches of this nation unharmed [even without the "reward" of a restored Temple].'[1]

וְאַפְּתֹם מַלְכִים — *And the royal duty.* This is *Rashi's* translation. Others render *revenues (Metzudos), expenditures (Ibn Ezra),* or *treasury (R' Yeshayah MiTrani).*

**14.** מְלַח הֵיכְלָא מְלַחְנָא — *We are desirous of ruining the Temple.* [The verb מְלַחְנָא, from מְלַח, *salt,* can mean *to ruin* (as by sowing with salt), *to preserve* (as salt preserves food) or simply *to salt* food. All of these interpretations are used by the commentators.]

Our translation follows *Rashi,* who translates מְלַח, *ruin.* He understands the passage as an expression of intent. *Radak* and *R' Yeshayah MiTrani,* however, translate this phrase in the past tense: *We have ruined the Temple.* We Samaritans have already halted the Jewish attempts to reconstruct the Temple.

*Ralbag* translates מְלַח as *preserve* and הֵיכְלָא as *palace: Because the preservation of the palace is our concern* [lit. *because the salt of the palace we salt,* salt being an idiom for preservative]. We Samaritans are dedicated to preserving the interests of the palace.

*Malbim* also renders מְלַח, *salt,* but translates: *We season our food with the palace salt.* The sale of salt throughout

1. The Midrash (ibid.) compares this with the Biblical account of Abimelech, king of Gerar. After unjustly banishing Isaac from his domain, the king stated, *'We have done only good to you, for we discharged you peacefully' (Genesis 26:29).* The Midrash remarks that this was a flawed, unwholesome goodness, for Isaac gained nothing, but merely emerged unharmed from the clutches of the Gerarites *(Radak* and *Yefeh Toar).*

*be damaged.* 14 *Now, inasmuch as we are desirous of ruining the Temple — for it would be improper for us to witness the King's disgrace — therefore, we have dispatched and made known to the King* 15 *that the annals of your ancestors be examined and you shall discover in the annals and know that this city is a rebellious city, damaging to monarchs and states; insurrection has occurred in it since ancient times. This is why this city was destroyed.* 16 *We inform the King that if this city is built and its walls founded, then in consequence no part of the Trans-River will be yours.*

*The King's Reply*

17 *The king sent a message to Rehum the secretary, Shimshai the scribe, and the rest of their companions who dwelt in Samaria, the other Trans-Riverites,*

the empire was in the hands of the crown, and its sale provided a major source of income for the royal estate. [As *Malbim* points out, this was the custom in many European kingdoms as well.] By stating that they consumed the palace salt, the Samaritans were assuring the king that they were his loyal servants who contributed to his welfare.

וְעַרְוַת מַלְכָּא לָא־אֲרִיךְ לַנָא לְמֶחֱזֵא — *For it would be improper for us to witness the King's disgrace* [lit. *for the nakedness of the king it is not proper for us to witness*]. We petition the king not for personal gain, but purely out of concern for his interests *(Malbim).*

**15.** דִּי יְבַקַּר בִּסְפַר דָּכְרָנַיָּא דִּי אֲבָהָתָךְ — *That the annals of your ancestors be examined.* This verse is to be read together with the preceding one: *We have, therefore, dispatched to the King and informed* [*you,* so] *that the annals of your ancestors be examined,* i.e., the records kept by your royal ancestors *(Rashi).*

וּתְהַשְׁכַּח — *And you shall discover.* The King need not depend upon our personal testimony — our statements can be corroborated by a search of the national archives *(Malbim).*

וְאֶשְׁתַּדּוּר — *Insurrection.* The Jewish inhabitants of Jerusalem have always rebelled against gentile monarchs *(Rashi).*

*Radak* and *R' Yeshayah MiTrani* trace the source of אֶשְׁתַּדּוּר, *insurrection,* to the Aramaic שדר, *to send,* since rebels generally *send* requests for assistance to sympathetic powers.

*Malbim* translates אֶשְׁתַּדּוּר, *attempts,* from מִשְׁתַּדַּר, *to attempt (Daniel 6:15).* Jerusalem is a city wherein insurrection has always been attempted against the gentiles.

**16.** חֲלָק בַּעֲבַר נַהֲרָא לָא אִיתַי לָךְ — *No part of the Trans-River will be yours.* The Samaritans warned the king that the Jews would rebel and seize not only Israel but the entire area on that side of the Euphrates *(Rashi).*

*Ibn Ezra* offers another possible interpretation: Should the Jews be permitted to continue building, the gentile inhabitants of the land listed

ד
יח־כא

יח נַהֲרָה שְׁלָם וּכְעֶת׃ נִשְׁתְּוָנָא דִּי שְׁלַחְתּוּן
יט עֲלֶינָא מְפָרַשׁ קֱרִי קָדָמָי׃ וּמִנִּי שִׂים טְעֵם
וּבַקַּרוּ וְהַשְׁכַּחוּ דִּי קִרְיְתָא דָךְ מִן־יוֹמָת
עָלְמָא עַל־מַלְכִין מִתְנַשְּׂאָה וּמְרַד
כ וְאֶשְׁתַּדּוּר מִתְעֲבֶד־בַּהּ׃ וּמַלְכִין תַּקִּיפִין הֲווֹ
עַל־יְרוּשְׁלֶם וְשַׁלִּיטִין בְּכֹל עֲבַר נַהֲרָה
כא וּמִדָּה בְלוֹ וַהֲלָךְ מִתְיְהֵב לְהוֹן׃ כְּעַן שִׂימוּ
טְעֵם לְבַטָּלָא גֻּבְרַיָּא אִלֵּךְ וְקִרְיְתָא דָךְ לָא

above (vs. 9, 10) would rise up in revolt against the king.

*Malbim* notes that in this verse the emphasis is placed on the Samaritans' own role as informers — *We inform the King* — whereas the information in verse 13 is presented to the king anonymously — *Let the King be informed.* He explains that in the earlier verse the Samaritans wished to convey the impression that to anyone familiar with the Jerusalemites' rebellious nature, it was self-evident that the Jews would refuse to pay taxes. One had merely to place the intelligence before the king and he would draw the obvious conclusion. *Let the King be informed ... that the levies, taxes, and tithes will no longer be paid ...* However, it was not obvious that the Jewish revolt would enflame the populace and engulf the entire Trans-Euphrates territory; here the Samaritans emphasized their own capacity as analysts ... *We inform the King that ... no part of the Trans-River will be yours.*

### ◆§ The King's Reply

**17.** שְׁלָם וּכְעֶת — *Shelam and Che'eth. Shelam* and *Che'eth* were the names of cities. Che'eth was another name for the city of Che'eneth, mentioned above in vs. 10 and 11 *(Rashi).*

*Ibn Ezra,* followed by *Metzudos,* agrees that Che'eth is identical with Che'eneth, but renders שְׁלָם, *peace.* This was the king's salutation to the petitioners: *The king sent word to Rehum ... Shimshai ... and the other Trans-Riverites — Peace — and to the city of Che'eth.*

As in v. 10 above, *R' Yeshayah MiTrani* renders כְּעֶת as *the date,* which was recorded here in the letter.

According to *Malbim, Shelam* is translated *and so on.* The word is related to שָׁלֵם, *complete,* and means *et cetera,* or, *and so on.* The reference is to the names of the petitioners and their cities enumerated above in vs. 9 and 10, beginning with the Dinites and Apharsathechites and ending with the city of Che'eneth. Rather than list individually the names of all the petitioners, the king shortened the lengthy roster with the words *and so on until Che'eth,* meaning all of the names listed in vs. 9 and 10, until the final name, Che'eth or Che'eneth.

**18.** נִשְׁתְּוָנָא — *The letter.* נִשְׁתְּוָנָא is a shortened form of כְּתָב הַנִּשְׁתְּוָן in v. 7 *(Rashi).* See comm. there.

*Malbim,* however, takes נִשְׁתְּוָנָא to be the opposite of כְּתָב הַנִּשְׁתְּוָן. The former means *a copy* (since the king read only the translation, he only saw *a copy* of the original), whereas the letter [כְּתָב] is the original text from which the copy [נִשְׁתְּוָנָא] was made.

מְפָרַשׁ קֱרִי — *Explained and read.* The word *and* is understood *(Rashi).*

*Malbim,* however, renders this: *Has been read in translation before me.*

**19.** וּבַקַּרוּ — *And they investigated.* The royal archives were examined, as

*Shelam and Che'eth.* 18 *The letter which you dispatched to us has been explained and read before me.* 19 *A decree was issued by me and they investigated and discovered that since ancient times this city has risen above its monarchs, and rebellion and insurrection have occurred in it.* 20 *Mighty sovereigns reigned over Jerusalem, who ruled over the entire Trans-River, and levies, taxes and tithes were paid to them.* 21 *Now issue a decree halting these people; this city shall not be built until a decree is*

suggested by the petitioners *(Rashi).*

*Malbim* comments that the king did not believe that so many signatories would lie about something so easily ascertained. Nor did he suspect that his trusted translators, Rehum and Shimshai, would deliberately distort the translation by alleging that the Jews were restoring the city of Jerusalem, and not just the Temple [see comm., v. 12]. Thus, he did not order an investigation of their charges against the Jews, but merely examined the royal archives for evidence of the Jewish character, as suggested in the letter to the king (v. 15).

עַל־מַלְכִין מִתְנַשְּׂאָה — *Has risen above its monarchs.* The Jewish inhabitants of the city have historically risen above gentile monarchs *(Rashi)* — in rebellion *(R' Yeshaya MiTrani).*

**20.** וּמַלְכִין תַּקִּיפִין הֲווֹ עַל־יְרוּשְׁלֶם וְשַׁלִּיטִין בְּכֹל עֲבַר נַהֲרָה — *Mighty sovereigns reigned over Jerusalem, who ruled over the entire Trans-River.* [Mighty Jewish kings ruled in Jerusalem over the entire Trans-River region. Thus, the threat of a Jewish kingdom is not to be taken lightly.]

This refers to King Solomon, of whom it is written *(I Kings* 5:4): *For he ruled over the entire Trans-River*[1] *(Rashi).*

וּמִדָּה בְלוֹ וַהֲלָךְ מִתְיְהֵב לְהוֹן — *And levies, taxes and tithes were paid to them.* Tribute was paid by the non-Jewish subjects to the Jewish kings *(Rashi).*

The information that Jewish monarchs had subdued the Trans-River peoples and collected taxes from them convinced the king that the Samaritans were correct in their warning (v. 16). If the city were rebuilt, no part of the Trans-River would be his *(Malbim).*

**21.** כְּעַן שִׂימוּ טְעֵם — *Now issue a decree.* Proclaim the decree halting these Jewish people from building.[2]

*Malbim* maintains that the king did not desire to end the Temple construction, which had been sanctioned by irreversible royal decree (1:2-4). His sole intention was to bring the restoration of the city of Jerusalem to a halt, since this was an unauthorized activity [see comm., v. 12]. Accordingly, his instruction to the Samaritans to issue a

1. The Trans-River area mentioned in *I Kings* 5:4 refers to the Babylonian side of the Euphrates. Solomon was so powerful that even those on the far side of the river from Jerusalem were his vassals *(Targum, Radak* there). The Persian king, however, spoke only of the Jewish side of the river *(Rashi)* [since this was the area now under discussion].

2. The Rabbis teach that the activities of Abraham, Isaac, and Jacob narrated throughout the *Book of Genesis* represent symbolically the experiences of the Jewish people in later generations.

In accordance with this precept, *Ramban (Genesis* 26:1) observes that the restoration of the

ד
כב־כד

כב תִתְבְּנֵא עַד־מִנִּי טַעְמָא יִתְּשָׂם: וּזְהִירִין הֱווֹ
שָׁלוּ לְמֶעְבַּד עַל־דְּנָה לְמָה יִשְׂגֵּא חֲבָלָא
כג לְהַנְזָקַת מַלְכִין: אֱדַיִן מִן־דִּי
פַּרְשֶׁגֶן נִשְׁתְּוָנָא דִּי אַרְתַּחְשַׁשְׂתְּא מַלְכָּא
קֱרִי קֳדָם־רְחוּם וְשִׁמְשַׁי סָפְרָא וּכְנָוָתְהוֹן
אֲזַלוּ בִבְהִילוּ לִירוּשְׁלֶם עַל־יְהוּדָיֵא וּבַטִּלוּ
כד הִמּוֹ בְּאֶדְרָע וְחָיִל: בֵּאדַיִן
בְּטֵלַת עֲבִידַת בֵּית־אֱלָהָא דִּי בִּירוּשְׁלֶם
וַהֲוָת בָּטְלָא עַד שְׁנַת תַּרְתֵּין לְמַלְכוּת
דָּרְיָוֶשׁ מֶלֶךְ־פָּרָס:

ה
א

א °נְבִיָּא ק׳ וְהִתְנַבִּי חַגַּי °נביאה וּזְכַרְיָה בַר־עִדּוֹא

degree *halting these people* was meant only to restrain the Jews from the construction of the city, as explained in the following phrase — *this city shall not be built* — but not to cause the abandonment of the restoration of the Temple. Rehum and Shimshai, however, in their capacity as the translators of the king's Persian correspondence into Aramaic, deliberately misinterpreted the letter, representing the instructions to *halt these people* as an order to halt the construction of the Temple. The distortion was successful, and the work on the Temple was halted [see comm., v. 23].

עַד־מִנִּי טַעְמָא יִתְּשָׂם — *Until a decree is issued by me.* The building of the city shall cease until explicit instructions authorizing its resumption are issued by me *(Rashi).*

**22.** שָׁלוּ לְמֶעְבַּד — *To create a disruption* [lit. *negligence*]. Make sure to disrupt the activities of the Jews and cause the cessation of their building *(Rashi).*

*Metzudos,* however, translates, *take heed not to be negligent* in halting the Jewish activities.

לְהַנְזָקַת מַלְכִין — *To the injury of the kings. Metzudos* notes the usage of the plural *kings.* Artahshast warned that if the Jews gained power, they would destroy all the monarchs of the land.

### ◆§ The Temple Construction Halted

**23.** פַּרְשֶׁגֶן נִשְׁתְּוָנָא דִּי אַרְתַּחְשַׁשְׂתְּא מַלְכָּא — *The text of King Artahshast's letter.* The translation follows *Rashi.*

*Malbim,* as above, translates *the copy* of the king's letter. Rehum and Shimshai had translated the king's Persian correspondence into Aramaic, and falsely inserted into the the Aramaic copy of the letter the demand that

Babylonian exiles to the Land of Israel may be traced to the encounter of Isaac and Rebecca with Abimelech, king of the Philistines. Abimelech initially decreed that anyone disturbing the Patriarch and his wife should be put to death. But this attitude of reverence soon turned to envy and resentment, and Isaac and his family were banished. Later, however, Abimelech reversed himself, journeying to Beersheba to join Isaac in a covenant sealed with pledges of peace and benevolence *(Genesis* 26:1-3).

The fortunes of the exiles returning from Babylon followed an identical course. First, Cyrus invited the exiles to go up to Jerusalem to build the Temple, and he instructed the officials in the Holy Land to treat them favorably — just as Abimelech had decreed that no one disturb Isaac. But Cyrus soon heeded the advice of the enemies of Judah and Benjamin and halted the Temple construction, as foreshadowed by Abimelech's banishment of Isaac and Rebecca. Some years later, Cyrus' successor Darius reversed the policy of hostility towards the Jews,

IV 22-24

issued by me. 22 Take care to create a disruption of this activity, for why should destruction grow great to the injury of the kings?

*The Temple Construction Halted*

23 Then, when the text of King Artahshast's letter was read before Rehum, Shimshai the scribe, and their companions, they went in haste to Jerusalem to the Jews, and halted them with force and power. 24 Then the work of the Temple of God in Jerusalem was discontinued; the disruption lasting until the second year of the reign of Darius, king of Persia.

V 1

*Now the prophets Haggai the prophet and Zechariah the son of Iddo prophesied to the Jews*

the Temple construction be halted [see comm., v. 21]. It was on the basis of this falsified Aramaic copy of the king's letter — *the copy of King Artahshast's letter* — that Rehum and Shimshai and their cohorts now rushed to Jerusalem and halted construction of the Temple.

**24.** בֵּאדַיִן בְּטֵלַת עֲבִידַת — *Then the work ... was discontinued.*[1] For a period of eighteen years [see prologue].

עַד שְׁנַת תַּרְתֵּין לְמַלְכוּת דָּרְיָוֶשׁ — *Until the second year of the reign of Darius.* Artahshast/Cyrus was succeeded by Ahasuerus, husband of Esther. He was followed by their son Darius. The second year of Darius' rule, when the construction of the Temple was resumed, fell in the seventieth year after the destruction of the First Temple *(Rashi).* [See prologue and comm., v. 5.]

# V

**1.** וְהִתְנַבִּי חַגַּי נְבִיָּא וּזְכַרְיָה בַר־עִדּוֹא נְבִיַּאיָּא — *Now the prophets Haggai the prophet and Zechariah the son of Iddo prophesied. Now* refers to the second year of Darius mentioned in the concluding verse of the preceding chapter: *Until the second year of the reign of Darius (Rashi).* The books of *Haggai* (1:1) and *Zechariah* (1:1) state explicitly that the prophecies of Haggai and Zechariah exhorting the Jews to rebuild the Temple took place in the second year of Darius.

בַר־עִדּוֹא — *The son of Iddo.* Zechariah was actually Iddo's grandson *(Malbim),*

authorizing the completion of the Temple structure and even stipulating that prayers be offered there for his welfare — just as Abimelech had ultimately sought out Isaac requesting a final reconciliation.

1. *Ramban* (to *Leviticus* 26:42,43) finds an allusion to Cyrus' original proclamation permitting the reconstruction of the Temple (1:2-4) and its subsequent reversal, in the closing passages of *Leviticus* 26. Verse 42 of that chapter reads, *I shall remember my covenant with Jacob ... Isaac ... and Abraham, and I shall remember the land.* This is a pledge of redemption. Yet the following verse reads, *and the land shall be bereft of them* — referring to a period of desolation. The first verse, *Ramban* explains, alludes to the stirrings of redemption evidenced by Cyrus' proclamation and the resultant founding of the Second Temple (chs. 1-3). The next

נְבִיַּאיָּא עַל־יְהוּדָיֵא דִּי בִיהוּד וּבִירוּשְׁלֶם
ב בְּשֻׁם אֱלָהּ יִשְׂרָאֵל עֲלֵיהוֹן: בֵּאדַיִן קָמוּ
זְרֻבָּבֶל בַּר־שְׁאַלְתִּיאֵל וְיֵשׁוּעַ בַּר־יוֹצָדָק
וְשָׁרִיו לְמִבְנֵא בֵּית אֱלָהָא דִּי בִירוּשְׁלֶם
וְעִמְּהוֹן נְבִיַּאיָּה דִי־אֱלָהָא מְסַעֲדִין
לְהוֹן:
ג בֵּהּ־זִמְנָא אֲתָה עֲלֵיהוֹן תַּתְּנַי פַּחַת עֲבַר־
נַהֲרָה וּשְׁתַר בּוֹזְנַי וּכְנָוָתְהוֹן וְכֵן אָמְרִין
לְהֹם מַן־שָׂם לְכֹם טְעֵם בַּיְתָא דְנָה לִבְּנֵא

as is evident from *Zechariah* 1:1. As explained above (comm. to 3:2, s.v. *Zerubabel the son of Shealtiel),* Scripture occasionally identifies people by their grandfather's name rather than by their father's *(Radak).*[1]

עַל־יְהוּדָיֵא — *To the Jews.* The word עַל is used in the sense of אֶל, *to (Rashi).* [C.f. 4:11,17,18.]

בְּשֻׁם אֱלָהּ יִשְׂרָאֵל עֲלֵיהוֹן — *In the name of the God of Israel.* In the name of God as said to them — that is, to the prophets *(Rashi).*

The text does not reveal the prophetic message. *Rashi* explains that the prophets commanded the Jews, in the name of God, to begin completing the Temple even without Darius' sanction.

The actual text of this prophecy is recorded in *Haggai* ch. 1 *(Radak* there).

That this was the message is evident, in context, from the next verse which states that the Jewish leaders, aided by the prophets, commenced building the Temple — obviously, on the basis of the prophecy mentioned in v. 1 *(Metzudos).*

*R' Yeshayah MiTrani* notes that the prophets assured them that this time the Temple would be completed successfully *(Haggai* 1:8, *Zechariah* 1:16).

*Malbim* remarks that since seventy years had elapsed since the destruction of the First Temple, the time had now arrived for the completion of the Second Temple [see Prologue].

**2.** קָמוּ זְרֻבָּבֶל בַּר־שְׁאַלְתִּיאֵל וְיֵשׁוּעַ בַּר־יוֹצָדָק — *Zerubabel the son of Shealtiel and Jeshua the son of Jozadak ... arose.* Immediately upon hearing the prophecy, Zerubabel and Jeshua arose *(R' Yeshayah MiTrani)* [see comm. 2:2].

*Haggai* (1:12-14) relates that *Zerubabel the son of Shealtiel, Joshua the son of Jehozadak Kohen Gadol,* and *the rest of the people then heeded the voice of* HASHEM *their God and the words of the prophet Haggai ... and they came and labored in the Temple of* HASHEM.

**3.** תַּתְּנַי ... וּשְׁתַר בּוֹזְנַי וּכְנָוָתְהוֹן — *Tattenai ... Shethar Bozenai, and their companions. Rashi* comments that these were members of the party of the enemies of Judah and Benjamin [who had thwarted

verse hints at the repeal of Cyrus' decree and the years of desolation until the final completion of the Temple during the reign of Darius.

1. *Radak (Haggai* 1:1) speculates that this occurs when the grandfather was a more famous figure than the father. Indeed, in *Zechariah* 1:1 *Radak* quotes a tradition that Iddo had also been a prophet. See also *Rashi* to *Exodus* 18:1.

V
2-3

*that were in Judah and Jerusalem in the name of the God of Israel to them.* 2 *Then Zerubabel the son of Shaltiel and Jeshua the son of Jozadak arose and commenced building the Temple of God in Jerusalem, accompanied and assisted by the prophets of God.*

3 *At that time, Tattenai, satrap of the Trans-River, Shethar Bozenai, and their companions approached them and said as follows: 'Who issued a decree to you to construct this Temple and to found these*

the original attempts to rebuild the Temple; see ch. 4]. When they learned of the renewed construction they set out to disrupt it again by informing on them for this unauthorized activity.

*Rashi* is supported by *Shir HaShirim Rabbah* 5:7, which states that Tattenai, satrap of the Trans-River, and his cohorts attempted to disrupt the Jewish efforts to rebuild the Temple.[1] The source for this interpretation is, evidently, the phrase אֲתָה עֲלֵיהוֹן, lit., *they came upon them,* suggesting that the approach was antagonistic.

*Malbim,* however, suggests that Tattenai and the others, in their capacity as officers of the king, acted in good faith, questioning the legality of the project. According to *Malbim,* the verse tells us that, *at that time,* i.e. just at the time that the construction of the Temple was resumed, the satrap of the province happened to pass through Judah. This apparent coincidence was actually Divine Providence because the satrap, who was not an enemy of the Jews, allowed them to continue building until a ruling on the matter could be received from the king [see below]. Had the enemies of the Jews discovered that the construction had been resumed before the satrap had given his temporary approval, they would have rushed to Jerusalem and immediately halted all activity.

פַּחַת עֲבַר־נַהֲרָה — *Satrap of the Trans-River.* Tattenai and Shethar Bozenai were the king's representatives governing the Jewish cities of the Holy Land *(R' Yeshayah MiTrani).*

מַן־שָׂם לְכֹם טְעֵם — *Who issued a decree to you.* [The king had stated 18 years before that the building be discontinued *until a decree be issued by me* [authorizing the resumption of the project] (4:21). In accordance with that, the satrap asked, *Who issued a decree to*

1. *Pirkei d'R' Eliezer* (ch. 38) and *Yalkut Shimoni* (to *II Kings* 17) record that the Samaritans now threatened to attack the builders with an army of 180,000 men. In consequence of this, and of the Samaritans' role in the original disruption of the Temple construction (ch. 4) during the reign of Cyrus [they also plotted to murder Nehemiah — see *Nehemiah* 6:12], Ezra, Zerubabel, and Jeshua the *Kohen Gadol* condemned them to eternal excommunication from the Jewish people. The entire Jewish congregation gathered together at the Temple site, and, in the presence of 300 schoolchildren bearing 300 Torah scrolls, 300 *Kohanim* sounding the blasts of 300 shofars, and the chants of the Levites, they invoked the esoteric, ineffable Name of God, and pronounced the solemn oath of excommunication. From that time onward, Jews were forbidden to eat bread baked by a Samaritan (Cuthite) [see *Tosafos* to *Chulin* 13a], and no Samaritan could ever be accepted as a proselyte. They were banished from the World to Come [following the resurrection of the dead], and stripped of any portion, legacy, or memorial in Israel. The decree of excommunication was immediately ratified by the Jewish community of Babylon and by King Darius himself, who added his own imprecation against them [see 6:12].

ד וְאֻשַּׁרְנָא דְנָה לְשַׁכְלָלָה: אֱדַיִן כְּנֵמָא
אֲמַרְנָא לְהֹם מַן־אִנּוּן שְׁמָהָת גֻּבְרַיָּא דִּי־
ה דְנָה בִנְיָנָא בָּנַיִן: וְעֵין אֱלָהֲהֹם הֲוָת
עַל־שָׂבֵי יְהוּדָיֵא וְלָא־בַטִּלוּ הִמּוֹ עַד־טַעְמָא
לְדָרְיָוֶשׁ יְהָךְ וֶאֱדַיִן יְתִיבוּן נִשְׁתְּוָנָא עַל־
ו דְנָה: פַּרְשֶׁגֶן אִגַּרְתָּא דִּי־שְׁלַח
תַּתְּנַי | פַּחַת עֲבַר־נַהֲרָה וּשְׁתַר בּוֹזְנַי
וּכְנָוָתֵהּ אֲפַרְסְכָיֵא דִּי בַּעֲבַר נַהֲרָה עַל־
ז דָּרְיָוֶשׁ מַלְכָּא: פִּתְגָמָא שְׁלַחוּ עֲלוֹהִי וְכִדְנָה
כְּתִיב בְּגַוֵּהּ לְדָרְיָוֶשׁ מַלְכָּא שְׁלָמָא כֹלָּא:
ח יְדִיעַ | לֶהֱוֵא לְמַלְכָּא דִּי־אֲזַלְנָא לִיהוּד
מְדִינְתָּא לְבֵית אֱלָהָא רַבָּא וְהוּא מִתְבְּנֵא

*you* [authorizing the resumption of work]?

וְאֻשַּׁרְנָא דְנָה לְשַׁכְלָלָה — *And to found these walls.* This is *Rashi's* translation.[1]

*Metzudos* translates לְשַׁכְלָלָה, *to complete:* Who authorized you *to complete these walls?*

**4.** אֱדַיִן כְּנֵמָא אֲמַרְנָא לְהֹם מַן־אִנּוּן שְׁמָהָת גֻּבְרַיָּא דִּי־דְנָה בִנְיָנָא בָּנַיִן — *They then said the following to them: 'What are the names of the persons constructing this building?'* The translation follows *Rashi,* who translates אֲמַרְנָא as *they said.*

According to *R' Yeshayah MiTrani,* however, the word אֲמַרְנָא is translated, *we said.* The passage does not describe the question now put to the Jews, but the Jewish reply to the question of the preceding passage. Having been asked: *Who authorized you to build this Temple?* the verse continues: *We then said to them what the names of the persons constructing this building are.* I.e., in reply to their question we told them the names of the people responsible for the resumption of the construction of the Temple — Zerubabel, Jeshua, and the elders.

*Malbim* adds that they emphasized Zerubabel's name because he was the king's appointee. [See *Haggai* 2:2 and comm. to 1:8 above, s.v. *Sheshbazzar.*] Tattenai then conferred with the elders who explained to him their justification for the rebuilding of the Temple. Their arguments are contained in Tattenai's letter to the king (vs. 11-17).

*Metzudos* also understands this verse as the Jewish reply. The response has two parts: (1) *We said to them as will be stated,* referring to the justification for the building of the Temple recorded below in vs. 11-16. To avoid repetition, the phrase כְּנֵמָא, *as will be stated,* is used, meaning that the Jews now responded as recorded below in the letter to the king. (2) *The names of the persons constructing this building* refers to a second reply. We also told them the names of those responsible for resuming the construction.

### ◆§ Providence

**5.** וְעֵין אֱלָהֲהֹם הֲוָת עַל־שָׂבֵי יְהוּדָיֵא — *But*

1. *Rashi* equates אֻשַּׁרְנָא with אֻשַּׁיָּא (above 4:12). The walls being founded were the stone walls of the Temple, not the fortified walls of the city.

*Providence*

*walls?' 4 They then said the following to them: 'What are the names of the persons constructing this building?' 5 But Divine Providence shielded the Jewish elders, and they did not disrupt them until the matter could be brought before Darius, whereupon they would write a reply concerning it.*

*The Letter to the King*

*6 [This is] the text of the letter sent to King Darius by Tattenai, satrap of the Trans-River, Shethar Bozenai and his companions, the Apharsechites of the Trans-River. 7 [This is] the message which they sent to him, wherein the following was written: to King Darius, all peace. 8 Let the king be informed that we have visited the province of Judah, at the Temple of the great God; it is being built of marble,*

*Divine Providence shielded* [lit. *the eye of their God was upon*] *the Jewish elders.*

וְלָא־בַטִּלוּ הִמּוֹ — *And they did not disrupt them.* The enemies did not forcibly disrupt the construction but waited ... *(Rashi).*

עַד־טַעְמָא לְדָרְיָוֶשׁ יְהָךְ — *Until the matter could be brought before Darius.* The elders persuaded the enemies to refrain from disrupting the Temple work until the matter could be brought before the king for his decision *(Rashi).*

וֶאֱדַיִן יְתִיבוּן נִשְׁתְּוָנָא עַל־דְּנָה — *Whereupon they would write a reply concerning it.* The subject of this phrase is ambiguous. *Rashi* understands *they* to refer to the Jewish elders. When the king's reply would be received, *they* [the Jewish elders] would write a reply to it, presenting their arguments to him.

*Metzudos* understands the subject of this phrase to be the king and his counselors. The work would be allowed to proceed *until ... their* [the royal court's] *reply was received.*

*Malbim* has it refer to Tattenai and his associates: *Whereupon they would deliver the copy* [of the letter] *concerning this.* Tattenai and his associates would translate the king's Persian reply and deliver an Aramaic copy to the Jews.

### ◆§ The Letter to the King

**6.** וּכְנָוָתֵהּ אֲפַרְסְכָיֵא — *And his companions, the Apharsechites.* The Apharsechites, one of the peoples of the Trans-River [see above 4:9], were supporters of Shethar Bozenai *(Rashi).*

According to *Malbim,* the text of our verse was written on the outside of the letter, and its purpose was to identify the authors of the correspondence: *The text of the letter was sent to King Darius by Tattenai, satrap of the Trans-River, Shethar Bozenai and his companions, the Apharsechites of the Trans-River.*

**7.** פִּתְגָמָא שְׁלַחוּ עֲלוֹהִי וְכִדְנָה כְּתִיב בְּגַוֵּהּ — *[This is] the message which they sent to him, wherein the following was written.* The translation follows *Metzudos. Malbim,* however, translates: *They sent to him for a statement,* meaning that the letter was neither a request for the king's favor nor a complaint against other citizens; it was simply an inquiry to ascertain the king's ruling concerning the construction of the Temple. Thus the letter was described as a request for the king's *statement* of reply.

לְדָרְיָוֶשׁ מַלְכָּא שְׁלָמָא כֹלָּא — *To King Darius, all peace. Rashi* explains this as

אֶבֶן גְּלָל וְאָע מִתְּשָׂם בְּכֻתְלַיָּא וַעֲבִידְתָּא דָךְ
ט אָסְפַּרְנָא מִתְעַבְדָא וּמַצְלַח בְּיֶדְהֹם׃ אֱדַיִן
שְׁאֵלְנָא לְשָׂבַיָּא אִלֵּךְ כְּנֵמָא אֲמַרְנָא לְּהֹם
מַן־שָׂם לְכֹם טְעֵם בַּיְתָא דְנָה לְמִבְנְיָה
י וְאֻשַּׁרְנָא דְנָה לְשַׁכְלָלָה׃ וְאַף שְׁמָהָתְהֹם
שְׁאֵלְנָא לְהֹם לְהוֹדָעוּתָךְ דִּי נִכְתֻּב שֻׁם־
יא גֻּבְרַיָּא דִּי בְרָאשֵׁיהֹם׃ וּכְנֵמָא פִתְגָמָא
הֲתִיבוּנָא לְמֵמַר אֲנַחְנָא הִמּוֹ עַבְדוֹהִי דִי־
אֱלָהּ שְׁמַיָּא וְאַרְעָא וּבָנַיִן בַּיְתָא דִּי־הֲוָא
בְנֵה מִקַּדְמַת דְּנָה שְׁנִין שַׂגִּיאָן וּמֶלֶךְ
יב לְיִשְׂרָאֵל רַב בְּנָהִי וְשַׁכְלְלֵהּ׃ לָהֵן מִן־דִּי
הַרְגִּזוּ אֲבָהֳתַנָא לֶאֱלָהּ שְׁמַיָּא יַהַב הִמּוֹ בְּיַד

a salutation to the king — all peace be to him. *Malbim,* however, interprets the phrase as an introductory description of the contents of the letter. *All is peaceful,* i.e. this letter contains no accusations or reports of any danger to the empire.

[As *Malbim* explains below, Tattenai emphasized that the construction of the Temple did not pose a threat to the Persians. He merely wished to confirm the Jewish assertion that their action was authorized by royal edict. This is consistent with *Malbim's* explanation that Tattenai was not an enemy of the Jews. See v. 4.]

**8.** אֶבֶן גְּלָל — *Marble.* The translation follows *R' Yeshayah MiTrani* and *Metzudos.*

*Midrash Rabbah* [to *Shir HaShirim* 5:7; see *Yefeh Kol*] states that the word גְּלָל alludes to the relatively small size of the building stones of the Second Temple compared to those of the first Temple. אֶבֶן גְּלָל is translated *rolling stones.* The stones were small and could have been rolled with relative ease. This is in contrast with the massive stones, measuring eight and ten cubits in length, which were used in the First Temple.

*Ibn Ezra* also translates *rolling stones,* but sees the phrase as an indication of the heaviness of the stones, for they could only be rolled, not lifted.

וְאָע מִתְּשָׂם בְּכֻתְלַיָּא — *The walls reinforced with wood* [lit. *wood has been placed in the walls*]. The translation follows *Rashi,* who explains that the purpose of the wood was to strengthen the walls. *Ibn Ezra* agrees, adding that cedar wood, which does not easily rot, was used to reinforce the walls.

*Malbim* suggests that the wood was mentioned to win favor for the Jews. Wooden walls may be easily destroyed by fire [see comm. 6:4]. Thus the king was assured that the Jews were not constructing an impregnable fortress.

וַעֲבִידְתָּא דָךְ אָסְפַּרְנָא מִתְעַבְדָא וּמַצְלַח בְּיֶדְהֹם — *This work has proceeded rapidly and successfully.* [The work done so far has proceeded rapidly and successfully.]

*Malbim* interprets these remarks, too, as advantageous to the Jews. Since the work has proceeded rapidly and successfully, it is evident that none of the neighboring peoples has offered resistance. Thus, the king was reassured that the Jews were not planning a rebellion, for such a plot would

*the walls reinforced with wood. This work has proceeded rapidly and successfully.*
9 *Then we questioned these elders as follows: 'Who issued to you a decree to construct this Temple and lay the foundation for these walls?'*
10 *We also asked them for their names, in order to inform you — so that we might record the names of their leaders.*
11 *They replied to us as follows: 'We are the servants of the God of heaven and earth, and we are reconstructing a Temple built many years ago — a great king of Israel built and founded it.*
12 *But now, because our ancestors incurred the wrath of the God of heaven,*

certainly have aroused opposition among the neighboring peoples loyal to the king.

**9.** אֱדַיִן — *Then.* When we first saw the building *(Rashi).*

וְאֻשַּׁרְנָא דְנָה לְשַׁכְלָלָה — *And lay the foundation for these walls.* This is *Rashi's* translation. *Metzudos* renders, *to complete these walls.*

**10.** שְׁמָהָתְהֹם — *Their names.* I.e., the names of their leaders who had advised them to build *(Rashi),* as explained in the last phrase of this verse *(Metzudos).*

דִּי נִכְתֻּב שֻׁם־גֻּבְרַיָּא דִּי בְרָאשֵׁיהֹם — *So that we might record the names of their leaders.* Here, again, *Malbim* suggests that the letter was helpful to the Jewish cause. The leader of the Jews — Zerubabel — was the king's appointee [see *Malbim's* comm. to v. 4 above]. Thus, the mention of his name would tend to lend legitimacy to the Jewish claim that the construction was sanctioned by the king.

**11.** וּכְנֵמָא פִתְגָמָא הֲתִיבוּנָא לְמֵמַר — *They replied to us as follows:* [lit. *as we will state the matter*]. This is *Rashi's* translation. *R' Yeshayah MiTrani,* however, renders: *When we said this thing, they replied as follows;* i.e., when we made the inquiries mentioned in vs. 9-10 they replied the following.

אֲנַחְנָא הִמּוֹ עַבְדוֹהִי דִי־אֱלָהּ שְׁמַיָּא וְאַרְעָא ... וּבָנַיִן — *We are the servants of the God of heaven and earth and we are reconstructing ...* And [therefore] we are reconstructing His Temple *(Metzudos).*

בַּיְתָא דִּי־הֲוָא בְנֵה מִקַּדְמַת דְּנָה שְׁנִין שַׂגִּיאָן וּמֶלֶךְ לְיִשְׂרָאֵל רַב בְּנָהִי וְשַׁכְלְלֵהּ — *A Temple built many years ago — a great king of Israel built and founded it.* The king was Solomon *(Rashi,* see *I Kings* 5-8). Thus, the ancient origin of the Temple and the greatness of its founder justify its reconstruction *(Malbim).*

**12.** לָהֵן — *But now.* The translation follows *Rashi. Metzudos* translates *only.*

מִן־דִּי הַרְגִּזוּ אֲבָהָתַנָא לֶאֱלָהּ שְׁמַיָּא ... וּבַיְתָה דְנָה סַתְרֵהּ וְעַמָּה הַגְלִי לְבָבֶל — *Because our ancestors incurred the wrath of the God of heaven ...* [*Nebuchadnezzar*] *destroyed this Temple and exiled the people to Babylon.* The Temple was destroyed because of the sins of our ancestors and these have been expiated through the suffering of the exile. Thus, the time for reconstruction has arrived *(Malbim).*

נְבוּכַדְנֶצַּר מֶלֶךְ־בָּבֶל °כסדיא וּבַיְתָה דְנָה °כַּסְדָּאָה ק׳
יג סַתְרֵהּ וְעַמָּה הַגְלִי לְבָבֶל׃ בְּרַם
בִּשְׁנַת חֲדָה לְכוֹרֶשׁ מַלְכָּא דִּי בָבֶל כּוֹרֶשׁ
מַלְכָּא שָׂם טְעֵם בֵּית־אֱלָהָא דְנָה לִבְּנֵא׃
יד וְאַף מָאנַיָּא דִי־בֵית־אֱלָהָא דִּי דַהֲבָה
וְכַסְפָּא דִּי נְבוּכַדְנֶצַּר הַנְפֵּק מִן־הֵיכְלָא דִּי
בִירוּשְׁלֶם וְהֵיבֵל הִמּוֹ לְהֵיכְלָא דִּי בָבֶל
הַנְפֵּק הִמּוֹ כּוֹרֶשׁ מַלְכָּא מִן־הֵיכְלָא דִּי בָבֶל
וִיהִיבוּ לְשֵׁשְׁבַּצַּר שְׁמֵהּ דִּי פֶחָה שָׂמֵהּ׃
טו וַאֲמַר־לֵהּ | °אלה מָאנַיָּא שֵׂא אֱזֶל־אֲחֵת °אֵל ק׳
הִמּוֹ בְּהֵיכְלָא דִּי בִירוּשְׁלֶם וּבֵית אֱלָהָא
טז יִתְבְּנֵא עַל־אַתְרֵהּ׃ אֱדַיִן שֵׁשְׁבַּצַּר
דֵּךְ אֲתָא יְהַב אֻשַּׁיָּא דִּי־בֵית אֱלָהָא דִּי

**13.** לְכוֹרֶשׁ מַלְכָּא דִּי בָבֶל — *Cyrus, king of Babylon.* [Although Cyrus was actually king of Persia (1:1), he ruled over the Babylonian empire conquered by his predecessor, Darius the Mede (see *Daniel* 6:1, 29).]

[This verse may indicate that Babylon was not considered merely a conquered province of the Persian empire but that the king of Persia — Cyrus — ruled as king of Babylon as well. This is in keeping with *Daniel* 6:1 which states: *And Darius the Mede received the kingship* (of Babylon) ...]

כּוֹרֶשׁ מַלְכָּא שָׂם טְעֵם — *King Cyrus decreed.* The present reconstruction was authorized by King Cyrus' decree [see in ch. 1], the existence of which had been forgotten in the interim *(Malbim).*

**14.** לְהֵיכְלָא דִּי בָבֶל — *To the temple in Babylon.* To Nebuchadnezzar's pagan temple in Babylon *(Rashi).*

וִיהִיבוּ — *And gave.* The fact that the Jews were now in possession of these vessels attested to the truth of their claim to Cyrus' authorization *(Malbim).*

לְשֵׁשְׁבַּצַּר — *To Sheshbazzar.* According to *Rashi,* Sheshbazzar was another name for Daniel; according to *Ralbag, Ibn Ezra* and *Metzudos,* he was Zerubabel [see comm. 1:8].

דִּי פֶחָה שָׂמֵהּ — *Whom he appointed satrap. Minchas Shai* notes that many old texts have the last word of this verse as שָׂמֵהּ (with a *sin)* but that *Rashi's* reading seems to have been שְׁמֵהּ (with a *shin).*

The translation follows *Ralbag* and *Metzudos* who follow the standard reading שָׂמֵהּ. Cyrus, at one point, made Sheshbazzar the satrap of Judah, as related in 1:8.

*Rashi,* following his reading, explains that Sheshbazzar was given the name *Pehah* upon his rise to leadership, from the word פֶּחָה [*pahah*], *satrap.*

Sheshbazzar's appointment by the king was stressed so that the construction would be considered as occurring under the king's auspices *(Malbim).*

**15.** וַאֲמַר־לֵהּ — *And he said to him.*

*He delivered them to Nebudchadnezzar the king of Babylon, the Chaldean who destroyed this Temple and exiled the people to Babylon.*

*13 However, in the first year of Cyrus, king of Babylon, King Cyrus decreed that this Temple of God be reconstructed. 14 In addition, the gold and silver vessels of the Temple of God — which Nebuchadnezzar had removed from the Sanctuary in Jerusalem and brought with him to the temple in Babylon — King Cyrus removed them from the temple in Babylon and gave to the one named Sheshbazzar, whom he appointed satrap. 15 And he said to him: "Take these vessels and go and bring them to the Sanctuary in Jerusalem, and let the Temple of God be built on its place."*

*16 This Sheshbazzar then proceeded to set in place*

Cyrus said to Sheshbazzar *(Rashi).*

אֲחֵת הִמּוֹ — *Bring them.* The translation follows *Rashi.*

*Ibn Ezra* and *Metzudos* render אֲחֵת, *place: place them* in the Sanctuary.

עַל־אַתְרֵהּ — *On its place.* On its original site [where the First Temple stood] *(Metzudos).*

16. שֵׁשְׁבַּצַּר ... אֲתָא — *Sheshbazzar ... proceeded.*

This passage indicates that Sheshbazzar led the Jewish laborers in the laying of the Temple foundation. The prophet Zechariah identifies the leader who did this as Zerubabel: *The hands of Zerubabel have founded this Temple (Zechariah* 4:9). It seems, then, that Sheshbazzar and Zerubabel were the same person (see comm. 1:8).

*Yalkut Shimoni,* however, identifies Sheshbazzar as the prophet Daniel, of whom it is stated in the Scripture that he *arose and performed the work of the king (Daniel* 8:27). In recognition of Daniel's zeal in performing this work, he was rewarded with the opportunity to establish the Temple. God said to him, 'You have served zealously. In the past you guarded the gateway reserved for mortals. As it is written, *and Daniel was at the royal gate* [*Daniel* 2:49]. You may now absorb yourself with the construction of the Temple.'

Daniel was instructed not to disclose the future occurrences which he had foreseen in his prophetic vision. Although deeply shocked by the catastrophic events he had witnessed, he exercised the utmost self-discipline in concealing his inner turmoil, and rose to perform the work of the king with the outer appearance of serenity *(Daniel* 8:26,27; see ArtScroll *Daniel).* Because of his great zeal in exercising self-restraint, he was elevated from guardianship of mortal kings to the service of God.

יְהַב אֻשַּׁיָּא — *To set in place the walls.* The translation follows *Rashi. Metzudos* [following his translation of 4:12] has our phrase refer to the setting of the foundation for the walls. [The walls themselves were not yet built, as stated at the end of this verse.]

*R' Yeshayah MiTrani* translates יְהַב אֻשַּׁיָּא, *showed the walls* [to us]. Tattenai, in his letter to the king, mentioned that

ה בִּירוּשְׁלֶם וּמִן־אֱדַיִן וְעַד־כְּעַן מִתְבְּנֵא וְלָא
יז שְׁלִם׃ וּכְעַן הֵן עַל־מַלְכָּא טָב יִתְבַּקַּר בְּבֵית
גִּנְזַיָּא דִּי־מַלְכָּא תַמָּה דִּי בְּבָבֶל הֵן אִיתַי דִּי־
מִן־כּוֹרֶשׁ מַלְכָּא שִׂים טְעֵם לְמִבְנֵא בֵּית־
אֱלָהָא דֵךְ בִּירוּשְׁלֶם וּרְעוּת מַלְכָּא עַל־דְּנָה
ו א יִשְׁלַח עֲלֶינָא׃ בֵּאדַיִן
א־ג דָּרְיָוֶשׁ מַלְכָּא שָׂם טְעֵם וּבַקַּרוּ | בְּבֵית
סִפְרַיָּא דִּי גִנְזַיָּא מְהַחֲתִין תַּמָּה בְּבָבֶל׃
ב וְהִשְׁתְּכַח בְּאַחְמְתָא בְּבִירְתָא דִּי בְּמָדַי
מְדִינְתָּא מְגִלָּה חֲדָה וְכֵן־כְּתִיב בְּגַוַּהּ
ג דִּכְרוֹנָה׃ בִּשְׁנַת חֲדָה
לְכוֹרֶשׁ מַלְכָּא כּוֹרֶשׁ מַלְכָּא שָׂם טְעֵם
בֵּית־אֱלָהָא בִירוּשְׁלֶם בַּיְתָא יִתְבְּנֵא
אֲתַר דִּי־דָבְחִין דִּבְחִין וְאֻשּׁוֹהִי מְסוֹבְלִין

Sheshbazzar had shown him the foundation of the Temple walls.

וּמִן־אֱדַיִן וְעַד־כְּעַן מִתְבְּנֵא — *Since then it has been constructed.* The translation follows *Rashi. R' Yeshayah MiTrani,* however, translates: *since then it is being constructed.* The elders did not wish to emphasize to Darius that it was King Cyrus who had halted the construction. They preferred merely to indicate to him that the work was not yet complete.

**17.** בְּבֵית גִּנְזַיָּא ... דִּי בְּבָבֶל — *The ... archives ... in Babylon.* [See comm. below, 6:2.]

וּרְעוּת מַלְכָּא עַל־דְּנָה יִשְׁלַח עֲלֶינָא — *And let the King convey to us his will in this matter.* Let the King inform us whether he favors or opposes the reconstruction of the Temple *(R' Yeshayah MiTrani; Metzudos).*

# VI

**1.** בֵּאדַיִן — *Then.* When the king received the correspondence described in the previous chapter *(Rashi).*

גִּנְזַיָּא — *The archives.* The royal archives specified in the letter to the king [(5:17): *let a search be made in the royal archives*] *(R' Yeshayah MiTrani).*

מְהַחֲתִין תַּמָּה — *Were stored* [lit. *stored there*]. The translation follows *Rashi.*
*Ralbag* and *Ibn Ezra* render *bring down:* The Babylonian library to which the record-keepers bring down their archives was examined. [Though the capital was in the Persian city of Shushan, old records were sent to the library in Babylon for storage.]

**2.** בְּאַחְמְתָא — *In a pouch. Rashi* and *Ibn Ezra* explain that אַחְמְתָא [derived from חֵמֶת, *pouch*] was a container used for storing books, documents and letters.

V
17
the walls of God's Temple in Jerusalem, but since then it has been constructed without being completed.' 17 Now if it pleases the King, let a search be made of the royal archives which are in Babylon to determine whether King Cyrus decreed that this Temple of God in Jerusalem be constructed; and let the King convey to us his will in this matter.

VI
1-3
King Darius then issued a decree, and they searched in the library in which the archives were stored in
Babylon. 2 A scroll was discovered in a pouch in
a palace in the province of Media and the following was recorded in it:
3 In the first year of King Cyrus, King Cyrus issued a decree [concerning] the Temple of God in Jerusalem: Let the Temple be built as a place for the offering of sacrifices, with its walls strongly founded;

בְּבִירְתָא — *In a palace.* The translation follows *Ibn Ezra* and *Metzudos.*

*Ralbag* and *Malbim* translate *in the capital city* [as בְּשׁוּשַׁן הַבִּירָה, *in the capital city of Shushan (Esther* 1:2)].

דִּי בְּמָדַי מְדִינְתָּא — *In the province of Media.* The preceding verse describes the search of the archives in Babylon. Yet our verse recounts the discovery of the record in Media. *Metzudos* explains that when the examination of the Babylonian library proved fruitless, a new search was conducted in Media, yielding the missing document.

*Malbim* elaborates: The capital of the Babylonian [and subsequently the Persian] empire was originally in the city of Babylon, and it was there that Cyrus' proclamation sanctioning the Temple reconstruction was recorded. Ahasuerus, who succeeded Cyrus, transferred the seat of government to Shushan [Susa] *(Esther* 1:2), and Cyrus' decree was lost, perhaps through the efforts of Ahasuerus' prime minister, the infamous Haman. [*Radal* to *Midrash Esther* (1:1) suggests that it was Tattenai and his cohorts (5:3) who destroyed the evidence of Cyrus' decree.] Thus, when Ahasuerus's successor, Darius, ordered a search of the Babylonian archives, nothing was found. But the hand of Providence intervened — and a copy was miraculously recovered at the new capital in Media.

וְכֵן־כְּתִיב בְּגַוַּהּ דִּכְרוֹנָה — *And the following was recorded in it:* The record was an abbreviated version of Cyrus' original decree *(Malbim).* [I.e., Cyrus' introductory remarks and his call for his gentile subjects to aid the Jews (1:2-4) are deleted here. However, the details concerning the materials for the Temple building and its dimensions are mentioned here (vs. 3,4) but not in ch. 1.]

*Ralbag* translates: *And the following was written in it: A record.* I.e., the document identified itself with the heading, *A record.*

**3.** וְאֻשּׁוֹהִי מְסוֹבְלִין — *With its walls strongly founded.* As above (4:12), *Rashi* translates אֻשּׁוֹהִי, *walls.* מְסוֹבְלִין [from לִסְבֹּל, *to bear*] means, literally, *able to bear great weight* The walls should be constructed so as to be able to support great weight *(Metzudos),* i.e. *strongly founded (Rashi).* [Since the walls would be massive — sixty cubits in

רוּמֵהּ אַמִּין שִׁתִּין פְּתָיֵהּ אַמִּין שִׁתִּין׃
ד נִדְבָּכִין דִּי־אֶבֶן גְּלָל תְּלָתָא וְנִדְבָּךְ דִּי־אָע
ה חֲדַת וְנִפְקְתָא מִן־בֵּית מַלְכָּא תִּתְיְהִב׃ וְאַף
מָאנֵי בֵית־אֱלָהָא דִּי דַהֲבָה וְכַסְפָּא דִּי
נְבוּכַדְנֶצַּר הַנְפֵּק מִן־הֵיכְלָא דִי־בִירוּשְׁלֶם
וְהֵיבֵל לְבָבֶל יַהֲתִיבוּן וִיהָךְ לְהֵיכְלָא
דִי־בִירוּשְׁלֶם לְאַתְרֵהּ וְתַחֵת בְּבֵית
ו אֱלָהָא׃ כְּעַן תַּתְּנַי פַּחַת עֲבַר־
נַהֲרָה שְׁתַר בּוֹזְנַי וּכְנָוָתְהוֹן אֲפַרְסְכָיֵא דִּי

height — they would need a very strong foundation to support their weight.]

*R' Yeshayah MiTrani,* however, translates מְסוֹבְלִין, *massive:* let the walls be massive, towering.

*Ibn Ezra* and *Metzudos* translate אֻשַּׁיָּא as *foundation* (above 4:12). Accordingly, they render the verse here as *let its foundations be weighty* — let the foundation be built of massive, heavy stones.

רוּמֵהּ אַמִּין שִׁתִּין פְּתָיֵהּ אַמִּין שִׁתִּין — *Its height sixty cubits and its width sixty cubits. Ibn Ezra* notes that the dimensions of the Second Temple recorded here exceeded those of the First Sanctuary built by King Solomon. See *I Kings* 6:2: *The Temple which King Solomon built for HASHEM was ... twenty cubits wide and thirty cubits high.* The Second Temple's length is not mentioned, since it was identical with that of the First Temple — sixty cubits. *(Ibn Ezra).*

*R' Yeshayah MiTrani* comments that the width of the Second Temple building was equivalent to its great height (sixty cubits) so that its walls would not collapse.

*Malbim* thinks that the size of the building is mentioned as evidence of the guiding hand of Providence, which caused Cyrus to authorize unquestioningly the construction of the Temple exactly according to the required specifications. [These were presumably instructed by the prophets and the elders.] This was essential, since any deviation from the proper dimensions would have disqualified the Temple from use. [Similarly, the First Temple was built in strict conformity with the commanded specifications. See *I Chronicles* 28:19: *It* (the Temple specifications) *was all in writing, by the hand of HASHEM to me ...*]

**4.** נִדְבָּכִין דִּי־אֶבֶן גְּלָל תְּלָתָא וְנִדְבָּךְ דִּי־אָע חֲדַת — *Three marble rows and one of new wood. Rashi* explains that the three exterior rows were of marble and the interior one was of wood, resembling King Solomon's Temple [see I *Kings* 6:36: *He* (King Solomon) *built ... three rows of stone, and one of hewn cedar wood*].

[Evidently, the walls consisted of three adjoining stone layers, with an additional layer of wood paneling the inside. Similarly, the walls of the First Temple were build of stone with an inner wooden paneling *(I Kings* 6:15).]

*Ibn Ezra* and *Metzudos* disagree, explaining that the verse refers to the tiers of the Temple walls. They were to consist of three marble tiers, one above the other, followed by one wooden tier, with this series repeated over and over to the top of the wall. This arrangement provided maximum strength, and a similar pattern was used for the walls of

*its height sixty cubits and its width sixty cubits.*
4 *Three marble rows and one of new wood; the expenses to be provided by the royal palace.*
5 *Also, the gold and silver vessels of the Temple of God — which Nebuchadnezzar removed from the Sanctuary in Jerusalem and brought to Babylon — let them be given over and brought to the Sanctuary in Jerusalem, to their place, and let them remain in the Temple of God.*

*The King Warns Tattenai*

6 *Now, Tattenai, satrap of the Trans-River, Shethar Bozenai, and their companions, the*

the courtyard in Solomon's Temple [see *I Kings* 6:36].[1]

וְנִפְקְתָא מִן־בֵּית מַלְכָּא תִּתְיְהִב — *The expenses to be provided by the royal palace.* The expenses for the Temple building and other Temple requirments *(Rashi)* [such as the daily Temple sacrifices (v. 9)].

**5.** יַהֲתִיבוּן — *Let them be given over.* This is *Rashi's* translation [see 5:14]. *Ibn Ezra, R' Yeshayah MiTrani* and *Metzudos* render יַהֲתִיבוּן, *returned.*

ויְהָךְ — *And brought* [lit. *and let it go*]. Let this entire collection be brought to Jerusalem *(Rashi).*

[The singular — let *this* be brought — refers to the entire collection.]

לְאַתְרֵהּ — *To their* [lit. *its*] *place.* [To their rightful place. Since this refers to the entire collection, the singular is again used.]

וְתַחֵת בְּבֵית אֱלָהָא — *And let them* [lit. *it*] *remain in the Temple of God.* This is *Rashi's* translation. *Ibn Ezra's* rendition, however, is: *and you* [Sheshbazzar; see 5:14] *shall place* [*them*] *in the Temple of God.*

### The King Warns Tattenai

**6.** כְּעַן תַּתְּנַי — *Now, Tattenai.* This was the king's reply to Tattenai and his supporters [see 5:3] *(Rashi).*

1. The Talmud *(Rosh Hashanah* 4a), however, asserts that Darius' intentions were far different from Solomon's. Solomon ordered that the walls be partially built of wood to enhance the Temple structure. His wooden sections were placed in the upper portion of the walls, imbedded in the width of the wall, and covered with plaster. Darius, however, added the wood so that he might have the Temple burnt should the Jews rebel. His wooden beams were positioned even in the lower levels of the walls, and exposed at the surface of the wall, so that they might be readily ignited. This indicates, says the Talmud, that Darius' virtue was blemished.

*Tosafos* there observes that although Darius was merely reinstating Cyrus' original specifications for the wooden walls and not ordering them himself, the Talmud properly concludes that Darius himself was blemished. Darius could easily have altered Cyrus' plan for exposed wooden walls. By leaving them intact he exhibited his desire for a Temple that might be readily ignited.

[*Rashi* and *Metzudos,* who compare Darius' arrangement of the walls with King Solomon's, would seem to consider the Persian king's intentions honorable. Evidently they prefer the differing opinions cited in *Rosh Hashanah,* which contend that his virtue was compromised not by his wooden walls, but by his desire for personal gain from the Temple services (see comm. v. 10) or his immorality (see comm. 7:8).]

ו
ז־י

ז בְּעֵבַר נַהֲרָה רַחִיקִין הֲווֹ מִן־תַּמָּה׃ שְׁבֻקוּ
לַעֲבִידַת בֵּית־אֱלָהָא דֵךְ פַּחַת יְהוּדָיֵא
וּלְשָׂבֵי יְהוּדָיֵא בֵּית־אֱלָהָא דֵךְ יִבְנוֹן עַל־
ח אַתְרֵהּ׃ וּמִנִּי שִׂים טְעֵם לְמָא דִי־תַעַבְדוּן
עִם־שָׂבֵי יְהוּדָיֵא אִלֵּךְ לְמִבְנֵא בֵּית־אֱלָהָא
דֵךְ וּמִנִּכְסֵי מַלְכָּא דִּי מִדַּת עֲבַר נַהֲרָה
אָסְפַּרְנָא נִפְקְתָא תֶּהֱוֵא מִתְיַהֲבָא לְגֻבְרַיָּא
ט אִלֵּךְ דִּי־לָא לְבַטָּלָא׃ וּמָה חַשְׁחָן וּבְנֵי תוֹרִין
וְדִכְרִין וְאִמְּרִין | לַעֲלָוָן | לֶאֱלָהּ שְׁמַיָּא חִנְטִין
מְלַח | חֲמַר וּמְשַׁח כְּמֵאמַר כָּהֲנַיָּא דִי־
בִירוּשְׁלֶם לֶהֱוֵא מִתְיְהֵב לְהֹם יוֹם | בְּיוֹם דִּי־
י לָא שָׁלוּ׃ דִּי־לֶהֱוֺן מְהַקְרְבִין נִיחוֹחִין לֶאֱלָהּ
שְׁמַיָּא וּמְצַלַּיִן לְחַיֵּי מַלְכָּא וּבְנוֹהִי׃ וּמִנִּי

רַחִיקִין הֲווֹ מִן־תַּמָּה — *Keep distant from that place.* Keep away from the Temple construction site; i.e., do not disrupt the construction *(Rashi).*

I command you to refrain from all contact with the Jews *(R' Yeshayah MiTrani).*

**7.** פַּחַת יְהוּדָיֵא וּלְשָׂבֵי יְהוּדָיֵא בֵּית־אֱלָהָא דֵךְ יִבְנוֹן עַל־אַתְרֵהּ — *The Jewish leaders and* [lit. *to*] *the Jewish elders shall construct this Temple in its place.* The translation follows *Rashi* and *Metzudos. Rashi* notes that the prefix לְ, *to,* in the word וּלְשָׂבֵי, lit. *and to the elders,* indicates that the king was now issuing a command to them.

Although the word פַּחַת [lit. *satrap*], *leaders,* is not prefixed by the usual לְ, *to,* the prefix from the word לַעֲבִידַת at the beginning of the verse is to be understood as introducing this word as well *(Ibn Ezra).*

*Midrash Rabbah* (to *Esther* 1:1) relates that since Ahasurerus had banned the Temple reconstruction, his son Darius was advised that he was not empowered under Persian law to reverse the ban. But Darius' close reading of Ahasuerus' edict revealed that his father had not imposed an absolute restriction, but had specified that *this city shall not be built until a decree is issued by me* (4:21). Reasoning that his father might have rescinded the restriction were he now alive, Darius assumed the authority to issue a decree authorizing the resumption of the Temple construction.

### ◆§ The King's Directive

**8.** וּמִנִּי שִׂים טְעֵם לְמָא דִי־תַעַבְדוּן עִם־שָׂבֵי יְהוּדָיֵא אִלֵּךְ לְמִבְנֵא בֵּית־אֱלָהָא דֵךְ — *I issue a decree to you authorizing your activities with these Jewish elders — to construct this Temple of God.* The translation follows *Rashi* and *Metzudos.*

In the preceding verses (6,7), Tattenai and his companions were merely commanded not to restrain the Jews from building [*keep distant from that place ... leave the work to the Jewish elders*]; but there was no requirement for them to aid in the construction. Yet, in our verse, the king commanded that Tattenai and his cohorts participate actively in the Temple restoration. *Malbim* explains that vs. 6-7 were written in accordance with Cyrus' original proclamation, wherein the gentiles were merely told not to obstruct the Jews, who would build by them-

VI 7-10

*The King's Directive*

*Apharsechites of the Trans-River. Keep distant from that place.* [7] *Leave the work of this Temple of God; the Jewish leaders and the Jewish elders shall construct this Temple in its place.* [8] *I issue a decree to you authorizing your activities with these Jewish elders — to construct this Temple of God; it shall come out of the royal estate, from the Trans-River taxes, and be speedily done. Expenses shall be disbursed to these people, so that they are not disrupted.* [9] *And anything of concern to them, [such as] young cattle, rams, and sheep for the burnt offerings to the God of heaven; wheat, salt, wine, and oil — according to the specifications of the Kohanim in Jerusalem — shall be supplied to them daily without delay.* [10] *So that they may offer pleasing sacrifices to the God of heaven, and pray for the lives of the King*

selves. But in v. 8, Darius added his own decree [*I issue a decree*], requiring the non-Jews to aid the Jewish elders by immediately appropriating funds from the Trans-River taxes.

וּמִנִּכְסֵי מַלְכָּא דִּי מִדַּת עֲבַר נַהֲרָה אָסְפַּרְנָא — *It shall come out of the royal estate, from the Trans-River taxes, and be speedily done. Rashi* relates this whole phrase to the preceding phrase. The cost of the project shall be borne by the royal treasury, to be paid out of the taxes collected in the Trans-River, and it [the construction] shall be done speedily.

*Metzudos,* however, connects this phrase with the end of the verse: *From the royal estate, out of the Trans-River taxes, expenses ... shall be speedily disbursed to these people, so that they are not disrupted.*

**9.** וּמָה חַשְׁחָן — *And anything of concern to them.* Anything causing concern, i.e., any need *(Rashi),* specifically, the needs of the altar *(Metzudos).*

וּבְנֵי תוֹרִין וְדִכְרִין וְאִמְּרִין — *Young cattle, rams, and sheep.* Darius' contribution surpassed that of Cyrus. Cyrus aided only in the construction of the Temple, but Darius also supplied the daily sacrificial requirements *(Malbim).*

חִנְטִין מְלַח חֲמַר וּמְשַׁח — *Wheat, salt, wine, and oil.* Wheat and oil were used for the מִנְחָה, *meal offering;* salt, for the sacrifices [all of which were salted]; and wine for the נְסָכִים, *libations (Rashi).*

כְּמֵאמַר כָּהֲנַיָּא — *According to the specifications* [lit. *word*] *of the Kohanim.* In the amounts that the *Kohanim* will specify *(Metzudos).*

דִּי־לָא שָׁלוּ — *Without delay.* This is *Rashi's* translation. Others render *without laxity (Metzudos);* or *without fail (R' Yeshayah MiTrani).*

**10.** נִיחוֹחִין — *Pleasing sacrifices.* [This translation may be found in *Rashi* to *Leviticus* 1:9. There the sacrifices are described as נִיחוֹחַ, which *Rashi* translates as *pleasing:* God is *pleased* with the bringing of sacrifices, since He has commanded that they be brought and His will has been fulfilled.]

וּמְצַלַּיִן לְחַיֵּי מַלְכָּא וּבְנוֹהִי — *And pray for the lives of the King and his sons.* The

יא שִׂים טְעֵם דִּי כָל־אֱנָשׁ דִּי יְהַשְׁנֵא פִּתְגָמָא
דְנָה יִתְנְסַח אָע מִן־בַּיְתֵהּ וּזְקִיף יִתְמְחֵא
יב עֲלֹהִי וּבַיְתֵהּ נְוָלוּ יִתְעֲבֵד עַל־דְּנָה׃ וֵאלָהָא
דִּי שַׁכִּן שְׁמֵהּ תַּמָּה יְמַגַּר כָּל־מֶלֶךְ וְעַם דִּי
יִשְׁלַח יְדֵהּ לְהַשְׁנָיָה לְחַבָּלָה בֵּית־אֱלָהָא דֵךְ
דִּי בִירוּשְׁלֶם אֲנָה דָרְיָוֶשׁ שָׂמֶת טְעֵם
יג אָסְפַּרְנָא יִתְעֲבִד׃ אֱדַיִן תַּתְּנַי
פַּחַת עֲבַר־נַהֲרָה שְׁתַר בּוֹזְנַי וּכְנָוָתְהוֹן
לָקֳבֵל דִּי־שְׁלַח דָּרְיָוֶשׁ מַלְכָּא כְּנֵמָא
יד אָסְפַּרְנָא עֲבַדוּ׃ וְשָׂבֵי יְהוּדָיֵא בָּנַיִן וּמַצְלְחִין
בִּנְבוּאַת חַגַּי °נביאה וּזְכַרְיָה בַּר עִדּוֹא
וּבְנוֹ וְשַׁכְלִלוּ מִן־טַעַם אֱלָהּ יִשְׂרָאֵל

°נְבִיָּא ק׳

Talmud *(Rosh Hashanah* 4a) faults Darius for his impure intentions. His purpose in supporting the Temple services was for the sake of his own welfare and that of his family, rather than for the glorification of God.

**11.** וּמִנִּי שִׂים טְעֵם — *I issue a decree* ... This decree mandating that any deviators be severely punished was Darius' own innovation, over and above the provisions of Cyrus' proclamation. This is why Darius stressed his own involvement: *I ... decree (Malbim).*

יִתְנְסַח אָע מִן־בַּיְתֵהּ וּזְקִיף יִתְמְחֵא עֲלֹהִי — *Should have the beams torn out of his house, and a gallows raised high for him.* And have the deviator hanged from that gallows *(Rashi).*

*Metzudos* translates: *A beam should be torn out of his house and set in place as a gallows for him.*

**12.** ... וֵאלָהָא — *And let the God* ... Should some king or nation over whom I wield no influence threaten the Temple, let God punish them *(Malbim).*

דִּי שַׁכִּן שְׁמֵהּ תַּמָּה — *Who has caused His name to dwell there. Rashi* translates the verb שַׁכִּן in the past tense [referring to the Divine Presence which rested on the First Temple]. *Metzudos,* however, translates שַׁכִּן in the future tense [referring to the expected visitation of the Divine Presence at the completion of the construction of the Second Temple].

יְמַגַּר כָּל־מֶלֶךְ וְעַם — *Topple any monarch or people.* The Rabbis assert that Darius' curse was directed primarily against the Samaritans [see 4:1,10], who had gathered an army to attempt to crush the Temple reconstruction. Ezra and the Jewish elders, in the presence of the entire community, had then pronounced a solemn oath of excommunication against them. Darius followed suit with his own imprecation, proclaiming *'Let ... God topple any monarch or people extending a hand to destroy this Temple' (Yalkut, II Kings* 17; *Pirkei d'R' Eliezer* 38; see comm. 5:3).

לְהַשְׁנָיָה — *To ruin.* This is *Rashi's* translation. *Metzudos,* however, translates *to deviate: And let God ... topple any monarch or people extending a hand to deviate* [*from my command*] *and destroy this Temple* ...

*and his sons.* 11 *I issue a decree that anyone deviating
from this matter should have the beams torn out of
his house, and a gallows raised high for him, and his
house designated a dunghill for this.* 12 *And let the
God Who has caused His name to dwell there topple
any monarch or people extending a hand to ruin or
destroy this Temple of God in Jerusalem: I, Darius,
have decreed that this be implemented expeditiously.*
13 *Then Tattenai, satrap of the Trans-River,
Shethar Bozenai and their companions, in considera-
tion of King Darius' foregoing dispatch, acted
expeditiously.*

*Successful Construction*

14 *And the Jewish elders built and were successful,
as foretold by the prophet Haggai and Zechariah the
son of Iddo; they built and founded by the command*

אֲנָה דָרְיָוֶשׁ שָׂמֶת טְעֵם אָסְפַּרְנָא יִתְעֲבִד — *I, Darius, have decreed that this be implemented expeditiously.* The construction of the Temple should proceed as quickly as possible *(Rashi).*

*Malbim* suggests that the king's command for immediate implementation meant two things: (1) Tattenai and his companions were to publicize the decree immediately, and (2) the construction should proceed rapidly.

Noting further that the demand for immediate action begins with the statement, *I, Darius, have decreed ...* , *Malbim* explains that the command for promptness was a result of Darius' own initiative. In this he surpassed Cyrus who had decreed only that the Temple be rebuilt without requiring quick compliance. Hence the words *'I, Darius, have decreed,'* connote: I, Darius, surpassing Cyrus and acting on my own initiative, have decreed that this be implemented immediately.

### ◆§ Successful Construction

**14.** בִּנְבוּאַת חַגַּי נְבִיָּא וּזְכַרְיָה — *As foretold by the prophet Haggai and Zechariah.* [See comm. 5:1.]

וּבְנוֹ וְשַׁכְלִלוּ — *They built and founded.* The translation follows *Rashi. Metzudos* translates *they began constructing and then completed.*

מִן־טַעַם אֱלָהּ יִשְׂרָאֵל — *By the command of the God of Israel.* The effort to successfully complete the building was launched by God's command to Israel [through Haggai and Zechariah (above 5:1)] *(Rashi).*

According to *Malbim,* the reference to God's command refers to God's special providence. *By the command of God as expressed through the decrees of Cyrus ...* The workings of Divine Providence, cloaked in the proclamations of mortal kings, caused the construction of the Temple. In a hidden miracle, the will of God turned the hearts of Cyrus and Darius and caused them to grant permission for the Temple restoration.

The Second Temple was built through hidden miracles because the returning exiles were unworthy of the revealed miracles which brought about the first conquest of the Holy Land during the times of Joshua [such as the miraculous collapse of the walls of

ו וּמִטְּעֵם כּוֹרֶשׁ וְדָרְיָוֶשׁ וְאַרְתַּחְשַׁשְׂתְּא
טו־יז טו מֶלֶךְ פָּרָס׃ וְשֵׁיצִיא בַּיְתָה דְנָה עַד יוֹם
תְּלָתָה לִירַח אֲדָר דִּי־הִיא שְׁנַת־שֵׁת
טז לְמַלְכוּת דָּרְיָוֶשׁ מַלְכָּא׃ וַעֲבַדוּ
בְנֵי־יִשְׂרָאֵל כָּהֲנַיָּא וְלֵוָיֵא וּשְׁאָר בְּנֵי־גָלוּתָא
יז חֲנֻכַּת בֵּית־אֱלָהָא דְנָה בְּחֶדְוָה׃ וְהַקְרִבוּ
לַחֲנֻכַּת בֵּית־אֱלָהָא דְנָה תּוֹרִין מְאָה

Jericho, the halting of the sun in midday at Gibeon, and the routing of the Canaanite hordes by a relative handful of Jewish warriors — see *Joshua*]. As stated by the Talmud (*Berachos* 4a): Ezra's generation was destined for redemption as miraculous as in the days of Joshua — but their misdeeds prevented this.

וּמִטְּעֵם כּוֹרֶשׁ — *And by the consent* [*lit.* *decree*] *of Cyrus.* The Temple construction was begun on the basis of Cyrus' permission [chs. 1-3] *(Rashi).*

וְדָרְיָוֶשׁ וְאַרְתַּחְשַׁשְׂתְּא — *And Darius Artahshast* [lit. *Darius and Artahshast*]. *Rashi* states that both these names refer to Darius, the present monarch who allowed the completion of the Temple construction. He was also entitled Artahshast, a name shared by all of the Persian kings, like the Egyptian *Pharaoh (Rashi;* see *Rashi* to *Nehemiah* 2:1). [*Rashi's* remarks are based on the Talmud *(Rosh Hashanah* 3b) which identifies Artahshast as Darius.]

*Ralbag* and *Baal HaMaor* (to *Rosh Hashanah* 3b, cited by *Malbim)* suggest that the Talmud's remarks are meant homiletically and that the simple meaning of this verse is that Artahshast is yet a third Persian king who reigned at a later date and gave his permission for the construction of the walls around Jerusalem.

*Ibn Ezra,* however, identifies Artahshast as Ahasuerus (see comm. to 4:7) and Darius as Darius the Mede, Cyrus' predecessor. The building was completed in the reign of yet a fourth king, Darius the Persian, Ahasuerus' son (next verse).

**15.** שְׁנַת־שֵׁת לְמַלְכוּת דָּרְיָוֶשׁ מַלְכָּא — *The sixth year of the reign of King Darius.* Thus, the Temple construction lasted four years *(Rashi).* [It began during the second year of Darius' reign (4:24).]

Actually, the construction lasted four and a half years, since *Haggai* (1:15) relates that the work began during the sixth month of the second year of Darius' reign, and it was completed in Adar, the twelfth month of the sixth year of his reign *(Malbim).*

### The Celebration

**16.** וַעֲבַדוּ בְנֵי־יִשְׂרָאֵל ... וּשְׁאָר בְּנֵי־גָלוּתָא — *Then the children of Israel ... and the rest of the exiles.* The *children of Israel* refers to the Israelites and the *rest of the exiles* to the Nethinites and the descendants of King Solomon's slaves listed in 2:43-58 *(Metzudos).*

חֲנֻכַּת בֵּית־אֱלָהָא דְנָה — *The inauguration of this Temple of God. Malbim* comments that the word *this* suggests that the celebrants also had in mind the celebration of another Temple — the third, final Sanctuary [to be constructed by the hand of God. *Rashi* to *Succah* 41a states that the Third Temple will be built by *Hashem* and will descend from Heaven, as *Exodus* 15:17 states: מִקְּדָשׁ ה׳ כּוֹנְנוּ יָדֶיךָ, *the Sanctuary, HASHEM, established by Your hands*].

*of the God of Israel, and by the consent of Cyrus and Darius Artahshast king of Persia.* 15 *This Temple was completed on the third day of the month of Adar during the sixth year of the reign of King Darius.*

*The Celebration*

16 *Then the children of Israel, the Kohanim, the Levites and the rest of the exiles celebrated the inauguration of this Temple of God joyously.* 17 *They offered up for the inauguration of this Temple of*

The Jewish settlers hoped that their celebration would be immediately followed by the miraculous appearance of the Third Temple and another inaugural in its honor [as described in *Ezekiel* 43:18-27, 45:18-25]. Thus, the text describes their celebration of the inauguration of *this* Temple — to be followed by another celebration marking the hoped for inauguration of the Third Temple.

בְּחֶדְוָה — *Joyously.* Since the festivities took place over Purim, which falls, in Jerusalem, on 15 Adar, Scripture emphasizes that the inauguration was celebrated *joyfully* — indicating that the rejoicing over the Temple was uppermost, surpassing even the Purim festivities *(Malbim).*

*Malbim* asserts that the celebration continued until 23 Adar, in order to last until the date foretold by the prophet Ezekiel for the inauguration of the Third Temple.[1] [This follows *Malbim's* comment that the celebrants hoped to proceed immediately to the inauguration of the Third Temple. See above.]

**17.** וְהַקְרִבוּ לַחֲנֻכַּת בֵּית־אֱלָהָא דְנָה — *They offered up for the inauguration of this Temple of God.* The particular offerings brought here do not coincide with the order of sacrifices detailed in *Leviticus* (although only Biblically prescribed sacrifices may be offered on the altar). Thus, these inaugural offerings must have been brought under a הוֹרָאַת שָׁעָה, *temporary ruling,* which the Rabbinic authorities are empowered to institute, on a temporary basis, in unusual circumstances. Such a ruling was issued at the time of the inaugural ceremony *(Rashi).* The ruling also had the approval of the prophets of the day *(Malbim).*

[*Malbim* and *Metzudos* cite a Talmudic statement to this effect in *Temurah* 15b and *Horios* 6a. However, the statement they refer to asserts only that the sacrifices brought at a later date by Ezra himself, at his emigration to the Holy Land (8:35), were sanctioned by a temporary ruling. The Talmud does not discuss the sacrifices brought now at the Temple inaugural. *Malbim* and *Metzudos* evidently feel that this Talmudic statement applies also to the sacrifices brought during the inauguration ceremony.]

According to *Ramban,* offering sacrifices at the inauguration is required by Biblical law. *Ramban* [to *Numbers* 7:13] sees in the passage — [The princes] *shall offer their sacrifice for the inauguration of the altar (Numbers* 7:11) — a Biblical command for the future which requires that special inaugural sacrifices be brought at the opening of the Temple service. This commandment was fulfilled by Ezra's generation, as stated in our passage.

However, *Rambam's* opinion is that the inaugural sacrifices were not required, but were brought voluntarily (see *Maaseh HaKorbanos* 2:15, 6:19, *Mishneh LeMelech).*

1. This is in keeping with *Malbim's* own opinion concerning the date of that inauguration. See ArtScroll to *Yechezkel* 43:18, 45:18.

ו דִּכְרִין מָאתַיִן אִמְּרִין אַרְבַּע מְאָה וּצְפִירֵי
יח־כ עִזִּין °לחטיא עַל־כָּל־יִשְׂרָאֵל תְּרֵי־עֲשַׂר °לְחַטָּאָה ק׳
יח לְמִנְיָן שִׁבְטֵי יִשְׂרָאֵל: וַהֲקִימוּ כָהֲנַיָּא
בִּפְלֻגָּתְהוֹן וְלֵוָיֵא בְּמַחְלְקָתְהוֹן עַל־
עֲבִידַת אֱלָהָא דִּי בִירוּשְׁלֶם כִּכְתָב סְפַר
יט מֹשֶׁה: וַיַּעֲשׂוּ בְנֵי־הַגּוֹלָה אֶת־
הַפָּסַח בְּאַרְבָּעָה עָשָׂר לַחֹדֶשׁ הָרִאשׁוֹן:
כ כִּי הִטַּהֲרוּ הַכֹּהֲנִים וְהַלְוִיִּם כְּאֶחָד

תְּרֵי־עֲשַׂר לְמִנְיָן שִׁבְטֵי יִשְׂרָאֵל — *Twelve — corresponding to the number of tribes of Israel. Metzudos* observes that twelve sacrifices were brought to correspond with the twelve tribes of Israel, although only two of the tribes — Judah and Benjamin — now returned to the Holy Land.

[*Tosafos* to *Arachin* 32a, however, states that some members of all of the twelve tribes took part in the return to the Land of Israel (see comm. 2:64 and v. 22).]

### ◆§ Priests and Levites Organized

**18.** כָהֲנַיָּא בִּפְלֻגָּתְהוֹן וְלֵוָיֵא בְּמַחְלְקָתְהוֹן — *The Kohanim in their groups and the Levites in their divisions.* The *Kohanim* and Levites were each organized into groups for their particular services *(Rashi).* [For the services performed by each group, see below.] They were divided into the same groups as in the first Temple *(R' Yeshayah MiTrani).*

The *Kohanim* were divided by the prophet Samuel and by King David into twenty-four groups, each of which served at the Temple for a period of one week. Each group was further divided into families, and each family was appointed to perform all of the priestly Temple functions during one day of the week *(Rambam, Klei HaMikdash* 4:3).

Similarly, the Levites were divided into twenty-four groups, each of which served at the Temple for one week, and each group was subdivided into families. Each family served in the Temple for one day, and carried out for that day all of the duties of the Levites *(Klei HaMikdash* 3:9). [*Rambam's* remarks are derived from *Taanis* 27a, which is based on *I Chronicles* 9:24-26, and chapters 23-26.]

*Malbim* notes that the word פְּלֻגָּתְהוֹן [*groups*], is used in relation to the *Kohanim,* while the word מַחְלְקָתְהוֹן [*divisions*], appears with respect to the Levites, indicating that the Levites were sub-divided into more clearly fixed units than the *Kohanim.* He bases this on *Kesef Mishneh* [to *Rambam, Klei HaMikdash* 3:9], who differentiates between the appointment of the *Kohanim* and the Levites. Although the families of *Kohanim* were appointed to each day's work at the Temple, the service to be performed by each *Kohen* was left open, to be decided by the daily drawing of lots. In the case of the Levites, however, the individual Levite was appointed to his particular task during the day. Thus, Scripture refers to the organization of the *Kohanim* into *groups,* assigned by family to serve during a particular week and on a particular day. The Levites, however, are described in terms of *divisions,* not only assigned by family to a weekly and daily period of service, but also assigned individually to particular tasks during the day.

עַל־עֲבִידַת אֱלָהָא דִּי בִירוּשְׁלֶם — *For the service of God in Jerusalem.* The *Kohanim* were commanded to perform the sacrificial services at the altar, and the Levites to chant the Temple liturgy *(Metzudos).* Additionally, the Levites were to guard the Temple, and serve as

VI 18-20

God one hundred oxen, two hundred rams, four hundred sheep, and goats as sin offerings for all of Israel, twelve — corresponding to the number of tribes of Israel. 18 And they established the Kohanim in their groups and the Levites in their divisions, for the service of God in Jerusalem, as written in the Book of Moses.

*Priests and Levites Organized*

19 The exiles brought the Passover offering on the fourteenth day of the first month. 20 For the Kohanim and Levites had purified themselves as one — all were

gatekeepers, opening and closing the Temple portals *(Rambam, Hil. Klei HaMikdash* 3:2).

כִּכְתָב סְפַר מֹשֶׁה — *As written in the Book of Moses. Leviticus* 21:8 designates the *Kohen Gadol* (High Priest) Aaron (and his descendants) as those assigned to perform the sacrificial services *(Klei HaMikdash* 4:1). *Numbers* 18:23 specifies that the Levites were to serve in the Temple *(Klei HaMikdash* 3:1). The particular forms of service are not Biblically explicit, but are derived in the Talmud *(Arachin* 11a,b) from various passages. They are defined in *I Chronicles* ch. 23-26.

**19.** בְנֵי־הַגּוֹלָה — *The exiles.* Those who returned to the Holy Land from the exile *(Malbim).*

לַחֹדֶשׁ הָרִאשׁוֹן — *Of the first month.* I.e., Nissan, which follows the twelfth month, the month of Adar, in which the Temple was completed *(Rashi).*

**20.** כִּי הִטַּהֲרוּ הַכֹּהֲנִים וְהַלְוִיִּם — *For the Kohanim and Levites had purified themselves.* Those who are טָמֵא, *tamei* (ritually contaminated), when the Passover lamb is to be brought are disqualified from bringing the offering. They must purify themselves and then bring the substitute Passover offering a month later on 14 Iyar. Since the *Kohanim* and Levites had purified themselves beforehand, they were able to bring the Passover sacrifice at the proper time on 14 Nissan. Thus, *the exiles* [i.e., all the exiles, including the *Kohanim* and Levites] brought the Passover offering on the fourteenth day of the first month (v. 19) because they purified themselves from their contamination, as stated in our verse: *For the Kohanim and Levites had purified themselves (Ralbag).*

Those who are contaminated may purify themselves by immersion in the *mikveh,* ritual bath, and in certain cases, bringing the required sacrifices. In case of contact with the dead, the process of purification involves a series of sprinklings with water mixed with the ashes of the red heifer *(parah adumah)* and immersion in the ritual bath (see *Numbers* ch. 19; *Rambam, Parah Adumah* 11).

כְּאֶחָד כֻּלָּם טְהוֹרִים — *As one — all were pure.* All the *Kohanim* and Levites were purified, barring none *(Metzudos).*

*Malbim* points out that *all* of the *Kohanim* were involved in the purification, as well as the Levites. The *Kohanim's* involvement here stands in contrast to their failure to purify themselves during the times of King Hezekiah, when the Levites who were more righteous than the *Kohanim* purified themselves in greater numbers[1] *(II Chronicles* 29:34). Now, however, during the dedication of the Second Temple, the *Kohanim* were as zealous as the Levites, and *all* cleansed themselves.

1. *II Chronicles* 29 relates that, during the period of the First Temple, the Judean king,

כֻּלָּם טְהוֹרִים וַיִּשְׁחֲטוּ הַפֶּסַח לְכָל־בְּנֵי
כא הַגּוֹלָה וְלַאֲחֵיהֶם הַכֹּהֲנִים וְלָהֶם׃ וַיֹּאכְלוּ
בְנֵי־יִשְׂרָאֵל הַשָּׁבִים מֵהַגּוֹלָה וְכֹל הַנִּבְדָּל
מִטֻּמְאַת גּוֹיֵ־הָאָרֶץ אֲלֵהֶם לִדְרֹשׁ לַיהוָה
כב אֱלֹהֵי יִשְׂרָאֵל׃ וַיַּעֲשׂוּ חַג־מַצּוֹת שִׁבְעַת
יָמִים בְּשִׂמְחָה כִּי | שִׂמְּחָם יהוה וְהֵסֵב לֵב
מֶלֶךְ־אַשּׁוּר עֲלֵיהֶם לְחַזֵּק יְדֵיהֶם בִּמְלֶאכֶת

וַיִּשְׁחֲטוּ הַפֶּסַח — *And they slaughtered the Passover offering.* As the next phrase makes clear, it was the Levites who slaughtered the Passover lamb *(Metzudos).*

[Although most of the sacrificial service may only be performed by *Kohanim (Zevachim* 2:1, 15b), the slaughter may be performed even by a non-*Kohen (Zevachim* 3:1, 31b).]

*Malbim* notes that *II Chronicles* (30:17; 35:6,10,11) records other occasions, during the times of the First Temple, when the Levites slaughtered the Passover lamb.

וְלַאֲחֵיהֶם הַכֹּהֲנִים — *For their brothers the Kohanim.* The *Kohanim* are also descended from Levi and can therefore be referred to as the brothers of the Levites *(Metzudos).*

**21.** וַיֹּאכְלוּ בְנֵי־יִשְׂרָאֵל — *And the children of Israel ... ate.* They ate the Passover lamb *(Metzudos).*

הַנִּבְדָּל מִטֻּמְאַת גּוֹיֵ־הָאָרֶץ אֲלֵהֶם — *Who had separated himself from the defilement of the nations of the land to join them.* This refers to proselytes who had separated themselves from the defilements of the idolatrous nations in order to join the Jewish nation *(Rashi* from *Kiddushin* 70a).

*Ibn Ezra* suggests the possibility that those *who had separated themselves* refers not to proselytes, but to errant Jews who had sinned by following the abominations of the nations and had now repented.

*R' Yeshayah MiTrani* agrees, asserting that the verse refers to Jews who had taken gentile wives and now cast them off. The *defilement of the nations of the land* refers to the forbidden wives. אֲלֵהֶם is understood as [*which had cleaved*] *to them:* The defilement of the nations — the forbidden wives — had cleaved to the sinners before they separated themselves [see Wertheimer, notes to *R' Yeshayah MiTrani*].

**22.** וְהֵסֵב לֵב מֶלֶךְ־אַשּׁוּר — *And he turned the heart of the king of Assyria.* [The *Book of Ezra* has until now only made mention of the Persian kings Cyrus and Darius Artahshast, who permitted their Jewish subjects — the members of the tribes of Judah and Benjamin — to rebuild the Temple. The abrupt reference in this passage to the aid that the king of Assyria gave the builders is the subject of much discussion among the commentators.

The Ten Tribes of the Northern Kingdom of Israel (i.e., all of the tribes

Hezekiah, reversed the evil trends of his father Ahaz, and removed the idols from the Temple, thereby initiating its rededication. Many of the people then brought sacrifices to the Temple, but there were not sufficient *Kohanim* present to handle them. It was necessary for the Levites, who were more righteous than the *Kohanim,* and who had purified themselves in greater numbers, to assist the *Kohanim* in skinning the animals.

*pure; and they slaughtered the Passover offering for
all the exiles, for their brothers the Kohanim and for
themselves.*
21 *And the children of Israel who
returned from exile ate, together with everyone who
had separated himself from the defilement of the
nations of the land to join them and seek* HASHEM, *
God of Israel.*
22 *They celebrated the festival of
matzoth joyfully for seven days, for* HASHEM *caused
them to rejoice; and he turned the heart of the king of
Assyria in their favor, so that he strengthened them*

except for Judah and Benjamin and the *Kohanim* and Levites) were exiled to Assyria during the period of the First Temple *(II Kings* 17). More than a hundred years later, the remaining tribes were exiled to Babylon *(II Kings* 25). The Medes and Persians later conquered the Babylonians *(Daniel* 6:1), and the Persian kings Cyrus and Darius, who ruled over the Jews who had been exiled to Babylon, permitted them to build the Second Temple (1:2,3; 6:8).]

*Ramban* maintains that the Ten Tribes did not return to the Land of Israel. The Jewish settlers in Jerusalem consisted only of members of the tribes of Judah and Benjamin and a few representatives of other tribes who had been banished with them to Babylon. According to *Ramban,* the king of Assyria mentioned here who aided in the construction of the Temple was actually the Persian king Darius, who extended aid to his subjects, the people of Judah and Benjamin. He is called the *king of Assyria* because Scripture uses Assyria interchangeably with Babylon [see *Genesis* 10:10,11: *The beginning of his kingdom was Babylon ... Ashur* [Assyria] *came from this land*]. Since Darius presided over the Babylonian kingdom, he is entitled *king of Assyria (Sefer HaGeulah;* see *Ramban, Leviticus* 26:16; comm. 2:64).

*R' Yeshayah MiTrani* also identifies the *king of Assyria* as Darius and explains that he was so entitled because he ruled over the kingdom of Assyria as well as Babylon. The Assyrian empire had been vanquished by Nebuchadnezzar and the Babylonians, and had in turn fallen to the Persians, now ruled by Darius *(Metzudos).*

*Ibn Ezra* adds that there is a special poignancy to the description of the Persian king as the king of Assyria. The Assyrians had desolated the Land of Israel during the First Temple period and exiled the Ten Tribes. But now the king of Persia — who also ruled over Assyria, and was thus a successor to the Assyrian kings — reversed their policy under the influence of Divine inspiration and supported the construction of the Temple. Thus the use of this title emphasizes the Divine Providence involved in this restoration.

*Rashi* comments that God influenced the king of Assyria to give support to the Jews in his kingdom and aid in the construction of the Temple.

*Ralbag* suggests that the mention of the Assyrian king's aid in the Temple construction indicates that, in addition to the tribes of Judah and Benjamin who returned from exile in Babylon, members of the Ten Tribes also returned from Assyria to Jerusalem (see comm. to 2:64), and were aided in the construction of the Temple by the king of Assyria.

[Assyria was, at that time, a Persian

ז א בֵּית־הָאֱלֹהִים אֱלֹהֵי יִשְׂרָאֵל: וְאַחַר
א־ו הַדְּבָרִים הָאֵלֶּה בְּמַלְכוּת אַרְתַּחְשַׁסְתְּא
מֶלֶךְ־פָּרָס עֶזְרָא בֶּן־שְׂרָיָה בֶּן־עֲזַרְיָה בֶּן־
ב חִלְקִיָּה: בֶּן־שַׁלּוּם בֶּן־צָדוֹק בֶּן־אֲחִיטוּב:
ג־ד בֶּן־אֲמַרְיָה בֶן־עֲזַרְיָה בֶן־מְרָיוֹת: בֶּן־זְרַחְיָה
ה בֶן־עֻזִּי בֶן־בֻּקִּי: בֶּן־אֲבִישׁוּעַ בֶּן־פִּינְחָס
ו בֶּן־אֶלְעָזָר בֶּן־אַהֲרֹן הַכֹּהֵן הָרֹאשׁ: הוּא
עֶזְרָא עָלָה מִבָּבֶל וְהוּא־סֹפֵר מָהִיר

province. Apparently, *Rashi* and *Ralbag* understand our passage as referring to the ruler of this province whom the Persians had established as monarch and who now provided significant assistance to the Jews.]

*Malbim* interprets מֶלֶךְ אַשּׁוּר as *the king* [of Persia who ruled] *over Assyria.* Assyria, at this time a part of the Persian empire, had once held Israel subject, and had then persecuted the Jews. Now, however, even the Assyrian satraps who served the Persian king as governors over the Jews aided in constructing the Temple.

בִּמְלֶאכֶת בֵּית־הָאֱלֹהִים — *In the labor for the Temple of God.* The king strengthened them by paying for the costs of the Temple and by protecting the builders from their enemies *(Metzudos).*

# VII

### ☙ Ezra Arrives

**1.** וְאַחַר הַדְּבָרִים הָאֵלֶּה — *Following these events.* Following the construction of the Temple, Ezra ascended from Babylon to Eretz Yisrael *(Rashi* and *Metzudos).* He did so only after the death of his teacher, Baruch ben Neriah, who was too weak to make the journey *(Shir HaShirim Rabbah* 5:5). This teaches that the study of Torah supersedes even the construction of the Temple *(Megillah* 16b).

בְּמַלְכוּת אַרְתַּחְשַׁסְתְּא — *During the reign of Artahshast.* Artahshast here is Darius *(Rashi).*

*Rashi's* view is stated by the Talmud (*Rosh Hashanah* 3b) which asserts that Ezra and his party arrived in Jerusalem during the year following the completion of the Temple construction. The Temple was completed during the sixth year of King Darius-Artahshast (6:15) and Ezra and his party reached Jerusalem in the king's seventh year (v. 7).

[According to this interpretation, the phrase, *Following these events,* implies *closely* following the Temple construction described in the preceding chapter.]

*Malbim,* however, cites *Baal HaMaor* (to *Rosh Hashanah* 3b; see comm. above, 6:14) who suggests that the Artahshast who ruled during Ezra's journey to Jerusalem was not Darius who completed the Temple construction, but a later Persian monarch. Thus, Ezra's arrival in Jerusalem in the seventh year of Artahshast occurred many years after the completion of the Temple in the sixth year of his predecessor Darius.

[Accordingly, the meaning of the opening phrase, *Following these events,* is *some time* following these events — many years following the completion of the Temple.]

עֶזְרָא — *Ezra.* According to one opinion in the Talmud *(Megillah* 16a), Ezra was

VII
1-6

*in the labor for the Temple of God, the God of Israel.*

Ezra Arrives

*Following these events, during the reign of Ar-*
*tahshast king of Persia — Ezra the son of Seraiah,*
*the son of Azariah, the son of Hilkiah,* 2 *the son of*
*Shallum, the son of Zadok, the son of Ahitub,* 3 *the*
*son of Amariah, the son of Azariah, the son of*
*Meraioth,* 4 *the son of Zerahiah, the son of Uzzi, the*
*son of Bukki,* 5 *the son of Abishua, the son of*
*Pinehas, the son of Elazar, the son of Aaron, the first*
*Kohen —* 6 *this Ezra ascended from Babylon. He was*

the prophet Malachi *(Metzudos).* The Talmud observes that the prophet Malachi castigated the sinners of Judah and Israel for taking gentile wives *(Malachi* 2:11, *Rashi).* Similarly, Ezra compelled the sinners to cast off their non-Jewish wives (10:2), indicating that Ezra was, indeed, Malachi.

בֶּן־שְׂרָיָה — *The son of Seraiah.* [A comparison to the list in *I Chronicles* 5:29-41 (see ArtScroll comm. there) shows that the Seraiah of our verse is the same as the one mentioned there as the father of Jehozadak. Accordingly, Ezra was the brother of Jehozadak and the uncle of Jeshua ben Jozadak, the first *Kohen Gadol* of the Second Temple (see comm. to 3:2 above). Seraiah served as *Kohen Gadol* in the First Temple and was executed by Nebuchadnezzar at the time of the destruction *(II Kings* 25:18-21).]

**3.** עֲזַרְיָה בֶּן־מְרָיוֹת — *Azariah, the son of Meraioth.* Six generations of Ezra's ancestors listed in *I Chronicles* (5:33-37) between Azariah and Meraioth are omitted here. Since the purpose of the list here is to trace Ezra's ancestral line to the first *Kohen Gadol,* Aaron, it was unnecessary to mention each ancestor *(Metzudos).* [See further ArtScroll comm. to *I Chronicles* 5:32.]

**5.** הַכֹּהֵן הָרֹאשׁ — *The first Kohen.* [This is *Metzudos'* translation. The identical phrase is used in reference to Seraiah in *II Kings* 25:18, and is rendered by the commentators there as *Kohen Gadol* (High Priest). However, in our passage, where the reference is to Aaron, the rendition *first* [original] *Kohen* seems more appropriate.]

**6.** הוּא עֶזְרָא עָלָה מִבָּבֶל — *This Ezra ascended from Babylon.* The Sages *(Sanhedrin* 21b) derive from this passage that Ezra would have been worthy of bringing the Torah to the Jewish people had he not been preceded by Moses [see comm., v. 10]: 'Of Moses it is written, *And Moses ascended to God (Exodus* 19:3); of Ezra it is written, *This Ezra ascended from Babylon.* Just as the ascension of Moses was for Torah, so was the ascension of Ezra for Torah.'

*Maharsha* (there) explains that Moses qualified as the Torah-giver by ascending to God, the source of wisdom. Similarly, Ezra ascended to the Holy Land whose very atmosphere, the Rabbis remark, gives forth wisdom — thus qualifying as an instrument for the giving of Torah, had Moses not preceded him.

The Rabbis combine the closing words of v. 5, *Aaron, the first Kohen,* with the opening words of v. 6, *This Ezra,* producing the phrase *Aaron; the first Kohen, is this Ezra.* This homiletically created phrase, the Rabbis remark, 'indicates that Ezra, who ascended from Babylon as the leader of his people, would have been esteemed even over his

ז
ז־ח

בְּתוֹרַת מֹשֶׁה אֲשֶׁר־נָתַן יהוה אֱלֹהֵי
יִשְׂרָאֵל וַיִּתֶּן־לוֹ הַמֶּלֶךְ כְּיַד־יהוה אֱלֹהָיו
ז עָלָיו כֹּל בַּקָּשָׁתוֹ: וַיַּעֲלוּ מִבְּנֵי־
יִשְׂרָאֵל וּמִן־הַכֹּהֲנִים וְהַלְוִיִּם וְהַמְשֹׁרְרִים
וְהַשֹּׁעֲרִים וְהַנְּתִינִים אֶל־יְרוּשָׁלִָם
ח בִּשְׁנַת־שֶׁבַע לְאַרְתַּחְשַׁסְתְּא הַמֶּלֶךְ: וַיָּבֹא
יְרוּשָׁלִַם בַּחֹדֶשׁ הַחֲמִישִׁי הִיא שְׁנַת

illustrious ancestor Aaron had the latter been alive then. This means that God's chosen leader of each generation is esteemed, during his times, over all others, even those of greater stature *(Yalkut Shimoni* 114).

סֹפֵר מָהִיר בְּתוֹרַת מֹשֶׁה — *A brilliant* [lit. *quick*] *scholar of the Torah of Moses.* [The word סֹפֵר is generally translated *scribe* (see *Targum* to *Judges* 5:14: מֹשְׁכִים בְּשֵׁבֶט סֹפֵר, *those who write with the pen of the scribe).* Our verse, however, specifies that he was the סֹפֵר *of the Torah of Moses,* indicating that the reference is to Ezra's standing as a great Torah scholar.]

[סֹפֵר is used in this sense by *Targum* to *Genesis* 49:10 who renders the word מְחֹקֵק, [lit. *lawgiver*] as סָפְרָא, *scholar* [i.e., one who can interpret the law]. Thus, the great Torah Sages of this period and forward were referred to as סֹפְרִים, *scholars.* See *Kelim* 3:7, *Rosh Hashanah* 34a, *Sanhedrin* 88b *(Doros HaRishonim* vol. 5, בבל וארץ ישראל, ch. 4, p. 174).]

A scholar quick to grasp the fine points of Torah *(Radak, Shorashim),* penetrating them with ease *(Metzudos). R' Yonah Ibn Janach* renders a *careful scholar,* while *Rashi (Psalms* 45:2) renders the word מָהִיר as *skillful.*[1]

*Ralbag* remarks that the word סֹפֵר is derived from ספר, *to count* or *enumerate.* Ezra could quickly enumerate all possible interpretations of each passage of the Torah. In addition, he could also enumerate quickly the proofs indicating which interpretations were most acceptable.

*Malbim* cites the following Mishnaic statement *(Avos* 1:2): Shimon the righteous was among the remnants of the Men of the Great Assembly [supreme judicial and legislative Tribunal headed by Ezra; see *Rambam, Hil. Tefillah* 1:4-7]. He was wont to say, 'The world stands on three things — on the Torah, on the services [i.e., the sacrifices; see commentaries to *Avos*], and on the practice of kindness.' These three pillars of the world were embodied in the personalities of the leading figures of Ezra's age. Zerubabel and Jeshua oversaw the construction of the Temple (3:2,8; 5:2), thus establishing the sacrificial services; Ezra organized the spread of Torah scholarship and strict adherence to its principles (7:10), thereby serving as the Torah personality; and Nehemiah strengthened the walls of Jerusalem and engaged in social reform [see *Book of Nehemiah*], thereby sponsoring the precept of kindness. Here, Ezra emerges as the *brilliant scholar of the Torah of Moses,* requesting the king's support for the advancement of the pillar of Torah.

וַיִּתֶּן־לוֹ הַמֶּלֶךְ כְּיַד־ה׳ אֱלֹהָיו עָלָיו כֹּל בַּקָּשָׁתוֹ — *The king granted him his every request, according to the command of* HASHEM, *his God, to him* [lit. *as the hand of* HASHEM, *his God, upon him*]. The translation follows *Rashi,* who explains that וַיִּתֶּן־לוֹ הַמֶּלֶךְ ... כֹּל בַּקָּשָׁתוֹ should be understood as one phrase parenthetically interrupted by ... כְּיַד־ה׳. The king granted all the requests God had commanded Ezra to make of him.

*Rashi's* translation, *according to the command of* HASHEM *to him,* indicates that Ezra was a prophet, commanded by God to gain the king's aid in sustaining the Temple. This is borne out by the

1. The word סֹפֵר there means *scribe* but, as pointed out in the commentary, it means scholar in our context.

*a brilliant scholar of the Torah of Moses, which*
*HASHEM, God of Israel, had given. The king granted*
*him his every request, according to the command of*
*HASHEM, his God, to him.*
7 *And some of the Israelites, Kohanim, Levites —*
*the choristers and gatekeepers — and Nethinites also*
*ascended to Jerusalem during the seventh year of*
*King Artahshast.* 8 *He arrived in Jerusalem in the*
*fifth month of the seventh year of the king.* 9 *For on*

Sages' tradition (*Megillah* 15a) identifying Ezra as the prophet Malachi.

*Metzudos*, following *Ibn Ezra*, translates the phrase כְּיַד־ה׳ אֱלֹהָיו עָלָיו, *according to the power HASHEM, his God, extended to him.* [I.e., the king agreed to all of Ezra's requests because the power of influence over the king was extended to him by God.]

*Malbim's* interpretation of the phrase is: *as the providence of HASHEM, his God, watched over him.* Ezra was given special Divine protection and guidance to guarantee his success in gaining the king's support, so that he could perpetuate the national commitment to the study of Torah and the strict adherence to its precepts (see above).

**7.** הַלְוִיִּם — *Levites.* The Levites did not initially join Ezra. The circumstances of their recruitment are related in 8:15-18 (*Ibn Ezra*).

וְהַמְשֹׁרְרִים וְהַשֹּׁעֲרִים — *The choristers and gatekeepers.* The Levites were composed of two groups — the choristers and gatekeepers (*Ralbag;* see comm. 2:41).

וְהַנְּתִינִים — *Nethinites.* [See above 2:43.]

וַיַּעֲלוּ ... אֶל־יְרוּשָׁלִָם — [*Also*] *ascended to Jerusalem.* In addition to those who had originally ascended with Zerubabel (2:2), those listed here now came with Ezra (*Metzudos*).

בִּשְׁנַת־שֶׁבַע לְאַרְתַּחְשַׁסְתְּא הַמֶּלֶךְ — *During the seventh year of King Artahshast.* See comm., v. 1.

**8.** וַיָּבֹא ... בַּחֹדֶשׁ הַחֲמִישִׁי — *He arrived ... in the fifth month.*[1] I.e., the month of Av (*Rashi*).

1. The Rabbis (*Rosh Hashanah* 3b, 4a) derive from this passage the information that the Persian king Darius was at first a righteous monarch, but later 'soured.' This is deduced from a close study of the relevant texts, which reveal a subtle alteration of the Scriptural treatment of the king.

To clarify this, a short introduction to the dating system of Scripture is necessary. Based on analysis of other verses, the Rabbis declare that the years of the gentile monarchs are always counted by Scripture from the month of Tishrei, with the first of Tishrei being reckoned the beginning of a new year of their reign regardless of when they actually ascended the throne. However, the years of the Jewish monarchs begin with Nissan. [See table below.]

| | | | |
|---|---|---|---|
| **Order of the Months** | 1. Nissan* | 7. Tishrei** | |
| | 2. Iyar | 8. Cheshvan | |
| | 3. Sivan | 9. Kislev | |
| | 4. Tammuz | 10. Teves | |
| | 5. Av | 11. Shevat | *First month for counting the years of Jewish kings. |
| | 6. Elul | 12. Adar | **First month for counting the years of gentile kings. |

[For example, if a Jewish king and a gentile king both ascended their respective thrones on the first of Adar, then the Jewish king would be reckoned as being in the second year of his reign one month later, on the first of Nissan, but the gentile king would not be considered in

ז ט הַשְּׁבִיעִית לַמֶּלֶךְ: כִּי בְּאֶחָד לַחֹדֶשׁ הָרִאשׁוֹן
ט-י הוּא יְסֻד הַמַּעֲלָה מִבָּבֶל וּבְאֶחָד לַחֹדֶשׁ
הַחֲמִישִׁי בָּא אֶל־יְרוּשָׁלַםִ כְּיַד־אֱלֹהָיו
י הַטּוֹבָה עָלָיו: כִּי עֶזְרָא הֵכִין לְבָבוֹ לִדְרוֹשׁ

9. יְסֻד הַמַּעֲלָה מִבָּבֶל — *The beginning* [lit. *foundation*] *of the ascent from Babylon.* The departure from Babylon took place on the first day of the first month *(Rashi).*

*Ralbag* translates: *the foundation for the ascent* [*was laid*] ... referring to the recognition of Ezra and his cause by the king and his advisors. This recognition, given on the first day of the first month, served as the *foundation* for the actual departure which occurred a short time thereafter. Or, according to *R' Yeshayah MiTrani,* it was on that day that Ezra departed from Babylon to the capital city of Shushan, to be appointed by the king as leader of the Jews. From there he completed the trip to Jerusalem.

According to *Ibn Ezra,* the word יְסֻד is rendered *advice* or *counsel.* The *counsel for the ascent from Babylon* took place on the first day of the first month. It was then that Ezra counseled those who ascended to accompany him to Jerusalem. The actual departure took place later.

כְּיַד־אֱלֹהָיו הַטּוֹבָה עָלָיו — *By the benevolence of his God* [lit. *according to the hand of his God which was goodly*

the second year of his reign until seven months later, on the first of Tishrei. Conversely, if they both ascended their thrones on the first of Elul, the gentile king would begin the second year of his reign one month later, on the first of Tishrei, but the Jewish king would not begin the second year of his reign until seven months later, on the first of Nissan.]

However, throughout Scripture, the numbering of the *months* begins with Nissan. When an incident is said to have occurred in the *first month* it means Nissan, the *second month* Iyar, the *third month* Sivan, etc. This is true even when referring to gentile kings, whose *years* are reckoned from Tishrei. Thus, if a gentile became king in Elul, an incident taking place one month later — in Tishrei — would be described as having occurred in the *seventh month* of the second year of his reign. The term *seventh month* is not a count but the *name* of a specific month — Tishrei.

Now the prophet Haggai records two passages taking place during Darius' *second year:* the first *(Haggai* 1:15) in the six month [Elul] and the second *(Haggai* 2:1) in the seventh month [Tishrei].

Since the second passage seems to have occurred after the first one, the recording of both passages in Darius' *second* year presents a problem. If Elul was during the second year of Darius' rule and the new third year began on the first day of Tishrei, then the following Tishrei must have been during the *third* year of Darius, not during the second as recorded in Scripture.

This discrepancy leads the Rabbis to the conclusion that the Persian king Darius, because of his great righteousness, was treated by Scripture like the Jewish kings, for whom the calendar year begins in the month of Nissan. Thus, the king's second year began in Nissan, and Tishrei was part of the same year; both Elul and the Tishrei immediately following were during Darius' second year.

The study of the *Book of Ezra,* however, raises new complications, which indicate to the Rabbis that by the sixth year of his reign, Darius' righteousness had dissipated and he was no longer deserving of the Nissan-based reckoning reserved for Jewish kings. The indications are as follows:

*Ezra* (6:15) relates that the Second Temple was completed on 3 Adar in Darius' sixth year. This was followed by the first Passover offering brought on 14 Nissan (6:19). On the first day of the following Nissan, Ezra began his ascent from Babylon (7:9) arriving in Jerusalem in the fifth month [Av] of the king's *seventh* year (7:8).

Here the Rabbis are faced with a dilemma. If, in view of his righteousness, Darius' year

VII 10

*the first day of the first month was the beginning of the ascent from Babylon; and he arrived in Jerusalem on the first day of the fifth month by the benevolence of his God.* 10 *For Ezra readied his heart to seek*

*upon him*]. Ezra's safe and successful journey to Jerusalem came about through the goodness of God *(Rashi).*

*Ralbag* asserts that this refers to the Divine assistance which prevailed upon the king to immediately grant all of Ezra's requests.

According to *Metzudos,* it is a reference to the Divine aid which greatly reduced Ezra's traveling time to Jerusalem.

**10.** ... כִּי עֶזְרָא הֵכִין לְבָבוֹ ... — *For Ezra readied his heart* ... This verse explains why Ezra was worthy of the success brought about by the Divine assistance described in the preceding verse — it was because he had readied his heart to seek, fulfill and teach the Torah *(Rashi; Ralbag).*

This shows that the Torah scholar who scrupulously observes the commandments and raises the people's spiritual level is blessed with absolute Providential protection. Because Ezra was a great Torah scholar, he was Divinely assisted in obtaining all that he desired from the king. Because he sought the word of God, fulfilled it, and taught it to the people, his requests were granted immediately *(Ralbag).*

*Yalkut* understands the readying of

began in Nissan, then the sixth year of his reign ended in Adar, when the Temple was completed, and the seventh year began the following month (i.e. the first Passover lamb was brought on 14 Nissan of Darius' *seventh* year). The first of Nissan a year later, when Ezra began his ascent from Babylon, should have been the beginning of Darius' *eighth* year, and the month of Av, when Ezra reached Jerusalem, should have been in Darius' *eighth* year. Yet the text states that Ezra arrived in Jerusalem during the king's *seventh* year (v. 8).

To reconcile the discrepancy, the Rabbis reason that by the sixth year of his reign Darius' righteousness had 'soured' and his status was reduced to that of the other gentile kings whose year begins in Tishrei. Thus Darius' seventh year began not in Nissan following the completion of the Temple but in the following Tishrei, and the year extended until the Tishrei thereafter to include the months of Nissan and Av, during which Ezra departed from Babylon and arrived in Jerusalem.

The following table illustrates the two ways of reckoning the years of Darius' reign.

| | | **Year of Darius' Reign According to** | |
|---|---|---|---|
| **Event** | **Month** | **Jewish Kings** | **Gentile kings** |
| Haggai's first passage | Elul | *2nd | *2nd |
| Haggai's second passage | Tishrei | *2nd | 3rd |
| Completion of Temple | Adar | *6th | *6th |
| First Passover offering | Nissan | 7th | 6th |
| Ezra's departure from Babylon | Nissan | 8th | *7th |
| Ezra's arrival in Jerusalem | Av | 8th | *7th |

*Scripture's reckoning.

The Talmud *(Rosh Hashanah* 36, 4a) cites several opinions concerning the specific misdeed which indicated the souring of Darius' righteousness. One view is that Darius' request that prayers be offered at the Temple for himself and his children (6:10, comm.) indicated that his intentions were selfish and not for the glory of God. Another is that Darius ordered that exposed wooden sections be built into the Temple walls (6:4, see comm.) in order to permit the quick burning of the Temple should the Jews rebel [see *Tosafos, Rosh Hashanah* 4a]. A third opinion cites Nehemiah's (2:6) mention of the king's *shegel* who sat beside him. The *shegel* is interpreted as a female dog with whom the king had immoral relations, indicating his disdain for the Biblical precept which forbids this abomination [see *Rashi, Rosh Hashanah* 4a].

אֶת־תּוֹרַת יהוה וְלַעֲשֹׂת וּלְלַמֵּד בְּיִשְׂרָאֵל
יא חֹק וּמִשְׁפָּט׃ וְזֶה ׀ פַּרְשֶׁגֶן הַנִּשְׁתְּוָן
אֲשֶׁר נָתַן הַמֶּלֶךְ אַרְתַּחְשַׁסְתְּא לְעֶזְרָא
הַכֹּהֵן הַסֹּפֵר סֹפֵר דִּבְרֵי מִצְוֺת־יהוה וְחֻקָּיו
יב עַל־יִשְׂרָאֵל׃ אַרְתַּחְשַׁסְתְּא
מֶלֶךְ מַלְכַיָּא לְעֶזְרָא כָהֲנָא סָפַר דָּתָא
יג דִּי־אֱלָהּ שְׁמַיָּא גְּמִיר וּכְעֶנֶת׃ מִנִּי שִׂים

Ezra's heart as a reference to his wholehearted prayer. 'One who prays wholeheartedly may be assured that his prayers will be heard.'

לִדְרוֹשׁ אֶת־תּוֹרַת ה׳ — *To seek* HASHEM*'s Torah.* Ezra devoted himself to a deep and intense study of Torah, amassing great knowledge, and mastering its profoundest meanings *(Malbim).*

וּלְלַמֵּד — *And teach.* Based on this passage, the Talmud (*Sanhedrin* 21b) states that Ezra was worthy of bringing the Torah to the Jewish people, had he not been preceded by Moses. This is derived from the two Scriptural passages describing Moses and Ezra in similar ways. Concerning Moses it is written: *HASHEM commanded me to teach you laws and precepts (Deut.* 4:14). Of Ezra it is written: *For Ezra readied his heart ... to teach precepts and laws in Israel*[1] [see also comm. v. 6].

בְּיִשְׂרָאֵל — *In Israel.* Ezra brought learning to the great masses of the people *(Ralbag).*

חֹק — *The statutes. Rashi (Genesis* 26:5), *Numbers* 19:1) defines *statutes* (חֻקִּים) as those commandments given without reasons, such as the prohibitions against eating pork or wearing *shaatnez* (a garment made of wool and linen). *Ramban* feels that חֻקִּים may refer to the Godly attributes men are required to emulate, such as kindness, compassion, charity, etc. *(Genesis* 26:5), or to customs established for the proper conduct of worldly affairs *(Exodus* 15:25).

*Malbim* explains that *statutes* refers to the body of Oral Law extrapolated by the Sages from the written words of the Torah.

### ◆§ The King's Letter

**11.** פַּרְשֶׁגֶן הַנִּשְׁתְּוָן — *The text of the letter.* [See above 4:23.]

סֹפֵר דִּבְרֵי מִצְוֹת־ה׳ וְחֻקָּיו — *Scholar of* HASHEM*'s commandments and statutes. Metzudos* explains that סֹפֵר here means one who has mastered the commandments and statutes.

*Malbim* renders סֹפֵר, *enumerator* [see comm. v. 6]. Ezra enumerated God's commandments and precepts. He counted the letters of the *Torah* — the Book of HASHEM's *commandments and statutes* — thereby preserving for posterity a precise count of its contents. Similarly, he counted the words of all of the Books of Scripture, issuing the approved, corrected version of the Scriptures free of any textual errors

1. *R' Ovadiah Bertinoro (Rav, Avos.* 1:15) derives from this verse that the Torah teacher's personal behavior should not deviate in any way from his teachings. The teacher's personal practice should be neither stricter nor more lenient than his instructions to his students. This may be seen from the depiction of Ezra — *for Ezra readied ... to fulfill ... and teach the precepts;* his fulfillment of *mitzvos* was consistent with his teachings.

*HASHEM's Torah, fulfill it, and teach in Israel the statutes and the laws.*

*The King's Letter*

11 *This is the text of the letter which King Artahshast gave to Ezra, the Kohen, the scholar scholar of HASHEM's commandments and statutes to Israel:*

12 *Artahshast, king of kings, to Ezra the Kohen, scholar of the Torah of the God of heaven and master of it; and to Che'eneth:* 13 *I decree that anyone in my*

which had occurred through erroneous copying. In addition, Ezra counted — i.e., enumerated and clarified — each of the statutes of the Oral tradition, as indicated by the use of the word חֻקָּיו, [*HASHEM's*] *statutes*, which refers to the Rabbinically extrapolated Oral Law [see above].

*R' Yitzchak Isaac Halevi (Doros HaRishonim* vol. 5 — בבל וארץ ישראל, ch. 4, p. 174) points out that this verse explains the origin of Ezra's unique title הַסֹּפֵר, *the scholar.* He was called Ezra, *the scholar,* because he was the consummate scholar of the commandments and statutes of the Torah.

עַל־יִשְׂרָאֵל — *To* [lit. *upon*] *Israel.* The words *to Israel* refer to the commandments and statutes. Ezra was the scholar of the commandments and statutes which Hashem had given to Israel *(Rashi).*

*Malbim,* however, relates these words not to *Hashem's* commandments but to the king's letter mentioned at the beginning of the verse. *This is the text of the letter which King Artahshast wrote to Ezra ... about Israel,* i.e., concerning the people of Israel.

**12.** אַרְתַּחְשַׁסְתְּא — *Artahshast.* This is the beginning of the text of the letter: 'I, Artahshast ...' *(Metzudos).*

*Malbim* is of the opinion that the letter opened with Artahshast's signature, and that this was customary in all royal correspondence.

גְּמִיר — *And master of it.* The translation follows *Rashi, Ibn Ezra* and *Ralbag.* גְּמִיר throughout the Talmud means *learned (Ralbag* and *Ibn Ezra).*

*Metzudos,* however, translates: *to everyone.* The letter was addressed to all the people of the land. *Ibn Ezra* also suggests this possibility and understands *everyone* as a reference to all the Jews now wishing to emigrate with Ezra.

*R' Yeshayah MiTrani* proposes that גְּמִיר means *complete.* It refers to the letter given by the king to Ezra. It was a *complete* letter, ready to be acted upon.

וּכְעֶנֶת — *And to Che'eneth.* The letter was addressed not only to Ezra but also to the empire at large and especially the residents of Che'eneth, the major city of the Trans-River [see above 4:10] *(Metzudos).* According to *Ibn Ezra,* Che'eneth is a reference to all the people of the Trans-River [as represented by the major city of Che'eneth].

*Malbim* translates גְּמִיר וּכְעֶנֶת as *etc., and Che'eneth.* He explains that this is an abbreviated reference to the gentile peoples listed above (4:9,10) who inhabited the Holy Land. The list there begins with the Dinaites and ends with the inhabitants of Che'eneth. The king's letter now was addressed to all of them and actually listed each of their names. Rather than list each of them here, the text uses the abbreviation *etc. and Che'eneth,* referring the reader to the complete list — *Dinaites, Apharsechites,* etc. to be found in 4:9, 10.

According to *Ralbag* and *R'*

ז
יד־יח

טְעֵם דִּי כָל־מִתְנַדַּב בְּמַלְכוּתִי מִן־עַמָּא
יִשְׂרָאֵל וְכָהֲנוֹהִי וְלֵוָיֵא לִמְהָךְ לִירוּשְׁלֶם
יד עִמָּךְ יְהָךְ׃ כָּל־קֳבֵל דִּי מִן־קֳדָם מַלְכָּא
וְשִׁבְעַת יָעֲטֹהִי שְׁלִיחַ לְבַקָּרָה עַל־יְהוּד
טו וְלִירוּשְׁלֶם בְּדָת אֱלָהָךְ דִּי בִידָךְ׃ וּלְהֵיבָלָה
כְּסַף וּדְהַב דִּי־מַלְכָּא וְיָעֲטוֹהִי הִתְנַדַּבוּ
לֶאֱלָהּ יִשְׂרָאֵל דִּי בִּירוּשְׁלֶם מִשְׁכְּנֵהּ׃
טז וְכֹל כְּסַף וּדְהַב דִּי תְהַשְׁכַּח בְּכֹל מְדִינַת
בָּבֶל עִם הִתְנַדָּבוּת עַמָּא וְכָהֲנַיָּא מִתְנַדְּבִין
יז לְבֵית אֱלָהֲהֹם דִּי בִּירוּשְׁלֶם׃ כָּל־קֳבֵל
דְּנָה אָסְפַּרְנָא תִקְנֵא בְּכַסְפָּא דְנָה תּוֹרִין |
דִּכְרִין אִמְּרִין וּמִנְחָתְהוֹן וְנִסְכֵּיהוֹן וּתְקָרֵב
הִמּוֹ עַל־מַדְבְּחָה דִּי בֵּית אֱלָהֲכֹם דִּי
יח בִּירוּשְׁלֶם׃ וּמָה דִי °עליך וְעַל־°אחיך יֵיטַב

°עֲלָךְ ק׳
°אֶחָךְ ק׳

*Yeshayah MiTrani,* וּכְעֶנֶת is translated as וּכְעַת, meaning *at this time* or *now.* The sense of the passage is *now the following message is presented* [see comm. to 4:10, 4:17].

**13.** מִתְנַדַּב — *Volunteering.* The translation follows *Rashi* and *Metzudos.*

מִן־עַמָּא יִשְׂרָאֵל ... עִמָּךְ יְהָךְ — *Among the Israelites ... may accompany you. Malbim* observes that Cyrus' original proclamation permitted his Jewish subjects to go up to Jerusalem for the purpose of building the Temple (1:3). Since the Temple was now completed, the Jewish exiles could no longer leave the land of their captivity without special permission from the king. Thus, it became necessary for the king to issue a new decree permitting the Jews to emigrate freely to Jerusalem.

**14.** ... כָּל־קֳבֵל — *For this purpose ...* This verse explains why the king permitted the Jews to accompany Ezra. Ezra's purpose was to investigate the extent of the fulfillment of the Torah in Jerusalem, and to teach Torah and the fear of Heaven. All those wishing to share in this spiritual elevation were invited to join Ezra in his journey to Jerusalem *(Malbim).*

שִׁבְעַת יָעֲטֹהִי — *His seven counselors.* The seven close advisers who had access to the king *(Rashi;* see v. 28, *Esther* 1:14).

עַל־יְהוּד וְלִירוּשְׁלֶם — *The Jews and Jerusalem.* The translation follows *Ibn Ezra.* According to *Rashi* the phrase refers to *the Jews of Jerusalem. Ralbag* and *Metzudos* render יְהוּד as *Judah.*

בְּדָת אֱלָהָךְ דִּי בִידָךְ — *Concerning the Torah of your God which is in your possession.* The purpose of the investigation is to ascertain whether the Jews of Jerusalem fulfill the Torah *(Rashi).*

*R' Yeshayah MiTrani,* however, translates *according to the Torah ... which is in your possession* — the investigation should be conducted on the basis of your Torah knowledge. As

VII
14-18

*kingdom among the Israelites, Kohanim and Levites*
*volunteering to journey to Jerusalem may accompany*
*you.* [14] *For this purpose you have been dispatched by*
*the king and his seven counselors: to investigate the*
*Jews and Jerusalem concerning the Torah of your God*
*which is in your possession,* [15] *And to transport the*
*silver and gold which the king and his counselors*
*have contributed to the God of Israel, whose dwelling*
*place is in Jerusalem,* [16] *and all the silver and gold*
*which you shall find in the entire province of*
*Babylon, together with contributions which the*
*people and the Kohanim contributed to the Temple*
*of their God in Jerusalem.* [17] *So that you may*
*purchase with this money, with all haste, oxen, rams*
*and sheep, and their meal offerings and libations, and*
*offer them on the altar of the Temple of your God in*
*Jerusalem.* [18] *You and your brethren may do with the*

*Contributions for the Temple*

the master of Torah, you are qualified to test them.

### ◆§ Contributions for the Temple

**15.** וּלְהֵיבָלָה כְּסַף וּדְהַב — *And to transport the silver and gold.* This is the king's second reason for granting permission for others to accompany Ezra (v. 13). They would serve as guardians for the safe transportation of such great valuables *(Malbim).*

הִתְנַדַּבוּ לֶאֱלָהּ יִשְׂרָאֵל — *Have contributed to the God of Israel.* The gold was contributed to provide for the needs of His Temple *(Rashi).*

**16.** וְכֹל כְּסַף וּדְהַב — *And all the silver and gold.* You are also commissioned to transport all the silver and gold *(Rashi).*

דִּי תְהַשְׁכַּח בְּכֹל מְדִינַת בָּבֶל — *Which you shall find in the entire province of Babylon.* This refers to the contributions made by the gentiles throughout Babylon *(Metzudos; Malbim).*

**17.** כָּל־קֳבֵל דְּנָה ... — *So that you may ...* The donations of gold and silver mentioned in the preceding verse are to be used for the following purpose *(Malbim).*

וּמִנְחָתְהוֹן וְנִסְכֵּיהוֹן — *And their meal offerings and libations.* [The sacrifices had to be accompanied by a meal offering and a libation of a certain size. See *Numbers* 15:1-12.]

**18.** וּמָה דִי עֲלָךְ ... יֵיטַב ... כִּרְעוּת אֱלָהֲכֹם — *Whatever seems right to you, according to the will of your God.* The money should be used to pay for the performance of God's commandments — whichever of them you and your brethren may choose *(Metzudos).*

*Malbim,* however, notes that according to Jewish law, money contributed by the people with the intention that it be used to buy the regular obligatory communal sacrifices [e.g., the cattle, wines, and grains for the daily *tamid* and the Sabbath *musaf*] may not be diverted to any other purpose. When these communal obligatory sacrifices have been bought and some unused money remains, the remaining

ז
יט־כג

בִּשְׁאָר כַּסְפָּא וְדַהֲבָה לְמֶעְבַּד כִּרְעוּת
יט אֱלָהֲכֹם תַּעַבְדוּן׃ וּמָאנַיָּא דִּי־מִתְיַהֲבִין לָךְ
לְפָלְחָן בֵּית אֱלָהָךְ הַשְׁלֵם קֳדָם אֱלָהּ
כ יְרוּשְׁלֶם׃ וּשְׁאָר חַשְׁחוּת בֵּית אֱלָהָךְ דִּי
יִפֶּל־לָךְ לְמִנְתַּן תִּנְתֵּן מִן־בֵּית גִּנְזֵי מַלְכָּא׃
כא וּמִנִּי אֲנָה אַרְתַּחְשַׁסְתְּא מַלְכָּא שִׂים טְעֵם
לְכֹל גִּזַּבְרַיָּא דִּי בַּעֲבַר נַהֲרָה דִּי כָל־דִּי
יִשְׁאֲלֶנְכוֹן עֶזְרָא כָהֲנָא סָפַר דָּתָא דִּי־אֱלָהּ
כב שְׁמַיָּא אָסְפַּרְנָא יִתְעֲבִד׃ עַד־כְּסַף כַּכְּרִין
מְאָה וְעַד־חִנְטִין כּוֹרִין מְאָה וְעַד־חֲמַר בַּתִּין
מְאָה וְעַד־בַּתִּין מְשַׁח מְאָה וּמְלַח דִּי־לָא
כג כְתָב׃ כָּל־דִּי מִן־טַעַם אֱלָהּ שְׁמַיָּא יִתְעֲבֵד
אַדְרַזְדָּא לְבֵית אֱלָהּ שְׁמַיָּא דִּי־לְמָה לֶהֱוֵא

money must be used for special voluntary communal burnt offerings called the *kayitz* of the altar.[1] Or it may be used for the salaries of those who performed certain services for the Temple *(Rambam, Hil. Shekalim* 4:5).

Thus, the king's directive to use the remaining silver and gold *according to the will of your God* means that the *Kohanim* were to divert the unused funds either to the purchase of this special *kayitz* sacrifice, or for salaries.

### ◆§ The Vessels

**19.** וּמָאנַיָּא — *And the vessels. Ramban (Megillah* 11b) suggests that these vessels were not contributions but original utensils used in the First Temple and plundered by the Babylonians during its destruction [see *Jeremiah* 52:17-23]. The king now returned them for use in the Second Temple [see comm. 1:7].

הַשְׁלֵם — *Give over. Rashi* and *Ralbag* explain that this word is derived from שַׁלֵּם, *pay. The vessels ... pay over to God,* i.e., give them over to the Temple.

*Metzudos* translates: *give over completely* [הַשְׁלֵם from the root שְׁלֵם, *complete*].

*Malbim* contrasts the king's instructions concerning the vessels with his directive (v. 18) concerning the gold and silver. Although the original intent of the donors of the gold and silver was that they be used for the obligatory communal sacrifices, the unneeded gold and silver could be diverted for other purposes [see comm. v. 18]. The vessels donated for the Temple services, however, were not to be used for any other objective. All of them were to be used in the services.

### ◆§ The King Finances the Temple Services

**20.** דִּי יִפֶּל־לָךְ לְמִנְתַּן — *Which you may be required* [lit. *which may fall to you*] *to provide.* Which you may happen to

1. The *kayitz* is offered on the altar at a time when the altar is otherwise unoccupied with the burning of other sacrifices. [*Kayitz* is literally a fig delicacy eaten as a dessert. Because the *kayitz* was brought to the altar after the other sacrifices had been consumed, or 'eaten,' it was considered a 'dessert' (see *Rambam, Shekalim* 4:9; *Shevuos* 12a, b).]

*remaining silver and gold whatever seems right to*
*you, according to the will of your God.* 19 *And the*
*vessels given to you for the service of the Temple of*
*your God give over to God in Jerusalem.* 20 *And any*
*other needs of the Temple of your God which you*
*may be required to provide, supply from the royal*
*treasury.* 21 *And in my name, I, King Artahshast,*
*issue a decree to all the treasurers in the Trans-River*
*that whatever Ezra the Kohen, scholar of the Torah*
*of the God of heaven, shall request of you, let it be*
*implemented expeditiously.* 22 *Up to one hundred*
*talents of silver, one hundred kors of wheat, one*
*hundred baths of wine, one hundred baths of oil, and*
*an unwritten amount of salt.* 23 *Everything*
*commanded by the God of heaven shall be done by*
*the [king's] seal, for the Temple of God; for why*

*The King Finances the Temple Services*

require for the Temple [besides the daily obligatory needs] *(Ralbag).*

תִּנְתֵּן — *Supply.* The translation follows *Rashi* who compares this verb to the Hebrew תִּתֵּן. *Metzudos,* however, renders *shall be supplied,* as in the Hebrew תִּנָּתֵן.

**21.** אַרְתַּחְשַׁסְתְּא — *Artahshast.* [See comm. to v. 1].

לְכֹל גִּזַּבְרַיָּא דִּי בַּעֲבַר נַהֲרָה — *To all the treasurers in the Trans-River.* This refers to the tax collectors beyond the river Euphrates, in the Holy Land, who collected taxes from the gentile peoples inhabiting the Land of Israel. This tax money was to be used to help Ezra *(Rashi).*

*Ibn Ezra* (v. 12) asserts that our verse marks the beginning of a new letter. The king sent two letters — one (beginning in v. 13) to the Jews who wished to accompany Ezra, granting them permission to do so, and a second (our verse) to the treasurers, instructing them to supply Ezra with funds.

**22.** עַד — *Up to* ... Any request up to the following amount for each category shall be honored *(Metzudos).*

כְּסַף כַּכְּרִין מְאָה — *One hundred talents of silver.* This would be used to purchase the animals for the sacrifices *(Rashi).*

חִנְטִין ... חֲמַר — *Wheat ... wine.* Wheat for the meal offering and wine for the libations *(Rashi).*

בַּתִּין מְאָה — *One hundred baths.* The *bath* was a liquid measure equivalent to three *seah (Metzudos).*

מְשַׁח ... וּמְלַח — *Oil ... and salt.* The oil was part of the meal offering. Salt was used on all sacrifices, as prescribed by *Leviticus* 2:13 *(Rashi).*

לָא כְתָב — *An unwritten amount.* The amount of salt was unlimited *(Rashi).* This was possible either because salt was inexpensive *(Metzudos)* or because the king owned the entire supply of salt in the kingdom *(Malbim)* [see comm. 4:14].

**23.** אַדְרַזְדָּא — *By the [king's] seal.* The translation follows *Rashi.* In the context of the passage the meaning is *quickly.*

כד קְצַף עַל־מַלְכוּת מַלְכָּא וּבְנוֹהִי׃ וּלְכֹם
מְהוֹדְעִין דִּי כָל־כָּהֲנַיָּא וְלֵוָיֵא זַמָּרַיָּא
תָרָעַיָּא נְתִינַיָּא וּפָלְחֵי בֵּית אֱלָהָא דְנָה
מִנְדָּה בְלוֹ וַהֲלָךְ לָא שַׁלִּיט לְמִרְמֵא עֲלֵיהֹם׃
כה וְאַנְתְּ עֶזְרָא כְּחָכְמַת אֱלָהָךְ דִּי־בִידָךְ מֱנִּי
°דָּיְנִין ק׳ שָׁפְטִין וְדַיָּנִין דִּי־לֶהֱוֺן °דאנין לְכָל־עַמָּא דִּי
בַּעֲבַר נַהֲרָה לְכָל־יָדְעֵי דָּתֵי אֱלָהָךְ וְדִי לָא
כו יָדַע תְּהוֹדְעוּן׃ וְכָל־דִּי־לָא לֶהֱוֵא עָבֵד דָּתָא

[A sealed decree is given the highest priority and is thus fulfilled quickly.]

*Malbim,* too, translates *seal,* asserting that the king commanded that a special seal be made bearing the insignia of the Temple of God. A decree bearing this seal would be considered a command of the God of heaven, and would carry the binding authority of the king's proclamation.

דִּי־לְמָה לֶהֱוֵא קְצַף ... — *For why should wrath befall ...* Let the treasurers supply the Temple needs, in order to avoid God's wrath *(Rashi).* This was the king's rationale for all of his decrees concerning the Temple contained in this letter *(Malbim).*

### ☙ Exemption for Temple Personnel

**24.** וּלְכֹם — *Therefore.* The translation follows *Rashi,* who compares לְכֹם to the Hebrew לָכֵן.

[*Rashi's* understanding is that the closing remark of the preceding verse, which expresses the king's belief that the Temple services protect the kingdom from Heavenly wrath, is the reason for the exemption from taxes of those involved in these services. Since the Temple services protect the kingdom, those performing the services are exempt from the taxes paid to the king in return for his protection. Taxing them would be like taxing soldiers in the king's army for the purpose of providing an army.]

*Metzudos* and *Malbim,* however, translate לְכֹם as *to you,* like the Hebrew לָכֶם. The passage reads, *we declare to you ...*

The Talmud *(Bava Basra* 7b; 8a) derives from our verse the ruling that a *talmid chacham* (Torah scholar, who devotes his time strictly to Torah study) is not required to pay taxes to the king. *Tosafos* there explains that the devotion to Torah study is equivalent to involvement in the Temple service. Just as the Temple personnel were exempt from taxes because of their participation in the sacred Temple services, so too *talmidei chachamim* are exempted because of their sacred Torah study.[1]

נְתִינַיָּא וּפָלְחֵי בֵּית אֱלָהָא דְנָה — *The Nethinites who work* [lit. *and those who work*] *in this Temple of God.* The translation follows *Rashi,* that the Nethinites were the Temple workers. [The conjunctive *vav* is sometimes added although no conjunction is meant. See *Radak's Michlol.*]

מִנְדָּה בְלוֹ וַהֲלָךְ לָא שַׁלִּיט לְמִרְמֵא עֲלֵיהֹם — *It shall not be lawful to impose upon them* [lit. *no one is empowered to levy upon them*] *levies, taxes and tithes.* [For an explanation of each of these various taxes, see comm. 4:13.]

### ☙ Enforcement of Torah

**25.** מֱנִּי — *Greater than.* מֱנִּי is like the Hebrew מִן *(Rashi).*

However, most commentators trans-

1. *Rashi* and *Meiri* to *Bava Basra* 8a and *Rosh* to *Nedarim* 62b state that the king exempted the Men of the Great Assembly from taxes. The statement is questioned by *Rashash* to *Bava Basra*

should wrath befall the king's realm and his children.
24 We therefore declare that for all Kohanim, Levite
choristers and gatekeepers, and Nethinites who work
in this Temple of God — it shall not be lawful to
impose upon them levies, taxes and tithes. 25 And
you, Ezra — by the Divine wisdom which you
possess, greater than that of the judges and
magistrates who judge all the people of the Trans-
River, for all who are knowledgeable in your God's
Torah — instruct those who do not know. 26 And

Exemption for Temple Personnel

Enforcement of Torah

late מַנִּי as *appoint: And you, Ezra, by the Divine wisdom which you possess, appoint judges and magistrates to administer all the people of the Trans-River.*

שָׁפְטִין וְדַיָּנִין — *Judges and magistrates.* According to *Malbim,* both judges and magistrates are mentioned because Ezra was commissioned to appoint the two types of judges recognized by Jewish law. One is the מֻמְחֶה, *expert,* who is qualified by his mastery of the law to preside alone over civil disputes (*Choshen Mishpat* 3:2). The second is the הֶדְיוֹט, *layman.* According to Jewish law, three laymen may sit on a civil tribunal provided one of them possesses *some* advanced legal knowledge (*Choshen Mishpat* 3:1). The king commanded Ezra to appoint both judges — masters of the law who would sit alone in judgment — and magistrates — laymen who would preside over civil cases in tribunals of three.

לְכָל־יָדְעֵי דָּתֵי אֱלָהָךְ — *For all who are knowledgeable in your God's Torah.* According to *Rashi,* this phrase describes the people of Trans-River — they were all knowledgeable in God's Torah.

According to those who interpret the preceding part of the verse as a command to Ezra to appoint judges and magistrates, this phrase is a description of the people to be judged by Ezra's appointees: *Appoint judges and magistrates ... for all those knowledgeable in your God's Torah,* i.e. in order to judge all who know Torah (*R' Yeshayah MiTrani*). [Only those knowing the law may be held accountable for their transgressions and judged by the courts.] *Metzudos* has it refer not to those being judged, but to the judges themselves. *Appoint judges and magistrates who are knowledgeable in God's Torah.*

וְדִי לָא יָדַע תְּהוֹדְעוּן — *Instruct those who do not know.* According to *Rashi,* the previous statements in this verse serve as a preface to the command expressed in this final phrase. The king, pointing out Ezra's great knowledge, commanded him to teach the judges and magistrates who were deficient in Torah knowledge.

According to *Metzudos,* however, our verse contains two commands: (1) To appoint judges, and (2) to teach all who were ignorant.

According to *R' Yeshayah MiTrani* our phrase refers to those who could not be held accountable in court because of their ignorance: *as for those who do not know* — and are therefore out of the courts' jurisdiction — *you must instruct them.*

**26.** וְכָל־דִּי־לָא לֶהֱוֵא עָבֵד דָּתָא דִי־אֱלָהָךְ — *And anyone failing to fulfill your God's Torah.* I.e., anyone who fails to heed the decisions of the courts (*Rashi*).

8a, however, who points out that Ezra mentions only the Temple personnel in the exemption, not the Men of the Great Assembly.

דִּֽי־אֱלָהָךְ וְדָתָא דִּי מַלְכָּא אׇסְפַּרְנָא דִּינָה ז
לֶהֱוֵא מִתְעֲבֵד מִנֵּהּ הֵן לְמוֹת הֵן °לשרשו כז־כח °לִשְׁרֹשִׁי ק׳
הֵן־לַעֲנָשׁ נִכְסִין וְלֶאֱסוּרִין׃ בָּרוּךְ כז
יהוה אֱלֹהֵי אֲבֹתֵינוּ אֲשֶׁר נָתַן כָּזֹאת בְּלֵב
הַמֶּלֶךְ לְפָאֵר אֶת־בֵּית יהוה אֲשֶׁר
בִּירוּשָׁלָםִ׃ וְעָלַי הִטָּה־חֶסֶד לִפְנֵי הַמֶּלֶךְ כח
וְיוֹעֲצָיו וּלְכׇל־שָׂרֵי הַמֶּלֶךְ הַגִּבֹּרִים וַאֲנִי
הִתְחַזַּקְתִּי כְּיַד־יהוה אֱלֹהַי עָלַי וָאֶקְבְּצָה
מִיִּשְׂרָאֵל רָאשִׁים לַעֲלוֹת עִמִּי׃
וְאֵלֶּה רָאשֵׁי אֲבֹתֵיהֶם וְהִתְיַחְשָׂם הָעֹלִים א ח א

*R' Yeshayah MiTrani,* however, understands this to refer to laxity in the fulfillment of the Torah in any way, not just to the refusal to follow the instructions of the courts.

אׇסְפַּרְנָא — *Expeditiously.* The translation follows *Rashi,* who attaches אׇסְפַּרְנָא, *expeditiously,* to the first part of the verse. *R' Yeshayah MiTrani,* however, and *Metzudos* place אׇסְפַּרְנָא with the latter part of the verse, reading: *shall be swiftly punished.*

לְמוֹת — *Executed* [lit. *to execution*]. This will occur should the offender be liable to any of the four Biblically prescribed forms of capital punishment meted out by the Rabbinic courts *(R' Yeshayah MiTrani;* see *Rambam, Sanhedrin* 14:1).

לִשְׁרֹשִׁי — *Uprooted* [lit. *to uproot*]. The Rabbis *(Moed Katan* 16a) interpret *uprooted* to mean excommunicated[1] [the sinner is uprooted from the world by excommunication] *(R' Yeshayah MiTrani).*

*Rashi* and *Metzudos* interpret *uprooting* as the destruction of the offender's roots through the execution of his family and children. [This seems inconsistent with Torah law, wherein only the sinner is punished, not his family and children. Evidently, this is a Persian punishment which the king empowered Ezra to invoke.] According to *Ibn Ezra,* uprooting the sinner means banishing him from his ancestral property.

וְלֶאֱסוּרִין — *Or torture.* This is *Rashi's* translation based on *Moed Katan* 16a [see footnote]. *Ralbag* and *R' Yeshayah MiTrani* translate: *imprisoned.*

1. The Biblically prescribed system of corporal and monetary punishment to be administered by the Jewish courts is strictly defined in Jewish law [see *Rambam, Sanhedrin*]. However, the Talmud *(Moed Katan* 16a), relying on our verse, instructs the Rabbinic courts to use special punitive options, decided upon at the discretion of the court, when unusual measures are needed to curb egregious offenders. The evildoers may be bound hand and foot and tied [to the whipping post *(Rashi)*], as it is written *to torture;* or they may be excommunicated, as it is written *uprooted* [see *Rambam, Sanhedrin* 24:4-9].

However, after delineating the broad discretionary use of these measures permitted to the courts, *Rambam (Sanhedrin* 24:10) cautions against judicial abuse in this area: 'Let [the judge's] intentions be for the sake of Heaven; let him not be insensitive to human dignity for the sake of which Rabbinic injunctions may be violated; certainly the dignity of the descendants of Abraham, Isaac and Jacob ... must be preserved ... except in order to enhance the glory of God.'

VII 27-28 *anyone failing to fulfill your God's Torah and the king's laws expeditiously, shall be punished — either executed, uprooted, subjected to loss of property or torture.*

*Ezra's Blessing*

27 *Blessed is HASHEM, God of our forefathers, for causing the king to desire this — to glorify the Temple of HASHEM in Jerusalem.* 28 *And He directed towards me the kindness of the king, his counselors and all of the king's powerful lords; I then strengthened myself, with the assistance of HASHEM, my God, and assembled leaders from among the Israelites to ascend with me.*

VIII 1 *The Family Heads*

*These are the heads of the families and genealogy of those who ascended with me during the reign of*

This concludes the king's letter of support *(Rashi).*

### ⁂ Ezra's Blessing

**27.** בָּרוּךְ ה׳ — *Blessed is HASHEM.* This is a thanksgiving prayer composed and added by Ezra when he wrote the *Book of Ezra (Rashi).*

This is an example of our obligation to praise God for his goodness to us. In addition to its own value as a mitzvah, this also serves as a means of making others aware of the role of Providence in human events. Thus, this Book records that Ezra offered praise to God for His goodness in helping him to obtain the needs of the people of Israel *(Ralbag).*

[In the first seven chapters of the *Book of Ezra,* events are recounted in the third person. However, from our verse until the close of ch. 9, Ezra narrates the events in first person. From the beginning of ch. 10 until the end the style returns once again to that of the beginning of the book and events are narrated in the third person.]

לְפָאֵר אֶת־בֵּית ה׳ — *To glorify the Temple of HASHEM.* God caused the king to desire to contribute to the upkeep of the Temple (vs. 15-23) *(Malbim).*

**28.** וְעָלַי הִטָּה־חֶסֶד לִפְנֵי הַמֶּלֶךְ — *And He directed towards me the kindness of* [lit. *before*] *the king.* God caused the king to empower me to enforce the Torah and appoint judges *(Malbim).*

כְּיַד־ה׳ אֱלֹהַי עָלַי — *With the assistance of HASHEM, my God.* [Lit. *as the hand of HASHEM, my God, was upon me.*] *(Rashi).*

מִיִּשְׂרָאֵל — *From among the Israelites.* From among those who remained in Babylon *(Rashi).*

רָאשִׁים — *Leaders.* Once the leaders agreed to ascend, others were attracted to accompany them *(Metzudos).*

## VIII

### ⁂ The Family Heads

**1.** וְהִתְיַחְשָׂם — *And genealogy.* The head of each family kept documents tracing his lineage to one of the twelve sons of Jacob *(Metzudos).* Additionally, each individual belonging to a family had records attesting to his membership in

ח
ב־יג

עִמִּי בְּמַלְכוּת אַרְתַּחְשַׁסְתְּא הַמֶּלֶךְ מִבָּבֶל׃
ב מִבְּנֵי פִינְחָס גֵּרְשֹׁם מִבְּנֵי אִיתָמָר דָּנִיֵּאל
ג מִבְּנֵי דָוִיד חַטּוּשׁ׃ מִבְּנֵי שְׁכַנְיָה מִבְּנֵי פַרְעֹשׁ
זְכַרְיָה וְעִמּוֹ הִתְיַחֵשׂ לִזְכָרִים מֵאָה
ד וַחֲמִשִּׁים׃ מִבְּנֵי פַּחַת מוֹאָב אֶלְיְהוֹעֵינַי בֶּן־
ה זְרַחְיָה וְעִמּוֹ מָאתַיִם הַזְּכָרִים׃ מִבְּנֵי שְׁכַנְיָה
בֶּן־יַחֲזִיאֵל וְעִמּוֹ שְׁלֹשׁ מֵאוֹת הַזְּכָרִים׃
ו וּמִבְּנֵי עָדִין עֶבֶד בֶּן־יוֹנָתָן וְעִמּוֹ חֲמִשִּׁים
ז הַזְּכָרִים׃ וּמִבְּנֵי עֵילָם יְשַׁעְיָה בֶּן־עֲתַלְיָה
ח וְעִמּוֹ שִׁבְעִים הַזְּכָרִים׃ וּמִבְּנֵי שְׁפַטְיָה
זְבַדְיָה בֶּן־מִיכָאֵל וְעִמּוֹ שְׁמֹנִים הַזְּכָרִים׃
ט מִבְּנֵי יוֹאָב עֹבַדְיָה בֶּן־יְחִיאֵל וְעִמּוֹ מָאתַיִם
י וּשְׁמֹנָה עָשָׂר הַזְּכָרִים׃ וּמִבְּנֵי שְׁלוֹמִית בֶּן־
יא יוֹסִפְיָה וְעִמּוֹ מֵאָה וְשִׁשִּׁים הַזְּכָרִים׃ וּמִבְּנֵי
בֵבַי זְכַרְיָה בֶּן־בֵּבָי וְעִמּוֹ עֶשְׂרִים וּשְׁמֹנָה
יב הַזְּכָרִים׃ וּמִבְּנֵי עַזְגָּד יוֹחָנָן בֶּן־הַקָּטָן וְעִמּוֹ
יג מֵאָה וַעֲשָׂרָה הַזְּכָרִים׃ וּמִבְּנֵי אֲדֹנִיקָם
אַחֲרֹנִים וְאֵלֶּה שְׁמוֹתָם אֱלִיפֶלֶט יְעִיאֵל

the family by proving his relationship to the family head *(Malbim).*

E.g., the members of the family of Pinehas (v. 2), who ascended with Ezra, were related to its family head Gershom. Gershom, in turn, kept documents showing that his lineage extended to one of the twelve sons of Jacob. [This lineage, however, is not recorded in the passages below.]

הָעֹלִים עִמִּי — *Of those who ascended with me.* They ascended with Ezra during his ascent, which occurred during the days of King Darius, after the reconstruction of the Temple [see 7:6-8]. The first emigration from the Babylonian exile had taken place during the reign of King Cyrus, and was led by Zerubabel and Jeshua (ch. 2) *(R' Yeshayah MiTrani).*

אַרְתַּחְשַׁסְתְּא הַמֶּלֶךְ — *King Artahshast.* I.e., the Persian king, Darius *(Rashi; R' Yeshayah MiTrani).* [See comm. to 7:1.]

מִבָּבֶל — *From Babylon.* [Even after the Persian conquest of Babylon, most Jewish people continued to reside there.]

**2.** מִבְּנֵי פִינְחָס גֵּרְשֹׁם — *Of the sons of Pinehas — Gershom.* The one who went up with Ezra from the sons of Pinehas was Gershom *(Metzudos).*

**3.** מִבְּנֵי שְׁכַנְיָה מִבְּנֵי פַרְעֹשׁ — *Of the sons of Shechaniah, of the sons of Parosh.* Shechaniah was a descendant of Parosh *(Ibn Ezra; Metzudos). Ibn Ezra* adds that the phrase *of the sons of Parosh* is added to distinguish this Shechaniah from his namesake mentioned in v. 5.

*King Artahshast from Babylon.* 2 *Of the sons of Pinehas — Gershom; of the sons of Ithamar — Daniel; of the sons of David — Hattush.* 3 *Of the sons of Shechaniah, of the sons of Parosh — Zechariah; and with him one hundred and fifty males traced their lineage.* 4 *Of the sons of the governor of Moab — Eliehoenai the son of Zerahiah; and with him two hundred males.* 5 *Of the sons of Shechaniah — the son of Jahaziel; and with him three hundred males.* 6 *Of the sons of Adin — Ebed the son of Jonathan; and with him fifty males.* 7 *Of the sons of Elam — Isaiah the son of Attaliah; and with him seventy males.* 8 *Of the sons of Shephatiah — Zebadiah the son of Michael; and with him eighty males.* 9 *Of the sons of Joab — Obadiah the son of Jehiel; and with him two hundred and eighteen males.* 10 *Of the sons of Shelomith — the son of Josiphiah; and with him one hundred and sixty males.* 11 *Of the sons of Bebai — Zechariah the son of Bebai; and with him twenty-eight males.* 12 *Of the sons of Azgad — Johanan the son of Hakkatan; and with him one hundred and ten males.* 13 *Of the sons of Adonikam, the last ones, these are their names — Eliphelet, Jeiel and Shemaiah;*

וְעִמּוֹ ... — *And with him.* Zechariah was the family head. The males of his family traced their lineage *with him (Rashi;* see comm. 1).

**4.** פַּחַת מוֹאָב — *The governor of Moab.* See comm. 2:6. The translation follows *Metzudos.*

**5.** בֶּן־יַחֲזִיאֵל — *The son of Jahaziel.* His name is omitted. He is called by the name of his father, who was better known than he *(Metzudos).*

**6.** עֶבֶד — *Ebed. Ebed* is a name *(Rashi).* [It does not denote *slave,* which is its Hebrew translation.]

**10.** בֶּן־יוֹסִפְיָה — *The son of Josiphiah.* His name is not recorded *(Ibn Ezra; Metzudos).*

**13.** אַחֲרֹנִים — *The last ones.* Of all those listed here who followed Ezra, they were the last to come *(Rashi; Metzudos).*

*R' Yeshayah MiTrani* and *Malbim,* however, translate: *and the last of the sons of Adonikam.* They explain that most of the members of this family had already emigrated from Babylon during the first immigration, in the days of Cyrus. [*Ezra* 2:13 lists 666 sons of Adonikam.] The last of the sons of the family of Adonikam — those who had remained in exile — now accompanied Ezra.

שְׁמוֹתָם — *Their names.* I.e., the names of the family heads *(Metzudos).*

יד וּשְׁמַעְיָה וְעִמָּהֶם שִׁשִּׁים הַזְּכָרִים׃ וּמִבְּנֵי בִגְוַי
°וְזַכּוּר ק׳ עוּתַי °וזבוד וְעִמָּהֶם שִׁבְעִים הַזְּכָרִים׃
טו וָאֶקְבְּצֵם אֶל־הַנָּהָר הַבָּא אֶל־אַהֲוָא וַנַּחֲנֶה
שָׁם יָמִים שְׁלֹשָׁה וָאָבִינָה בָעָם וּבַכֹּהֲנִים
טז וּמִבְּנֵי לֵוִי לֹא־מָצָאתִי שָׁם׃ וָאֶשְׁלְחָה
לֶאֱלִיעֶזֶר לַאֲרִיאֵל לִשְׁמַעְיָה וּלְאֶלְנָתָן
וּלְיָרִיב וּלְאֶלְנָתָן וּלְנָתָן וְלִזְכַרְיָה וְלִמְשֻׁלָּם
רָאשִׁים וּלְיוֹיָרִיב וּלְאֶלְנָתָן מְבִינִים׃
°וָאֲצַוֶּה ק׳ יז °ואוצאה אוֹתָם עַל־אִדּוֹ הָרֹאשׁ בְּכָסִפְיָא

### ◆§ The Search For Levites

**15.** אֶל־הַנָּהָר הַבָּא אֶל־אַהֲוָא — *At the flowing river, at the Ahava. Rashi's* understanding is that the name of the river was *Ahava.*

*Metzudos,* however, translates: *the river flowing to Ahava.* The river, which remains nameless, flowed to a place known as *Ahava.*

*Malbim* translates *that the river flowed into the Ahava.* The river at which Ezra assembled them was the nameless tributary of the river Ahava.

וַנַּחֲנֶה שָׁם יָמִים שְׁלֹשָׁה וָאָבִינָה בָעָם — *And we encamped there for three days. I then scrutinized the people* [lit. *meditated concerning the people*]. Ezra would not undertake the exacting task of scrutinizing the genealogies of those coming with them until three restful days had passed.

The Talmud derives from here that a traveler should rest for three days after the completion of his journey before praying, so that he may recover from his fatigue and then immerse himself in prayer with absolute concentration *(Eruvin* 65a).[1]

וּמִבְּנֵי לֵוִי לֹא־מָצָאתִי — *But I could find no Levites.* Above, in 2:40-42, we find that Levites had emigrated from Babylon to the Land of Israel at the time of the first ascent, and 2:70 records that, *the Levites ... settled in their cities.* This occurred some years before Ezra's arrival in the Holy Land, during the reign of Cyrus. Why then was it necessary for Ezra to search for Levites among the new immigrants from Babylon, when Levites had already been living in the Holy Land for a number of years?

*Rashi* and *Tosafos* (to *Kiddushin* 69b and *Yevamos* 86b; see *Sefer HaMikneh* there) explain that during the Babylonian exile the exiles had been ordered to entertain their captors with songs and music of the songs of Zion *(Psalms* 137:3). To avoid doing this, they amputated their thumbs so that they could no longer pluck the strings of the lyre.[2] All of the Levites who emigrated to the Land of Israel during the first ascent were of those who had mutilated themselves and who could therefore not perform the Temple service. [These

1. *Tur* and *Shulchan Aruch (Orach Chaim* 98) rule that this was applicable only during the Talmudic era, when absolute concentration during prayer was common. In post-Talmudic times, however, such total immersion in prayer is in any case virtually unachievable, and the three day restriction therefore does not apply. Nevertheless, one should still prepare for prayer by putting aside thoughts and sentiments which might interfere with proper concentration *(Mishnah Berurah* 98:6).

2. As the source, *Rashi (Kiddushin* 69b; see *Tosafos, Yevamos* 86b) cites *Yalkut's* (883) explanation of the Jewish captives' reply to the Babylonians depicted in *Psalms* 137:4: *How*

The Search For Levites

*and with them sixty males.* 14 *Of the sons of Bigvai — Uthai and Zaccur; and with them seventy males.*
15 *I assembled them at the flowing river, at the Ahava, and we encamped there for three days. I then scrutinized the people and the Kohanim, but I could find no Levites there.* 16 *So I dispatched the eminent Eliezer, Ariel, Shemaiah, Elnathan, Jarib, Elnathan, Nathan, Zechariah and Meshullam; and the sagacious Joiarib and Elnathan.* 17 *I directed them to Iddo, the leader in the place of Casiphia, and I gave*

Levites sang during the founding of the Temple (3:10,11), when it was not Biblically required, but not during the Temple services.] Ezra now sought among those who accompanied him Levites sound of limb who would qualify for service at the Temple. None of these had settled in the Holy Land previously, preferring the comforts of the Babylonian exile to the privations and hazards of the fledgling community in Jerusalem. When he remarked that he could find no Levites in the camp, Ezra was referring to Levites who were acceptable for the Temple service.[1]

However, *Ramban* and *Ritva (Kiddushin* 69b), *Kaftor Vaferach* (ch. 25) and *Tosefos Yom Tov (Kiddushin* 4:1) disagree, maintaining that qualified Levites had emigrated in the times of Cyrus, and still dwelt in the Holy Land. Ezra's concern was only that he could find no Levites to accompany him now. [*R' Yaakov Emden,* in his notes to *Yevamos* 86b, conjectures that Ezra's concern was because many of the original Levites had returned to Babylon in the interim and there was now a shortage of Levites in Eretz Yisrael.]

**16.** וָאֶשְׁלְחָה לֶאֱלִיעֶזֶר — *So I dispatched ... Eliezer* [lit. *to Eliezer*]. The translation follows *Ibn Ezra, Metzudos* and *Malbim,* who explain that Ezra dispatched Eliezer, Ariel, and the others to talk with Iddo [see v. 17]. Thus, Eliezer, Ariel, Shemaiah and the others were the bearers, rather than the recipients of the message.

*R' Yeshayah MiTrani,* however, translates I *dispatched* [a message] *to Eliezer, to Ariel,* etc. He explains that Eliezer, Ariel, and the others had remained in Babylon. Ezra dispatched a message to them asking them to approach Iddo with the request for Levites.

רָאשִׁים — *The eminent* [lit. *the heads*]. *Rashi's* rendition is *the great,* or *the eminent. Malbim,* however, translates *the leaders* (of the people).

Ezra felt that eminent men in positions of leadership would be most likely to succeed in exerting the influence necessary to gain Levite support *(Ralbag).*

**17.** וָאֲצַוֶּה אוֹתָם עַל־אִדּוֹ — *I directed* [lit. *commanded*] *them to* [lit. *upon*] *Iddo.* I sent them with orders to speak to Iddo *(Rashi).*

*can we sing the song of Hashem on foreign soil?* They did not simply refuse by saying, 'We shall not sing,' but answered, 'How can we sing?', implying that they *could not sing.* They had maimed themselves, and could not pluck the instruments which accompany the singing.

1. The Talmud *(Yevamos* 86b) relates that Ezra penalized the Levites for their failure to ascend from Babylon to the Holy Land. He decreed that מַעֲשֵׂר רִאשׁוֹן, *the first tithe* (one tenth of the produce of the Land of Israel), reserved for the Levites [see *Numbers* 18:21], be withheld from them. One opinion in the Talmud is that the first tithe was transferred to the poor. Another opinion is that it was given to the *Kohanim* [see *Rambam, Hilchos Maaser* 1:4].

ח
יח־כא

הַמָּקוֹם וָאָשִׂימָה בְּפִיהֶם דְּבָרִים לְדַבֵּר אֶל־
אִדּוֹ אָחִיו °הנתונים בְּכָסִפְיָא הַמָּקוֹם
°הַנְּתִינִים ק׳
יח לְהָבִיא־לָנוּ מְשָׁרְתִים לְבֵית אֱלֹהֵינוּ׃ וַיָּבִיאוּ
לָנוּ כְּיַד־אֱלֹהֵינוּ הַטּוֹבָה עָלֵינוּ אִישׁ שֶׂכֶל
מִבְּנֵי מַחְלִי בֶּן־לֵוִי בֶּן־יִשְׂרָאֵל וְשֵׁרֵבְיָה
יט וּבָנָיו וְאֶחָיו שְׁמֹנָה עָשָׂר׃ וְאֶת־חֲשַׁבְיָה
וְאִתּוֹ יְשַׁעְיָה מִבְּנֵי מְרָרִי אֶחָיו וּבְנֵיהֶם
כ עֶשְׂרִים׃ וּמִן־הַנְּתִינִים שֶׁנָּתַן דָּוִיד
וְהַשָּׂרִים לַעֲבֹדַת הַלְוִיִּם נְתִינִים מָאתַיִם
כא וְעֶשְׂרִים כֻּלָּם נִקְּבוּ בְשֵׁמוֹת׃ וָאֶקְרָא שָׁם
צוֹם עַל־הַנָּהָר אַהֲוָא לְהִתְעַנּוֹת לִפְנֵי

בְּכָסִפְיָא הַמָּקוֹם — *In the place of Casiphia. The place* is mentioned to differentiate it from an entire territory which was also called *Casiphia (Malbim).*

וָאָשִׂימָה בְּפִיהֶם דְּבָרִים לְדַבֵּר — *And I gave them a message to convey* [lit. *and I placed words in their mouths to speak*]. The translation follows *Metzudos.*

אֶל־אִדּוֹ אָחִיו — *To Iddo and Ahiv* [lit. *to Iddo Ahiv*]. According to *Rashi, Ahiv* is a name [not the common noun meaning *his brother*]. *Ibn Ezra,* however, translates: *to Iddo* [*and*] *his brother.*

הַנְּתִינִים בְּכָסִפְיָא — *Who were settled in ... Casiphia. Rashi* notes that, although the word is pronounced [קְרִי] נְתִינִים, the spelling [כְּתִיב] in the text is נְתוּנִים, *placed.* Therefore, *Rashi* translates: Who were *placed* or *settled* in Casiphia.

*Ibn Ezra* and *Metzudos,* however, render הַנְּתִינִים, *the Nethinites.* Iddo and Ahiv were Nethinites from whom Ezra's emissaries requested help in the search for Levites.

*Ralbag* offers a third translation: *Iddo, Ahiv, and the Nethinites.* In his opinion, Iddo and Ahiv were not themselves Nethinites, but others in Casiphia were. In addition to Iddo and Ahiv, Ezra's representatives approached the Nethinites, who had traditionally served at the Temple, and requested them to send some of their members to serve in the Temple. Indeed, this request bore fruit, and some 220 Nethinites joined Ezra's party (v. 20).

*Malbim's* translation is: *who were appointed* [*by the king*] *to Casiphia.*

### ◆§ Success in Finding Levites

**18.** כְּיַד־אֱלֹהֵינוּ הַטּוֹבָה עָלֵינוּ — *By the success given us by our God* [lit. *by the hand of our God which was good upon us*]. The translation is *Rashi's.*

אִישׁ שֶׂכֶל — *A wise man.* This is *Rashi's* translation. *R' Yeshayah MiTrani* explains that the travelers were unsure of their way and fearful for their safety. The wise man's counsel was needed to determine the proper route and to defend the travelers against marauders.

*Metzudos,* however, interprets אִישׁ שֶׂכֶל, *a skilled man.* He was skilled in the choral recitations of the Levites.

*Metzudos* remarks that the identity of the wise man is unknown. *Ibn Ezra,* however, identifies him as Sherebiah, mentioned later in the verse. The word Sherebiah is understood as referring to both the phrase preceding it and the

*them a message to convey to Iddo and Ahiv, who were settled in the place of Casiphia — to bring to us*

*Success in Finding Levites*

*servants for the Temple of our God.* 18 *And they brought us, by the success given us by our God, a wise man of the sons of Mahli the son of Levi the son of Israel; Sherebiah, his sons, and his brothers — eighteen.* 19 *And Hashabiah, accompanied by Isaiah, of the sons of Merari; his brethren and their sons — twenty.*

20 *And of the Nethinites whom David and the chiefs had designated for the service of the Levites; two hundred and twenty Nethinites, all specified by*

*The Fast*

*name.* 21 *There, on the river Ahava, I proclaimed a fast; to fast before our God and beseech him for*

phrase following it: *A wise man of the sons of Mahli, the son of Levi, the son of Israel* [—*Sherebiah*]; *Sherebiah, his sons, and his brothers — eighteen.*

מִבְּנֵי מַחְלִי ... — *Of the sons of Mahli* ... All of those named in this verse and the next were Levites *(Rashi).*

**20.** לַעֲבֹדַת הַלְוִיִּם — *For the service of the Levites.* The Nethinites were to aid the Levites in their tasks at the Temple *(Metzudos).*

[Nethinites had already gone up to Eretz Yisrael during the first ascent from Babylon (2:43), which took place a number of years before Ezra's journey. *Rashi* (there) identifies them as woodcutters and water-carriers who earned their livelihood by working for the people. The Nethinites mentioned here, however, were servants of the Levites. Although Ezra instructed all of those disqualified from intermarrying with other Jews to emigrate to the Holy Land *(Kiddushin* 69b, see comm. to 2:43), he had evidently allowed these Nethinites to remain in Babylon with their Levite masters. Perhaps he did so because their status as servants allowed them to be readily identified as disqualified for marriage, whereas the other disqualified Jews were not easily identified, and were thus prone to improper marriages.]

נִקְּבוּ בְשֵׁמוֹת — *Specified by name.* The Nethinites who now ascended to Israel were those whose names were known, i.e. prominent, well-known Nethinites *(Metzudos).*

### ☙ The Fast

**21.** וָאֶקְרָא ... צוֹם — *I proclaimed a fast.*

*Rambam (Taanis* 1:4; see *Shulchan Aruch Orach Chaim* 566:2) states: The Rabbis instruct that a fast day be proclaimed whenever the community is beset by peril, until heavenly mercy is obtained.

*Ralbag* explains why fasting is appropriate in times of peril: The fast is an effective aid to the prayers of both the wicked and the saintly. The denial of the flesh exalts the wicked, impelling them towards penitence and Godliness — and thus increases the effectiveness of their prayers. The fast also aids the prayers of the righteous, who suffer the privations of fasting over the people's sins while praying for forgiveness of those sins. Since God gives special consideration to the righteous, in order to relieve their suffering he grants their prayers, and the people's sins are forgiven.

*Taz (Orach Chaim* 562:8 based on *Berachos* 17a) asserts that the person fasting is credited with having offered himself as a

אֱלֹהֵינוּ לְבַקֵּשׁ מִמֶּנּוּ דֶּרֶךְ יְשָׁרָה לָנוּ וּלְטַפֵּנוּ
כב וּלְכָל־רְכוּשֵׁנוּ׃ כִּי בֹשְׁתִּי לִשְׁאוֹל מִן־הַמֶּלֶךְ
חַיִל וּפָרָשִׁים לְעָזְרֵנוּ מֵאוֹיֵב בַּדָּרֶךְ כִּי־
אָמַרְנוּ לַמֶּלֶךְ לֵאמֹר יַד־אֱלֹהֵינוּ עַל־כָּל־
מְבַקְשָׁיו לְטוֹבָה וְעֻזּוֹ וְאַפּוֹ עַל כָּל־עֹזְבָיו׃
כג וַנָּצוּמָה וַנְּבַקְשָׁה מֵאֱלֹהֵינוּ עַל־זֹאת וַיֵּעָתֵר
כד לָנוּ׃ וָאַבְדִּילָה מִשָּׂרֵי הַכֹּהֲנִים שְׁנֵים
עָשָׂר לְשֵׁרֵבְיָה חֲשַׁבְיָה וְעִמָּהֶם מֵאֲחֵיהֶם
כה עֲשָׂרָה׃ °ואשקולה לָהֶם אֶת־הַכֶּסֶף

°וָאֶשְׁקְלָה ק׳

sacrifice, since his own blood and fat are reduced from lack of food, just as the blood and fat of the sacrificial animal are consumed on the altar *(Leviticus* 4:5-10).

דֶּרֶךְ יְשָׁרָה — *Favorable passage* [lit. *straight road*]. We beseeched God to lead us on a peaceful journey *(Rashi),* and to guide us on a route out of the reach of our enemies *(Metzudos).*

*Ralbag* conjectures that when Ezra and his party reached the river, they learned of the deadly designs of their Samaritan enemies. The fast was then proclaimed to pray for protection during the perils of the remaining journey.

לָנוּ וּלְטַפֵּנוּ וּלְכָל־רְכוּשֵׁנוּ — *For ourselves, our infants, and all our possessions. Malbim* observes that their prayer reflected their proper sense of priorities. It opened with a prayer for their most essential need — safe passage for themselves and their infants — and only then did it follow with a request for the safety of their valuables.

**22.** כִּי־אָמַרְנוּ לַמֶּלֶךְ — *Since we had told the king.* Ezra stresses that his failure to request military support was *only* because the king had been told that God is good to those who seek Him and wrathful against those who oppose Him. Had this not been told to the king, Ezra would have asked for troops and would not have relied solely on God's protection, even though he and his entourage were engaged in fulfilling a major mitzvah — that of going up to the Holy Land. This is in accordance with the precept, אֵין סוֹמְכִים עַל הַנֵּס, *We do not rely on miracles.* Indeed, the Talmud *(Pesachim* 8b) states that even while engaged in performing a mitzvah (when the merit of the mitzvah provides a protective shield), it is improper to expose oneself to a *likely* danger. Thus, had he been able to, Ezra would have requested military aid. He was unable to do so, since the king had been told that the returning exiles enjoyed special Divine protection *(Malbim).*

**23.** עַל־זֹאת — *For this.* The Talmud *(Taanis* 8b) observes that they prayed exclusively for *this* — a peaceful journey — but no other request was made, although they faced other dangers. *(Maharsha* explains that the use of the word *this — and beseeched our God for 'this'* — implies the presence of other unspecified perils, for which supplication was *not* offered.) Based on this the Talmud states that a community beset by more than one peril must limit its prayers at any one time to only one of the dangers. [See also *Shulchan Aruch, Orach Chaim* 515:15.]

וַיֵּעָתֵר לָנוּ — *And He granted our prayers.* He accepted our prayers, for we reached Jerusalem in peace *(Rashi).*

*favorable passage for ourselves, our infants, and all*
*our possessions.* 22 *For I was embarrassed to request*
*of the king troops and horsemen to assist us against*
*the enemy during the journey, since we had told the*
*king that our God visits His favor upon all who seek*
*Him, and His might and wrath against all who*
*forsake Him.* 23 *So we fasted and beseeched our God*
*for this — and He granted our prayers.* 24 *I then drew*
*aside twelve of the chiefs of the Kohanim: Sherebiah*
*and Hashabiah, accompanied by ten of their*
*brethren.* 25 *And I weighed out to them the silver, the*

*Guardians for the Valuables*

*Ibn Ezra* and *Ralbag*, however, feel that there was an immediate revelation that the prayer was accepted, even before the peaceful completion of the journey made this self-evident. [This is indicated by the placing of the statement, *and He granted our prayers*, immediately after the prayer was uttered, and before the journey was resumed.] The Divine revelation came through a message to one of the prophets, perhaps Ezra himself, according to the opinion (*Megillah* 15a) that Ezra was the prophet Malachi.

*Malbim* cites the experience of Rabbi Chanina ben Dosa (*Berachos* 34b) who could sense, by the facility with which he was able to utter his prayers, whether they would be accepted. When his prayers could be easily spoken, they would be heard. When he experienced difficulty in expressing the prayers, he knew they would not be accepted. Similarly, Ezra may have known by the ease of the recitation of his prayers that they would be effective.

### ◆§ Guardians for the Valuables

**24.** ...וָאַבְדִּילָה — *I then drew aside* ... Ezra drew aside twelve leading warriors and appointed them as guardians of the valuables. The entourage was about to travel through a wild area, and the warriors were to protect the valuables against possible attacks by marauders (*Malbim*).

מִשָּׂרֵי הַכֹּהֲנִים שְׁנֵים עָשָׂר לְשֵׁרֵבְיָה חֲשַׁבְיָה — *Twelve of the chiefs of the Kohanim: Sherebiah and Hashabiah.* This verse seems to state that Sherebiah and Hashabiah were the *Kohanim* appointed to guard the gold, the silver, and the vessels. However, above (vs. 18,19), Sherebiah and Hashabiah were identified as Levites, not *Kohanim. Ralbag* resolves the problem by translating: *I drew aside twelve* [of those under the authority] *of the chiefs of the Kohanim — Sherebiah, Hashabiah* ... The verse refers to twelve Levites — Sherebiah, Hashabiah, and their ten brethren — who were *under the authority* of the *Kohanim*, but were not *Kohanim* themselves.

*Yalkut* (v. 28, see comm. there), however, indicates that the *Kohanim* themselves guarded the valuables. *Yalkut's* reading is: *I then drew aside twelve of the chiefs of the Kohanim 'and' Sherebiah and Hashabiah.* I.e., besides the twelve *Kohanim*, who are unnamed, Ezra also drew aside the Levites, Sherebiah, Hashabiah, and their ten brethren. Thus, the guard was comprised of twelve *Kohanim* and twelve Levites.

**25.** ... וָאֶשְׁקֳלָה לָהֶם — *And I weighed out to them* ... I gave them the valuables by weight [i.e., the valuables were

וְאֶת־הַזָּהָב וְאֶת־הַכֵּלִים תְּרוּמַת בֵּית־
אֱלֹהֵינוּ הַהֵרִימוּ הַמֶּלֶךְ וְיֹעֲצָיו וְשָׂרָיו
כו וְכָל־יִשְׂרָאֵל הַנִּמְצָאִים׃ וָאֶשְׁקֲלָה עַל־
יָדָם כֶּסֶף כִּכָּרִים שֵׁשׁ־מֵאוֹת וַחֲמִשִּׁים
וּכְלֵי־כֶסֶף מֵאָה לְכִכָּרִים זָהָב מֵאָה כִכָּר׃
כז וּכְפֹרֵי זָהָב עֶשְׂרִים לַאֲדַרְכֹנִים אָלֶף וּכְלֵי
נְחֹשֶׁת מֻצְהָב טוֹבָה שְׁנַיִם חֲמוּדֹת כַּזָּהָב׃
כח וָאֹמְרָה אֲלֵהֶם אַתֶּם קֹדֶשׁ לַיהוָה וְהַכֵּלִים
קֹדֶשׁ וְהַכֶּסֶף וְהַזָּהָב נְדָבָה לַיהוָה אֱלֹהֵי

weighed, as an accounting procedure, then given to them] *(Metzudos).*

תְּרוּמַת בֵּית־אֱלֹהֵינוּ — *Contributions to the Temple of our God.* Citing our phrase as an example, *Ramban* (to *Deut.* 12:6) asserts that the word תְּרוּמָה [*terumah*], *contribution,* literally *the object set aside,* is used in Scripture only in reference to objects or funds set aside for the *Kohanim* or the Temple.

הַנִּמְצָאִים — *Who were to be found.* Who were living in Babylon *(Rashi).*

**26.** עַל־יָדָם — *To them* [lit. *on their hands*]. For the purpose of giving over to them *(Metzudos).*

*Malbim,* however, translates: *by them.* The valuables were weighed twice: first by Ezra, as described in the preceding verse — *I weighed out to them,* and then a second time *by them* [the recipients], as stated in this verse (see *Malbim's* comm. to *Jeremiah* 32:9,10).

וּכְלֵי־כֶסֶף מֵאָה לְכִכָּרִים — *One hundred silver vessels by talents. By talents* indicates that each of the vessels weighed one talent *(Rashi).*

*Ibn Ezra,* however, translates: *silver vessels totaling one hundred talents.*

**27.** וּכְפֹרֵי זָהָב — *Golden bowls.* These bowls were used for the catching and sprinkling of the blood of the sacrifices *(Rashi).*

לַאֲדַרְכֹנִים אָלֶף — *At one thousand darkons.* The *darkon* was a coin. The twenty golden bowls were valued at a total of one thousand *darkons (Rashi).*

According to *Metzudos,* however, *each* of the bowls was valued at one thousand *darkons.*

וּכְלֵי ... שְׁנַיִם — *And two vessels.* The Talmud *(Arachin* 10b) states that the two precious copper vessels mentioned in this verse were instruments which had been used in the First Temple. They were actually two *pairs* of vessels. One was a pair of delicate cymbals [producing a soft tone *(Rashi)*]. The other was a mortar in which the incense used for the Temple services was ground. Both were delicately crafted to produce the proper tones. [*Rashi* explains that the sounds of the pounding of the incense against the mortar affected the quality of the aroma of the incense. Therefore, the mortar was carefully constructed to emit exactly the right sound when pounded.]

*R' Yeshayah MiTrani* suggests that all of the vessels now returned by Ezra had been used in the First Temple and then looted by the Babylonians during the destruction of the Temple [see comm. 7:16].

נְחֹשֶׁת מֻצְהָב — *Golden copper.* Copper having the hue of gold *(Ralbag; Radak; Metzudos;* see *Middos* 2:3). [מֻצְהָב, *golden-hued,* from זָהָב, *gold.*]

*gold, and the vessels — contributions to the Temple of our God which were donated by the king and his counselors and nobles, and all of Israel who were to be found.*
26 *I weighed out to them six hundred and fifty talents of silver, one hundred silver vessels by talents, one hundred talents of gold.*
27 *Twenty golden bowls at one thousand darkons, and two vessels of fine golden copper, precious as gold.*
28 *I said to them, 'You are sacred to HASHEM, and the vessels are sacred; and the silver and gold are a contribution to HASHEM, God of your forefathers.*

טוֹבָה — *Fine* [lit. *good*]. *Rashi* notes that the adjective טוֹבָה, *fine*, is in the feminine gender, and it describes נְחֹשֶׁת, *copper*, also feminine.

*Ralbag*, however, notes an inconsistency. מֻצְהָב, *golden*, is in the masculine form. Since both מֻצְהָב and טוֹבָה are adjectives describing *copper*, it is grammatically inconsistent for the first adjective to be masculine and the second feminine. He cites another passage in Scripture where both masculine and feminine adjectives are used in describing the same object: וְרוּחַ גְּדוֹלָה וְחָזָק, *a great, powerful wind* (*I Kings*, 19:11). גְּדוֹלָה, *great*, is feminine; חָזָק, *powerful*, masculine. Both words describe רוּחַ, *wind* [see *Rashi, Genesis* 32:9].

*Malbim* proposes that the adjectives do not describe just one word — נְחֹשֶׁת, *copper*, but two words — כְּלֵי נְחֹשֶׁת, *copper vessels*. These two words combine the masculine and the feminine: כְּלִי, *vessel*, is masculine; נְחֹשֶׁת, *copper*, feminine. Correspondingly, the adjectives describing the כְּלֵי נְחֹשֶׁת are also a mixture of masculine and feminine.

חֲמוּדֹת כַּזָּהָב — *Precious as gold.* According to one Talmudic interpretation, each vessel was as precious as two golden vessels. [*Korban Eidah* (*Yerushalmi, Succah* 5:6) explains that *two vessels* is redundant, since the plural usage (*vessels*) always indicates *two*, when no greater number is specified. The word שְׁנַיִם, *two*, is therefore read with the next phrase, שְׁנַיִם חֲמוּדֹת כַּזָּהָב — *twice as precious as gold*.] Another opinion in the Talmud is that both vessels combined were equivalent to one of gold (*Arachin* 10b).

**28.** אַתֶּם קֹדֶשׁ לַה׳ וְהַכֵּלִים קֹדֶשׁ — *You are sacred to HASHEM, and the vessels are sacred.* And it is befitting to place the sacred vessels under the protection of the sacred servants of God (*Metzudos*).

According to *Yalkut*, this pronouncement was made to the guards who were *Kohanim*[1] [see comm., v. 24].

*Ralbag*, however, maintains that the guardians were all Levites [see comm., v. 24]. Accordingly, his interpretation is that the statement, *you are sacred to HASHEM* ... was made to the Levites. [The Levites were also sanctified by their dedication to the Temple service. See *Rambam, Shemittah* 13:13.]

נְדָבָה לַה׳ — *Are a contribution to HASHEM*. Therefore, they are also sacred (*Metzudos*).

1. *Yalkut* observes that the pronouncement compares the *Kohanim* with the sacred vessels, i.e. *you* [the *Kohanim*] *are sacred to HASHEM, and the vessels are sacred.* This teaches that it is forbidden to benefit personally from the labors of a *Kohen* [see *Rambam, Klei HaMikdash* 4:2], just as it is forbidden to use the sacred Temple vessels for personal purposes [see *Rambam, Meilah* 1:1]. *Yalkut* relates that two of the rabbis were waited upon by R' Zeira, who was a *Kohen*. They were admonished by R' Abba who quoted Shmuel's statement that deriving benefit from the work of a *Kohen* constitutes desecration of the sacred, comparable to using the Temple vessels for profane purposes. Shmuel's Scriptural source is this verse.

כט אֲבֹתֵיכֶם׃ שִׁקְדוּ וְשִׁמְרוּ עַד־תִּשְׁקְלוּ לִפְנֵי
שָׂרֵי הַכֹּהֲנִים וְהַלְוִיִּם וְשָׂרֵי־הָאָבוֹת
לְיִשְׂרָאֵל בִּירוּשָׁלָםִ הַלְּשָׁכוֹת בֵּית יְהוָה׃
ל וְקִבְּלוּ הַכֹּהֲנִים וְהַלְוִיִּם מִשְׁקַל הַכֶּסֶף
וְהַזָּהָב וְהַכֵּלִים לְהָבִיא לִירוּשָׁלַםִ לְבֵית
לא אֱלֹהֵינוּ׃ וַנִּסְעָה
מִנְּהַר אַהֲוָא בִּשְׁנֵים עָשָׂר לַחֹדֶשׁ הָרִאשׁוֹן
לָלֶכֶת יְרוּשָׁלָםִ וְיַד־אֱלֹהֵינוּ הָיְתָה עָלֵינוּ
לב וַיַּצִּילֵנוּ מִכַּף אוֹיֵב וְאוֹרֵב עַל־הַדָּרֶךְ׃ וַנָּבוֹא
לג יְרוּשָׁלָםִ וַנֵּשֶׁב שָׁם יָמִים שְׁלֹשָׁה׃ וּבַיּוֹם
הָרְבִיעִי נִשְׁקַל הַכֶּסֶף וְהַזָּהָב וְהַכֵּלִים בְּבֵית
אֱלֹהֵינוּ עַל יַד־מְרֵמוֹת בֶּן־אוּרִיָּה הַכֹּהֵן
וְעִמּוֹ אֶלְעָזָר בֶּן־פִּינְחָס וְעִמָּהֶם יוֹזָבָד
לד בֶּן־יֵשׁוּעַ וְנוֹעַדְיָה בֶן־בִּנּוּי הַלְוִיִּם׃ בְּמִסְפָּר
בְּמִשְׁקָל לַכֹּל וַיִּכָּתֵב כָּל־הַמִּשְׁקָל בָּעֵת
לה הַהִיא׃ הַבָּאִים מֵהַשְּׁבִי
בְנֵי־הַגּוֹלָה הִקְרִיבוּ עֹלוֹת ׀ לֵאלֹהֵי יִשְׂרָאֵל

**29.** שִׁקְדוּ — *Be zealous.* Be energetic, industrious and assiduous *(Radak, Shorashim)*

וְשִׁמְרוּ — *And guard* [*the valuables*]. Spare no effort in guarding the gold, the silver, and the vessels *(Ibn Ezra; Ralbag; Metzudos).*

*Ralbag* translates: *Be zealous in your guard.*

עַד־תִּשְׁקְלוּ לִפְנֵי שָׂרֵי הַכֹּהֲנִים וְהַלְוִיִּם — *Until you weigh* [*them*] *over before the chiefs of the Kohanim and Levites.* Until you weigh the valuables over to the chiefs — i.e. until you return the valuables by weight [to account for them] *(Metzudos).*

הַלְּשָׁכוֹת בֵּית ה׳ — *For the chambers of* HASHEM*'s Temple.* In order that they be conveyed by the chiefs to the chambers of God's Temple *(Rashi).*

*Malbim's* interpretation is that the prefix בּ, which appears in the preceding word, בִּירוּשָׁלָיִם, *in Jerusalem,* is also applied to הַלְּשָׁכוֹת, *the chambers,* yielding *in the chambers* — guard the valuables until you weigh them before the chiefs in Jerusalem *in* the chambers of the Temple.

*Ibn Ezra* presents a different interpretation. The word שָׂרֵי, *chiefs,* which appears in the previous phrase applies to the closing phrase as well. The passage thus reads, *until you weigh* [*them*] *over before the chiefs of the Kohanim and Levites and the heads of the families...in Jerusalem—the heads of the chambers of* HASHEM*'s Temple.* [The valuables were to be given to the *chiefs* of the *Kohanim,* Levites and Israelites.

[29] *Be zealous and guard [the valuables] until you*
*weigh [them] over before the chiefs of the Kohanim*
*and Levites and the heads of the families of Israel in*
*Jerusalem for the chambers of* HASHEM*'s Temple.*
[30] *And the Kohanim and the Levites will receive the*
*weight of the silver, the gold, and the vessels to*
*convey to Jerusalem for the Temple of our God.'*

[31] *We departed from the river Ahava on the*
*twelfth of the first month to journey to Jerusalem.*
*And our God gave us success, and He saved us from*
*the hand of enemies and ambushers along the way.*
[32] *We arrived in Jerusalem, and remained there for*
*three days.* [33] *On the fourth day, the silver, gold, and*
*vessels were weighed over at the Temple of our God*
*to Meremoth the son of Uriah the Kohen,*
*accompanied by Elazar the son of Pinehas; they were*
*accompanied by Jozabad the son of Jeshua and*
*Noadiah the son of Binnui, the Levites.* [34] *By number*
*and by weight, all; and the entire weight was*
*recorded at that time.*

*The Valuables Delivered and Weighed*

*The Burnt Offerings*

[35] *The exiles returning from captivity brought*

They were the heads or the officials in charge of the Temple chambers.]

**30.** וְקִבְּלוּ הַכֹּהֲנִים וְהַלְוִיִּם ... — *And the Kohanim and the Levites will receive ...* Our verse is a continuation of Ezra's instructions to the guardians (v. 29). *Be zealous and guard [the valuables] until you weigh over before the chiefs ... And the Kohanim and the Levites will receive the weight ...* That is, the *Kohanim* and Levites who would later receive the valuables from the guardians *(Ibn Ezra).*

לְבֵית אֱלֹהֵינוּ — *For the Temple of our God.* For the needs of the Temple *(Ibn Ezra).*

### ◆§ The Valuables Delivered and Weighed

**33.** נִשְׁקַל הַכֶּסֶף וְהַזָּהָב וְהַכֵּלִים ... עַל יַד־ מְרֵמוֹת — *The silver, gold, and vessels were weighed over ... to Meremoth.* The valuables were accounted for by weight and then handed over to Meremoth *(Metzudos).*

**34.** בְּמִסְפָּר בְּמִשְׁקָל לַכֹּל — *By number and by weight, all.* They were all delivered by number and by weight; i.e. the number and the weight of all the valuables now delivered by the guardians to Meremoth and his companions matched their number and weight when they were received from Ezra *(Rashi).*

וַיִּכָּתֵב כָּל־הַמִּשְׁקָל — *And the entire weight was recorded.* The weight of all the valuables — and certainly their number was recorded *(Malbim).*

### ◆§ The Burnt Offerings

**35.** הַבָּאִים מֵהַשְּׁבִי בְנֵי־הַגּוֹלָה — *The exiles returning from captivity.* This refers to

ח פָּרִ֨ים שְׁנֵים־עָשָׂ֜ר עַל־כָּל־יִשְׂרָאֵ֗ל אֵילִ֣ים ׀
לו תִּשְׁעִ֣ים וְשִׁשָּׁ֗ה כְּבָשִׂ֕ים שִׁבְעִ֣ים וְשִׁבְעָ֔ה
צְפִירֵ֥י חַטָּ֖את שְׁנֵ֣ים עָשָׂ֑ר הַכֹּ֖ל עוֹלָ֥ה
לו לַֽיהוָֽה׃ וַיִּתְּנ֞וּ ׀ אֶת־דָּתֵ֣י הַמֶּ֗לֶךְ לַֽאֲחַשְׁדַּרְפְּנֵ֤י
הַמֶּ֙לֶךְ֙ וּפַחֲו֖וֹת עֵ֣בֶר הַנָּהָ֑ר וְנִשְּׂא֥וּ אֶת־הָעָ֖ם
ט א וְאֶת־בֵּ֥ית הָאֱלֹהִֽים׃ וּכְכַלּ֣וֹת
א אֵ֗לֶּה נִגְּשׁ֨וּ אֵלַ֤י הַשָּׂרִים֙ לֵאמֹ֔ר לֹֽא־נִבְדְּל֨וּ

those who now returned with Ezra *(Rashi).*

הַכֹּל עֹלָה — *All burnt offerings.* The particular sacrifices listed here do not conform with the Torah laws governing the sacrifices, and could not ordinarily have been offered at the Temple.[1] They were now offered because Ezra and his colleagues issued a הוֹרָאַת שָׁעָה, *temporary ruling* — the temporary suspension of the law which may be decreed by the highest Rabbinical authorities in order to meet overriding momentary needs [see comm. 6:17] — instructing that these particular offerings be brought *(Rashi; Horios* 6a; *Temurah* 15b).

*Malbim* (to 6:17) adds that the prophets of the day were commanded, by Divine revelation, to issue this *temporary ruling* instructing that these sacrifices be offered.

### ◆§ The Royal Decrees Transmitted

**36.** וַיִּתְּנוּ אֶת־דָּתֵי הַמֶּלֶךְ — *They transmitted the royal decrees.* The returning exiles informed the king's appointee's of his decrees [in his letter to Ezra (7:11-26)] *(Rashi),* and showed them the letter *(Ralbag).* [The decrees authorized Jewish emigration to the Holy Land, ordered that all of the Temple requirements be immediately fulfilled, and instructed Ezra to establish courts to enforce Torah law. Scripture records only that the king sent a letter concerning his decrees to Ezra (7:11). There is no mention, however, that the king sent letters to the governors of the Trans-River. Thus, it was only through the exiles themselves that the local satraps learned of the decrees.]

לַאֲחַשְׁדַּרְפְּנֵי הַמֶּלֶךְ — *To the king's satraps.* The word is a composite of אחש דר פני, *the great ones* [אחש] *who enter* [דר, lit. *live*] *the inner chambers* [פני]; i.e. the highest officials of the realm, who have regular access to the inner circles of the palace *(Radak, Shorashim* in the name of his father). This seems to be *Rashi's* explanation of

1. This verse states that twelve bulls were brought for all of Israel, ninety-six rams, seventy-seven sheep, and twelve goats as sin offerings. In addition, *all* are described at the close of the sentence as burnt offerings (עֹלָה), although the twelve goats are described previously in the verse as sin offerings (חַטָּאת).

The Talmud *(Temurah* 15b, *Horios* 6a) examines each of these specifications, and points out that in some ways these offerings conform with the ordinary sacrificial regulations, and in other ways they do not.

The twelve bulls for all of Israel and the twelve goats as sin offerings were brought to atone for the idol worship practiced by the Jewish people during the times of King Zidkiyah immediately preceding the fall of the First Temple [see *II Chronicles* 36:14]. The bulls and goats correspond to the Biblically prescribed sacrifices to be brought when the entire congregation has sinned by committing idol worship — one bull as a burnt offering, and one goat as a sin offering *(Numbers* 15:22-26; see *Rashi, Temurah* 15b, *Horios* 6a). But why were *twelve* bulls and goats brought, when only one of each is prescribed by the Torah?

VIII 36 *burnt offerings to the God of Israel: twelve bulls for all of Israel, ninety-six rams, seventy-seven sheep, twelve goats as sin offerings — all burnt offerings to*

*The Royal Decrees Transmitted*

*HASHEM.* 36 *They transmitted the royal decrees to the king's satraps and the governors of the Trans-River; and they raised up the people and the Temple of God.*

*Intermarriage*

IX 1 *When this was concluded, the chiefs approached me, saying: The people of Israel, the Kohanim,*

the word as well.

*Malbim* notes that the king's decrees were also addressed to the gentile nations [see his comm. to 7:11]. Each nation was governed by a satrap and governor. The king's decree was now publicized to all the nations through their ministers and governors.

וּפַחֲוֹת — *And the governors.* They governed the affairs of each city *(R' Yeshayah MiTrani).*

וְנִשְּׂאוּ אֶת־הָעָם — *And they raised up the people.* They raised the esteem of the people by assisting them *(Rashi, Metzudos,* see comm. 1:4). [One of the king's decrees was that the treasurers provide funds to be used for the Temple. See 7:21-23.]

# IX

### ◆§ Intermarriage

**1.** וּכְכַלּוֹת אֵלֶּה — *When this was* [lit. *when these were*] *concluded.* When the recounting of the king's decrees *(Rashi)* and the consequent elevation of the people's status *(R' Yeshayah MiTrani)* described in the final verse of the preceding chapter had been completed ...

At this point, four months had already passed since Ezra's arrival in Jerusalem. He had arrived in the fifth month (7:9) of the year, and it was now the ninth month, as indicated in 10:9 *(Malbim).*

אֵלַי — *Me* [lit. *to me*]. Ezra is the narrator.

הַשָּׂרִים — *The chiefs.* These were the chiefs of Israel *(Rashi)* [and not the

According to some Talmudic opinions, the twelve bulls and goats were offered for the twelve tribes of Israel, who shared the guilt for the idol worship. [Some members of all the tribes remained in the Land of Israel to the very end of the First Temple. See comm. 6:22.] Another opinion in the Talmud is that the idolatry was repeated twelve times, necessitating twelve bulls and twelve goats.

The Talmud also explains why all of the sacrifices are called burnt offerings at the end of the verse. Actually, the twelve goats were not burnt offerings, but sin offerings. However, they differed from the ordinary sin offering and resembled the burnt offering in the following way: Ordinary sin offerings are partly consumed on the altar and partly eaten by the *Kohanim,* but the burnt offering is completely consumed, and not eaten at all. The sin offering to be sacrificed when the community has committed idolatry is exceptional in that it, too, is totally consumed like the burnt offering. Thus, the twelve sin offering goats are called burnt offerings, which they resembled. Since they were brought as atonement for community-wide idol worship, they were totally consumed, like the burnt offering.

In the ways just described, the sacrifices brought when Ezra and his group reached Jerusalem conformed to the prescribed rules for sacrifices. However, Ezra's offerings differed from the ordinary sacrificial regulations in two ways: (1) Ezra's sacrifices were brought for

ט
ב־ד

הָעָם יִשְׂרָאֵל וְהַכֹּהֲנִים וְהַלְוִיִּם מֵעַמֵּי
הָאֲרָצוֹת כְּתֹעֲבֹתֵיהֶם לַכְּנַעֲנִי הַחִתִּי הַפְּרִזִּי
ב הַיְבוּסִי הָעַמֹּנִי הַמֹּאָבִי הַמִּצְרִי וְהָאֱמֹרִי: כִּי־
נָשְׂאוּ מִבְּנֹתֵיהֶם לָהֶם וְלִבְנֵיהֶם וְהִתְעָרְבוּ
זֶרַע הַקֹּדֶשׁ בְּעַמֵּי הָאֲרָצוֹת וְיַד הַשָּׂרִים
וְהַסְּגָנִים הָיְתָה בַּמַּעַל הַזֶּה רִאשׁוֹנָה:
ג וּכְשָׁמְעִי אֶת־הַדָּבָר הַזֶּה קָרַעְתִּי אֶת־בִּגְדִי
וּמְעִילִי וָאֶמְרְטָה מִשְּׂעַר רֹאשִׁי וּזְקָנִי
ד וָאֵשְׁבָה מְשׁוֹמֵם: וְאֵלַי יֵאָסְפוּ כֹּל חָרֵד

king's gentile functionaries mentioned in the final verse of the preceding chapter. The subject discussed in this chapter is an internal Jewish matter].

כְּתֹעֲבֹתֵיהֶם לַכְּנַעֲנִי — [Doing] *like the abominations of the Canaanites.* Their deeds are like the abominations of the Canaanites *(Metzudos; Malbim).*

**2.** כִּי־נָשְׂאוּ מִבְּנֹתֵיהֶם — *For they have taken their daughters in marriage.* The preceding verse faults the people of Israel with performing the abominations of the nations. This verse states the cause — *for they have taken their daughters in marriage.* They have married the daughters of the gentile peoples (listed in v. 1) and have followed their wives' abominable traditions *(Metzudos; Malbim).*

זֶרַע הַקֹּדֶשׁ — *The sacred seed.* I.e., the Jewish people *(Metzudos).*

בְּעַמֵּי הָאֲרָצוֹת — *With the nations of the land.* They married gentile women who had not converted to Judaism. If they had converted, the Jews would have been permitted to marry them (with the exception of Egyptian converts[1]), and they would not be criticized now for having done so *(Ralbag).*

וְיַד הַשָּׂרִים וְהַסְּגָנִים הָיְתָה בַּמַּעַל הַזֶּה רִאשׁוֹנָה — *And the chiefs and the officers* [lit. *And the hand of the chiefs and officers*] *were first in this transgression.* They were the first to marry heathens and the rest of the people followed their example *(Metzudos).*

The chiefs who approached Ezra (v. 1) were national leaders of great piety *(R' Yeshaya MiTrani).* They informed Ezra of the other nobles who had sinned grievously by marrying gentiles.

*Malbim* (to 10:2), however, explains that the chiefs did not actually intermarry but were condemned for having done so because of their failure to protest and exert their influence against these sinful marriages. [See comm. to 10:2.]

### ◆§ Ezra's Anguish

**3.** וּמְעִילִי — *And my cloak.* Ezra tore his

מֵזִיד, *deliberate sin* [of idol worship]; ordinarily, sacrifices are brought only when the transgressors have, through negligence, sinned בְּשׁוֹגֵג, *unintentionally.* (2) The sacrifices included ninety-six rams and seventy-seven sheep. Nowhere in the Torah's laws of sacrifices is this number of rams and sheep prescribed. Therefore, the Talmud concludes, the sacrifices offered when Ezra and his companions reached Jerusalem were prescribed by הוֹרָאַת שָׁעָה, the Rabbis' *temporary ruling* used to alter normal procedures in extraordinary times.

1. An Egyptian or Edomite convert is forbidden to marry a native Jew until the third generation after conversion *(Deut.* 23:8-9). A Jew is permitted to marry any other woman who

IX 2-4

*and the Levites have not separated themselves from the peoples of the land — [doing] like the abominations of the Canaanites, the Hittites, the Perizzites, the Jebusites, the Ammonites, the Moabites, the Egyptians, and the Emoraites.* 2 *For they have taken their daughters in marriage for themselves and their sons, and the sacred seed have intermingled with the nations of the land — and the chiefs and officers were first in this transgression.*

*Ezra's Anguish*

3 *When I heard this, I rent my garment and my cloak, tore the hair from my head and beard, and sat stunned.* 4 *And all who hastened at the word of the*

outer garment in anguish *(Metzudos).*

וָאֶמְרְטָה מִשְּׂעַר רֹאשִׁי — *Tore the hair from my head. Leviticus* (21:5) prohibits tearing the hair out (קָרְחָה). *Beis Yosef (Yoreh Deah* 180) rules that the prohibition applies only when the hair is torn in mourning for the dead, not when it expresses any other sorrow. *Bach* disagrees, insisting that tearing the hair out for other sorrows is also forbidden.

All authorities agree, however, that the hair may be torn out in sorrow over a loss of Torah *(Tosafos, Sanhedrin* 68a; see *Minchas Chinuch* 467). Accordingly, Ezra was justified in tearing his hair as an expression of anguish over the people's terrible desecration of the Torah.

מְשׁוֹמֵם — *Stunned.* Speechless with anguish *(Metzudos). Malbim* renders *desolated.*

The following are *Rambam's (Isurei Biah* 12:1-8) remarks concerning the gravity of intermarriage: 'A Jew or Jewess who marries a gentile and then has relations with the non-Jew is punished with מַלְקוּת, Biblically prescribed flogging ... When out of wedlock, such relations are punished by מַכַּת מַרְדּוּת, Rabbinically prescribed flogging ... Anyone who is publicly [perceived as] having relations with a non-Jewess (i.e., before 10 Jewish witnesses) whether after marriage or out of wedlock, may be executed by the קַנָּאִי [*kanna'i*], *zealot,* whose attack is praiseworthy and zealous. This precept was handed down orally to Moses at Sinai, and is verified by Pinehas' action against Zimri. [Pinehas executed the Shimonite prince, Zimri, for having relations with a Midianite woman. As a result, a plague which had caused the death of 24,000 Jews was halted, and Pinehas was rewarded with becoming a *Kohen (Deut.* 25:7-15).] However, the *kanna'i* may strike only while the immoral act is being performed, but not afterward ...

'... Should he [the sinner] escape the

converts to Judaism, including, according to some opinions, members of the seven ancient Canaanite peoples *(Deut.* 7:1) who inhabited Eretz Yisrael in Biblical times. Of those seven peoples, only the Gibeonites, later known as the Nethinites, converted, and they were forbidden in marriage to Jews by Rabbinical decree (see comm. 2:43).

However, since the Assyrian king Sennacherib uprooted all of the gentile peoples from their homelands and resettled them elsewhere (see 4:10), nationality is no longer indicative of national origin — i.e., those living in Egypt are not necessarily descended from the ancient Egyptians. Consequently, a present day convert, even an "Egyptian," may marry into the Jewish community *(Rambam, Isurei Biah,* 12:17-25) (see *Mishnah, Yadayim* 4:4).

ט בְּדִבְרֵי אֱלֹהֵי־יִשְׂרָאֵל עַל מַעַל הַגּוֹלָה וַאֲנִי
ה ה יֹשֵׁב מְשׁוֹמֵם עַד לְמִנְחַת הָעָרֶב: וּבְמִנְחַת
הָעֶרֶב קַמְתִּי מִתַּעֲנִיתִי וּבְקָרְעִי בִגְדִי וּמְעִילִי

the *kanna'i* and the punishment of the courts, then his punishment is ... that his progeny [by a Jewish wife] will never be numbered among the wise men or their disciples; if he is a *Kohen*, his children will never bring an offering before God. We are taught that a person having relations with a non-Jewess is considered as having married the false deity itself, and he is entitled "the desecrator of God's sanctity."

'Although this sin is not subject to capital punishment, its gravity should not be underestimated, for it leads to harm unmatched by any other immoral act. For a child born of adultery or incest, although illegitimate, is fully related to its father and is totally Jewish – but the child of a non-Jewess is unrelated to its father [i.e., non-Jewish]. This results in attachment to the idolaters from whom God has separated us; in forsaking him; in sinning against him ...' *(Rambam).*

*Rama,* too, considers intercourse with a non-Jewess among the gravest of transgressions, ruling that, as in the case of adultery or incest, '... a Jew is required to suffer death rather than engage in relations with a non-Jewess' *(Even Haezer* 16:2). [For the ruling concerning a Jewess who is ordered, upon pain of death, to submit to a gentile, see *Rama, Yoreh Deah* 157:1.]

*Ralbag* remarks that, although the penalty meted out by the courts is flogging – a mild punishment compared to the capital punishment reserved for the gravest Biblical transgressions – in terms of Divine retribution, its consequences are disastrous. Witness the Divine punishment for King Solomon's marriages to gentile women who had actually converted[1] – for this transgression the Jewish people were exiled.

The Talmud *(Eruvin* 19a) asserts that the patriarch Abraham raises up the damned from *Gehinom* – except for those guilty of having relations with a gentile woman, whom Abraham does not identify as Jews.

### ◆§ The Gathering

**4.** כֹּל חָרֵד בְּדִבְרֵי אֱלֹהֵי־יִשְׂרָאֵל – *And all who hastened at the word of the God of Israel.* The translation follows *Metzudos,* citing *I Samuel* 16:4, *And all who hastened at the word* ... (see *Rashi* to *Isaiah* 66:5). Those who hastened to carry out the word of God then gathered.

*Malbim* translates חָרֵד as *trembled.* According to him, the phrase is to be understood as if it read: כֹּל חָרֵד עַל מַעַל הַגּוֹלָה בְּדִבְרֵי אֱלֹהֵי־יִשְׂרָאֵל, *All who trembled at the exile's transgression of the word of the God of Israel.*

עַל מַעַל הַגּוֹלָה – *Concerning the transgression of the exile.* The righteous among the settlers gathered to Ezra to report to him the extent of the transgressions so that the transgressors might be stoppped (*Rashi* , *Taanis* 13a).[2]

1. *Rambam (Isurei Biah* 13:15,16) explains that King Solomon's wives were bona fide converts, but their motives for converting were improper. This is indicated by their continued practice of idolatry even after their marriages to Solomon. Thus, they were morally (though not legally) equivalent to gentiles, and King Solomon was guilty of the moral equivalent of intermarriage.

2. The Talmud *(Taanis* 12b) rules that on a day of communal fasting and penitence, the morning hours (following the morning prayers) should be spent in correcting the transgressions of the members of the community. This is derived from the statement here that *those who hastened at the word of the God of Israel* [discussed] *the transgressions of the exile* [with Ezra] *until the afternoon.* [See *Shulchan Aruch Orach Chaim* 577:16.]

IX

5 *God of Israel then gathered around me concerning*

*The Gathering* *the transgression of the exile, while I sat stunned until the afternoon offering.*

5 *At the afternoon offering I arose from my fast,*

*Ezra's Prayer* *having torn my garment and my cloak, and fell to my*

עַד לְמִנְחַת הָעָרֶב — *Until the afternoon offering. Rashi* to *Taanis* 13a explains that עֶרֶב refers to the beginning of the afternoon period, i.e. after the sun has reached its zenith and has begun its westward decline, casting shadows towards the east. [See also *Rashi* to *Exodus* 12:6.]

*Metzudos* translates מִנְחָה as *gift,* in this case *offering.* The expression מִנְחַת הָעָרֶב [literally, *the afternoon gift*] refers to the regular afternoon sacrifice *(Tamid)* which was offered daily at the Temple (see comm. above 3:3). Ezra sat stunned until the time of the afternoon offering.

*Ramban (Exodus* 12:6), however, translates מִנְחָה as *rest* or *setting.* מִנְחַת הָעָרֶב is translated the *afternoon setting* of the sun. As in the interpretations of *Rashi* and *Metzudos,* though, the reference is to the beginning of the afternoon when the sun begins its move towards setting. [See also *Tosefos Yom Tov, Berachos* 4:1.]

### ☙ Ezra's Prayer

**5-15.** Great wisdom is required in properly meting out criticism so that it is accepted by those being rebuked.

Ezra knew that his demands for the expulsion of wives and children would arouse deep opposition. He did not attempt, therefore, a direct attack against the sinners but chose, instead, a stratagem designed to convey the full severity of the matter indirectly.

With rent garments Ezra prayed and lamented aloud before a shocked multitude, describing aloud in his prayer before God the calamities which would befall the nation should the awful sin remain unrectified. As a result of this indirect rebuke against the transgressors, the shaken, remorseful people gave their unanimous consent to the painful task of ejecting the non-Jewish wives and children [ch. 10] *(Ralbag).*

**5.** קַמְתִּי מִתַּעֲנִיתִי — *I arose from my fast.* Ezra did not eat all that day *(Rashi).* He did not end his fast now, but arose in his weakened condition and began to pray *(Metzudos),* hoping that the fast would enhance the effectiveness of his prayer *(Rashi* to *Taanis* 13a).

*Ralbag's* interpretation, however, is: *I ended my fast.* While Ezra had sat stunned he took no food or drink. Now, however, he arose and took nourishment [perhaps because he was incapable of prayer in his weakened condition]. *Ralbag* adds that, although the term *fast* generally refers to a full day's abstinence from food [see *Shulchan Aruch Orach Chaim* 562:1], Ezra's morning abstinence is also considered fasting.[1]

וּבְקָרְעִי בִגְדִי וּמְעִילִי — *Having torn my garment and my cloak. Rashi (Taanis* 13a) explains that though one does not generally pray in such a disheveled condition, Ezra now did so, feeling that his willingness to endure the discomforts of fasting and of wearing tattered clothing would increase the effectiveness of the prayer.

1. *Shulchan Aruch Orach Chaim* (562:1,6,11) rules that a תַּעֲנִית שָׁעוֹת, *fast of hours,* is as binding as a full day's fast. Thus, a person accepting upon himself the obligation of fasting for several hours is required to do so, just as the person undertaking to fast all day must do so. However, as far as the special fast-day prayer (עֲנֵנוּ) is concerned, the fast of hours is not given equal status. This special prayer is recited only during the all-day fast but not during the *fast of hours.*

וָאֶכְרְעָה עַל־בִּרְכַּי וָאֶפְרְשָׂה כַפַּי אֶל־יְהֹוָה
ו אֱלֹהָי׃ וָאֹמְרָה אֱלֹהַי בֹּשְׁתִּי וְנִכְלַמְתִּי
לְהָרִים אֱלֹהַי פָּנַי אֵלֶיךָ כִּי עֲוֺנֹתֵינוּ רָבוּ
לְמַעְלָה רֹּאשׁ וְאַשְׁמָתֵנוּ גָדְלָה עַד לַשָּׁמָיִם׃
ז מִימֵי אֲבֹתֵינוּ אֲנַחְנוּ בְּאַשְׁמָה גְדֹלָה עַד
הַיּוֹם הַזֶּה וּבַעֲוֺנֹתֵינוּ נִתַּנּוּ אֲנַחְנוּ מְלָכֵינוּ
כֹהֲנֵינוּ בְּיַד | מַלְכֵי הָאֲרָצוֹת בַּחֶרֶב בַּשְּׁבִי
ח וּבַבִּזָּה וּבְבֹשֶׁת פָּנִים כְּהַיּוֹם הַזֶּה׃ וְעַתָּה
כִּמְעַט־רֶגַע הָיְתָה תְחִנָּה מֵאֵת | יְהֹוָה
אֱלֹהֵינוּ לְהַשְׁאִיר לָנוּ פְּלֵיטָה וְלָתֶת־לָנוּ

*Metzudos* explains that Ezra prayed in torn clothing in order to arouse penitent feelings among the observers [see 10:1].

וָאֶפְרְשָׂה כַפַּי — *And extended my palms.*[1] In a posture used when begging for kindness *(Metzudos).*[2]

**6.** בֹּשְׁתִּי וְנִכְלַמְתִּי — *I am embarrassed and ashamed. Malbim* explains that the word בֹּשְׁתִּי, *embarrassed,* refers to the mortification resulting from one's own recognition of personal shortcomings. However, the term נִכְלַמְתִּי, *ashamed,* indicates a sense of embarrassment brought about by degradation in the eyes of others.

*Radak (Shorashim)* explains that בּוּשָׁה is milder than כְּלִימָה; while the former may be the result of inadequacy, the latter always implies fault.

כִּי עֲוֺנֹתֵינוּ רָבוּ לְמַעְלָה רֹּאשׁ — *For our transgressions have multiplied above our heads.* The translation follows *Metzudos.*

*Malbim* adds that עָוֺן, *transgression,* refers to a sin of the mind [such as faulty judgment or denial of the truths of Torah]. Accordingly, the verse states that the transgressions *have multiplied above our heads,* or *our minds* — our minds overflow with transgressions.

*Ralbag* sees this expression as a reference to God, Master of the heavenly hosts. He renders לְמַעְלָה רֹּאשׁ, *the Master of those above.* The meaning of our phrase is: *Our transgressions against the Master of those above have multiplied.*

*Ralbag* also presents an alternate translation. רֹּאשׁ is translated *counting* or *reckoning* [as in *Numbers* 4:21]. Thus: *Our transgressions have multiplied beyond reckoning* — they are innumerable.

וְאַשְׁמָתֵנוּ — *And our sins.* This is the translation of *Metzudos. Malbim,* however, renders *our guilt.*

According to *Malbim,* the two statements at the end of the verse — *our transgressions*

1. Praying with extended palms is no longer customary among Jews, although the custom appears in Scripture and in the early Rabbinic literature. Once the practice was accepted as a form of gentile worship it was dropped by Jews, in keeping with the tradition of preserving the unique nature of Jewish prayer forms [see *Rashi* to *Deut.* 16:22] *(R' Akiva Eiger, Glosses to Orach Chaim,* 89:1, from *Beer Sheva,* 74).

2. Since Ezra made his supplication during the afternoon, the Talmud *(Taanis* 12b, 13a) requires that on days of communal fasting and penitence, the prayers and supplications for God's mercy and forgiveness take place during the afternoon *minchah* prayers [see *Orach Chaim* 577:16].

*knees and extended my palms to HASHEM, my God.*
*6 And I said: My God, I am embarrassed and*
*ashamed to lift my face to You, my God — for our*
*transgressions have multiplied above our heads, and*
*our sins extend unto heaven. 7 From the days of our*
*forefathers until this day we have sinned greatly;*
*because of our transgressions we were delivered, with*
*our kings and Kohanim, into the hands of the*
*monarchs of the lands — to the sword, captivity,*
*plunder, and shamefacedness — as in the present day.*
*8 Now, for a fleeting moment, favor has been*
*bestowed by HASHEM our God to leave us an escape*

*have multiplied above our heads and our guilt extends until heaven* — correspond with the two statements at the beginning of the passage — *I am embarrassed and I am ashamed.* The private recognition of the transgressions of the intellect [*transgressions ... above our heads*] is the cause of the privately felt embarrassment expressed in the first phrase, while *our guilt extends until heaven* results in Divine punishment, obvious to all, and causes me to be *ashamed* — publicly humiliated.

**7.** מִימֵי אֲבֹתֵינוּ אֲנַחְנוּ בְּאַשְׁמָה גְדֹלָה עַד הַיּוֹם הַזֶּה — *From the days of our forefathers until this day we have sinned greatly.* The sins which caused our punishment began in the days of our forefathers *(Malbim).*

וּבַעֲוֹנֹתֵינוּ נִתַּנּוּ ... בְּיַד מַלְכֵי הָאֲרָצוֹת — *Because of our transgressions we were delivered ... into the hands of the monarchs of the lands.* The same transgressions continue now, and we are still not worthy of redemption. God brought us back to the Land of Israel and restored the Temple to us out of His great kindness but not because we are deserving of this. Hence, it follows that the present return to the land is but a temporary respite unless we fully repent *(Malbim).*

כְּהַיּוֹם הַזֶּה — *As in the present day.* As indicated by the circumstances of the present day, the suffering and humiliation of exile continues. The ten tribes [see 2:64] and many members of the tribes of Judah and Benjamin still remain in exile *(Rashi).*

**8.** כִּמְעַט־רֶגַע — *For a fleeting moment* [lit. *a small moment*]. The redemption will not be a lasting one unless we repent *(Rashi* and *Malbim).*

*Ralbag* sees this not as a reference to the fleeting moment of redemption, but to the fleeting moment of exile. Considering the great guilt of our forefathers (v. 7), the seventy years of the Babylonian exile may be viewed as only a fleeting moment. [Now, after this fleeting moment of exile, God, in His lovingkindness, has left us a refuge.]

*Metzudos,* however, translates: *for a short time.* The redemption has so far been relatively insignificant, having thus far lasted only a short time.

הָיְתָה תְחִנָּה מֵאֵת ה׳ — *Favor has been bestowed by HASHEM* [lit. *There has been a favoring from HASHEM*]. תְּחִנָּה is derived from חֲנִינָה, meaning the giving of undeserved benefits *(Metzudos).* We have been redeemed not because we are deserving but out of God's lovingkindness *(Malbim).*

לְהַשְׁאִיר לָנוּ פְּלֵיטָה — *To leave us an escape.* God saved us from extinction in exile *(Malbim).*

יָתֵד בִּמְקוֹם קָדְשׁוֹ לְהָאִיר עֵינֵינוּ אֱלֹהֵינוּ
ט וּלְתִתֵּנוּ מִחְיָה מְעַט בְּעַבְדֻתֵנוּ׃ כִּי־עֲבָדִים
אֲנַחְנוּ וּבְעַבְדֻתֵנוּ לֹא עֲזָבָנוּ אֱלֹהֵינוּ וַיַּט־
עָלֵינוּ חֶסֶד לִפְנֵי מַלְכֵי פָרַס לָתֶת־לָנוּ מִחְיָה
לְרוֹמֵם אֶת־בֵּית אֱלֹהֵינוּ וּלְהַעֲמִיד אֶת־
חָרְבֹתָיו וְלָתֶת־לָנוּ גָדֵר בִּיהוּדָה וּבִירוּשָׁלִָם׃
י וְעַתָּה מַה־נֹּאמַר אֱלֹהֵינוּ אַחֲרֵי־זֹאת כִּי

וְלָתֶת־לָנוּ יָתֵד — *And to provide us a stake.* A *stake* refers to a firm place [like a stake which is firmly embedded], as in *Isaiah* 22:23 — *I will embed him as a stake in an enduring place (Rashi).*

בִּמְקוֹם קָדְשׁוֹ — *In His sacred place. Hashem* has provided us a stake in His sacred place by settling us in the Land of Israel and Jerusalem *(Rashi; Metzudos),* and by restoring the Temple *(Malbim).*

לְהָאִיר עֵינֵינוּ אֱלֹהֵינוּ — *So that our God may enlighten us* [lit. *illuminate our eyes*]. Through the restoration of the Temple, God enlightens us so that we may behave righteously and put an end to our punishment *(Malbim).*

[God chose Eretz Yisrael, and particularly the Temple in Jerusalem, as places where He would reveal His presence and awaken the people's desire to serve Him (see *Sefer HaChinuch* 95). Thus, the settlement of the Holy Land and the restoration of the Temple were conducive to following the ways of God and behaving righteously.]

בְּעַבְדֻתֵנוּ — *In our servitude.* To give us some life while we are still servants of the Persian king, Darius *(Rashi; Metzudos).*

*Malbim* translates: *despite our servitude.* God will *give us some life* — some measure of success — *despite our servitude,* although the time for true redemption [implying freedom from servitude] has not yet arrived, as revealed to Daniel (9:24). [See *Daniel* 8:13ff and ArtScroll comm. there.]

**9.** כִּי־עֲבָדִים אֲנַחְנוּ — *For we are slaves.* We are slaves to the Persian king Darius *(Rashi).*

וַיַּט־עָלֵינוּ חֶסֶד לִפְנֵי מַלְכֵי פָרַס לָתֶת־לָנוּ מִחְיָה — *He has directed the good will of the Persian kings towards us to give us life.* The Talmud *(Megillah* 11a) understands this as a reference to God's direction of the will of the Persian king Ahasuerus during the times of Haman. When Haman attempted to destroy the Jews, God's providence directed Ahasuerus' goodwill towards the Jewish people. This resulted in their deliverance from Haman's murderous designs, as told in the *Book of Esther.*

The allusion to Ahasuerus' good will is contained only in the first part of the phrase — *to give us life* — for Ahasuerus gave the Jewish people life by saving them from Haman. The concluding words, *to raise up the Temple of our God and to restore its ruins,* allude not to Ahasuerus but to the Persian kings who aided in the Temple construction — Cyrus and Darius.

לְרוֹמֵם אֶת־בֵּית אֱלֹהֵינוּ — *To raise up the Temple of our God.*[1] This refers to the decrees commanding the restoration of the Temple (1:2,3; 6:7,8) *(Malbim).*

1. The Talmud *(Shabbos* 11a) derives from this phrase the requirement that a Jewish house of worship must be elevated above all the other houses in its city. The Talmud warns that failure to observe this rule results in the destruction of the city.

*Rashi (Shabbos* 11a) explains that this is implied by the continuation of the statement, *and to provide us with a fence in Judah and Jerusalem.* Because of the lifting up of the Temple, *and to provide us a stake in His sacred place, so that our God may enlighten us, and give us some life in our servitude.* 9 *For we are slaves, but in our servitude, our God has not forsaken us. He has directed the good will of the Persian kings towards us to give us life, to raise up the Temple of our God and to restore its ruins, and to provide us with a fence in Judah and Jerusalem.*

*The Confession*

10 *Now what can we say after this, our God, for we*

וּלְהַעֲמִיד אֶת־חָרְבֹתָיו — *And to restore its ruins.* The Temple was restored in the face of the attempts by the enemies of Judah and Benjamin to keep it in ruins [see ch. 6] *(Malbim).*

וְלָתֶת־לָנוּ גָדֵר בִּיהוּדָה וּבִירוּשָׁלָם — *And to provide us with a fence in Judah and Jerusalem. Ibn Ezra* and *Metzudos* explain this as a reference to the protected position of the Jewish settlers in Judah and Jerusalem. They were *fenced* or guarded against enemy attacks.

According to *Ralbag,* the word *fence* is an idiom for a dwelling place [which is generally enclosed by a fence]. The passage refers to the settlement of the Jews in their homes in Judah and Jerusalem.

*R' Yeshayah MiTrani* comments that the mention of the fence indicates the weakness of the Jewish settlement in Judah and Jerusalem, which is described not even as a home but merely as a fence.

*Rashi* states that this refers figuratively to the fence of restrictions which were added by the Rabbis to protect the Biblical prohibitions. This ring of Rabbinical rules prevents the violation of the Torah precepts just as a fence protects the area it encloses from damage. [See *Avos* 1:1 — *Make a fence around the Torah.* See also *Rambam, Mamrim* 2:4.]

[The allusion, apparently, is to the ten regulations which Ezra instituted *(Bava Kama* 82a), among them the inclusion of Torah reading as part of the synagogue service three times weekly; the designation of Mondays and Thursdays as the days when the Rabbinical courts would hold sessions; and the requirement that a woman's hair must be thoroughly cleansed before immersion in the *mikveh* (ritual bath). See *Bava Kama* for a thorough discussion of all of Ezra's regulations.]

*Malbim's* opinion is that the fence represents the preservation of Jewish identity. The Jews of the time operated their own independent administrative apparatus with Jewish governors, judges and political leaders. They were thus insulated — fenced — against the undesired influence of their heathen neighbors.

### ◆§ The Confession

**10.** וְעַתָּה מַה־נֹּאמַר אֱלֹהֵינוּ אַחֲרֵי־זֹאת כִּי עָזַבְנוּ מִצְוֹתֶיךָ — *Now what can we say after this, our God, for we have forsaken Your commandments.* Can we express dissatisfaction at the limited nature of our redemption [i.e., our continued servitude, as expressed in the

they merited the provision of the fence, implying that should the Temple [or house of worship] not be elevated, no protective fence will be provided and ruin will follow. [See *Maharsha* and *Rashash.*]

Unfortunately, this cannot be observed in many places where the non-Jewish structures rise above the synagogue *(Mishnah Berurah* 150:5).

יא עָזַבְנוּ מִצְוֺתֶיךָ׃ אֲשֶׁר צִוִּיתָ בְּיַד עֲבָדֶיךָ
הַנְּבִיאִים לֵאמֹר הָאָרֶץ אֲשֶׁר אַתֶּם בָּאִים
לְרִשְׁתָּהּ אֶרֶץ נִדָּה הִיא בְּנִדַּת עַמֵּי הָאֲרָצוֹת
בְּתוֹעֲבֹתֵיהֶם אֲשֶׁר מִלְאוּהָ מִפֶּה אֶל־פֶּה
יב בְּטֻמְאָתָם׃ וְעַתָּה בְּנוֹתֵיכֶם אַל־תִּתְּנוּ
לִבְנֵיהֶם וּבְנֹתֵיהֶם אַל־תִּשְׂאוּ לִבְנֵיכֶם
וְלֹא־תִדְרְשׁוּ שְׁלֹמָם וְטוֹבָתָם עַד־עוֹלָם
לְמַעַן תֶּחֶזְקוּ וַאֲכַלְתֶּם אֶת־טוּב הָאָרֶץ
יג וְהוֹרַשְׁתֶּם לִבְנֵיכֶם עַד־עוֹלָם׃ וְאַחֲרֵי כָּל־

preceding verse]? No, for we have forsaken God's commandments and are therefore undeserving of any kindness at all *(Metzudos).*

Furthermore, since the purpose of this partial redemption was to arouse us to complete repentance leading, in turn to the total redemption [see v. 8, s.v. לְהָאִיר עֵינֵינוּ], what can we say to justify ourselves after this partial redemption? Not only have we failed to repent, but we have forsaken Your commandments and have added new transgressions to the old.

**11.** אֲשֶׁר צִוִּיתָ — *Which You commanded.* [This phrase continues the sentence begun in the preceding verse: *For we have forsaken Your commandments which You commanded.*]

הָאָרֶץ ... אֶרֶץ נִדָּה הִיא — *The land ... is a land of repulsiveness.* The word נִדָּה is derived from נד, to *move* or *become distant* [נִדָּה is, literally, that which causes a distancing from it, i.e., *repulsiveness*] *(Ibn Ezra; Metzudos).*

*Malbim* observes that the land itself is defiled by the abominations of the nations: *For the nations whom I am casting out before you were defiled with all of these* [*immoral acts*]. *The land became defiled and I remembered its sins and the land spewed out its inhabitants* [*Lev.* 18:24,25] *(Malbim).*

בְּנִדַּת עַמֵּי הָאֲרָצוֹת — *Made so by the repulsiveness of the nations of the lands.* [The land, though desirable, has become repulsive by the practices of its corrupt inhabitants.]

בְּתוֹעֲבֹתֵיהֶם — *With their abominations.* The abominations of licentiousness and idolatry[1] *(Ralbag).*

### ◆§ The Evil of Intermarriage

**12.** וְעַתָּה בְּנוֹתֵיכֶם אַל־תִּתְּנוּ לִבְנֵיהֶם וּבְנֹתֵיהֶם אַל־תִּשְׂאוּ לִבְנֵיכֶם — *Now, do not give your daughters* [in matrimony] *to their sons, and do not wed their daughters to your sons.* [Verses 10 and 11 state: *For we have forsaken Your commandments — which You commanded through Your servants, the prophets.* This verse specifies the commandments.]

*Malbim* traces this to the Biblical and prophetic admonitions stated in connection with God's promise to drive out the gentile peoples of the land and the command to eradicate every vestige of their corrupt religion ... *Lest you enter into a covenant with the inhabitant of the land ... and take from his daughters for your sons (Exodus* 34:15,16).

1. The Torah condemns the pagan peoples who inhabited ancient Canaan for their numerous abominations, including immoral practices such as adultery, incest, and sodomy *(Leviticus* 18:1-30, 20:23), and idoltary *(Deut.* 7:4,25, 8:2, et al.).

IX 11-13

*have forsaken Your commandments.* [11] *Which You commanded through Your servants, the prophets, saying: The land which you are approaching to inherit is a land of repulsiveness, made so by the repulsiveness of the nations of the lands; with their abominations with which they have filled it from end to end, in their defilement.* [12] *Now, do not give your daughters to their sons, and do not wed their daughters to your sons, and never inquire after their peace and well-being — so that you may possess and eat of the goodness of the land, and bequeath it everlastingly to your sons.* [13] *And after all that has*

*The Evil of Intermarriage*

[The statement, *Now, do not give your daughters to their sons ... so that you may possess and eat of the goodness of the land, and bequeath it everlastingly to your sons,* is not Ezra's personal statement to the people but his quote of the commandment of Hashem to the prophets.]

Intermarriage between Jew and gentile, banned elsewhere in the Torah as well, is universally abhorrent. Here, in the context of the Jewish struggle to resettle Eretz Yisrael, Ezra warns that this detestable practice is the source of the defilement and eventual loss of the land.[1].

וְלֹא־תִדְרְשׁוּ שְׁלֹמָם וְטוֹבָתָם עַד־עוֹלָם — *And never inquire after their peace and well-being.* This particular injunction is stated only in reference to the Ammonites and Moabites mentioned in v. 1. This corresponds with the Biblical injunction concerning the Ammonites and Moabites: *Do not seek their peace and well-being (Deut.* 23:7).

*Ramban (Deut.* 23:7) explains that this prohibits Jews from soliciting the welfare of the Ammonites or Moabites in the manner of a relative, although those two peoples are in fact descended from the patriarch Abraham's nephew, Lot.

In addition, in the case of attack by Ammon or Moab, the Torah waives its customary regulations limiting the degree of retaliation permitted against an attacking enemy force.

This is because of the pernicious behavior of these two nations — their callous disregard for the needs of the Israelites wandering in the desert, and the hiring of the sorcerer Balaam, who attempted to curse the Jews, and then advised that they be seduced into acts of immorality, thus bringing God's retribution against them.

לְמַעַן תֶּחֶזְקוּ — *So that you may possess.* I.e., occupy and retain the land *(Metzudos).*

This statement indicates that abstention from intermarriage is a requirement for keeping the Holy Land. Conversely, *Joshua* 23:12-13 states that intermarriage is punished with expulsion from the land (Malbim).

עַד־עוֹלָם — *Everlastingly.* You will

1. *And ... for if you turn back and cleave to the remainder of these nations ... and intermarry with them ... know that* HASHEM *your God will no longer drive out the nations from before you, but they shall be a trap and a pitfall for you, marauders on your flanks and encampments before your eyes, until you are banished from this goodly land which* HASHEM *your God gave to you ... (Joshua* 23:12,13).

ט
יד־טו

הַבָּא עָלֵינוּ בְּמַעֲשֵׂינוּ הָרָעִים וּבְאַשְׁמָתֵנוּ
הַגְּדֹלָה כִּי | אַתָּה אֱלֹהֵינוּ חָשַׂכְתָּ לְמַטָּה
יד מֵעֲוֺנֵינוּ וְנָתַתָּה לָּנוּ פְּלֵיטָה כָּזֹאת: הֲנָשׁוּב
לְהָפֵר מִצְוֺתֶיךָ וּלְהִתְחַתֵּן בְּעַמֵּי הַתֹּעֵבוֹת
הָאֵלֶּה הֲלוֹא תֶאֱנַף־בָּנוּ עַד־כַּלֵּה לְאֵין
טו שְׁאֵרִית וּפְלֵיטָה: יהוה אֱלֹהֵי
יִשְׂרָאֵל צַדִּיק אַתָּה כִּי־נִשְׁאַרְנוּ פְלֵיטָה
כְּהַיּוֹם הַזֶּה הִנְנוּ לְפָנֶיךָ בְּאַשְׁמָתֵינוּ כִּי אֵין
א לַעֲמוֹד לְפָנֶיךָ עַל־זֹאת: וּכְהִתְפַּלֵּל

י
א

bequeath it to your sons, they to their sons, and so on *(Metzudos)*.

**13.** וְאַחֲרֵי כָּל־הַבָּא עָלֵינוּ — *And after all that has befallen us.* [Ezra's confessional prayer now continues.] After all that we have suffered in our exile *(Rashi; Ibn Ezra)*.

חָשַׂכְתָּ לְמַטָּה מֵעֲוֺנֵינוּ — *You have held back to less than our transgressions* [*deserve*]. You have refrained from punishing us according to our transgressions and have punished us to a lesser degree than our transgressions warrant *(Commentators)*.

*Rashi* also suggests the meaning: *You have reduced our transgression to the lowest level.* You have accepted our suffering in exile as atonement for our transgressions. Thus, the transgressions have been virtually eliminated, or reduced to the lowest level.

*Ibn Ezra* suggests: *You have held our transgressions below* — on earth. You have permitted some of our transgressions to remain below on earth [i.e., You have overlooked them], rather than raising them up to heaven above and recording them in the heavenly records [where we must eventually be punished for them].

וְנָתַתָּה לָּנוּ פְּלֵיטָה כָּזֹאת — *And have given us an escape of this kind.* God has given us an undeserved escape. Had the Jews been punished according to their misdeeds, there would have been no refuge. Since *You have held back to less than our transgressions deserve*, however, we were permitted to enjoy a deliverance which we did not deserve *(Metzudos; Malbim)*.

**14.** הֲנָשׁוּב — *If we were to revert* [lit. *shall we revert?*]. The translation follows *Rashi*.

*Metzudos*, however, reads הֲנָשׁוּב, *shall we revert?* The question is rhetorical. Would it be proper for us to revert to violating Your commandments after experiencing Your kindness in the reduction of our punishment?

הֲלוֹא תֶאֱנַף־בָּנוּ — *Would You not be enraged at us?* The question is rhetorical, meaning — You would surely be enraged at us *(Rashi)*.

*Malbim* adds that the verb לְהִתְאַנֵּף, *to be enraged*, is used in cases when the full wrath is unleashed, as in this verse, which ends — *and* [You would] *destroy us beyond remnant and survivors.*

עַד־כַּלֵּה לְאֵין שְׁאֵרִית וּפְלֵיטָה — *And destroy us* [lit. *until destruction*] *beyond remnant and escape. Safra (Leviticus* 18:30) derives from here that if the Jews were to follow the heathen abominations, they would be utterly destroyed

*befallen us for our evil deeds and great sins, our God, You have held back to less than our transgressions [deserve], and have given us an escape of this kind.*
14 *If we were to revert to violating Your commandments and intermarrying with the peoples of these abominations, would You not be enraged at us and destroy us beyond remnant and escape?*
15 *HASHEM, God of Israel, You are charitable, for we have been left this day as a remnant; we are before You in our iniquity, for we cannot stand before You concerning this.*

by God. This process is described in *Leviticus* 18, which lists the prohibitions against sexual transgressions and ends, *Do not defile yourselves with* [these abominations]; *I am HASHEM, your God (v. 30). Safra* explains that the words, *I am HASHEM your God,* are added to teach that 'If you abstain from these abominations then I will be your God, and protect you. Conversely, should you become defiled, you shall become isolated from Me, and merit destruction.'

**15.** צַדִּיק אַתָּה כִּי־נִשְׁאַרְנוּ פְלֵיטָה כְּהַיּוֹם הַזֶּה — *You are charitable, for we have been left this day as a remnant.* Your goodness in leaving us, this day, as a remnant was charitable [צַדִּיק from צְדָקָה, *charity*]; we did not deserve it *(Metzudos; Malbim). Malbim* points out that this statement corresponds to the description of God's leniency in v. 13: *You have held back to less than our transgressions deserve* — You have punished us to a degree less than we deserve according to our transgressions.

הִנְנוּ לְפָנֶיךָ בְּאַשְׁמָתֵינוּ — *We are before You in our iniquity.* We continue committing, even now, this grave iniquity of intermarriage *(Metzudos; Malbim).*

כִּי אֵין לַעֲמוֹד לְפָנֶיךָ . . . זֹאת — *For we cannot stand before You concerning this.* We have no other credits great enough to outweigh the transgression of intermarriage and permit us to endure before You *(Rashi; Metzudos).*

*Metzudos* relates this statement to the beginning of the verse: *You are charitable, for we have been left this day as a remnant.* Our inquity is so great, that we cannot stand before You. Yet we have been left as a remnant. This is surely evidence that You are charitable.

*Malbim,* however, understands the mention of God's leniency at the beginning of the phrase differently. The kindness covers two periods, the past and the future. *You are charitable, for we have been left this day as a remnant.* Although we deserved great punishment *in the past,* You left us as a remnant.

Even if, in the future, You will become *enraged at us, and destroy us beyond remnant and escape* (v. 14), this will not disprove your charitableness, since we are well deserving of such punishment. For *we are before You in our iniquity; we cannot stand before You concerning this.* We cannot extenuate our guilt.

*R' Yeshayah MiTrani* interprets our phrase as a reference to prayer: *None can stand before You* in prayer for forgiveness *concerning this* appalling sin.

י עֶזְרָא וּכְהִתְוַדֹּתוֹ בֹּכֶה וּמִתְנַפֵּל לִפְנֵי בֵּית
ב־ג הָאֱלֹהִים נִקְבְּצוּ אֵלָיו מִיִּשְׂרָאֵל קָהָל
רַב־מְאֹד אֲנָשִׁים וְנָשִׁים וִילָדִים כִּי־בָכוּ
הָעָם הַרְבֵּה בֶכֶה׃
°עֵילָם ק׳ ב וַיַּעַן שְׁכַנְיָה בֶן־יְחִיאֵל מִבְּנֵי °עולם וַיֹּאמֶר
לְעֶזְרָא אֲנַחְנוּ מָעַלְנוּ בֵאלֹהֵינוּ וַנֹּשֶׁב נָשִׁים
נָכְרִיּוֹת מֵעַמֵּי הָאָרֶץ וְעַתָּה יֵשׁ־מִקְוֶה
ג לְיִשְׂרָאֵל עַל־זֹאת׃ וְעַתָּה נִכְרָת־בְּרִית

# X

### ◆§ Assembly and Confession

**1.** וּכְהִתְפַּלֵּל עֶזְרָא וּכְהִתְוַדֹּתוֹ בֹּכֶה — *As Ezra prayed and confessed, weeping.* Ezra prayed and confessed loudly so that the sinners would be aroused to repentance *(Ralbag).*

וְנָשִׁים — *Women. Malbim* suggests that among the women who gathered around Ezra were the Jewish wives of the husbands who had also taken gentile wives. *Malbim* quotes the related statement of the prophet Malachi (*Malachi* 2:13) to the sinners: *This is a second thing that you do — envelop the altar of HASHEM in tears, weeping, and lamenting. Rashi* there explains that this refers to the lamenting of the Jewish wives who had been superseded in their husbands' affections by gentile women.[1]

כִּי־בָכוּ הָעָם הַרְבֵּה בֶכֶה — *For the people wept profusely* [lit. *much weeping*]. Because the people around Ezra wept profusely, the sounds of their weeping attracted a great multitude of men, women, and children *(Metzudos).*

**2.** וַיַּעַן — *Cried out.*

The translation here is *cried out,* although the word יַעַן is generally rendered *replied.* Our translation is based on *Rashi's* assertion (to *Song of Songs* 2:10, *Deut.* 26:5) that the root ענה may be rendered *cried out* in a loud voice. As his source, *Rashi* quotes *Deut.* 27:14, וְעָנוּ הַלְוִיִּם וְאָמְרוּ ... קוֹל רָם, *Let the Levites cry out and say ... in a loud voice.* See comm. 8:23.

אֲנַחְנוּ מָעַלְנוּ — *We have transgressed.* The Talmud *(Sanhedrin* 116a) asserts that Shechaniah was not guilty of the transgression but included himself among the sinners in order to minimize the embarrassment of the true culprits who would later confess. Similarly, the Talmud adds, a number of Sages, using Shechaniah's action as a source, 'confessed' to wrongs of which they were innocent so that the guilty would not be humiliated.

*Malbim* also notes that Shechaniah and the vast majority of the people had *not* married gentiles. [The offenders listed below (vs. 18-44) constituted a small fraction of the Jewish community then residing in the Holy Land.] Nevertheless, Shechaniah and all the people were included in the statement *we have transgressed,* because the illicit marriages took place publicly and the Jewish leaders did not protest to the transgressors. Since all of the Jewish

1. One opinion in the Talmud *(Megillah* 15a) identifies Ezra as the prophet Malachi, citing, as evidence, the similarity of their activities. Malachi (2:11) assailed those who had taken gentile wives, saying: *Judah was traitorous, and an abomination was done in Israel and Jerusalem, for*

X
1-3

*Assembly and Confession*

*As Ezra prayed and confessed, weeping and prostrating himself in front of the Temple of God, there gathered about him an exceedingly large assemblage of Israelites — men, women and children — for the people wept profusely.*

2 *Then, Shechaniah the son of Jehiel, of the sons of Elam, cried out, and exclaimed to Ezra: We have transgressed against our God and have taken in alien women of the peoples of the Land, but now there is hope for Israel concerning this.*

*The Covenant*

3 *Now let us enter*

people are bound up together, and mutually responsible for each other's actions (כָּל יִשְׂרָאֵל עֲרֵבִים זֶה בָזֶה), the transgression assumed the dimensions of a *national* infamy, as expressed by Shechaniah's statement, *We* — all of us — *have transgressed.* [Similarly, the accusation made by those reporting to Ezra (9:2): *And the chiefs and officers were the first in this transgression,* i.e., the responsibility for the transgression may be traced to the nobles and lords, who did not use their power and influence to restrain the practice.]

וְעַתָּה יֵשׁ־מִקְוֶה — *But now there is hope.* There is hope for the Israelites, since they can cast out the gentile women and their offspring *(Rashi).*

*Malbim* explains the use of the word *now.* Until Ezra's arrival in Jerusalem, the Jewish leadership did not have the power to forcibly stop the offenders. Now, however, Ezra had been granted official jurisdiction in matters pertaining to Torah observance (7:26). Thus, the present situation created unprecedented responsibilities as well as new hope. The leadership was now fully responsible for the illicit marriages but at the same time, with the king's backing, it could compel the transgressors to cast out the forbidden wives and their children. Now there was *hope* for Israel.

Unlike *Rashi,* who translates מִקְוֶה, *hope, Ralbag* renders it *mikveh,* or ritual purification bath. Accordingly, the verse reads: *There is now a mikveh for Israel.* The *mikveh* refers to the process of abandoning the alien wives. Sinners cleansing themselves of corruption by abandoning their forbidden wives are compared to unclean individuals cleansing themselves of ritual impurity (טוּמְאָה) by immersing themselves in the waters of the *mikveh* [see *Rambam, Hil. Mikvaos* 11:12].

### ☙ The Covenant

**3.** נִכְרָת־בְּרִית — *Let us enter into a covenant.* [The covenant was established when the people took a solemn oath pledging to expel the alien wives (v. 5).]

Ezra and his supporters were well aware that the order to cast off the forbidden wives and children would meet with determined resistance. They were resolved, therefore, to impose the strictest sanctions against those refusing to comply. They knew that they could not exceed the standard penalties authorized by Torah law, and they thought that those penalties would be insufficient. To meet the extraordinary circumstances, they asked the people to take a solemn oath to rid themselves of the alien wives. When such a pledge expressing the will of the nation is made, the courts may exceed the regularly prescribed Torah punishments

*Judah desecrated his sacredness to HASHEM by loving and marrying the daughter of an alien god.* Similarly, Ezra rid the people of their gentile wives.

לֵֽאלֹהֵינוּ לְהוֹצִיא כׇל־נָשִׁים וְהַנּוֹלָד מֵהֶם
בַּעֲצַת אֲדֹנָי וְהַחֲרֵדִים בְּמִצְוַת אֱלֹהֵינוּ
ד וְכַתּוֹרָה יֵעָשֶׂה׃ קוּם כִּֽי־עָלֶיךָ הַדָּבָר וַאֲנַחְנוּ
ה עִמָּךְ חֲזַק וַעֲשֵׂה׃ וַיָּקׇם עֶזְרָא
וַיַּשְׁבַּע אֶת־שָׂרֵי הַכֹּהֲנִים הַלְוִיִּם וְכׇל־
ו יִשְׂרָאֵל לַעֲשׂוֹת כַּדָּבָר הַזֶּה וַיִּשָּׁבֵעוּ׃ וַיָּקׇם
עֶזְרָא מִלִּפְנֵי בֵּית הָאֱלֹהִים וַיֵּלֶךְ אֶל־לִשְׁכַּת

if necessary. They may levy fines and mete out extreme punishment, including the death penalty, according to the needs of the moment *(Malbim).* [For further support of *Malbim's* theory, see *Judges* ch. 20 and *Malbim's* commentary to there, and *Ramban* to *Leviticus* 27:29.]

*Malbim* equates this power given to the people with the broad punitive powers given by the Torah to Jewish kings, who may confiscate property and even inflict capital punishment, if necessary. [*Rambam, Hilchos Melachim* 3:8,10 enumerates the special powers of the Jewish monarch.]

*Malbim's* reasoning in equating the power of the entire people with that of the king may be explained as follows: The Jewish king serves as the executor of the national will, as stated by *Rambam (Melachim* 3:6), *'His* [the king's] *heart is the heart* [i.e., desire] *of the entire congregation of Israel.'* Because he is the instrument of the entire people, and his decrees represent their wishes, he is granted extraordinary powers. It follows, then, that the express will of the people themselves, as articulated by a public national oath, carries the same legal and moral force as the king's decree.

לְהוֹצִיא כׇל־נָשִׁים — *To cast out all of the women.* I.e., the gentile women *(Metzudos).*

וְהַנּוֹלָד מֵהֶם — *And their offspring.* The children of the gentile wives were themselves gentiles, in accordance with the Torah law *(Yevamos* 23a, derived from *Deut.* 7:4) that a child born of a Jewish father and a gentile mother is not a Jew *(R' Yeshayah MiTrani; Ibn Ezra).*

*Ibn Ezra* notes that מֵהֶם, *their,* is the masculine form, although the passage refers to the *women's* children. The meaning is the same as the feminine form מֵהֶן.

בַּעֲצַת ה׳ — *According to the will* [lit. *counsel*] *of God.* The translation is *Rashi's.* The reference is to the Biblical injunction against marrying a non-Jew: *Do not intermarry with them (Deut.* 7:3; *Metzudos).*

*Ibn Ezra,* however, translates *according to the counsel of God.* His interpretation is that the counsel of God was needed to determine whether some of the women had converted properly and could therefore be accepted. In the end, none of the alien women were accepted, because none of them had properly converted to Judaism.

וְהַחֲרֵדִים בְּמִצְוַת אֱלֹהֵינוּ — *And* [*the efforts of*] *those who hasten at the commandment of our God.* The translation follows *Rashi* and *Ibn Ezra,* who apparently wish to avoid the suggestion that the community equated the counsel of the righteous people with the will of God. Those who hasten at the commandment of God would act to assure that His will was carried out.

*Metzudos* and *Malbim,* however, translate, *according to the will of God and* [*the counsel of*] *those who tremble* ... Those who tremble and hasten at the command of God would add their *will* and *counsel,* i.e., influence, to arouse the sinners to cast out their wives and offspring.

וְכַתּוֹרָה יֵעָשֶׂה — *Let action be taken in*

*into a covenant with our God to cast out all of the women and their offspring, according to the will of God and [the efforts of] those who hasten at the commandment of our God; let action be taken in conformity with the Torah.* 4 *Arise, for the matter is incumbent upon you and we are with you. Be stalwart and act.*

*The Oath*

5 *Ezra then arose, and bade the chiefs of the Kohanim, the Levites and all of Israel swear to fulfill this, and they swore.* 6 *Ezra then rose from in front of the Temple of God and went to the chamber of*

*Ezra's Grief*

*conformity with the Torah.*[1] By expelling the gentile wives and children, the people would conform to the Torah's requirement [as specified in *Deut.* 7:3-4] *(Rashi).*

*Ibn Ezra* translates: *And action shall be taken in conformity with the Torah.* This was a warning to the effect that those unwilling to cast out their wives and offspring would be coerced into doing so. In *Ibn Ezra's* opinion, the verse states that the casting out of the gentile wives and children would be accomplished in two ways: (1) by husbands willing to do so — *by those who tremble at the commandment of our God;* and (2) by the coercion of those husbands unwilling to comply. Concerning these men, the verse states: *And action shall be taken in conformity with the Torah.*

*Malbim,* following his commentary to the beginning of the verse, explains this phrase as follows: *Let action be taken* — action in excess of the normal punishment — *in conformity with the Torah* rule which permits extraordinary penalties in the case of a communal oath.

**4.** קוּם — *Arise.* Act swiftly. The word קוּם, *arise,* is used when the intention is to arouse to immediate action, as in God's command to Joshua, קוּם עֲבֹר אֶת הַיַּרְדֵּן, *arise and cross the Jordan* [*Joshua* 1:2] *(Metzudos).*

כִּי־עָלֶיךָ הַדָּבָר — *For the matter is incumbent upon you* [lit. is *upon you*]. Since you are our leader *(Metzudos).*

וַאֲנַחְנוּ עִמָּךְ — *And we are with you.* We shall follow your decisions *(Rashi).* [We are with you in terms of implementation, but the decisions are in your hands, Ezra, since you are our leader.]

### ◈§ The Oath

**5.** שָׂרֵי הַכֹּהֲנִים הַלְוִיִּם וְכָל־יִשְׂרָאֵל — *The chiefs of the Kohanim, the Levites, and all of Israel.* The word *chiefs* refers to each of the groups mentioned — the chiefs of the *Kohanim,* the chiefs of the Levites, and the chiefs of all of Israel *(Metzudos; Malbim).*

With this oath, taken by the representatives of all the people, the matter became the expression of the will of the entire nation [see comm. v. 3] *(Malbim).*

1. *Yerushalmi (Yevamos* 2:6) rules, on the basis of this phrase, that a child born of a Jewish father and gentile mother is Biblically considered a non-Jew. This is indicated by the statement that the casting out of the gentile women and their offspring would be *in conformity with the Torah,* i.e. the source of this casting out of the offspring is the Torah law. *Yerushalmi* traces the origin of this rule to the Biblical passage in *Deut.* 7:4. [See also *Yevamos* 23a, and *Zecher Yitzchok* responsa 2.]

יְהוֹחָנָן בֶּן־אֶלְיָשִׁיב וַיֵּלֶךְ שָׁם לֶחֶם לֹא־אָכַל
וּמַיִם לֹא־שָׁתָה כִּי מִתְאַבֵּל עַל־מַעַל הַגּוֹלָה:
ז וַיַּעֲבִירוּ קוֹל בִּיהוּדָה וִירוּשָׁלַםִ לְכֹל בְּנֵי
ח הַגּוֹלָה לְהִקָּבֵץ יְרוּשָׁלָםִ: וְכֹל אֲשֶׁר לֹא־
יָבוֹא לִשְׁלֹשֶׁת הַיָּמִים כַּעֲצַת הַשָּׂרִים
וְהַזְּקֵנִים יָחֳרַם כָּל־רְכוּשׁוֹ וְהוּא יִבָּדֵל
מִקְּהַל הַגּוֹלָה:
ט וַיִּקָּבְצוּ כָל־אַנְשֵׁי־יְהוּדָה וּבִנְיָמִן | יְרוּשָׁלַםִ
לִשְׁלֹשֶׁת הַיָּמִים הוּא חֹדֶשׁ הַתְּשִׁיעִי
בְּעֶשְׂרִים בַּחֹדֶשׁ וַיֵּשְׁבוּ כָל־הָעָם בִּרְחוֹב
בֵּית הָאֱלֹהִים מַרְעִידִים עַל־הַדָּבָר
י וּמֵהַגְּשָׁמִים: וַיָּקָם עֶזְרָא הַכֹּהֵן וַיֹּאמֶר
אֲלֵהֶם אַתֶּם מְעַלְתֶּם וַתֹּשִׁיבוּ נָשִׁים נָכְרִיּוֹת
יא לְהוֹסִיף עַל־אַשְׁמַת יִשְׂרָאֵל: וְעַתָּה תְּנוּ

**Ezra's Grief**

**6.** וַיֵּלֶךְ שָׁם לֶחֶם לֹא־אָכַל וּמַיִם לֹא־שָׁתָה — *He went there, but he neither ate bread nor drank water.* Although the fast day had already ended, Ezra was unable to eat or drink because of his intense grief *(Malbim).*

**The Call to Jerusalem**

**8.** כַּעֲצַת הַשָּׂרִים וְהַזְּקֵנִים — *As advised by the chiefs and the elders.* The chiefs and elders had set the three-day time limit *(Metzudos).*

יָחֳרַם כָּל־רְכוּשׁוֹ — *Should have all his property destroyed.* Based on this verse, the Talmud *(Yevamos* 89b) asserts that the Rabbinical courts may expropriate private property (הֶפְקֵר ב״ד הֶפְקֵר), if necessary, for advancing Torah observance.

In addition, the Talmud *(Moed Katan* 16a) derives from this verse the ruling that property expropriation is imposed as a penalty for contempt of a Rabbinical court. [Failure to appear after three days constituted contempt of the order to appear issued by Ezra and his court.]

*Malbim,* however, feels that the extraordinary penalty of the destruction of property was imposed on the strength of the oath taken by the chiefs of the *Kohanim,* Levites, and Israelites to cast out the illegal wives and children (v. 5; see his comm. to vs. 3,5).

וְהוּא יִבָּדֵל מִקְּהַל הַגּוֹלָה — *And himself separated from the congregation of the exile.*[1] He would be excluded from all

1. *Yerushalmi (Moed Katan* 3; *Yalkut)* relates that a certain individual disregarded three subpoenas issued by R' Yehoshua, whereupon R' Yehoshua dispatched the following communication to him: Were it not for my custom never to inflict excommunication, I would do so against you, for excommunication is imposed in twenty-four instances of contempt for Rabbinical authority, and this (the failure to answer a subpoena) is one. As Scripture states: *Anyone failing to appear after three days ... [should] be separated from the congregation.*

*Jehohanan the son of Eliashib; he went there, but he*
*neither ate bread nor drank water, for he grieved over*
*the transgression of the exile.* 7 *And a call was issued*
*throughout Judah and Jerusalem to all of the exiles,*
*to assemble in Jerusalem.* 8 *And that anyone failing to*
*appear after three days, as advised by the chiefs and*
*the elders, should have all his property destroyed,*
*and himself separated from the congregation of the*
*exile.*

*The Call to Jerusalem*

9 *All the men of Judah and Jerusalem gathered to*
*Jerusalem after three days, on the twentieth of the*
*ninth month; and all the people sat in the broad plaza*
*before the Temple of God, trembling over the matter*
*and from the rains.* 10 *And Ezra the Kohen arose and*
*said to them: You have transgressed and harbored*
*alien wives, adding to Israel's iniquity.* 11 *Now,*

*Ezra's Charge to the People*

of the affairs of the congregation *(Metzudos).*

**9.** הוּא חֹדֶשׁ הַתְּשִׁיעִי — *The ninth month* [lit. *it being ... the ninth month*]. I.e. the month of Kislev *(Rashi).*

It is evident from here that Ezra was not told of the intermarriages until more than four months after his arrival. As is clear from the verses, all the events described in chapter 9 took place in the span of a few days. Since this verse states that the gathering took place on the twentieth day of the ninth month, it follows that the events took place during that month, more than four months after Ezra's arrival on the first day of the fifth month (7:8) *(Malbim* to 9:1).

וַיֵּשְׁבוּ כָל־הָעָם בִּרְחוֹב בֵּית הָאֱלֹהִים — *And all the people sat in the broad plaza before* [lit. *of*] *the Temple of God.* The people sat *in front of* the Temple but not *in* the Temple, where sitting was not permitted [see *Rambam, Hil. Beis HaBechirah* 7:6] *(Ralbag).* This plaza was one of several on the Temple Mount. These plazas had been in existence during the First Temple as well [see *II Chronicles* 29:4].

מַרְעִידִים עַל־הַדָּבָר — *Trembling over the matter.* The people were fearful about the transgression of which they were guilty *(Rashi).*

וּמֵהַגְּשָׁמִים — *And from the rains.* The people were also shivering and miserable because of the drenching rainfall *(Rashi).*

### ⚜ Ezra's Charge to the People

**10.** אַתֶּם מְעַלְתֶּם — *You have transgressed.* Ezra addressed all the Jews, reminding them that although most of them had not married gentiles they were all guilty, because all Jews are bound together and held mutually accountable. Ezra's purpose was to unite the people in recognition of this collective guilt. Then anyone continuing to live in sin would be dissociated from them and could be prosecuted as a traitor to the nation under the special powers given to the people to punish evildoers [see comm., v. 3] *(Malbim).*

לְהוֹסִיף עַל־אַשְׁמַת יִשְׂרָאֵל — *Adding to Israel's iniquity.* You have added new transgressions to the old *(Metzudos).*

י
יב־טז

תּוֹדָה לַיהוָה אֱלֹהֵי־אֲבֹתֵיכֶם וַעֲשׂוּ
רְצוֹנוֹ וְהִבָּדְלוּ מֵעַמֵּי הָאָרֶץ וּמִן־הַנָּשִׁים
יב הַנָּכְרִיּוֹת: וַיַּעֲנוּ כָל־הַקָּהָל
°כִּדְבָרְךָ ק׳ וַיֹּאמְרוּ קוֹל גָּדוֹל כֵּן °כדבריך עָלֵינוּ
יג לַעֲשׂוֹת: אֲבָל הָעָם רָב וְהָעֵת גְּשָׁמִים וְאֵין
כֹּחַ לַעֲמוֹד בַּחוּץ וְהַמְּלָאכָה לֹא־לְיוֹם
אֶחָד וְלֹא לִשְׁנַיִם כִּי־הִרְבִּינוּ לִפְשֹׁעַ בַּדָּבָר
יד הַזֶּה: יַעַמְדוּ־נָא שָׂרֵינוּ לְכָל־הַקָּהָל וְכֹל
אֲשֶׁר בֶּעָרֵינוּ הַהֹשִׁיב נָשִׁים נָכְרִיּוֹת יָבֹא
לְעִתִּים מְזֻמָּנִים וְעִמָּהֶם זִקְנֵי־עִיר וָעִיר
וְשֹׁפְטֶיהָ עַד לְהָשִׁיב חֲרוֹן אַף־אֱלֹהֵינוּ
טו מִמֶּנּוּ עַד לַדָּבָר הַזֶּה: אַךְ יוֹנָתָן בֶּן־עֲשָׂהאֵל
וְיַחְזְיָה בֶן־תִּקְוָה עָמְדוּ עַל־זֹאת וּמְשֻׁלָּם
טז וְשַׁבְּתַי הַלֵּוִי עֲזָרֻם: וַיַּעֲשׂוּ־כֵן בְּנֵי הַגּוֹלָה

**11.** תְּנוּ תוֹדָה לַה׳ אֱלֹהֵי־אֲבֹתֵיכֶם וַעֲשׂוּ רְצוֹנוֹ — *Confess before* [lit. *give confession to*] *HASHEM, God of your forefathers, and perform His will.* Confess to your guilt [תוֹדָה from וִדּוּי, *confession*], be remorseful, and perform His will in the future *(Metzudos).* [*Metzudos* includes here the three major components of repentance: *confession* (וִדּוּי), *remorse* (חֲרָטָה), and *resolve never to repeat the transgression* (קַבָּלָה לְהַבָּא). See *Rambam, Hilchos Teshuvah* 1:1.]

וְהִבָּדְלוּ מֵעַמֵּי הָאָרֶץ — *And separate yourselves from the peoples of the land.* Do not give your daughters in marriage to gentile husbands *(Metzudos).*

[This avoids the apparent redundancy of the call to separate themselves from: (1) *the peoples of the land* and (2) *the alien wives.* The separation from *the peoples of the land* refers to non-Jewish husbands, while the closing phrase is directed towards alien wives.]

### The Congregation Replies

**12.** וַיַּעֲנוּ — *Cried out.* [See comm. v. 2.]

**13.** וְהָעֵת גְּשָׁמִים וְאֵין כֹּחַ לַעֲמוֹד בַּחוּץ — *And it is the rainy season* [lit. *and the time is one of rain*] *and it is not possible* [lit. *and there is no strength*] *to remain outdoors.* Those who have married gentile wives are too numerous to be housed, and one cannot remain outdoors during the present rainy season *(Metzudos).* [However, they were only a small percentage of the community, as is evident from the second half of this chapter *(Malbim* to v. 2).]

וְהַמְּלָאכָה — *And this ... task.* The task of expunging this transgression by expelling the gentile wives cannot be accomplished quickly *(Rashi; Metzudos).*

כִּי־הִרְבִּינוּ לִפְשֹׁעַ — *For we have sinned much.* The sinners are numerous *(Metzudos).*

**14.** יַעַמְדוּ־נָא שָׂרֵינוּ לְכָל־הַקָּהָל — *Let our chiefs now remain with the entire congregation.* This is *Rashi's* translation.

*Metzudos,* however, translates *let our*

confess before HASHEM, God of your forefathers, and perform His will, and separate yourselves from the peoples of the land and from the alien wives.

*The Congregation Replies*

12 The entire congregation then cried out, and exclaimed in a loud voice: True! We must do as you say! 13 But there are many people, and it is the rainy season and it is not possible to remain outdoors; and this is not a task for one or two days, for we have sinned much in this matter. 14 Let our chiefs now remain with the entire congregation, and let all those in our cities who harbored alien wives appear at designated times, accompanied by the elders and judges of each city, until the wrath of our God shall recede from us, until this matter [is resolved]. 15 Only Jonathan the son of Asahel and Jahzeiah the son of Tikvah stood against this, and Meshullam and Shabbethai the Levite abetted them.

*The People Comply*

16 And the exiles

*chiefs of the entire congregation now remain* [in Jerusalem].

*Malbim's* rendition is *let our chiefs remain 'for' the entire congregation* — let the chiefs remain on behalf of the entire congregation.

לְעִתִּים מְזֻמָּנִים — *At designated times.* These to be arranged by the chiefs *(Metzudos).*

וְעִמָּהֶם זִקְנֵי־עִיר וָעִיר וְשֹׁפְטֶיהָ — *Accompanied by the elders and judges of each city.* The elders and judges would report on whether any others harboring gentile wives had remained behind in their cities *(Metzudos).*

עַד לְהָשִׁיב חֲרוֹן אַף־אֱלֹהֵינוּ מִמֶּנּוּ — *Until the wrath of our God shall recede from us. Metzudos* relates this statement to the beginning of the sentence: *Let our chiefs remain* in Jerusalem to oversee the expelling of the gentile wives, until their activities are successful, and cause *the wrath of our God to recede from us.*

עַד לַדָּבָר הַזֶּה — *Until this matter* [*is resolved*]. The translation follows *Metzudos.*

*Malbim,* however, interprets our phrase as a reference to all other transgressions which might arouse the wrath of God, up to and including intermarriage. Let our chiefs remain in Jerusalem until the wrath of our God shall recede from us — the wrath caused by all transgressions up *until this matter* — i.e., intermarriage.

**15.** אַךְ יוֹנָתָן ... וְיַחְזְיָה ... עָמְדוּ עַל־זֹאת — *Only Jonathan ... and Jahzeiah ... stood against* [lit. *on*] *this.* They stood against this matter and ridiculed it *(Rashi),* but all the rest of the people agreed *(Malbim).*

*Metzudos,* however, explains that Jonathan and Jahzeiah stood *for* the matter. Of all the people, they were the staunchest supporters of the casting out of gentile wives.

### ◆§ The People Comply

**16.** וַיַּעֲשׂוּ־כֵן בְּנֵי הַגּוֹלָה — *And the exiles did so.* They expelled the gentile wives *(Metzudos).*

י וַיִּבָּֽדְלוּ֙ עֶזְרָ֣א הַכֹּהֵ֔ן אֲנָשִׁ֞ים רָאשֵׁ֧י הָאָבֹ֛ות
יז־יט לְבֵ֥ית אֲבֹתָ֖ם וְכֻלָּ֣ם בְּשֵׁמ֑וֹת וַיֵּ֨שְׁב֜וּ בְּי֤וֹם
יז אֶחָד֙ לַחֹ֣דֶשׁ הָעֲשִׂירִ֔י לְדַרְי֖וֹשׁ הַדָּבָֽר׃ וַיְכַלּ֣וּ
בַכֹּ֔ל אֲנָשִׁ֕ים הַהֹשִׁ֖יבוּ נָשִׁ֣ים נָכְרִיּ֑וֹת עַ֚ד
יח י֣וֹם אֶחָ֔ד לַחֹ֖דֶשׁ הָרִאשֽׁוֹן׃ וַיִּמָּצֵ֗א
מִבְּנֵ֤י הַכֹּהֲנִים֙ אֲשֶׁ֣ר הֹשִׁ֔יבוּ נָשִׁ֖ים נָכְרִיּ֑וֹת
מִבְּנֵ֨י יֵשׁ֤וּעַ בֶּן־יֽוֹצָדָק֙ וְאֶחָ֔יו מַֽעֲשֵׂיָ֣ה
יט וֶאֱלִיעֶ֔זֶר וְיָרִ֖יב וּגְדַלְיָֽה׃ וַיִּתְּנ֥וּ יָדָ֖ם לְהוֹצִ֣יא
נְשֵׁיהֶ֑ם וַאֲשֵׁמִ֛ים אֵֽיל־צֹ֖אן עַל־אַשְׁמָתָֽם׃

[This is a general statement. The remainder of the chapter delineates the details of the expulsion.]

וַיִּבָּדְלוּ עֶזְרָא הַכֹּהֵן אֲנָשִׁים — *Ezra the Kohen [and] the men ... separated themselves.* The translation follows *Ibn Ezra* and *Ralbag,* who understand the phrase as if it were written *'and' [the] men.*

*R' Yeshayah MiTrani,* however, understands the phrase as if it were written וַיִּבָּדְלוּ (לְ)עֶזְרָא ... אֲנָשִׁים, *men were separated* [*for*] *Ezra.* The family heads were separated in order to serve as assistants to Ezra in implementing his program.

These leaders separated themselves from the people by remaining in Jerusalem to examine the matter of illicit wives, while the rest of the people returned home to their personal affairs *(Malbim).*

*Metzudos,* however, interprets the verse as follows: *The exiles did so and they were separated* [from their wives]; [by] *Ezra the Kohen and the men who were the family heads.*

[The word אֲנָשִׁים, *men,* generally implies *distinguished men* (see 2:2). In this case, the family heads were the distinguished men.]

וְכֻלָּם בְּשֵׁמוֹת — *All renowned* [lit. *all by names*]. All the family heads were celebrated men, whose names were widely known *(Metzudos).*

לְדַרְיוֹשׁ הַדָּבָר — *To investigate the matter.* The word דריוש does not appear anywhere else in Scripture *(Minchas Shai)* but is to be understood as לִדְרוֹשׁ, *to investigate (Rashi, Ibn Ezra).*

**17.** וַיְכַלּוּ בַכֹּל אֲנָשִׁים הַהֹשִׁיבוּ נָשִׁים נָכְרִיּוֹת — *They concluded with all the men who had harbored alien wives.* They concluded rectifying the deeds of all the men who had harbored alien wives and finished the process of having them cast out their wives *(Rashi).*

*Ralbag* interprets: *They concluded the investigation of all the men who had installed alien wives* — they finished clarifying which wives were to be cast out.

*Ibn Ezra* (followed by *Malbim),* however, feels that the prefix בַּ, *with,* in בַּכֹּל, *with all,* is to be understood as extending to the word אֲנָשִׁים, *men,* as well. The sentence is now understood: *They concluded everything* [the investigation]; *with the men who had harbored alien wives.*

This is necessary, *Malbim* argues, because of the appearance of the word בַּכֹּל. [This word is used throughout Scripture to complete a phrase, while בְּכָל is used in the middle of a phrase.] Thus בַּכֹּל here completes the first phrase וַיְכַלּוּ בַכֹּל, *they concluded everything.*

לַחֹדֶשׁ הָרִאשׁוֹן — *Of the first month.* The month of Nissan *(Rashi).*

*did so. Ezra the Kohen and the men who were the*
*family heads, all renowned, separated themselves and*
*convened on the first day of the tenth month to*
*investigate the matter.* 17 *They concluded with all the*
*men who had harbored alien wives by the first day of*
*the first month.*

*The Transgressors*

18 *And there were discovered among the sons of*
*the Kohanim some who had harbored alien wives: of*
*the sons of Jeshua the son of Jozadak and his*
*brethren — Maaseiah, Eliezer, Jarib, and Gedaliah.*
19 *And they advised them to cast out their wives, and*
*that they owed a guilt offering of a ram for their guilt.*

### ◆§ The Transgressors

**18.** מִבְּנֵי יֵשׁוּעַ בֶּן־יוֹצָדָק — *Of the sons of Jeshua the son of Jozadak.* Jeshua the son of Jozadak was the *Kohen Gadol* (High Priest) [see above, comm. 2:2][1] *(R' Yeshayah MiTrani).*

**19.** וַיִּתְּנוּ יָדָם — *And they advised them* [lit. *gave their hand*]. *Rashi* explains that יָד [literally *hand*] may mean *advice* [as in *II Samuel* 14:19]. Here too, וַיִּתְּנוּ יָדָם may be translated *they gave their advice.*

[According to *Rashi,* then, the subjects of this verse are Ezra and the heads of the families. When their investigation disclosed that these *Kohanim* had married gentile women, *they* (Ezra and his associates) *advised them* (the guilty parties) *to cast out their wives and that they owed a guilt offering ...*]

*Ibn Ezra,* however, translates literally — *they gave their hand* — meaning they shook hands. Giving the hand is the traditional symbol of the acceptance of an oath, or of acquiescence and submission, indicating that they would accept his demand to expel their wives. [According to *Ibn Ezra* the subjects of the verse — *they* — are the guilty *Kohanim.*] *They gave their hands,* either swearing or at least binding themselves to cast out their wives.

וַאֲשֵׁמִים אֵיל־צֹאן — *And that they owed a guilt offering of a ram.* The translation follows *Metzudos.*

*Ibn Ezra,* however, reads וַאֲשֵׁמִים as the equivalent of וְהָאֲשֵׁמִים, *and the guilty ones. And they gave their hand* [i.e., they pledged] — *the guilty ones — a ram for their transgression.*

עַל־אַשְׁמָתָם — *For their guilt.* There is no precedent in Jewish law for the bringing of a sacrificial ram in atonement for the transgression of intermarriage. Thus, the decision that the *Kohanim* bring the rams must have been a הוֹרָאַת שָׁעָה, *temporary ruling.* [The Rabbis may, under certain conditions, temporarily suspend the Torah laws; see comm. 6:17.] The leading Rabbis of the day temporarily suspended the normal sacrificial rules, and ordered the *Kohanim* to bring the rams as guilt offerings *(Rashi; Ibn Ezra; Ralbag; Metzudos).*

*Malbim,* however, maintains that there was no special ruling. The *Kohanim* had had relations with *betrothed maidservants.* [The betrothed

1. *Zechariah* 3:1 relates: *He showed me Joshua the Kohen Gadol standing before the angel of HASHEM, and the satan stood on his right side to accuse him. Rashi* there explains that the accusation was that his sons had taken gentile wives, as recorded in our verse.

כ־כא וּמִבְּנֵי אִמֵּר חֲנָנִי וּזְבַדְיָה: וּמִבְּנֵי חָרִם
מַעֲשֵׂיָה וְאֵלִיָּה וּשְׁמַעְיָה וִיחִיאֵל וְעֻזִּיָּה:
כב וּמִבְּנֵי פַּשְׁחוּר אֶלְיוֹעֵינַי מַעֲשֵׂיָה יִשְׁמָעֵאל
כג נְתַנְאֵל יוֹזָבָד וְאֶלְעָשָׂה: וּמִן־הַלְוִיִּם יוֹזָבָד
וְשִׁמְעִי וְקֵלָיָה הוּא קְלִיטָא פְּתַחְיָה יְהוּדָה
כד וֶאֱלִיעֶזֶר: וּמִן־הַמְשֹׁרְרִים אֶלְיָשִׁיב וּמִן־
כה הַשֹּׁעֲרִים שַׁלֻּם וָטֶלֶם וְאוּרִי: וּמִיִּשְׂרָאֵל
מִבְּנֵי פַרְעֹשׁ רַמְיָה וְיִזִּיָּה וּמַלְכִּיָּה וּמִיָּמִן
כו וְאֶלְעָזָר וּמַלְכִּיָּה וּבְנָיָה: וּמִבְּנֵי עֵילָם מַתַּנְיָה
כז זְכַרְיָה וִיחִיאֵל וְעַבְדִּי וִירֵמוֹת וְאֵלִיָּה: וּמִבְּנֵי
זַתּוּא אֶלְיוֹעֵנַי אֶלְיָשִׁיב מַתַּנְיָה וִירֵמוֹת וְזָבָד
כח וַעֲזִיזָא: וּמִבְּנֵי בֵּבָי יְהוֹחָנָן חֲנַנְיָה זַבַּי עַתְלָי:
כט וּמִבְּנֵי בָּנִי מְשֻׁלָּם מַלּוּךְ וַעֲדָיָה יָשׁוּב וּשְׁאָל
ל °ירמות: וּמִבְּנֵי פַּחַת מוֹאָב עַדְנָא וּכְלָל °וְרָמוֹת ק׳
בְּנָיָה מַעֲשֵׂיָה מַתַּנְיָה בְּצַלְאֵל וּבִנּוּי וּמְנַשֶּׁה:

maidservant (שפחה חרופה) is a gentile female slave (שפחה כנענית) owned by a Jew who is betrothed to a slave. Biblical law (see *Leviticus* 19:20-22) requires that a Jew having relations with this maidservant bring a guilt offering as atonement.] Thus, the guilt offerings brought by the *Kohanim* were mandated by the Biblical command requiring the guilt offering for relations with the betrothed maidservant. This is based on the opinion of R' Chisda in the Talmud *(Kerisos* 11a) that the *Kohanim* who brought guilt offerings had had relations with betrothed maidservants.[1]

Based on this interpretation, *Malbim* renders וַאֲשֵׁמִים אֵיל־צֹאן עַל־אַשְׁמָתָם: *and they 'conceded' their obligation of a ram for their transgression.* The sinners themselves admitted that they had had relations with the betrothed maidservants, and were therefore obligated to

1. *Rashi's* statement that the *Kohanim* brought their sacrifices on the basis of a temporary ruling suspending the ordinary Torah law contradicts R' Chisda's assertion in the Talmud that the *Kohanim* had taken betrothed maidservants and were obligated by Biblical command to bring the guilt offerings. *Malbim* offers the following explanation for *Rashi's* departure from the Talmudic interpretation.

Two opinions appear in the Talmud concerning the betrothed maidservant. The minority view is that the reference is to a gentile maidservant betrothed to a non-Jewish slave. The majority opinion [cited by *Rambam, Isurei Biah* 3:13 and *Rashi* to *Leviticus* 20:19], however, is that the maidservant under discussion is defined as a gentile maidservant betrothed to a Hebrew slave. [A Jewish man is not permitted to have relations with a gentile maidservant. However, a Hebrew slave (עֶבֶד עִבְרִי) may take such a maidservant as a wife *(Exodus* 21:4).]

*Rashi's* opinion is that the institution of Hebrew slavery (עֶבֶד עִבְרִי) did not exist after the return from the Babylonian exile [see *Tosafos* to *Gittin* 36a], but there may have been gentile slaves at the time. Therefore, the phenomenon of a maidservant betrothed to a Hebrew slave,

X
20-31

20 *Of the sons of Immer: Hanani and Zebadiah.* 21 *Of
the sons of Harim: Maaseiah, Elijah, Shemaiah,
Jehiel, and Uzziah.* 22 *Of the sons of Pashchur:
Elioenai, Maaseiah, Ishmael, Nethanel, Jozabad, and
Elasah.* 23 *Of the Levites: Jozabad, Shimei, Kelaiah,
known as Kelita, Pethahiah, Judah, and Eliezer.* 24 *Of
the choristers: Eliashib. Of the gatekeepers: Shallum,
Telem, and Uri.*

25 *Of the Israelites: of the sons of Parosh, Ramiah,
Izziah, Malchijah, Mijamin, Elazar, Malchijah, and
Benaiah.* 26 *Of the sons of Elam: Mattaniah,
Zechariah, Jehiel, Abdi, Jeremoth, and Elijah.* 27 *Of
the sons of Zattu: Elioenai, Eliashib, Mattaniah,
Jeremoth, Zabad, and Aziza.* 28 *Of the sons of Bebai:
Jehohanan, Hananiah, Zabbai, and Athlai.* 29 *Of the
sons of Bani: Meshullam, Malluch, Adaiah, Jashub,
Sheal, and Ramoth.* 30 *Of the sons of the governor of
Moab: Adna, Chelal, Benaiah, Maaseiah, Mattaniah,
Bezalel, Binnui, and Menasheh.* 31 *The sons of*

bring a ram for the transgression. The admission of guilt was significant because, according to Talmudic law, the courts cannot force someone accused of having illicit relations with a betrothed maidservant to bring a guilt offering if he denies the allegation (*Kerisos* 12b). Thus, it was only because the sinners conceded their obligation that they brought the rams as guilt offerings.

**20.** וּמִבְּנֵי אִמֵּר ... — *Of the sons of Immer* ... All of these listed until v. 23 were *Kohanim (Rashi).*

**23.** וּמִן־הַלְוִיִּם — *Of the Levites.* These were the Levites who had taken gentile wives *(Metzudos).*

וְקֵלָיָה הוּא קְלִיטָא — *Kelaiah, known as Kelita.* He was called by both names — *Kelaiah* and *Kelita (Metzudos).*

**30.** פַּחַת מוֹאָב — *The governor of Moab.* [See comm. 2:6.]

as defined by the majority opinion in *Kerisos* 11a, did not exist during Ezra's times, since there were no Jewish slaves. The maidservant, however, could have been betrothed to a *gentile* slave, as specified in the minority opinion in *Kerisos.*

It follows, then, that R' Chisda's assertion that the *Kohanim* were Biblically mandated to bring guilt offerings for sinning with betrothed maidservants is viable only according to the minority Talmudic opinion which defines the betrothed maidservant as a female slave betrothed to a gentile slave. This was possible even during the days of Ezra. *Rashi,* however, follows the majority Talmudic view [held by R' Akiva and R' Yishmael in *Kerisos* 11a] that perceives the betrothed maidservant as a female slave betrothed to a *Hebrew* slave. Accordingly, the sinners during Ezra's period could not have had relations with the Biblically prohibited betrothed maidservants, since there were no Hebrew slaves at the time. Thus, the sacrifices brought by the *Kohanim* for their transgressions could not have been Biblically mandated, but were offered on the basis of a temporary ruling which suspended the normal Torah rules.

י
לא־מד

לא וּבְנֵי חָרִם אֱלִיעֶזֶר יִשִּׁיָּה מַלְכִּיָּה שְׁמַעְיָה
לב־לג שִׁמְעוֹן: בִּנְיָמִן מַלּוּךְ שְׁמַרְיָה: מִבְּנֵי חָשֻׁם
מַתְּנַי מַתַּתָּה זָבָד אֱלִיפֶלֶט יְרֵמַי מְנַשֶּׁה
לד־לה שִׁמְעִי: מִבְּנֵי בָנִי מַעֲדַי עַמְרָם וְאוּאֵל: בְּנָיָה
לו בֵדְיָה °כלוהי: וַנְיָה מְרֵמוֹת אֶלְיָשִׁיב:
לז־לח מַתַּנְיָה מַתְּנַי °ויעשו: וּבָנִי וּבִנּוּי שִׁמְעִי:
לט־מ וְשֶׁלֶמְיָה וְנָתָן וַעֲדָיָה: מַכְנַדְבַי שָׁשַׁי שָׁרָי:
מא־מב עֲזַרְאֵל וְשֶׁלֶמְיָהוּ שְׁמַרְיָה: שַׁלּוּם אֲמַרְיָה
מג יוֹסֵף: מִבְּנֵי נְבוֹ יְעִיאֵל מַתִּתְיָה זָבָד זְבִינָא
מד °ידו וְיוֹאֵל בְּנָיָה: כָּל־אֵלֶּה °נשאי נָשִׁים
נָכְרִיּוֹת וְיֵשׁ־מֵהֶם נָשִׁים וַיָּשִׂימוּ בָּנִים:

°כְּלֻהוּ ק׳
°וְיַעֲשָׂי ק׳
°יַדַּי ק׳
°נָשְׂאוּ ק׳

## Alien Wives and Children

**44.** וַיָּשִׂימוּ בָּנִים — *With whom* [lit. *and*] *they gave forth* [lit. *placed*] *children.* With whom they had children. All were expelled — the alien wives and the children *(Rashi).*

[The expulsion of the alien wives and their children, although not mentioned in this verse, is stated explicitly in 10:3.]

*Malbim* notes the use of the term וַיָּשִׂימוּ בָּנִים, *and they gave forth children,* rather than the more common expression, וַיּוֹלִידוּ בָּנִים, *and they fathered children.* The reason for the change, *Malbim* asserts, is that a child born of a Jewish father and gentile mother follows the mother's lineage, and is a